FREE FALL

FREE FALL

Why South African Universities
are in a Race Against Time

MALCOLM RAY

With a foreword by Vuyo Jack

BOOK**STORM**

ISBN: 978-1-928257-27-1
e-ISBN: 978-1-928257-28-8

First edition, first impression 2016

Published by Bookstorm (Pty) Ltd
PO Box 4532
Northcliff 2115
Johannesburg
South Africa
www.bookstorm.co.za

Edited by John Henderson
Proofread by Kelly Norwood-Young
Author photo by Suzy Bernstein
Cover design by publicide
Book design and typesetting by Triple M Design
Printed by Creda Communications, Cape Town

For my son, Liam

In honour of my mother and in loving memory of my father

[People] make their own history, but they do not make it just as they please; they do not make it under circumstances chosen by themselves, but under circumstances directly encountered, given and transmitted from the past. The tradition of all the dead generations weighs like a nightmare on the brain of the living.

KARL MARX, *The 18th Brumaire of Louis Bonaparte*

Contents

Abbreviations and acronyms

AAI	African-American Institute
ADA	Americans for Democratic Action
AHI	Afrikaanse Handelsinstituut
AMSAC	American Society of African Culture
ANC	African National Congress
ANS	Afrikaanse Nasionale Studentebond
ASA	African Students Association
AsgiSA	Accelerated and Shared Growth Initiative for SA
ASM	African Students' Movement
Assocom	Associated Chambers of Commerce
ASUSA	African Students' Union of South Africa
BPC	Black People's Convention
CAS	Central Applications Service
CBM	Consultative Business Movement
CCF	Congress for Cultural Freedom
CDE	Centre for Development and Enterprise
CEO	Chief Executive Officer
CIA	Central Intelligence Agency
CMS	Consolidated Mines Selection
CODESA	Convention for a Democratic South Africa
COSATU	Congress of South African Trade Unions
CPSA	Communist Party of South Africa
DHET	Department of Higher Education and Training
dti	Department of Trade and Industry
EFF	Economic Freedom Fighters
FAK	Federasie van Afrikaanse Kultuurvereniginge
FCI	Federated Chamber of Industries

GDP	Gross Domestic Product
GEAR	Growth, Employment and Redistribution
GM	General Motors
HESA	Higher Education South Africa
HSRC	Human Sciences Research Council
ICJ	International Court of Justice
ICT	Information and Communications Technology
JIPSA	Joint Initiative on Priority Skills Acquisition
MEC	Member of the Executive Council
MK	Umkhonto we Sizwe
MP	Member of Parliament
NAACP	National Association for the Advancement of Colored People
NAFCOC	National African Federated Chamber of Commerce
NAYO	National Youth Organisation
NBI	National Business Initiative
NSA	National Student Association
NSC	National Security Council
NSFAS	National Student Financial Aid Scheme
NUMSA	National Union of Metalworkers of South Africa
NUSAS	National Union of South African Students
OPC	Office for Policy Coordination
PAC	Pan Africanist Congress
PU for CHE	Potchefstroom University for Christian Higher Education
PYA	Progressive Youth Alliance
RDP	Reconstruction and Development Plan
SABRA	South African Bureau for Racial Affairs
SACOB	South African Chamber of Business
SACP	South African Communist Party
SARS	South African Revenue Service
SASCO	South African Students Congress
SASM	South African Students Movement
SASO	South African Students' Organisation
SETA	Sector Education and Training Authority
SOE	State-owned Enterprise
SRC	Student Representative Council
SSRC	Soweto Students Representative Council
SWF	Sovereign Wealth Fund
TRAYO	Transvaal Youth Organisation

UCM	University Christian Movement
UCT	University of Cape Town
UDF	United Democratic Front
UJ	University of Johannesburg
UKZN	University of KwaZulu-Natal
UN	United Nations
UNISA	University of South Africa
USSALEP	United States–South Africa Leader Exchange Program
Wits	University of the Witwatersrand
YMCA	Young Men's Christian Association

Author's note

Kierkegaard once wrote that history is lived forward but written backwards.* My task in writing about the South African education system has followed this epigram, with a difference, however: When I set out to write this book in November 2015 – just as students suspended their protest action to write exams – bigger events were about to strike. Like a virus that had suddenly infected an organism, a surge of student and worker militancy had been spreading across university campuses, in some instances linking student demands to frequent and unequivocal condemnations of the government and student organisations politically aligned to the African National Congress (ANC).

In addition to this crossing of wires, the student movement had by February 2016 faced another change variable: the ANC's tendency to blame the increasingly violent form of protests on a 'third force'. These charges were usually made within an assumed American-sponsored regime change frame of reference: if black students continued to support regime change, they would not only drive South Africa into the hands of 'foreign forces', the ANC's Secretary General, Gwede Mantashe, claimed, but they would also help forge a domestic alliance between the beneficiaries of American foreign policy and opposition parties. The possibility that there might be truth in such claims could not be ruled out, as is shown in Part III of this book by the infiltration of the local anti-apartheid student movement and academic community by the United States in the 1960s and seventies. Still, there came a point when such remarks ceased being supportive of student demands and seemed increasingly like minor deflections from major issues.

What's unquestionable is that the present moment is a country convulsed by the consequences of what is likely the most stunning failure of the higher

---

* Quoted in Dobbs, M, *One Minute to Midnight* (London: Mixed Sources, 2009), p. xvii.

education system in post-apartheid history, since the clampdown on the black student movement led by the likes of Steve Biko, Saths Cooper, Barney Pityana, Strini Moodley and others in the early to mid-1970s, and the uprising by schoolchildren in Soweto on 16 June 1976.

Having said that, nothing, I felt, in the silence between the dramatic outbreak of campus protests in 2015 and the growing intensity of student action between January and early March 2016, was fixed yet. In any case, no story is complete – not least in the historical sense.

Yet there was nothing inevitable about the revolt. What happened in 2015, and continues to unfold into an indeterminate future, had been preceded, and would be followed, by fluctuating triumphs and failures in something relatively new to the democratic government – the sub rosa battleground of protest politics.

As I began reflecting on the situation, I came to understand more clearly the perpetual conflict between those who want to see genuine change and the powers that control and own economic wealth; the arguments between those in political office and university authorities and black student proponents of a broader, more radical transformation of the education system; and the ambitions and frustrations of politicians who have had to navigate the contradictions.

I had become familiar with the post-1994 record. Individually, the rise of 'integrated' universities from the segregated institutional configuration of apartheid state planning seemed to reflect the mundane rhythms of change; at most, they were gradual adjustments to the new order that imploded under their contradictions.

But how much of our past lay buried beneath the heavy calumny of the present? To answer this question required coming to terms with the particular place of elitism in the preservation of privilege since 1994.

By January 2016, I was more convinced than ever that, apart from the organisations and personalities behind the student revolts, the gaps lay in the business of disentangling the present from the detritus of the past.

True, this book had by this time grown beyond my original plans: from a recording of the people and circumstances behind the #RhodesMustFall (hereafter 'Rhodes Must Fall') and #FeesMustFall (hereafter 'Fees Must Fall') movements into a wider historical treatment of education and capitalism since the end of slavery in South Africa. In the process, I stuck to a fundamental question that insistently framed my research: who (or what) was behind the rise of student anger in post-apartheid South Africa – and, more importantly, *why?*

The story was an unbroken line from another era. The situation required careful historical treatment and, perhaps more importantly, urgent solutions.

*

Writing this book has not been easy. I have had to tell a very large story as if the whole calumny of colonialism and apartheid-capitalism had suddenly become compressed in a sharp, piercing moment.

Despite the vast scholarly work on South African education before and after 1994, there are at least two respects in which it strikes me, at least, as inadequate. First, no previous work has comprehensively examined the education of black South Africans since the end of apartheid in historical terms. What literature there is has been largely written within the apartheid context. Peter Kallaway and others, for example, in an impressive volume of essays in *Apartheid and Education*, poured the foundations for an understanding of the limits of late-apartheid educational reforms; but they could do no more than write in the context of the 1980s, when apartheid was reaching its end.

Secondly, the narrative since the end of apartheid has so persistently peddled historical 'challenges' and 'progress' towards integrating and expanding the schooling and university landscape as truth that it has become an acceptable reference point for even independent historians and scholars. Typically, the corporatised institutional framework within which the demographic profile of student enrolment has transformed had, until the resurgence of students protests in 2015, been widely accepted. Yet, half-hearted and fragmentary attempts to transform universities have had their logic and consistency: the democratic government had known all along that it could not prise open the doors of higher learning without serious consequences for the fiscus. And so the transformation agenda has operated at arm's length from universities, leaving the institutions themselves to change things, or leave them unchanged, as the case may be.

Now all those attempts by the government to change the educational landscape seem vain. Indeed, in this hour of truth, black students themselves appear as the harbingers of a radically transformed system. My attempt to comprehensively map the origins and development of apartheid education from the contemporary setting of present-day student revolts is thus a historical treatment of limited attempts by the democratic government to transform the education system.

This book has two main aims. One is to provide an account of the political, cultural and socio-economic foundations of the education system since the end of slavery in 1834 till its modernisation during the apartheid era more than a century later. By portraying the history of education and student protests in a rounded manner, my hope is that we will shed new light not only on pre-1994 history, but also on the challenges of transforming the system in the early 21st century.

Why and how students eventually turned unresolved challenges into protests is the other aim of this book. It describes attempts at transforming the higher education system since 1994, their limits, and the circumstances that led to the Rhodes Must Fall and Fees Must Fall movements in 2015. If there is a thesis to this book, it is this: the restructuring of higher learning institutions that began in 2002/2003 under former education minister Kader Asmal merely gave a progressive veneer to a corporatisation process begun by former apartheid president PW Botha. The net effect has been merged universities open to all but largely untransformed and financially inaccessible to the poor. In the latter regard, free education is a constitutional right. It means finding sustainable sources of funds and funding models; it means transforming the cultural matrix, demographic profile and teaching content of universities; it means expanding the creativity and imagination of teaching staff and students as producers and consumers of society's cultural and intellectual capital; and, finally, it means transforming universities from encrusted monasteries of a hegemonic white and subsidiary black intellectual vanguard into inclusive, generative sources of intellectual adventurousness and subversion in the production of knowledge, and of self-surpassing excellence in academic achievement, thereby giving far greater scope for the making of critically trained and creative minds.

A NOTE ON THE STRUCTURE OF THIS BOOK

A full appreciation of the contemporary South African educational landscape requires an analysis of the evolution of the system in three historically contingent contexts. In the first place, any attempt to grasp the history and dynamics of education for black people of South Africa must be set in the context of European colonialism. Such a process, as writers as varied as Franz Fanon, Amílcar Cabral, Nosipho Majeke, Dan O'Meara, Peter Kallaway, Merle Lipton, and Willie Esterhuyse have shown, was a cultural as well as an economic and political event.[†] The colonised peoples of southern Africa, wrote Kallaway in his introduction to *Apartheid and Education*,

> were not simply conquered in a military sense; did not lose only their political independence; were not simply divorced from an independent economic base; were not just drawn into new systems of social and economic life as urban dwellers or wage labour. Though all these aspects of the process of colonisation have great importance, the key aspect to be noted here is that it also entailed cultural and ideological transformation in which the schools were major agents.[‡]

The theoretical starting point for such an endeavour is the influence of structural, institutional and human agency in the process of co-opting and controlling subjugated groups. What follows, then, is a historical treatment of the role Christian mission schools, and later Bantu education, came to play in the creation of a subservient and denationalised class of black youth and workers as a complementary force to state repression that ultimately framed the development of the apartheid-capitalist structure. Schools (and later segregated 'bush colleges') negated common-sense knowledge of the colonised "by reinforcing the self-image of incompetence and ignorance" and promoting "the notion of congruence between acceptance of the legitimacy of colonial rule and the capitalist system that it represented".[¶] In the late-apartheid era, the most notable characteristic of this system was perhaps the degree to which Bantu education, rather than meeting the demands of the apartheid-capitalist economy, actually tried to accommodate the general fate of the black student population to the economic logic of a grand neo-liberal strategy during the reign of President PW Botha during the late 1970s and eighties.

Set against this background, the remainder of the book explores the impact of government policies since the formal dissolution of the apartheid legal–administrative system and its implications for the newly elected democratic government's pursuit of particular transformation goals. Shortly after the birth of the Organisation of African Unity in 1963, Amílcar Cabral observed that psychological and socio-economic patterns of development in

---

[†] Quoted in Kallaway, P (ed), *Apartheid and Education: The Education of Black South Africans* (Johannesburg: Ravan Press, 1984), p.8.
[‡] Ibid., pp. 8-9.
[¶] Ibid., p. 9.

post-liberation African states were mirrors of colonialism's contradictions.[§] South Africa, close to 22 years since the end of apartheid, is likewise a mirror of the contradictions inherent in the decampment of a new generation of black youth – the so-called born-frees – on a neo-liberal educational and economic landscape. Thus, just as the black university student movement of 1971 to 1975 and the Soweto generation of school-going youth in 1976/1977 had a chance in forms of anti-apartheid resistance to Bantu education and succeeded in raising their grievances with mixed tragedy and hope, so the post-liberation student movement now meets its crisis in shifting geographic and institutional frontiers, shrinking financial opportunities, and the rise of identity politics and exclusionary populism[#] in South African universities.

In a nutshell, what is offered here is a narrative history of education toward our understanding of how the ANC government, by advocating a fairly liberal paradigm of institutional integration and corporatisation in 2003, unintentionally adapted and entrenched the terms of late-apartheid reforms to the higher education system that astonishingly matches the present.

This, then, is more than a record of the student protests. The story is as much about South Africa's descent into economic ruin since the end of apartheid as the forces that connived and acted on the country in previous centuries. It is, at base, a historical treatment of a country in upheaval in the second decade of the 21st century, torn between the past and the future, between privilege and disadvantage, between an educated elite and a glut of people on the fringes. Ultimately, it is a story of a malevolent history behind a country's long descent into racialised inequality, and the havoc this has wreaked since the end of apartheid. As such, this book requires sequenced reading – from beginning to end.

Our story begins with the Rhodes Must Fall movement at the anti-climax of the ANC's mission 21 years since 1994. For, if liberation could hardly have been purchased at greater cost to the poor, this approach, surpassing victory, is neither an apologia for the stony and turbulent slide into student revolt, nor is it free from recognition of complex, often contradictory, choices that are made by government in a lived experience.

---

§ Quoted in Cabral, A, 'The weapon of theory'. Address delivered to the First Tricontinental Conference of the Peoples of Asia, Africa and Latin America (Havana: January 1966). Accessed at http://www.marxists.org/subject/africa/cabral/1966/weapon-theory.htm.

The core of this ideological platform has variously been described as 'ethno-nationalism', 'religious nationalism', or 'exclusionary welfarism'. See Hans-George Betz, *Socialist Register*, 2003, pp. 194-195.

To this end, this book concludes by advancing a model of social engagement between students, academic and non-academic staff on campuses, university principals and management, business, and the government that, in turn, forms the conceptual scaffolding for the construction of a model of economic engagement in the higher education value chain we call *Ubuntu* economics – that is, the mutually reinforcing investment by all stakeholders in radical outcomes.

The concept of a sovereign wealth fund for higher education is recommended as a financial instrument for raising funds and allocating them to universities and students on a more sustainable basis than the range of proposals and disparate initiatives that have come to light since the protests began. The rationale for such a fund is its rich potential to provide incentives for all stakeholders in the higher education value chain. For business, it is the incentive to invest in and benefit from the production of sorely needed talent. For universities, it is the incentive to transform the institutional landscape and benefit from funds in a context of scarce resources. For black students from disadvantaged homes, it is the opportunity to earn a degree and plough back into the economy that which is gained from a free education. For government, it is a virtuous cycle of free education, skills, and economic growth as the surest path to meeting its constitutional mandate of open and accessible higher learning institutions.

MALCOLM RAY
Johannesburg
June 2016

Acknowledgements

I benefited from the generous support of many people, without whom this book would never have materialised. I am grateful to Vuyo Jack, who has been an inspiring critic, and a colleague and friend devoted to telling this story. Vuyo's ideas are embodied in the Epilogue to this book. In my attempt to capture the background and climate of the 1960s, 1970s and 1980s, my sincere gratitude goes to all participants who gave generously of their time and recollections of the period, and who offered advice. I am especially grateful to Saths Cooper, who has been an inspiring critic and a living repository of knowledge on student struggles, past and present. I am also deeply indebted to a large number of people who granted me interviews, both as a journalist over the past two decades and in direct preparation for this manuscript.

Much of the documentation on which a significant part of this narrative is based has been drawn from unpublished material at the Historical Papers research archive at the University of the Witwatersrand. I have drawn heavily, for instance, on minutes of meetings and conferences of the United States–South Africa Leader Exchange Program, which offer rich insights into the covert ideological agenda of the organisation in South Africa since the late 1950s. Archivists Gabi and Zofia at Historical Papers were a valuable compass in trawling mounds of manuscript collections and publications that formed some of the background material for this book. Michele Pickover, in particular, was a model of professional scholarship and collegiality.

A special note of gratitude to Jimmy and staff at the Mugg & Bean in Killarney Mall, which doubled as my office away from the office during the writing of this book; Louise, Russell and Nicola at Bookstorm for guiding me through the production of this book; and Tammy for reigniting that creative force.

Most of all, I am forever indebted to the apple of my life, my son Liam, for his forbearance and loving support during my single-minded obsession with this book; and my mother, Sheila, whose courage, strength and fighting spirit in her lifetime have been my inspiration.

Last but by no means least, I want to thank the present generation of university students whose struggle is this book. Their capacity for bold and often imaginative action is, without doubt, a sterling affirmation of the heroic struggles of previous generations. For, if history is indeed lived forwards, the dead weight of past generations, in Karl Marx's famous words, is being reawakened and written into the future.

Foreword

Malcolm and I have spent long hours talking about the impact of the student protests that started in South Africa in 2015, about why they happened, where they came from and what we should do in response to the crisis that has unfolded. Our commitment to a process to become part of the solution to this crisis was the result.

We saw the popular protests of the Arab Spring advocating for #MubarakMustFall, #GaddaffiMustFall, #BenAliMustFall. The regimes fell but there was a vacuum left after their fall; nothing was rising to build on the successes of these revolutions.

In South Africa in 2015, we had the #RhodesMustFall movement which advocated first for the removal of colonial symbols of oppression, but mostly centred on the comprehensive transformation of universities in South Africa. Late in 2015 we had the #FeesMustFall movement which protested against fee increases at Wits in the short term, but in the main campaigning for free education. These were great and laudable initiatives.

However, there are questions that need to be answered: #RhodesMustFall, but what is going to rise in its stead, and how do we want to be defined? #FeesMustFall, but what must rise to ensure that we have students of the highest caliber that can compete anywhere in the world? How do we ensure that we have universities with world-class infrastructure and a relevant curriculum grounded in an Afrocentric identity and reality? How do we attract and retain top academics who produce practical and groundbreaking research, and who apply the most innovative teaching methods that generate high graduation rates?

The common weakness that runs through the different movements from the Arab Spring to the Rhodes Must Fall and Fees Must Fall movements, is a lack of creativity in finding solutions to ensure we build strong replacements from the rubble of the things that must fall. The reality of the matter is that it is much easier to destroy than it is to build something from nothing. This is the challenge facing us.

If you don't create something in our hyper-connected world, you are going to be disrupted at the speed of light. If you don't build something that is enduring, what legacies will you leave in the next twenty years? What will it take to prevent disruption of our politics, economy and society in the coming years?

We need leadership from all sectors of our society, leadership that is able to drive the nation, economy and society in the right direction within the realities of a volatile, uncertain, complex and ambiguous world. I will use a musical analogy to explain this.

In South Africa we have gone through both classical and struggle leadership styles, both of which have their value. In stable and predictable times, classical leadership works as it gives a semblance of order and certainty, which is what investors like. In times when oppression has gone overboard, the struggle leadership style may be appropriate. However, struggle leadership is not capable of building anything that lasts as the skillset acquired through this leadership style is focused on destruction. By equal measure, classical leadership is not able to break its restrictive structure because the skillset built over 10 000 hours is too precious to be used for destruction, despite our great need for leadership at this moment.

So what is the answer? We need to move to jazz leadership. This leadership style is comfortable with all contexts, including the classical and struggle contexts. Jazz leadership respects form, order and the basic training needed to play jazz. It is collaborative and gives other soloists a chance to showcase their chops. There is space for everyone to shine. Improvisation is the mantra of jazz. It becomes okay to break the normal form in order to be creative and meet the needs of the moment. It creates music that is relevant to the moment and yet has enough clarity and sense of timing to return to its original form. It thrives on the unknown and requires attunement with other band members. Jazz leadership responds positively to whatever notes are thrown at the group, and manages to calibrate band members to new notes without losing their identity. Jazz leadership is antifragile because it gains value as more challenges are thrown at it. This is the radical approach advocated as a way out of the current crisis, a way to ensure we have a legacy to leave the next generation.

Jazz leadership is needed in politics, where we see new ideologies created that talk to our present moment. We should not be constrained by socialism, communism and capitalism, but should talk about *Ubuntu* ideology as we see it applied today.

Jazz leadership is needed in the economy, where new fields are discovered and new value is created in those fields for the good of everyone.

Jazz leadership is needed in education, where we can uncover and shape the inherent potential contained in students, rather than forcing them to be something they are not.

Jazz leadership is needed in our society, where everyone takes responsibility to create something out of nothing.

Jazz leadership is transformative in that the volatility of our world is turned to vision, where uncertainty emerges as understanding, where complexity vanishes into clarity, and where ambiguity leaps into agility.

We have used this thinking to conceptualise a funding solution to help move beyond the current crisis and on to a stronger future. We used Einstein's approach to problem solving: if one hour is available to solve a problem, Einstein would spend 55 minutes understanding the problem and 5 minutes coming up with the solution. Malcolm has done a stellar job of plumbing the depths of the problem, going back to the history of education from colonial times to the present. He presents a compelling narrative of a sensitive subject by shedding light on issues and points-of-view never seen before.

Now we need to begin the journey of building a productive and prosperous South Africa we can all be proud of. We are taking the educational baton from the generation of 1976, and we need to build an economic legacy that will speak for itself beyond our time. We have to use our skills to honour and build on the foundations laid by our ancestors for the good of all our people, now and in the future. We need to show them that they did not sacrifice everything they had in vain.

Hence we are building a mix of private equity and sovereign wealth fund structures called the Nation Building Fund. This Fund will, by using pragmatic tools, address key socio-economic issues such as education, culture, energy and economic growth that South Africa sorely needs to attend to at this time of its development. In the epilogue to this book, Malcolm sketches out the basic elements of the solution that needs to be rolled out.

The Nation Building Fund is about protecting and projecting our light as South Africans to build something that transcends us. We hope you will join us on this journey.

VUYO JACK
Johannesburg
September 2016

Introduction

THE STUDENT WHO GOT RID OF RHODES

IN ALL OF CAPE TOWN THERE ARE FEW VANTAGE POINTS AS DAZZLING AS Table Mountain. At the foot of the mountain is a sloping rise commanded by the University of Cape Town (UCT). Tranquil and picturesque, UCT's magnificent grey-stone buildings, breezy boulevards and manicured gardens are a great architectural exclamation point to British liberal culture and ideology towering above the city. Behind the campus runs one of Cape Town's busiest tree-lined thoroughfares: De Waal Drive.

It was on the crest of De Waal Drive that a small crowd gathered on a languid summer evening in February 2010. A black university student was shoved at gunpoint into one of six blue-light VIP vehicles in a presidential motorcade with President Jacob Zuma in one of them. His hands were tied behind his back and his head covered with a black hood.

Shortly after the episode, the 25-year-old student appeared on the front page of the *Sunday Times*. The name Chumani Maxwele was then unknown to ordinary South Africans. He was born in the Eastern Cape and arrived in Cape Town some time in the late 1990s to find opportunity in the city's bustling economy. Now living the life of a student at UCT, he was plagued by financial hardship. For black students, UCT was an exclamation point alright, but to a hollow reality and lie presented by the British. In 2010, UCT was a decaying cultural sanctuary for white privilege.

That summer afternoon, in 2010, Maxwele broke silence on his arrest. In his version, he was picked up by presidential bodyguards while jogging on De Waal Drive. Accused by the bodyguards of pointing his middle finger at President Zuma's blue-light motorcade, which he fiercely denied, he was taken to Mowbray police station and held overnight in a cell without a bed or food. The next morning he was moved to a communal cell at the Wynberg Magistrate's Court. At 4.30 p.m. that afternoon he was released, without appearing in court.

Much heat has been generated by the theory that Chumani Maxwele's arrest was the tipping point in a chain of events that continues to unravel. His personal odyssey, it has been said, may have dramatically changed the entire course of events. Others have made lesser claims, but still describe the 'Maxwele affair' as the most bizarre set of events to have occurred during the larger, often tumultuous, battle to transform South African society.

For, after all, who was Chumani Maxwele?

The student was certainly hard to read. But so, too, he must have thought, were his foes in the government. It was not always clear whether he was being interrogated, debriefed or diagnosed. "I was asked about my political allegiance,"[1] he once told journalists during a press briefing, in obvious reference to allegations by some high-ranking officials in the ruling African National Congress (ANC) government that a 'third force' had been behind an agenda to destabilise the government. Months later, Maxwele had sought the assistance of the FW de Klerk Foundation, set up by South Africa's last apartheid president, in bringing a case before the Human Rights Commission against the police, lending succour to conspiracy theories that there was more to the episode than met the eye.

Could it be true? The official standpoint of the government in the days and months after Maxwele's arrest was opaque, leading students and ordinary citizens to doubt the official story. Did Maxwele show his middle finger to the presidential motorcade? And why were his political allegiances questioned by presidential bodyguards? Whether in response to the finger, or the hand of a third force, as the government claimed, another story was playing out, quietly at first, and then rapidly gathering steam.

Unbeknown was that there was also considerable debate in student circles about how best to secure a propaganda advantage from this remarkable turn of events. In the months that followed Maxwele's arrest, there was talk within government of the student as a reckless malcontent "to whom we have nothing to say". To which Maxwele responded with palpable relief, "That is, of course, precisely what we wanted to hear."

In the years that followed, Maxwele on more than one occasion told journalists that his case had become bigger than him. "This is not about me," he told *City Press*. "This thing is about black people. It is about the history of black people. It is in front of you."[2] He wanted the court to make an order.

1 Author's unpublished notes from a press briefing by Chumani Maxwele, Cape Town, 21 June 2013.
2 See http://www.news24.com/Archives/City-Press/Newsmaker-Chumani-Maxwele-No-regrets-for-throwing-faeces-at-Rhodes-statue-20150429.

It took Maxwele three years to get his day in court. At the end of the case, a reader understood why he had sought legal recourse. It all may have provoked a sharp backlash in 2015.

*

How the idea came about we don't know, although he'd witnessed first-hand the indignity of racism and raw emotions of black students at UCT and was perfectly primed to see the student movement coming out of the fog. Like so many black students of his generation, Maxwele's hardened bitterness began in tragedy and hope. In numerous interviews he gave to journalists, he liked to tell of the sound of a plane flying over his home in the Eastern Cape. In the hovels of black poverty in the largely rural province, planes were a rare sighting; only powerful, influential people flew in them. A wall of lies separated the reality from the myth during apartheid. But Maxwele was right about one thing: power was held by the apartheid state. He once recalled watching on a television set in the village nurse's house military armoured vehicles manned by white soldiers tearing into crowds of black protesters. That was the height of apartheid-state repression during the late 1980s.

Now a democratic government was, theoretically, in control of the state, the police, the army, the schools, the universities – almost everything. Yet Maxwele's generation knew and felt every day the fictional promise of a better life for all. Maxwele knew the lie.

The son of a miner who died on the job and a domestic-worker mother, he left the Eastern Cape in 2006 to settle in an area 20 kilometres outside the city of Cape Town called Delft, where he had hoped to find a place in the sun. But Delft turned out to be an unforgiving place. Almost half its residents lived with a carnival of wants, always desperate for opportunities to make ends meet.

Nearby, the black township of Khayelitsha was a sprawl of tin shacks on a windswept landscape nestled in the shadow of postcard Cape Town. "In a one-kilometre stretch of road, you'd pass a thousand people," Maxwele recalled. "For me, that was shocking."[3] Its inhabitants were migrants from the Eastern Cape – a pejorative moniker that would cling to their status as

---

3 See Fairbanks, E, 'Why South African students have turned on their parent's generation', 18 November 2015. Accessed at https://www.theguardian.com/news/2015/nov/18/why-south-african-students-have-turned-on-their-parents-generation.

'foreigners' in Cape Town. Most had escaped the homelands of the Transkei and Ciskei, two creations of the apartheid government in its drive to partition the country into ethnic cantons. The official system was severe. The apartheid authorities had devoted enormous effort to wiping out the spirit of entrepreneurialism and property ownership and nurturing wants in the homelands that forced many homeland occupants into a life of cheap labour in white cities like Cape Town. Even so, the basic human instinct to survive literally drove successive waves of migration to Cape Town during the 1980s and nineties.

Life in Cape Town's black townships after 1994 was as hostile to survival, however. There were human rights for all – except that the struggle to access them was more modern, fuelled by a borderless socio-economic chasm that has marked the indelible boundaries of racial divisions since 1994. Left to their own devices, residents survived without running water and electricity; families defecated in plastic boxes collected once a week by the municipality.

In 2006, Maxwele got a job at Woolworths in the upscale suburb of Claremont. On his first day, he once recalled in an interview, he and his mostly black colleagues were given uniforms: "a pressed shirt, a tie, and shiny patent leather shoes".[4] His colleagues, he said, felt proud – they were real 'businesspeople' now. Not Maxwele; he saw the reality. The vast majority of Woolworths customers were white; he their servant.

Maxwele and his generation wanted more – much more – than the system had to offer. The apartheid past, he realised, still imprisoned blacks behind unyielding walls. An entire generation of youths had been told they were born-frees; they were a cohort of youth born during the early 1990s with almost no memory of apartheid, a generation undeserving, in Human Settlements Minister Lindiwe Sisulu's estimation, of state-subsidised housing and socio-economic reparations.

As the system heaved into the first decade of democracy, Maxwele baulked. Then he grew anxious. Without a higher education and prospects for success, he was, to all social appurtenances, an outcast. When he finally got a chance to enrol at UCT, in 2009, on a student bursary, his daily sojourn from Delft to the university in Rondebosch was a tale of two worlds. He was still an economic migrant, a foreigner. In the city's swanky university precinct and cloistered campus community, hardly anyone noticed. The university governing body was as indifferent to the racial status quo.

---

4 Ibid.

4

Meanwhile, the initial months of 2009 began on thin ice. But by April, once again the ANC and the government rose from the quagmire of political instability and economic uncertainty. By May, the newly elected government of Jacob Zuma was in control; a guarded optimism was expanding, at first haltingly, and then by leaps and bounds after the chaos and indecision of the early removal from office of his predecessor, Thabo Mbeki; and a new, unabashed clutch of black tycoons were swopping thrifty sports jackets for designer suits, expensive eateries, showy sushi parties and exquisite champagne.

They had good reason for optimism. Though Zuma never openly expressed it, his allies in the ANC Youth League and trade union federation COSATU (Congress of South African Trade Unions) at the ruling party's Polokwane conference expected nothing less than the disavowal of an earlier period of elitism that had taken shape initially under Nelson Mandela and then Mbeki. The previous system had at its core a quick-profit ethos forged in the mid- to late 1990s when a handful of politically connected black tycoons in cosy corporate deals with large white businesses suddenly appeared on the scene, reaching full strength in a frenzy of leveraged shares doled out by banks and mining houses, and ripening into a wealthy caste of black capitalists by the new millennium.

By the close of the first decade of the new millennium, a fundamental rule of South African capitalism – control over the state – was directed less at a handful of black winners than their moneyed corporate benefactors and political handlers in government in a new push for a more dramatic makeover of economic power relations from white and black elitism to a broader base of black beneficiaries.

'Broader', in hindsight, is a bit optimistic. The new era would demonstrate just the opposite. The frustrations of the previous decade – the resentments of every group that felt ignored, marginalised, helpless and slighted since the end of apartheid – would be taken out on party moderates. To them, those were lost years: under Mbeki there had been far too much focus on a business-centred growth path and economic-stabilisation measures.

Apparently, the election of Zuma hardly changed their thinking. By early 2010, South Africa was in trouble again. Old stable hands and astute economists in government had been virtually exiled from leadership, and were even retiring in large numbers. Corruption was endemic. Party discipline – the most tangible measure of the Mbeki era – was wilting and waning, and voter turnout on the ANC's side in the 2009 local-government elections had been declining in the face of rising opposition parties.

It was a sign of just how dysfunctional the state was becoming. By every observable measure, South Africa was sinking swiftly into a new phase of the transition; a terrain where the scramble for wealth and power was cutting an anarchic swathe across the country. The first signs that something was amiss were hints of a new form of enrichment within the state procurement system that had been steadily expanding from a few localised episodes during Mbeki's government into an acidic pattern of larceny on a grand scale no sooner than his removal, adding a sombre depth to the tragedy.

Coming on the heels of a spate of corruption stories that thronged the front pages of newspapers across the country, the reports added fuel to media speculation of a silent coup, where control of the state and security apparatus had by then become the battleground for rival factions in the ruling party.

Standing above all others in the scramble for power and wealth was a new clutch of young black militants in the ANC Youth League who, in their public avowals, wanted nothing less than the disavowal of an earlier period of elitism; in reality, they wanted control of the state and its resources. Their chief foe was Zuma, and he knew them better: they were in plain view. They had hoped to bend him to their will after Mbeki's removal, but, if they could not bend him, they decided, they must defeat him.

As confidence in the survival of Zuma's presidency began to falter, in mid-2012, a restive coterie of youth, encouraged by the ANC Youth League's calls for the nationalisation of mines and expropriation of land, introduced a new virus into the Rainbow construct that had been assiduously cultivated during the Mandela presidency – rebellion. They had publicly charged that Zuma betrayed his mandate at the fateful party conference that toppled Mbeki in December 2007.

A depression had settled over the land, with dark political clouds intensifying a sense of dystopia even among those in the white business establishment who, out of greed or cowardice during apartheid or love of privilege since 1994, endowed the ANC government that now ruled them with spurious virtues. The confidence that South Africa had transcended its past and was different from some of its tormented African neighbours – that trust was vanishing.

It was as if a huge historic conflict had suddenly become a calumnious feud. "The ANC," the country's then Deputy President Kgalema Motlanthe observed in August 2012, "was being taken over by alien tendencies."[5]

Thus it was when Jacob Zuma took the reins in 2009 that the new era produced not only lucrative fiefdoms – a clutch of powerful businessmen who became known as 'tendepreneurs' – but also power alliances that eventually paved the way for the rise of a generation of young radicals: the born-frees.

The new administration did not turn out as they had hoped. Whites kept their grip on economic power, and soon the coalition behind Zuma's rise lost theirs and slipped from most South African minds. But throughout the months between the end of the Mbeki presidency and the morning of February 2010, inequality remained an irritant and constant reminder of unfinished business.

In this poisonous atmosphere, the name Chumani Maxwele came to fit in a peculiarly evocative way.

AFTER AN INVESTIGATION INTO MAXWELE'S ARREST, THE HUMAN RIGHTS Commission came to the profound conclusion that his constitutional rights were violated. Supposedly, the Minister of Police, Nathi Mthethwa, a respondent in the matter, had acted in an unreasonable and unacceptable manner by initially failing to cooperate with the Commission and respond timeously and substantively to its request for information.

In a March 2011 draft report on the case, the Commission also found that the Minister should "be held vicariously liable for the acts of members and employees of the South African Police Service who are found to have been acting within the course and scope of employment".[6]

What's more, the Commission recommended that the Minister, on behalf of all employees involved in the Maxwele incident, "should make a full written apology to Maxwele for their unlawful and unconstitutional behaviour".[7] This apology, the Commission wrote to the Minister, "should be submitted to the Commission within 30 days of the Minister's receipt of

---

5 Author's notes on the occasion of Deputy President Kgalema Motlanthe's speech to the ANC's National Elective Conference, Mangaung, 2012.

6 See Centre for Constitutional Rights, 'Police brutality failing the Constitution', 1 March 2013. Accessed at www.cfcr.org.za/index-php/docs-statements?download=190:police-brutality-failing-the-constitution

7 Quoted in Donnelly, L, 'Police told to apologise to jogger', *Mail & Guardian Online*, 8 July 2011. Accessed at http://mg.co.za/article/2011-07-08-police-told-to-apologise-jogger.

the Commission's report".[8]

The day before Chumani Maxwele's R1.4 million civil claim against Mthethwa was about to be heard in court, he was made a settlement offer of R80 000. Still traumatised by the police abuse he claimed he suffered, the student told the *Mail & Guardian* afterwards he felt the amount of money offered did not match his damages claim following his arrest in February 2010. "I don't think justice will be served by reaching a settlement behind closed doors,"[9] he said shortly after the settlement offer was made. What he really wanted was his day in court.

He knew that prostrating himself to the government by accepting the settlement offer was a sure way to mark indelibly the legally permissible boundaries of a political and moral issue. As long as the grand metaphor – the bad-land we call the transition – was floating above the confusion of power struggles in the ruling party, the bigger picture would at best be elusive, and no one in the inner sanctums of power bothered to challenge that.

In 2013, an appeal finding by the Human Rights Commission upheld its earlier ruling that Mthethwa apologise to Maxwele. When the appeal by Mthethwa was finally settled, the Minister wrote a terse letter to the Commission, apologising for the conduct of members of the security establishment.

By the end of 2013, Maxwele's High Court case appeared to have become a moral victory – for him, if not an entire generation of black students. Where once he was a loyal member of the ANC, he had defied the highest office in the land and got away with it. "On that day," Maxwele later recalled, "the party was over for me."[10]

And so, after his brief moment in the media glare, he returned to student life. In the eternal void, his lawsuit went predictably ignored – until early 2015, when Maxwele, now emboldened by his victory, came out of obscurity to put the transformation of the higher education system at the centre of South Africans' consciousness.

*

8 Muaga, V, 'Chumani Maxwele's rights were violated – SAHRC', *Politicsweb*, 7 July 2011. Accessed at http://www.politicsweb.co.za/opinion/chumani-maxweles-rights-were-violated-sahrc.

9 Underhill, G, 'Man who "insulted" Zuma in limbo', *Mail & Guardian Online*, 7 June 2013. Accessed at http://mg.co.za/article/2013-06-07-00-man-who-insulted-zuma-in-limbo.

10 Author's notes, Cape Town, 21 June 2013.

If his arrest provided Maxwele with the flammable pretext for his cause, the atmosphere of perceived crisis and disappointment was the spark that would set off a national movement. What distinguished those early days of 2015 was that so many black students had no funding for tuition fees and accommodation. Many like Maxwele lived nomadic lives between impoverished townships and the rarefied halls and lecture rooms of campus. Around that time, Maxwele attended a public talk by a Lonmin black executive to students on the massacre of striking mine workers at Marikana in the North West province.

"The whole house was white," Maxwele recalled, saying: "I was so upset. How can a black executive from Lonmin come and defend a white, London-based company? I made my views heard and guess what, the chairman was a very apologetic black academic. He threatened to call security."[11]

*

The fate of black students at UCT was to dream and wait and decay. But Maxwele wasn't decaying. Beneath his slightly bewildered manner lay a fierce intensity and even stubbornness.

The story, told by those close to him, is that Chumani Maxwele had come face to face with racism at university. Two weeks after the Lonmin meeting, Maxwele was in the university library. He recalled being approached by a white student who said, "'Are you that kaffir who disturbed our talk?' I wanted to engage with him but the insult made me report it to UCT," Maxwele claimed.[12] It took the university eight months to report back, but the investigation into the complaint had not been finalised.

The Rainbow nation and the transformation of higher education were not for historically white ivory towers like UCT, which belonged to an older, Anglo-Saxon liberal tradition.

In this rarefied atmosphere it was not unusual to see black and white students and bespectacled professors walking past a bronze statue of Cecil John Rhodes on the terraced slopes of the upper campus with an air of dishevelled preoccupation and indifference. But beneath the humdrum routine,

---

11 Quoted in Fekisi, L & Vollenhoven, S, 'We love UCT, says student who covered Rhodes in shit', *The Journalist*, June 2015. Accessed at http://www.thejournalist.org.za/spotlight/we-love-uct-says-student-who-covered-rhodes-in-shit.
12 Ibid.

black student anger at racism on campus had been steadily gathering energy during the previous two years.

Then came the tipping point.

*

On 8 March 2015 – almost five years to the day Chumani Maxwele rose from nowhere to publicly challenge his arrest by presidential bodyguards – the 30-year-old student filled a container with human waste from one of the portable toilets in the crowded black townships on the windswept plains outside Cape Town. The next morning, he took the container to the Rhodes statue. Sculpted by Marion Walgate in the repose of Rodin's *The Thinker* gazing over the university rugby fields and peripatetically toward Rhodes's imperial dream of a British colonial Africa, the statue was unveiled in 1934 in tribute to Rhodes's donation of the Groote Schuur estate for the founding of the university in 1918.

Rhodes imagined Anglo-Boer War enmity between English and Afrikaner being laid to rest. He wanted the interaction of promising young people from these backgrounds in a collegiate academic environment. Yet, just as many young Afrikaners in the 1930s and forties were uncomfortable on a campus which provided daily reminders of Rhodes and his close ally, Leander Starr Jameson, many black students began to question the continued memorialisation of the statue.

Just a decade earlier, the Rhodes Foundation had sought to rebrand itself, to re-imagine its legacy through an alliance with the Mandela Foundation. The new board referred to it by a name that seemed to have come straight out of a Kafkaesque novel. They called it, more prosaically, the Mandela Rhodes Foundation. There were no protests. In fact, throughout the anti-apartheid struggle the Rhodes statue had received no special attention; it was barely mentioned in transformation policy and discourse since 1994.

Against this diffidence, Maxwele launched a cheeky analytical attack. At 7:30 p.m. on Monday, 21 September 2015, he gave a succinct statement to an *Independent Online* reporter. Seeking to revive the spirit of black consciousness, he reached back to the ideas of Steve Biko and the Algerian revolutionary, Franz Fanon, for inspiration. He told the reporter that his one-man protest was on behalf of "the collective pain and suffering" of all black people. He was calling for the removal of the statue. UCT, he said, had no collective history, alleging that students were "offended" by the architecture and names of buildings on the campus. "This poo that we are throwing on the statue represents the shame of black people," he snarled. "By throwing it on the statue we are throwing our shame to (sic) whites' affluence."[13]

Maxwele then emptied the container over the statue. If the protest was a propaganda coup, a clever provocation meant to inflame university authorities, confront public sensibilities, and incite black students, the gambit worked. Amid all the disbelief and denial, a mild tremor had shaken the foundations of the country.

*

All who knew him agree, the storm that had broken in February 2010, when Chumani Maxwele was arrested, was also the theatrical denouement of his life. Until that point, the apotheosis of an ordinary student whose grasp of the country's complex problems was perhaps limited even helped sustain the myth of a principal protagonist.

Whatever the exact details, Maxwele had kept transformation from being a complete abstraction. If not for him, the Rhodes statue might not have crossed our minds. During the days that followed the Rhodes incident, the story was given prominence in newspapers across the country at a time when the country seemed adrift, torn apart by social and political discord.

But another story was running beneath the surface: the development of certain ideas about universities and their mission in South Africa. Some students in Maxwele's circle had begun to think about what it would mean for Rhodes to be removed from campus. They concluded that it would be good for the transformation of the higher education system.

In many ways, then, the day Maxwele desecrated the Rhodes monument offered a tangible metaphor for a grander narrative caught between circumstance and power. With the ANC in power and the old apartheid dominion still in control of the economy, the student youth would inhabit the space in between – a ubiquitous terrain known as 'the transition' – to brandish their own struggle in an opaque world somewhere between conspiracy and a newly emerging moneyed class.

In the days and weeks that followed, the protest had spread to other campuses in South Africa – including Rhodes University, where students

---

13 Quoted in Bester, J, 'Protestors throw poo on Rhodes statue', *Independent Online*, 10 March 2015. Accessed at http://www.iol.co.za/news/south-africa/western-cape/protesters-throw-poo-on-rhodes-statue-1829526.

demanded a name change, and the University of KwaZulu-Natal (UKZN), where students defaced a statue of King George V and draped a banner bearing the words 'End white privilege'. The students at UKZN had begun their own hashtag #GeorgeMustFall.

A new movement had begun. Chumani Maxwele had lit the flame.

THE ROAD THAT LED TO THE STUDENT MOVEMENT IS LONG AND NOT AT ALL direct. The genesis of this book lies in the basic question: Why did Rhodes become the leading cause of students? The answer, as we shall see, is not straightforward. The elite sectors of higher education have had a large number of distinctive characteristics: collegial self-management, self-confidence in criticism of a highly selected elite, excellence in the specific skills of each aesthetic and intellectual practice, high social esteem, and high incomes for senior managers. The reward for students and academic staff in this productive system has also been distinctive: not high incomes and opportunities per se, but cultural insularity. The interrelatedness of these characteristics suggests that this system is a niche culture, flowering only under conditions similar to those previously found in higher education institutions where its beneficiaries had received their cultural and intellectual formation.

Herein lay its fragility. In Desmond Ryan's splendid critique of the British education system since the Thatcher reforms of the 1980s, higher education has existed in an "economic enclave protected by vested interests".[14] This protection ("that formative racial matrix", as Ryan reminds us) has depended on a long-established but contingent view of its interests taken by privileged classes. In historical perspective, the development of South African higher education between the early 20th century and 1994 has been similar. Since the end of apartheid, those controllers had not changed, even though the proclaimed view of the democratic state's interests had been transformed. Higher education now appears, in Ryan's take on the British experience, "as the state-sponsored workshop of the discipline of control for an elite destined for leadership roles across those parts of the culture which gave scope to critically trained and creative minds".[15] As the generative source of a culture of intellectual snobbery and cultural insulation, of

---

14 Ryan, D, 'The Thatcher government's attack on higher education in historical perspective', in *New Left Review*, No. 227 (London: January-February 1998), p. 5.
15 Ibid.

self-surpassing individual achievement, and of Western norms, the South African higher education system has been all but transformed – not by disruptive students and declining standards against superior competition from the systems of other countries, but by its own former and current governing authorities and sponsors in the private sector.

In being organisationally reconfigured to take on a politically decreed transformative role in society and the economy, universities have not individually and collectively changed their institutional culture. They have, in a sense, remained productive of racial hierarchies of power. In being economically reconfigured, they have abrogated the responsibility to self-manage their own work, a vital ingredient of the discipline of originality. Losing the discipline of creativity under criticism has brought the consequential loss of their transformative role as producers of critical thinking and intellectual dynamism.

PART I

An Imperial Prologue

1835–1902

CHAPTER I

A polite war

THE ROLE OF MISSION SCHOOLS IN CONQUEST

THERE IS NO SEMINAL OPENING ACT FOR OUR STORY, BUT LET'S START with a solitary affair – long discarded in the currency of time – that provided a foretaste of the years that lay ahead. In what is clearly one of the least-heralded events in South African history, we find in an archived notebook of British missionary, Reverend John Campbell, scrawls of a report to London outlining the dangers of a new conflict. Upon the successful conclusion of slavery, warned Campbell, the Dutch would become a menace in southern Africa more formidable to the British Crown than any yet known. Campbell's entry, some time in March 1832, tells of plans for a secret treaty between a Griqua interpreter named Andries Waterboer and the British governor of the Cape Colony at that stage, in which Waterboer agreed to 'keep the peace' in the area.[16]

We do not have an exact date of the treaty, but we can hazard a guess at 1835, a year after the end of slavery and the outbreak of the Third Cape Frontier War. By this time, freed slaves and indigenous communities in the Cape were resisting schooling for subordinate positions in the Cape Colony. Until the first suggestion of segregation in schooling, when the Church recommended separate schools for slaves, Dutch children shared common facilities with slaves, and endured similar subject status. Thus, from the earliest days of formal education in the Cape, the colonialists' implementation of policy was met by slave-Dutch student resistance.

Their most effective defence, the historian, Frank Molteno, has written, was flight.[17] And so, in the early 1830s, the outcast Khoikhoin were fleeing the Cape inland to the area known as Griqualand West (now the Northern

---

16 McNish, JT, *The Road to El Dorado* (Cape Town: Struik, 1968), p. 8.
17 Molteno, F, 'The origins of black education: The historical foundations of the schooling of Black South Africans', in Kallaway (n ‡ above), p. 46.

Cape) via Namaqualand; so, too, were Dutch hunters and farmers at the Cape gradually moving north, some along the coastline, others spreading fanwise toward the Orange Free State and the Transvaal.

In Griqua oral testimony, related to me by one of the oldest surviving members of the community named Eddie Fortune, the presence of the Dutch in the Northern Cape became a menace by the mid-1830s. The number of Afrikaner trekboers had grown considerably, from a handful in 1832 to about 1 500 by the end of slavery in 1834, with some 700 settled on land beyond the Orange River during 1836. Some settled land occupied by the Griqua; others leased considerable tracts from the Griqua chief, Adam Kok I, known as the "'missionary chief' because the church had a great deal to do with his election".[18] Once occupied, they ignored the Griqua and emulated as best they could the institutions of the British colony they had recently fled.

When I met Eddie Fortune in early 2010, he told me that many Afrikaners who had crossed the Orange River remained on Kok's land around Campbell, and later an area known as Philippolis (later Kokstad). Others asked Sotho Chief Moshoeshoe for pasturage between the open scrubby veld and mountains in the Caledon Valley. A few isolated parties under separate leaders reached the Vaal River, where they encountered Chief Mzilikazi's mighty Ndebele; still others trekked eastwards into the land of King Tshaka's amaZulu.

Apartheid history has, since the late 1930s, mythologised this stage in the Dutch trekboers' journey from the Southern Cape as the Great Trek and ascribed the split between Afrikaners and English in the white power bloc to liberal policies of the British government in the latter's relations with black people. Conceptualising the process from an alternative standpoint, the historian, Nosipho Majeke, has described how the trekboers "were in danger of being submerged" because of their small numbers, lack of military strength and complete lack of cohesion. "For the procuring of guns," she wrote, "they were dependent on the British, whose subjects they were."[19]

In this climate of conflict and betrayal, the majority of trekboers were given free rein as long as they didn't resist Britain's advance into the interior and northern parts of the country. Between the early and late 1930s, the

18 See McNish (n 16 above), p. 6.
19 Quoted in Majeke, N, *The Role of the Missionaries in Conquest* (Cape Town: APDUSA, 1986). Accessed at http://vi.sahistory.org.za/pages/library-resources/onlinebooks/role-missionaries/missionaries-index.htm.

budding republics the trekboers had gone on to establish in the Orange Free State and the Transvaal did pose a threat to Britain's expansion. Subject to Afrikaner ideology, the Afrikaners now looked both back to their own culture and language, and onward to an aggressive struggle against Britain for self-determination that would span the better part of a century. The chief beneficiaries of Britain's imperial ambitions in southern Africa, for the first time since the migration of trekboers and the Khoikhoin from the Cape, were now tribal chiefs such as Moshoeshoe in the Caledon Valley and Waterboer in Griqualand, who stood to benefit from a new capitalist economy under British rule.

By mid-1835, the threat of a land grab persuaded Adam Kok in Philippolis that Britain would have to intervene directly to avert annexation by the Boer republics. But the chronology of time leading to the treaty reveals that it was at least three months earlier, in March 1835, that Andries Waterboer met British agents to discuss the finer shadings of his role in Britain's annexation of the area. In this treaty, Waterboer, who had gone on to usurp the chieftainship of a rival Griqua faction, had also to use his military forces against any 'rebel' Griqua loyal to Kok under constant supervision by a British government agent and emissary of London.

Here was Britain's finest hour. Unfortunately for the Griqua, it was Waterboer's darkest hour. Britain needed the vast South African interior in order to advance north from the Cape Colony, where it had ruled since the turn of the 19th century; and tribal chiefs like Andries Waterboer were its 'jackpot'.

It could be argued that the keynote for our story was struck at just this moment, 172 years after the first school was opened in 1663 to educate the original shipment of Dutch East India Company slaves to the Cape in Christianity and the Dutch language.[20] As will become evident later in this book, the manner of their banishment to a life of inferiority and despair after the end of slavery in 1834 would, going on two centuries later, foreshadow the decampment of a generation of born-frees onto a new political landscape.

The aim of this chapter is not to probe a vast speculative literature, or certain dubious histories that have edged closer towards falsification, on the role Britain came to play in the conquest, first of the Khoikhoin and then African communities in southern Africa, although this forms a significant

---

20 Molteno (n 17 above), p. 45.

backdrop. Rather, it is to explore how and why Britain's principal front organisation for educational indoctrination and cultural assimilation – the London Missionary Society – and its main instrument, mission schools, came about before returning to their role in the conquest and dismemberment of the Griqua.

*

There is an image in the private collection of Gamsha Gool, who married into the Kok family in Kimberley, of Andries Waterboer wearing a suit; his necktie is fastened to a stiff, white wing collar and his greying hair is neatly combed back behind a wide forehead and pinched face that tapers into a well-groomed moustache and pointy beard. The yellowy, creased portrait cuts an incongruous figure: his elegant attire appears to cast the man in the respectable image of an English aristocrat. His apparent air of pensive concentration gives the impression of almost studious poise. Only the austerity of a threadbare jacket and rumpled shirt exclaims the real background of his minor station in British colonial society.

By the time we see Waterboer in this photograph, already in his sixties, he is very much a 'black Englishman', not quite his own man. He is among a few black people to have been through mission schooling and believes that Christianity is civilised and divine; the Crown Colony is its anointed emissary.

In 1935, Waterboer's primary mission was a coup – dividing the Griqua nation and generating considerable support for Britain's occupation of the territories of Griqualand. Until this point, Britain maintained a formal alliance with Waterboer in Griqualand West, with the nominal backing of Adam Kok in Philippolis, against Afrikaner trekboers who, we recall, had fled British rule in the Cape Colony during the mid-1830s and established two republics. This creation of 'buffers' in the ensuing battle between the English and Chief Mzilikazi to the north and Afrikaners on farms at Winburg across the Vaal River and Potchefstroom would be a constant theme of British imperial designs on South Africa well into the 20th century.

In 2010, when I met Gamsha Gool already sixteen years into South Africa's democracy, I was struck by how deeply the legacy of Waterboer's treaty had been etched in the social fabric of the Griqua. "The bones of the Griqua," he told me, "were scattered far and wide by centuries of false promises, ideological indoctrination, co-option and division by British missionary schooling."[21] The broader current in which the education of chiefs was thus articulated ideologically, Gool seemed to be saying, was the work of liberal humanitarians in the aftermath of the Industrial Revolution in Britain. In fact, there arose a new stratum of colonialists fulfilling the role of moderate, post-feudal African governments, so important in sustaining the emerging secular ideology of 19th-century British imperialism.

Here, the wheels of history began to role, and, depending on your interpretation, ultimately shaped the alliances, boundaries and land-ownership patterns in what became modern monopoly capitalism. The role Britain came to play in the conquest, first of the Khoikhoin and then Nguni- and Sotho-speaking Africans beyond slavery, was not an ephemeral thing.

London's reach, as we shall see, was long.

IN THE MIDDLE AGES, THE ECONOMIC EXPANSION OF EUROPE WAS AT THE root of the Christian Crusades against the Mohammedans and the Spanish and Portuguese slave traders. It was the combined inspiration of Christian piety and profit that dispatched the Elizabethan adventurers in the late 16th century to join in the commercial crusade begun by their rivals, Spain and Portugal.

In the early to mid-19th century, this pattern of conquest merged with two moments that moved the missionaries into overdrive. One was the British Industrial Revolution. Within British society, years of industrialisation had wrought such changes that customary political notions and ideas became almost meaningless. Britain's and Europe's social structure had been overturned; the social classes which had so implacably wrestled with one another in the emerging bourgeois order were all, with the partial exception of the mercantile class, either destroyed or lying prostrate. Steam and machinery had revolutionised industrial production; workers were streaming into towns; the wheels of the industrial machine were turning faster and faster. In this milieu, Britain was searching for new markets, new raw materials, and a mass of new workers. On the battlefields of Britain's colonies, the classes which possessed power in the state were by this time the rising industrialists and landowners.

The other development was the end of slavery and the retreat of Britain

---

21 Interview with the author, Kimberley, 10 July 2012.

from direct military conquest of its colonial subjects in the colonies. Europe and Britain were in the throes of bourgeois revolutions. Both slavery and authoritarianism, a group of liberal humanitarians believed, were antiquated institutions that could only discredit Britain in its new spheres of influence around the world. Feudalism, wrote the Superintendent-General of the Cape Education Department, Langham Dale, in an article entitled 'Technical instruction and industrial training', had yielded great riches, but the new epoch and the new slave would yield even greater riches. He then posed the rhetorical question, "Do you prefer to spend public money on police, prisons and other repressive and protective agencies, or on the workshop and the teachers of handicraft?"[22]

In fact, a very underrated aspect of hegemony the British established in the first half of the 19th century was the role religion, language and cultural indoctrination came to play in training and nurturing large elements of elite strata in the Third World, directly in its own institutions and indirectly through 'national' institutions located in the colonies themselves, through the supply of teachers and syllabi. Karl Marx and Frederick Engels gave intellectual vigour to their theory of bourgeois revolution in *The Communist Manifesto*, published in 1848, when they declared that capitalism had unleashed enormous productive powers in the 100 years since the beginning of the Industrial Revolution in Britain. They observed the ruling classes as stable only to the extent that they were able to press the minds of subordinate classes into their service.

If this constituted an exclusive repertoire of ideological apparatuses through which the emerging African elite began to think, the decline of feudalism in the Cape during the early 1930s coincided with an international order of ideology and culture in which ideas of mental subjugation were to become universal.

*

In the apparent anarchy following Britain's second conquest of the Cape in 1806, a single end can be seen: a capitalist system into which both the Dutch and black populations had to be assimilated – the one as partners, the other as exploited wage labourers. Yet the conflict between Afrikaners,

---

22 Dale, L, 'Technical instruction and industrial training', *Christian Express* XXI, 1 March 1892, in Molteno (n 17 above), p. 51.

whose own history had begun in rebellion against British imperialism, and British industrialists over the nature of the emerging economic order also meant they shared a common, immediate aim: the confiscation of land from indigenous communities and the imposition of a racially exclusive social order on this melange.

Out of these early efforts emerged a vast system of indoctrination aimed at keeping black people pliant and subjugated. Large parts of indigenous culture and institutions in new British colonies were taken over simply through the cultural assimilation of many of their leaders. And it is here, not only in the social and economic formation of British imperialism, but also in the cultural influence of the British imperial colony in the Cape, that the articulation of a new informal capitalist empire within a framework of universal rights (in opposition to both slavery and direct colonialism) reached maturity.

None of what I have highlighted so far is particularly mysterious. The end of slavery, the birth of capitalism in the interstices of British modernity, the rise of imperialism: all these, and many other collateral matters, are well documented. What is particularly striking is a type of history that features a group of influential men, influenced by an ideology of evangelism during the industrial transformations of the 1820s, who helped invent the ideas and emblematic forms of human agency with which Britain influenced, refashioned, and ultimately dictated the conditions of colonial conquest in South Africa.

Particularly successful instruments of this new ideology were mission schools, "workshops of Christian civilisation and cultural assimilation", Cape Governor George Grey once called them, that were to become the foundational myth through which Britain sought the legitimation and security of the emerging bourgeois state. All this depended, in turn, on the historical evolution of a set of ideas and institutions under the leadership of a unique agency: the London Missionary Society.

AS EARLY AS 1775, A RELIGIOUS PARTY ORIGINATING AMONG SOME Cambridge theologians, known as the Evangelicals, formed the Society for Missions in Africa and the East, and, through their influence, missionaries of various denominations were deployed throughout British colonies in the East Indies, Jamaica, Trinidad, Nova Scotia, the West Coast of Africa, and southern Africa. In the British House of Commons, they had won a series of resolutions to work for the 'religious welfare' of Britain's richest colonial possession: India. There is no question that there was intense, sometimes explosive, rivalry between liberals and hawkish conservatives in London over Britain's imperial ambitions and methods. But, in this strategy, the two parties were never far apart. If economic expansion was the new battleground, the Evangelicals received strong support from an influential group of politicians representing the industrial and mercantile class. Known as the Clapham Sect, their political patron was William Wilberforce, the son of a wealthy merchant in Clapham, London. The group also included Lord Teignmouth, a former Governor General of India and representative of the aristocracy associated with the rising middle class, and Thomas Fowell Buxton, a politician and partner in a brewery concern, who, with Wilberforce, founded the Aborigines' Protection Society during a particularly menacing period of British colonial conquest in Australia.

Some time in 1776, the Evangelicals had the idea of founding the London Missionary Society based on the principle of united action by all denominations of orthodox Christianity. It was part of British capitalism, with its varied resources, that the Society sent its first party of missionaries to the Cape Colony in 1799, consisting of two Hollanders, Dr Van der Kemp and Kicherer, and two Englishmen named Edwards and Edmond. Van der Kemp, who seems to have been the leader of the party, became mission manager. On their arrival at the Cape of Good Hope, wrote Dr RHW Shepherd, Lovedale College's Principal in the 1950s, in his *History of Lovedale*, Van der Kemp travelled as far as the Tyumie River in the bushy scrubland of the Eastern Cape, where, decades later, the college would emerge. There, Van der Kemp tried to win over the Xhosa Chief, Ngqika. But such overtures were not matched by the intensely traditional ideological disposition of Ngqika, who had held his own against Dutch land invasions for about a quarter of a century.

Meanwhile, the Reverends Kicherer and Edwards travelled north to the baThwa at the Zak River, but encountered a community already decimated by the ravages of war. To attempt to regroup them into a community was unprofitable, and Van der Kemp set to work in Graaff-Reinet.

In his book, *A History of Christian Missions in South Africa*, the author, J du Plessis, records a number of Khoikhoin "drawn into mission schools and Christianity by Van der Kemp and placed in a temporary location at

Zwartkops River in Algoa Bay".[23] It was in the district near what is now Uitenhage, Du Plessis wrote, that Van der Kemp encountered resistance. The attempt to establish a mission station in the area operated doubly for the purpose of co-opting the missionary-controlled Khoikhoin; if their resistance could be crushed, it would be easier to pursue the attack against the amaXhosa. As it turned out, the Khoikhoin joined the Xhosa Chief Ndlambe in resisting the mission station and school. But, one by one, their surviving leaders were captured and Xhosa–Khoikhoin unity was shattered.

It is interesting to observe how, from this point forward, the pattern of subsequent labour policy emerged. The traveller, Lichtenstein, has left a picture of Bethelsdorp as a place of "shameful poverty".[24] "It was on a barren strip of land," he recorded, "insufficient to enable the Khoikhoin to live without going out to labour for emerging industrialists and farmers."[25]

In 1801, the Reverend Anderson, who had arrived in the Cape with a second batch of missionaries, established a footing among the Griqua and began a process of 'divide and rule'. The first schools in the Northern Cape and in the Orange Free State were set up in 1823, and in Natal and what became the Transvaal in 1835 and 1842, respectively. Using literacy classes, these schools proved irresistible to some black leaders.

And therein lay a paradox articulated clearly by Langham Dale's later description as "hostages for peace": the participation of chiefs in the missions set up in the Transkei, Thembuland and Griqualand.[26] Their participation made them, in effect, fellow travellers of British imperialist conquests in early 19th-century South Africa. But, upon examination of the first faltering steps of missionary work, it seems likely that schooling was still relatively detached from a strategy for capitalist expansion. As will become evident, the development of mission schools by the turn of the century was slow, until 1839 when the establishment of a Department of Education in the Cape Colony brought the control of missions under its jurisdiction.[27]

Fortunately for the Evangelicals, the same developments that had made winning the hearts and minds of the chiefs so crucial – territorial conquest and capitalist expansion – were also producing a generation of liberals in London who shared capitalists' interests in southern Africa, but not Britain's

---

23 Du Plessis, J, *A History of Christian Missions in South Africa* (London, 1911), pp. 29-30.
24 Molteno (n 17 above), p. 51.
25 Ibid.
26 Ibid.
27 Ibid., p. 49.

military disposition. By some accounts, the biggest developments in missionary education began with the entry of one man on the scene who had set the entire country on a course that would sunder from the historical record traditional claims to land and mineral resources through a string of beguiling manoeuvres and go on to pour the foundations of what, well over a century later, would become Bantu education. His name was Dr John Philip.

CHAPTER 2

'Evangelical workshops'

NATIVE EDUCATION

To FOLLOW JOHN PHILIP'S CAREER SINCE HIS ARRIVAL IN THE CAPE IN
1818 is a great political drama of the role of missionary education around
the time the ravages of British military conquest were in full frame. Some
time in early 1818, following a meeting of the London Missionary Society,
Philip was appointed Superintendent of the London Missionary Society in
Southern Africa and placed in charge of an ambitious project: establishing a
permanent agency of the Society in the region. Accomplishing this required
actors; only their dramatisations could remove the mental blinders that led
some black communities to regard with suspicion the strategy of divide and
rule beneath the model of civilised order of the missionaries.

Philip had by the time of his arrival in the Cape been moving through
the social and political set of London's middle-class elite. With his reput-
edly effete mannerisms and political machismo, he came to the Cape
Colony with liberal-humanitarian ideas of 'liberty and equality', freedom of speech, and 'free' labour with which the middle classes in England
had been liberated from feudal autocracy. He had the support of powerful men like Wilberforce, Buxton and other representatives in the British
Parliament. At a later stage in his career, he was able to write confidently
(and confidentially) to Buxton: "At present, the Colonial government does
nothing as to relations with the independent native tribes without consulting me."[28]

Philip had quickly established a reputation as the most far-sighted representative of British imperialism in southern Africa. The London Missionary
Society's cloak-and-dagger diplomacy appealed to the imagination of the
man; its main attraction was the promise of achieving strategic objectives

---

28 Quoted in Majeke (n 19 above), 'Chapter III: Dr Philip – defender of the Hottentot'.

on the cheap and sly, without involving Britain in all-out war. He saw no
daylight in the narrowly restrictive feudal economy of the Governor of the
Cape, Lord Charles Somerset, and his alliance with the emerging Cape
Afrikaner elite. Somerset was, to all appearances, a petty despot opposed to
the independence of the London Missionary Society. As the 1820s wore on,
Somerset's alarm reached dire pitch.

The character of liberals, and their discomfort with the plain adaptation
of Britain's strategy of military conquest of emerging capitalist societies,
gave their world view a human face. In reality, the rapacity of the Dutch
for land and labour never equalled in efficiency the systematic subjugation by the British, precisely because the British represented an expanding
capitalism.

At the same time as the Cape wine industry was declining, the entrepreneurial instincts of the 1820 generation of British settlers in the
Eastern Cape were opening up the Xhosa frontier and Port Natal as
major fields of investment and profit. And so, for a time in the 1820s,
a particular mercantile vision and liberalism merged in agitating for
the removal of restrictions on labour relations. It was with a degree of
equanimity, Philip once observed in a letter to Buxton, that any of the
Cape Town bourgeoisie witnessed the decline of the slave-based agricultural economy of the south-western Cape as the shallow and limited
prosperity of the economic boom.[29] As early as 1821, he envisaged the
establishment of a college in the Cape to train teachers and preachers.
In 1829, the South African College was established, although, at first,
it was little more than a high school. Emblematic of the fundamentally
conservative nature of the alliance between the Dutch and English at
the Cape, it would, however, take more than a century before black people were regarded as ready for admission into what would become the
University of Cape Town in 1918; only to be excluded again in 1959 when
the ironically named Extension of University Education Act was passed
by the government of Hendrik Verwoerd.[30]

In the meantime, Scottish teachers and ministers were arriving at the
Cape, many of them kindling the liberal impulse. As scions of Scotland's
intellectual elite, these men saw education as fundamental to the spread of
Christian civilisation.

---

29 Ibid.
30 Keegan, T, *Colonial South Africa and the Origins of Racial Order* (Cape Town: David Philip, 1996),
pp. 97-99.

But it was Philip who carried to a fine art the missionary policy of 'divide and rule'.

*

In 1828, Philip set out his treatise in a paper, rather prosaically entitled, 'Researches in South Africa'. The paper was written as an exploratory tract; and it caught the eye of British liberals, headed by Wilberforce and Buxton, who regarded it as a bureaucratic brief for the role of mission schools in the conquest of black communities. Writing to Philip that same year, Buxton stated admiringly: "Your 'Researches' have done the work. It gave a clear exposition of the value and function of missionary institutions in the interests of British imperialism, and at the same time the very basis of its argument was the superiority of the capitalist economy, with its 'free' labourer, over the backward feudal economy of the Dutch."[31]

A look at the Preface to Philip's thesis gives a clear sense of what may be called his credo: "While our missionaries ... are everywhere scattering the seeds of civilisation ...," he wrote, "they are extending British interests, British influence and the British Empire ... . Wherever the missionary places his standard among a savage tribe, their prejudices against the colonial government give way, their dependence upon the Colony is increased by the creation of artificial wants ... . Industry, trade and agriculture spring up."[32]

Here, Philip stated both an aim and a method. The method was Christianisation, which involved something much more than religion; the aim was the destruction of communal culture prevalent among African communities and its replacement with a system of wage labour under capitalism. By 'civilisation' he meant Christian capitalist civilisation. But Philip recognised that the transition from communalism to capitalism would not take place automatically. "The habits, customs, and ideas of the old system have to be broken down and replaced by those of the new system. That is one of the functions of the missionary," he wrote. "Having accepted him as a man of peace, the Christian convert has a desire to dress like his teacher and eat like his teacher. The tastes of the new civilisation – those 'artificial wants' – are thus insinuated into his habits ... . The first step towards civilising the savage is therefore to overcome his natural indolence."[33]

---

31 See Majeke (n 19 above), 'Chapter III: Dr Philip – defender of the Hottentot'.
32 Ibid.
33 Ibid.

For the first time, the link between mission stations, Christianity and labour was clear. Philip concluded his treatise thus: "Many who are acquiring a taste for civilised life by their connection with our mission stations will prefer labour, with a state of freedom, in the Colony."[34] His advocacy of the 'liberation' of the Khoikhoin from Dutch serfdom now fell into its proper perspective. He continued: "Make the Hottentots free. Give them a fair price for their labour, and their masters will have double the work and the value to the state will be trebled."[35]

If Philip's credo provided the theoretical rationale for the overt dimensions of colonial conquest, mission schools supplied the ideological basis for its covert aspects. His first aim was to convince British government officials who still had qualms about non-aggression. He then proceeded to describe specific interventions. The first step was to set up mission schools, which would serve as foci for indoctrinating chiefs. "By adopting a more liberal system of policy," he wrote, "tribes will be more productive, there will be an increased consumption of British manufactures, taxes will be paid, and farmers will have no cause to complain of a lack of labour."[36]

So pervasive was this strategy that Wilberforce later called Philip's handiwork the "basis of all politics";[37] and the arch-imperialist, Cecil John Rhodes, would decades later endorse and embroider it into his own stratagem for conquest. In fact, it was Philip, half a century before Rhodes, who aimed to extend British domination to the equator. But his imperialist vision had to wait until the discovery of gold and diamonds – and the final defeat of the Dutch and Africans. In reality, it was all part of the liberal myth of 'protection' of black tribes against external threats. It was trusteeship in its earliest form. As Majeke has written: "It was the beginning of the herrenvolk lie of the inferiority of the Non-European."[38]

It can be said that British capitalism scored its first victory with the 'liberation' of the Khoikhoin under the guise of liberalism. The amaXhosa now lay next in the path of conquest.

*

---

34 Ibid.
35 Ibid.
36 Ibid.
37 Ibid.
38 Ibid.

In the general chaos of the 1834–1836 war atmosphere, Philip was confident of the prospects of his pacification of the chiefs. While he waited at the Kat River Settlement for D'Urban's arrival, he did a great deal of writing, setting out his ideas on 'Native policy' to Buxton in London. In a letter to Buxton's daughter, with whom he had a friendly relationship and corresponded warmly throughout his station in South Africa, he wrote: "I am now ready for him with a grip of the whole situation …. I consider my work in this place done."[39]

Through his numerous correspondences, we find that Philip saw further than British military governors and commanders. In one of his letters to Buxton, he wrote, "We must be the masters, but rule as we do in India."[40] India, England's richest colonial possession, was by then torn apart by England's policy of 'divide and rule' over a period of 200 years.

By the close of the 1830s, missionary activity was spread throughout southern Africa. The London missions had been followed, in quick succession, by the Wesleyan, Scottish, Rhenish, Berlin, French and American missions in breaking down the resistance of the Xhosa Chief, Ngqika. The Rhenish mission concentrated on the Namaqua and the Herero in the far north-west of the Cape Colony beyond the Orange River. The Berlin mission added its quota of missionaries among the Xhosa and started a mission school at Bethel; they also ingratiated themselves with the Koranas beyond the Orange River in Griqualand, having acquired land from the Griqua Chief, Adam Kok, who, by that time, was himself under the influence of the Wesleyan missionaries.

To the east of Griqualand, the French missionaries, on Philip's advice, mollycoddled Chief Moshoeshoe; and the Americans, also at the instigation of Philip, attempted to gain a footing both among the amaZulu between the Drakensberg Mountains and the East Coast, and the Ndebele, a splinter group of the amaZulu who had broken from Tshaka and settled further inland on the Highveld.

Of all the missionaries, the Wesleyans came to be regarded by the Cape government as its most efficient agent. Their first mission was to the Namaqua, west of the Cape Colony, after crossing the Orange River into Great Namaqualand. But their most intensive operations were among the

---

39 Ibid.
40 See Majeke (n 19 above), 'Chapter V: Political role of the mission'.

Bantu[41] tribes, both to the east and north of the Cape. Under the leadership of Reverend William Shaw, they proceeded to chart a chain of mission stations from the Zuurveld to Port Natal, a vast distance of roughly 1 000 kilometres. Beyond the Orange River, they rivalled the London Missionary Society among the Griqua and played a small but significant part in the dismemberment of that community. Still further north, they gained a footing among the baTswana and soon followed the French missionaries into the land of Moshoeshoe.

But what Philip feared was the spirit of resistance of the chiefs. He had more subtle methods in mind, articulated in his 'Native policy'. He was convinced of the value of treaties with chiefs as a step toward outright annexation of their territories. In one of his musings to Buxton on native policy, he set out his case for persuading the chiefs (as a 'first step'), through missionaries, to accept the 'friendship and protection' of the British government. The next step, he argued, was to subsidise chiefs with a fixed salary, thus turning them into paid servants of the government. This was presumably what Philip had in mind when he emphasised the necessity of "ruling as we do in India".[42] It was the very cornerstone of the policy which he, as the self-appointed political adviser of the Cape government, proposed. And there was no doubt as to the purpose of his policy. "Had a few of the chiefs been subsidised," he wrote on one occasion, "by having small salaries paid to them, we might by this time have had the affairs of Kaffirland in our own hands."[43]

To the Cape governor, he now recommended the appointment of resident missionaries beside each Xhosa chief. "A total expenditure (on agents) of even £3,000 would cost much less than armies,"[44] he wrote to Somerset. Even the ruthless military officer, Colonel Harry Smith, was moved to remark that, "The man of the gospel is after all a worldly fellow ... more full of dragooning our new subjects than a hundred soldiers."[45]

As the Griqua Chief, Andries Waterboer, was a particular protégé of the missionaries, he became Philip's litmus test of the new system based on the Indian model. He pressed the necessity to Somerset of a treaty with

---

41 'Bantu' refers to over 400 ethnic groups in Africa, from countries ranging from Cameroon to South Africa. They form a common language family, called the Bantu language. However, the word 'Bantu' was used in the term Bantu education in a derogatory manner towards black South Africans.
42 Quoted in Majeke (n 19 above), 'Chapter V: Political role of the mission'.
43 Ibid.
44 Ibid.
45 Majeke (n 19 above), 'Chapter VI: The Wesleyans take hand'.

Waterboer on the northern frontier, where trekboers were seizing land but were unlikely, he feared, to protect either themselves or the colony from attack by the Ndebele Chief, Mzilikazi.

Thus it was that Waterboer was brought to Cape Town in 1835, via a circuitous route, to sign the first treaty with the Cape government.

THE YEAR 1854 MARKED AN IMPORTANT TURNING POINT IN THE DEVELopment of state interest in, and support for, the schooling of black people. In that year, Sir George Grey was appointed Governor of the Cape. Unlike Somerset, Grey and Philip were made for each other. Grey, like Philip, held missionary education to be the prime weapon in the subjugation of the indigenous population.

By 1854, conquered tribes were wrenched from their own material base and traditional social moorings. Schooling had assisted in incorporating into the new order those set loose from tribal structures of social control in such a way that they could be disciplined to serve the interests of Britain's territorial ambitions. As Grey saw it, the integration of the African people into the Cape economy was meant to turn them into "useful servants, consumers of goods, contributors to revenue; in short, a source of strength and wealth to the Colony, such as Providence designed them to be".[46]

However, Grey's treatment of education in the emerging new order was more shrewdly played. He saw the role of missionaries as indeterminate in the choking controversies within the Cape government between military repression and co-option. In this atmosphere, he had already come under the influence of Philip and the liberal humanitarians in the London Missionary Society. But, unlike Philip, Grey was a man of the mid-19th century. His central thesis, large and ambitious, was that the mission stations, as evangelical workshops with civilising missions, had outlived their day in the developing capitalist order.[47]

To most conservatives at the time, this was a dangerous delusion fit to be repeated in social confabs, but bearing little relation to the realities of a Victorian nation-consciousness and Empire-proud Britain. Only a remote future, it was thought, might bring about the repose of a capitalist nirvana.

---

46 Molteno (n 17 above), p. 51.
47 Ibid., p. 54.

Having with so much thunder pilloried military tactics, Grey's plans for South Africa were as sweeping as the ravages of military madness. The cornerstone of his policy was to break the power of the chiefs and destroy the tribal system, a task for which he had received ample training; he had just returned from the subjugation of the Maoris in New Zealand by methods that were to become familiar in his new station. He began, mildly at first, a dispatch from Cape Town on 22 November 1854, to the British Colonial Secretary that more profoundly matched the rise of a new economic order:

> The plan I propose with a view to the general adjustment of these questions of frontier policy is to attempt to gain an influence over all the tribes included between the present north-eastern boundary of this colony and Natal by employing public works which will tend to open their country; by establishing institutions for the education of the children and by these and other means to attempt to win them to civilisation and Christianity, and thus to change by degrees our present unconquered and apparently irreconcilable foes into friends who may have common interests with ourselves.[48]

Here was Grey's agenda for all Britain's political and ideological operations in the second half of the 19th century. Soon after his arrival at the Cape, he laid his plans before a meeting of missionaries at Lovedale College in the Eastern Cape. "Native education," he said, "was too bookish." In handling the Maoris of New Zealand, he promoted schemes for industrial education. He now proposed that missionary institutions should commence the same training for African students in "the more useful mechanical arts". His schemes for training Africans in these arts flowed from his original proposal to "eradicate native indolence".[49] Grafting this educational doctrine on missionary schools, he now saw their role as purveyors of a whole system of new ideas, needs, desires, allegiances, authorities, and a new morality. Christian dogma and moral instruction on good and evil formed the basis of British civilisation, aimed at undermining tribal authority and culture. But the particular point we stress here is the link between education and the new money-economy as two parts of a single process. In the early stages of conquest, the military had been enough; the object was land. Now a stage

---

48 Ibid., pp. 50-51.
49 Quoted in Majeke (n 19 above), 'Chapter III: Dr Philip – defender of the Hottentot'.

had been reached in the process of reproducing labour. In other words, a 'Native' policy was needed to fashion education into a modern instrument of racial capitalism.

For their labour, workers would receive payment in money. Grey had tried this on the indigenous communities of southern Australia and later New Zealand, and boasted that he never failed. "When half the day's toil was over, they would receive sixpence; at the end of the day, another sixpence," he wrote of the Australian aborigines. "Sometimes they received payment in kind, such as sugar, salt or coffee, the White man's food. When they were fined, the payment of the fine had to be in money."[50]

*

The first recorded black tertiary institution under Grey's native policy was established when a missionary named Reverend Ayliff became head of an industrial department at Lovedale College in the Eastern Cape. Consultations between Grey, Ayliff and the heads of Lovedale, wrote Shepherd, resulted in "a cordial understanding and agreement between them as to the institution, to be conducted by the mission, under the patronage and with the assistance of Government".[51]

While Lovedale was now to be combined with an industrial department, Ayliff, Shepherd went on to record, was instructed to "give higher education to a portion of the native youth – an educated class, from which might be selected teachers of the young, catechists, Evangelists, and ultimately even fully quali-fied preachers of the Gospel".[52] Moreover, African teacher–missionaries were to receive special government grants for their salaries. "Under such a plan [of payment]," wrote Grey, "every chief will be dependent on the government and will, therefore, have the strongest interest in its maintenance and success."[53]

All this took place worlds away from the real story, however. They were, in Majeke's words, "minor skirmishes that masked a bigger game of divide and rule played by the British". The secret of this grotesque apotheosis lay in Britain's grand imperial plan: far from forfeiting its claim to the Griqualand ter-ritory in the treaty with Waterboer, the British Empire would move once again to annex Griqualand with the discovery of diamonds in Griqualand West.

---

50 Majeke (n 19 above), 'Chapter VIII: Christianity and civilisation'.
51 Ibid.
52 Ibid.
53 Ibid.

From this point of view, the treaty of September 1835 with Andries Waterboer, which we recall gave Waterboer nominal jurisdiction over Griqualand, envisaged much more than fixing the temporary limits of land-plunder. It considered the subjugation of blacks on a broader scale and, as such, signalled the beginnings of a deliberate 'Native policy'.

IN THE FIRST TENTATIVE YEARS OF TERRITORIAL DISPUTES AND ALLIANCES, power relations were waxing and waning according to the politics of the day. In one of those bouts of flux, back-pedalling and realignment, a Special British Commissioner named Sir George Clerk arrived in Bloemfontein in early August 1853 with instructions to "abandon the Orange River Sovereignty". There was, Clerk declared, "now no alliance whatever with any native chief of tribes to the northward of the Orange River".[54]

On 11 March 1854, the British flag was lowered in the Orange Free State capital, Bloemfontein, and the Griqua chief, Nicholas Waterboer, who had succeeded Andries Waterboer, was left vulnerable to annexation by the Orange Free State republic. Britain's formal withdrawal from the area at a convention in Bloemfontein was to have a dramatic effect on future boundary disputes when a lawyer named David Arnot was assigned to act for the Waterboer Griqua territorial claim.

If Andries Waterboer had given Britain legal proxy over the interior as a buffer against the Afrikaners, only to hand the territory to the Afrikaners, Arnot would enact the final betrayal with the discovery of diamonds. Something of an incongruous figure by some accounts, Arnot gave every appearance of having the Griqua's interests at heart, he being of mixed British and Griqua descent. But his allegiance was to the British. He continually urged that a "wall of flesh"[55] should be raised as a buffer between the Griqua and the Orange Free State and the Transvaal Afrikaner trekboers.

It was some time in 1863, records JT McNish in his historical account of the 1869 diamond rush,[56] that Arnot travelled to Grahamstown and convinced as many British settlers as he could to occupy Griqualand. When word spread of diamonds on the banks of the Orange River, a party from

---

54 McNish (n 16 above), p. 10.
55 See Wilmot, A, *The Life and Times of Sir Richard Southey, K.C.M.Q.* etc. Accessed at https://archive.org/stream/lifetimesofsirrioowilm/lifetimesofsirrioowilm_djvu.txt.
56 McNish (n 16 above), p. 32.

Colesberg, along with Arnot, approached Nicholas Waterboer and secured a concession, giving them the sole right to search for diamonds in the area. Having goaded Waterboer to agree, Arnot, ever the schemer, set about persuading the Griqua chief to seek the protection of the Cape government in return for the Griqua agreeing to their territory becoming a British protectorate known as Griqualand West. Arnot all the while was quietly at work with agents of the British government to annex the territory. There was a special thrill, he once remarked, in urging, and ultimately convincing Waterboer to accept British protection and a pension of £1 000 annually once his territory became a British Crown Colony.[57]

When the Grahamstown party eventually arrived, they were advised by the Griqua tribal council that the land would be leased for a maximum 20-year period at a fee of £15 annually. Arnot gave Waterboer the written assurance that he would never act in word or deed, impugn, deny or cast doubt upon the righteous rights of Chief Waterboer.[58] Then he got the settlers to sign the leases in what amounted to the modern equivalent of a land-grab.

*

Such were the bitter fruits of Britain's missionary education. If Reverend John Philip poured the foundations for mission schools as forces for territorial conquest, Sir George Grey adapted the policy for black schooling as an instrument of modern capitalist exploitation. Perhaps, though, history will depict David Arnot's appearance on the scene as the start of a chain of events that bound Britain and South Africa together under the most bizarre circumstances.

What does not seem to be in doubt is that the drama from here on was a thoroughly modern saga. The feverish economic expansion when diamonds were discovered in large quantities along the southern bank of the Vaal River as well as close to the Riet River at Koffiefontein and Jagersfontein, the general dislocation among Griqua and black diggers that accompanied it, and the denial of their political and economic rights formed the grim backdrop to the rule of mining magnates.

From this point forward, the growth of black schooling would have a more direct bearing on racial-capitalist class relations. In general terms, as

---

57 Ibid., pp. 31-32.
58 Ibid., p. 31.

Frank Molteno has articulated, "schooling was one minor fact amongst many which went into the making of the black working class".[59]

---

59 Molteno (n 17 above), p. 59.

CHAPTER 3

From kaffir parsons to outcast ghettos

THE NEXT CONQUEST

ON A NORTHBOUND ROAD, PAST BARBED-WIRE FENCES AND SIGNS WITH loud warnings, there is a smouldering scrubland, scorched black, on the fringes of Kimberley in the Northern Cape. It is a bitterly cold June morning in 2010, shortly after the inauguration of Jacob Zuma as South Africa's third democratic president, and I am with Malcolm Goliath, a small diamond miner in Kimberley. In the distance there are silhouettes of youths walking with a slow shuffle, bending, lifting – back and forth in a sort of sombre march. "This is one of the oldest mine dumps in and around the city owned by De Beers," says Goliath. "These youth spend their days and nights scavenging for diamonds; and to keep the place wide open and visible De Beers regularly scorches the place. *Nothing* survives here."[60]

When Goliath said 'nothing survives', his penchant for irony may have shrunk into a piercing wit. There were people struggling to survive alright, but in peculiar circumstances fashioned by the area's chaotic past that belongs to a different generation; a different century, even. For two centuries, the Griqua community wandered the ever-shifting territorial frontiers of this barren interior between English colonialists and Afrikaner trekboers who settled the area during the Great Trek from the Cape in 1836. Never quite part of the one or the other and yet partial descendants of the Cape Dutch, there was a larger community of black people who eventually came to define Griqua identity: Sotho, Tswana, Xhosa, Ndebele, who had been migrants in the Northern Cape for centuries; and since the discovery of diamonds in 1867, wage labourers.

The scorched land is rubble from the famous De Beers Mine, discovered

---

60 Hereinafter, all direct references to Malcolm Goliath are attributed to an interview with the author, Kimberley, June 2010.

in 1872 and virtually mined out by the turn of that century. When I visited the area in 2010, the 'Big Hole', as the mine came to be colloquially known, was a commodified trade in 'cultural tourism', and, to all intents, a banal testimony to the philosophy of its founder, the British mining magnate, Cecil John Rhodes. "The weak," Rhodes once wrote to his business partner, Alfred Beit, "are vanquished and enslaved and the strong hold the title deeds to the future."[61]

In this story, the dystopic mine dump in Kimberley was, in a sense, the grand metaphor for colonialism. This was still frontier territory; not quite an old forgotten frontier, but its brooding adaptation to a new era. Pushed to the margins of modernity, the poor belonged to another century when men like Rhodes ascended the stage and South Africa fell victim to policies that would mark the plight of black people for generations.

It is here, in the rise of settler capitalism during the late 19th century, that this chapter of our story begins.

*

One evening in early 1890, Rhodes invited his friend and close associate, William Stead, to a meeting at his Groote Schuur estate on the grassy foot-hills of Table Mountain in Cape Town. "I think you will agree," he told a nodding Stead, "that we have set out on a great mission to create an Anglo-American empire."[62]

Here was the idealism and pillage of British imperialism. Rhodes, born in 1853 in Bishop's Stortford in England where his father was a pastor, arrived in Durban in 1870 at the tender age of 17, and, by 1890, had become Prime Minister of the Cape. For Rhodes, the world of politics he had entered was a great chess game of manipulation, patronage and personal ambition in which only wealthy educated whites, or those with connections on the fringes of the mining oligarchy, participated. It was personal ambition that brought Rhodes into this world; and by the time he met Stead he already had a bold plan.

If the end of the slave economy in 1834 cleared the decks for the rise of mission schools, the Glen Grey Bill, passed shortly after Rhodes's meeting

---

61 Sletz-Kessler, R, *Sylvia, Rachel, Meredith, Anna: A Novel* (Durham: Thatcher Forest Publishing, 2007), p. 134.
62 Crow, T, 'Cecil John Rhodes – warts and all', *Politicsweb*, 22 December 2015, in *South African History Online*. Accessed at http://www.sahistory.org.za/people/cecil-john-rhodes.

with Stead, was meant to tie Africans securely to the wheel of the now rapidly expanding capitalist economy, with mining as its flywheel. The Bill had come about because Rhodes had insisted on it. As a politician at the Cape, Rhodes had been involved in territorial questions between 1882 and 1884 over land to the north of Griqualand West and east of the Transvaal.

How intensely he was already engaged in pursuing his agenda can be seen from his battles in the mining industry. From his perch at Oxford University during a study break from Kimberley in 1875, five years after large quantities of diamonds were discovered, Rhodes saw a fist fight without order. The Kimberley diamond fields, he would write to his mother, were a moveable glut of 'anarchy': beneath the cacophony of hundreds of small diggers going about their business, there were no rules to regulate the market or corral the behaviour of black labour. The collective misery, he concluded his letter, was simply the result of the maniacal exuberance of competing diggers. In the chaos and sometimes bitter rage that swept the community of diggers and black workers, Rhodes saw plenty of justification for pushing his ideas.

Within five years, his curious seed had sprouted: he had already skilfully bought out the small diggers at a trough in the market and amalgamated their claims in the Kimberley area. With his diamond concessions safely sown up in the De Beers syndicate, he now gazed north, first to the exploitation of minerals in the Boer republic of the Transvaal. He counted this vast territorial swath as a 'road to the north' – to Matabeleland and Mashonaland between the Limpopo and the Zambezi. The road to the north was a British protectorate, which, as far as Rhodes was concerned, meant it stood open to him. There was just one hurdle: liberal mission stations, with their focus on 'annexing chiefs' through the Christianising influence of mission schools, were the dominant force in the colony.

As Rhodes and Stead puzzled over possible means of not only expanding their interests in southern Africa, but also rolling back British imperialism in favour of more direct control of land and natural resources in the colonies, they kept coming back to the same idea: the usefulness to their cause of a landless African labour force. Two years later, in 1894, the Glen Grey Act would provide a solution.

Before examining the implications of the Glen Grey legislation for black education and labour, it is first necessary to contextualise missionary education in the emerging bourgeois order. This means recapping the story of missionaries helping to reinvent the weapons of cultural and psychological

subjugation in late 19th-century South African capitalism, before colonialists such as Rhodes attempted to modernise the system.

*

Why did mission schools become such a menace to bourgeois settler society
when their origins, we remember, lay in the humanitarian and intellectual
impulses of Britain's industrial revolution that had put an end to feudalism?
An account of antagonisms between the free status of black labour that the
end of slavery in 1834 had produced and the political inclinations and personal ambitions of the British mercantile class, who had settled in the Cape
in 1820, provides an appropriate context.

Before the middle of the 19th century, there was little attempt to educate the growing industrial working class on the basis of the argument
that 'a little knowledge is a dangerous thing'. As Thomas Keegan has
recorded in his history of colonialism entitled *Colonial South Africa and
the Origins of Racial Order*, workers who were required to do simple
manual labour in factories were kept in ignorance "for their own good",
lest they become tainted by "foreign ideologies that might give them
ideas above their station and lead them to put forth unreasonable political demands for social change".[63] Although the legal underpinnings of
racial order did not require the law to be couched in overtly racial terms,
the few mixed Dutch schools for liberated slaves in Cape Town, founded
to teach English from the early 1820s onwards, were almost exclusively
white. Education for coloureds was left to the mission schools (attended
by poor whites as well).[64]

The first signs of clear policy shifts were Cape legislative interventions
during the late 1830s to regulate free slaves in the labour market. In July
1839, the Cape Legislative Council adopted an ordinance regulating the
rights and duties of 'masters and servants'; and, by 1840, liberal-humanitarian impulses thrived on a weak and underdeveloped settler economy in
the transition to bourgeois colonial society. But once settler capitalism had
become a vital force, these liberal impulses faded; an amended ordinance

---

63 Keegan (n 30 above), p. 126. Also see Johnson, R, 'Really useful knowledge: Radical education and
    working class culture, 1790–1848, in Dale, R et al. (eds), *Politics, Patriarchy and Practice: Education
    and the State*, Vol. 2 (Basingstoke: Farmer Ford/OU Press). Accessed at http://www.arasite.ord/
    johnson.htm.
64 Ibid.

was adopted in March 1841 to harness the subordination of black workers in the Cape to the emerging system of racial capitalism.

By the 1850s, a more virulent war of dispossession and conquest by the colonial government convinced conservative missionaries such as David Livingstone and George Grey that the future of mission schools lay in their role as 'industrial workshops' for Africans. Religion, while still a method of subjugation and cultural assimilation, was surpassed by the larger industrial transformations of the 1830s and forties. The new order was to be based on the ever-more rigid assertion of racial hegemony. The gist of it is this: because the colonial underclasses failed to conform to the ideal of a sub-servient workforce, new forms of social control and subjugation had to be invented to control labour and meet the demands of trade and industry.

These developments coincided with – in fact, were a result of – the rise of capitalist relations of production in agriculture. In 1953, a Commission of Inquiry in Natal was urging the apprenticeship of black youths to white farmers and tradespeople through resident magistrates. The Commission recommended the establishment of government industrial schools in each village and three years of compulsory schooling for all black children between 7 and 12 years of age. An ordinance, published in 1856, made pro-vision for grants-in-aid to mission schools and permitted the government to establish and maintain public schools. Subjects of instruction were to be religious education, industrial training, and instruction in the English language.

In 1863, the Superintendent of Education in the Cape, Langham Dale, proposed legal measures to increase the subsidisation of black schools that would encourage the teaching of needlework to girls and carpentry, shoe-making and printing to boys. Two years later, in 1865, legislation was enacted to provide state aid to three types of schools: public, mission and native. A state Inspectorate of Education was also established to monitor implemen-tation. Until this point, however, such developments would have made no major advances in the education of black people. It was the discovery of minerals and consequent changes in industrial and labour processes that led to the expansion of schooling to meet the needs of capitalist development.

Even then, the level of skill required was low. In any case, the racist form of class relations now precluded black workers from acquiring trade and other specialist skills. As early as 1836, the Interdepartmental Committee on Native Education was arguing that, "on the one hand, ... any rational system of education should make provision for vocational training, leading on to occupations which will give employment and a source of livelihood to a considerable proportion of the population. On the other hand, any such policy ... would in the present structure of South African economic conditions lead to competition of Native tradesmen with Europeans which is at present prohibited."[65]

The Education Act, passed in 1865, was a direct response to this dilemma. Because the Act aimed at training black youths for life in a racialised labour market, separate and unequal education now emerged to structure and control economic life, which, until the development of capitalist industrialisation, had been a provisional, haphazard and unregulated process. More than a century later, in 1950, the Eiselen Commission, set up by the National Party government, was to reflect on the logic of the Education Act thus: "Bantu education, as carried [out] by the missionary bodies, became increasingly the care of the government concerned because the Bantu were increasingly affecting the economy and political life of the country."[66]

By the late 1870s, the centrality of black schooling to capitalist development was reflected in the growing interest of the state in 'native education'. The consequent growth in the number of pupils in black schools was dramatic. Whereas, in 1865, there were a mere 2 827 African pupils enrolled in schools, by 1885 enrolment had risen to 15 568, and, by 1891, to 25 000.[67] By 1879, the first syllabuses for elementary black schools were introduced. Hygiene and traditional crafts were emphasised and a fifth of school time was to be spent on manual work, which included carpentry for boys, laundering for girls, and gardening for both boys and girls.[68]

The adaptation of schooling to new demands of the workplace had begun. Employers began to see that it might be in their interests to win from workers some measure of acceptance of the social place towards which conditions would propel them.

"Nostalgia," wrote Martin J Murray in his treatment of spatial politics in former mining towns like Johannesburg, "is a bittersweet

---

65 Quoted in Molteno (n 17 above), p. 59.
66 Ibid., p. 57.
67 Ibid., p. 58.
68 Ibid.

sentiment of loss and displacement."[69] Murray went on to describe "the collective memory of place" as the superimposition of two images: "a longing for the unrealised promises of the past juxtaposed with the unfulfilled present".[70]

If, in Murray's view, Johannesburg's changing landscape during the first decade of the 21st century emblematised a forgotten past, Kimberley described a remembered place suspended in time. In the selective memory of Kimberley, the shadows on the open veld did not count a full century and a half since the diamond rush in 1869; but the titleholders certainly did. By 2010, the scorched mine dump described what the historian, Martin Legassick, once called "stony heaps of Griqua graves".[71] The scavengers were, to paraphrase Franz Fanon, 'artificial citizens' in an abstract state that had yet to transcend historical fault lines.

And so there was a tendency for itinerant visitors to Kimberley to believe, as South Africa's second democratic president, Thabo Mbeki, put it in a speech to Parliament in 2006, that "yesterday was another country";[72] that an older generation wanted to forget, and the young couldn't remember. A handful of black youths were encouraged to succeed, a triumph no doubt of a culture of aspiration in the new South Africa. Not so for the larger sea of poverty. For to view Kimberley's tentative steps to reinvent itself through the construction of emblematic attributes and iconographies was to miss the point; it was to misconstrue form for substance, appearance for reality. It had the superficial trappings of democracy, but, in every relevant respect, its tragic legacy mocked, even abandoned, any pretence of economic equality and social bonhomie.

Certainly for the Griqua in the Northern Cape, their decampment on a new frontier since the end of apartheid in 1994 may have been legitimised by democracy, but through these unfulfilled promises a historical narrative was resurrected: the notion of "outcast ghetto", of "'permeable and fluid edges", as Murray described it,[73] was legible in the racial geography and fixed borders when the Victorian townscape Rhodes entered in the early 1870s inscribed itself on the ruins of the frontier mining town. It was one predicated on the incongruous relationship between mission schools as

69 See Murray, MJ, *City of Extremes: The Spatial Politics of Johannesburg* (Johannesburg: Wits University Press, 2011), p. 139.
70 Ibid.
71 Interview with the author, Cape Town, December 2011.
72 Mbeki, T, State of the Nation Address, Joint Sitting of Parliament, Cape Town, 3 February 2006.
73 Murray (n 69 above), p. 139.

producers of Christianised labour and the latter's outcast ghetto status in the emerging capitalist order.

In such a state of extraordinary innovativeness, Rhodes resisted the liberal blandishments of mission schools. By 1894, the conflict between missionaries and Rhodes was not so much over labour relations as policies in respect of independent African communities since the end of slavery. Because Rhodes wanted land in order to exploit the minerals beneath it, and in this way haul the emerging capitalist economy into a new racial order, the first issue to drive a wedge between him and liberals in the Cape government was mission schools.

To be sure, Rhodes saw mission schools as liberal excesses bound up with an obsolescent social system in the anarchic wars for land during the early to mid-19th century. He was restless by nature and anxious to replace the extravagance of a cumbersome and politically overwrought missionary system with the more repressive apparatus of territorial conquest and with enforced labour on the emerging mines in Kimberley and Johannesburg.

The Cape's Constitution ruled out compulsion or intimidation in labour relations; and it was on this issue that Rhodes developed an intense hostility toward the missionaries. If racial segregation in South Africa was a marriage between an economic system based primarily on migrant labour and a political system that ruled out black competition, mining towns such as Kimberley that sprung up in the 1870s were important formative influences. Rhodes looked at the issue of African labour supply from his position as a mining magnate and an employer in Kimberley. Here his De Beers Consolidated Mines controlled its African labour force tightly through passes, contracts and single-sex compounds where male workers lived. Initially, both white and black labour were to be housed in compounds, but white workers protested. Increasingly, a white–black labour division became institutionalised across all economic sectors in other towns and cities. When, in 1894, Rhodes looked around for a solution, the idea took root that the small scattered African reserves provided a home base for cheap black labour as well as their exclusion from political rights.

*

On 7 August 1894, the *Bloemfontein Express* reported a speech by Rhodes on the reserves in which he stated that, "certain parts of the country must be the home of the natives. Not everyone must have a piece of land, but it must be a place where people could go back after work."[74]

The idea of reserves as an integral part of both the economic and political system gathered momentum as Rhodes pushed ahead with his grand expansion schemes. He knew that his chances of driving his policy of annexation would be resisted by liberals in the Cape government. In this battle, he set out to woo the Afrikaner Bond,[75] led by Jan Hofmeyr, whom Rhodes had befriended. If the Cape Afrikaners would find it easier to assert themselves and stifle opposition, Hofmeyr was, in Rhodes's view, "undoubtedly the most capable politician in South Africa"[76] to argue his case in Parliament.

Ideologically, Hofmeyr was no extreme nationalist. He held the Afrikaner Bond back from the policy of a united Dutch-ruled South Africa, an outcome which was to be achieved in very different circumstances 60 years later. He favoured liberal forms of colonialism, which meant the Cape looking after its own interests, free from British imperial interference. But he also shared Rhodes's anxiety over the disastrous consequences to which a free labour market and liberal education system might expose whites generally; and in his eagerness to strengthen the position of whites, Hofmeyr weakened the Bond's own position in the new dispensation. No doubt, he counted on Rhodes's support just as Rhodes counted on his. Little though he thought of the British, he treated them as comrades whom he expected to behave towards the Bond with a certain propriety. He did not imagine that Rhodes would turn his comradely gestures to his own immediate and private advantage.

What Rhodes had that Hofmeyr did not, besides wealth, was a capacity and ideological facility for big thinking. One of Rhodes's biographers, Robert Rotberg, observed that Rhodes's aims at this juncture had been anti-imperial and pro-colonial: that is, seeking to advance a narrow, sectarian cause, motivated by an inexhaustible desire to conciliate the Bond and cultivate an alliance against liberalism. Rhodes himself had a better strategic grasp of Britain's economic expansion in the second half of the 20th century than the top political brass in London, telling his mother in a telegram that it was better to "annex land, not men".[77] The letter, written in a hurry while Rhodes was engaged in a policy battle in Parliament, was an indignant

---

74 Quoted in Giliomee, H, *The Afrikaners: Biography of a People* (Johannesburg: Tafelberg, 2003), p. 291.

75 Not to be confused with the Afrikaner Broederbond which emerged in 1918.

76 Quoted in Wheatcroft, G, *The Randlords* (Simon & Schuster, 1987), p. 145.

77 Rotberg, R, *The Founder, Cecil Rhodes and the Pursuit of Power* (New York, Oxford University Press, 1988), p. 150.

explosion, an angry retort to his liberal opponents.

At this stage, it seems what Rhodes wanted was a genial collaboration between English and co-opted Afrikaner elites. He was certainly guarded and a little suspicious of the Bond; but he was always willing to enter into compromises if they met his goals – among whites, at any rate, which would have ensured peace regardless of African rights. In the circumstances of the mid-1880s, the fact that it was Afrikaners in the Cape who were invested in capitalism (in contrast with their rural brethren in the Orange Free State and the Transvaal) had perhaps something to do with this. Winning the support of the Bond on labour policy, he felt, would help him secure Southern Bechuanaland in a way which would never be endangered by shifts in liberal British sentiment.

Whether he agreed with the plan or not, Hofmeyr was nonetheless not about to go up against Rhodes. As far as he was concerned, there was sufficient common ground between Rhodes and the Afrikaner Bond on the labour and education question. After winning Hofmeyr over to his cause, Rhodes worked with inexhaustible verve for what he would later call a 'Natives Bill for Africa'. Such a Bill would entrench white supremacy by restricting the education and economic advancement of blacks to native reserves, and, in this fashion, excluding from the vote those who lived on land held in communal property. And here we have, in the upheaval of Cape politics, an early signal of the legal framework of Bantu education as a 'gentle stimulant' Rhodes would use to force blacks living on reserves to work on the mines and for at least part of the year in the Cape Colony.

"IT IS THE DUTY OF THE GOVERNMENT TO REMOVE THESE POOR CHILDREN from this life of sloth and laziness," Rhodes told a sitting of the Cape Parliament in 1894, adding: "We will teach them the dignity of labour."[78] The statement, dripping irony, was Rhodes's introduction of the Glen Grey Bill. Least of all could he himself live by honest work. Not that he was slothful. Even at the most despairing and futile moments of his political and mining career his work took up a great deal of his energy. But his intentions in arguing for the Bill were predatory, gratuitous and political in a wider sense as well. His choice of the word 'dignity' in his push for a new repressive

---

78 Quoted in Crow (n 52 above).

labour and education dispensation for Africans gave perverse dimensions to Cape Governor George Grey's sentiments on native policy, four decades before, that more immediately suited Rhodes's own ambitions. He spoke in terms the Afrikaner Bond welcomed. Africans were "lazy", he said, at best "children" and at worst "barbarians".[79] "It had to be brought home to them that in future nine-tenths of them would have to spend their lives in manual labour. African workers need special education towards that end."[80] Schools were now overproducing a certain class of human being – 'the Kaffir parson', admirable as individuals but as a class "dangerously inciting other blacks by informing them that they were oppressed".[81]

In the Afrikaner historian Hermann Giliomee's recording, the laboratory for ideas of Rhodes and Hofmeyr was a small, overcrowded but coveted area north of Queenstown called Glen Grey. Forty years earlier, wrote Giliomee, Glen Grey had been assigned to the Tambookie branch of the Thembu people and was now a reserve, housing about 8 000 Thembu families. A number of men used it as a base, going out from there for short-term employment on white farms. In his recounting of life in the area, Giliomee found that "few white farmers also lived there and, along with the Thembu, they clamoured for land to be opened up to individual tenure". In 1892, Rhodes, with Bond support, appointed a commission to look into the problems in Glen Grey. Its report proposed a shift from communal to individual title, with the land divided up equally into 55-morgen plots among African families. The new law provided instead for farms of four morgen, each granted on the basis of ownership or freehold. The right of the eldest son was enforced with the intention of compelling other sons to learn "the dignity of labour and to seek work in the colony".[82] A tax of 10 shillings was imposed to press all the younger sons to find work in order to pay the tax.

The enactment of the Glenn Grey Bill was therefore not only an attempt to end mission schooling and redirect black schools to African reserves; concerned as he was since his first months in Kimberley to secure the diamond mines and the Cape generally, Rhodes's advocacy of the Bill had as much to do with using the native reserves to channel sufficient black labour to the mines and the Cape Colony.

As parliamentarian and prime minister, Rhodes defied liberal thinking

---

79 Ibid.
80 Ibid.
81 Quoted in Giliomee (n 74 above), p. 292
82 Quoted in Crow (n 52 above).

in the Cape and, through the Glen Grey legislation, laid the foundations for 20th-century apartheid in all but name. In defending his actions against Africans, he rationalised, persuading his liberal detractors that Africans would benefit neither by voting nor by freehold ownership of farms and education. As a capitalist, Rhodes depended on an expanding frontier not only of territorial conquest, but also unskilled labour. Without vast reservoirs of manpower, he once remarked, "the mines would shut down and [his] vision to finance his conquests would cease".[83]

It was with his self-interest in mind that Rhodes argued, soon after the enactment of the Glen Grey Bill, that the liberal-humanitarian underpinnings of missionary education turned out to be a "shallow and deceptive" thing.[84] True, African chiefs trained by mission schools were a mere handful by this time; but, all too often, relations between missionaries and chiefs, as Timothy Keegan observed in his study of the period, were fraught with ambiguity and conflict not only over allegiance to their followers, acolytes and Christian converts, but also more deeply over a battle for possession of salient signs and symbols, linguistic forms of rational argument, and positive knowledge.

Amid the chaos of capitalist expansion and drift of policies, Rhodes eschewed as the very seedbed of English liberal humanitarianism and Christian education the London Missionary Society, arguing that it had by the 1840s and 1850s already become deeply and pervasively infected with civil-rights sentiment. He instead backed proposals by conservative missionaries in the Cape such as David Livingstone that colonial mission stations should be sold to non-African inhabitants as freehold proprietors.

*

In truth, Rhodes was grappling all the while with a dilemma. As an agent and backer of capitalist interests, his primary mission was to drive policies that would take the education of workers in a free labour market seriously; and yet here he was advocating a return to a new form of slave labour!

"Rhodes, a man with big plans and great ambitions," according to one of his biographers, Robert Rotberg, "fell as politician, entrepreneur and empire extender to the persuasive belief that the greatness of the objective justified

---

83 Ibid.
84 See Rotberg (n 77 above), p. 688.

any method of achieving it."[85] The goal alone, wrote Duncan Innes, filled his vision. "Ends were everything; any means whatsoever could be justified if it served great goals."[86] As long as the emerging racial oligarchy was struggling to come of age, he put authority and control first.

By the end of the 19th century, Rhodes was concerned with legal measures to enforce lower forms of labour in a labour market that was technically free of slavery. He had already pushed through legislation in the Cape to expropriate black diggers of their mining rights and introduced the Hut Tax to force labour onto the Kimberley diamond fields. By this indirect form of extortion, more and more minerals, land and labour came under the ownership and control of the colony; the original black pastoralists became mere tenants in their own country. Britain would secure the vast territorial swath of goldfields in the Transvaal; the oligarchs would keep the keys.

If the abiding legacy of Rhodes, after his death in 1902, masked the virtual extinction of mission schools, the Glenn Grey Act was the opening salvo in an era that bore all the hallmarks of apartheid in all but name – the racial segregation of society.

Thus was Rhodes's legacy a pattern of black communities and Afrikaner authorities foiled by the wiles of foreign money. More narrowly, the plan itself lasted a mere decade; but the story of black schooling tied to mining compounds and native reserves would cover virtually the entire 20th century.

---

85 Rotberg (n 77 above), p. 685.
86 Quoted in Rotberg (n 77 above), p. 685.

PART II

From Christian Nationalism to Bantu Education

1902–1961

CHAPTER 4

God and Volk

CHRISTIAN NATIONALISM

THE WORLD OF POLITICS AFRIKANERS HAD ENTERED BY THE DAWN OF THE 20th century was a tableau of ruin in which the spectacle of 'poor whiteism' was breeding a menacing, ill-tempered martinet. South Africa was in the spasm of a modern industrial revolution; after centuries of territorial tussles, land dispossession and enforced proletarianisation, the new capitalist order had finally been consummated with brute force during the Anglo-Boer War of 1899–1902. But the old feudal order of Afrikaner pastoralists refused to die.

Reluctantly, Lord Alfred Milner, who became Governor of the Cape in the early 20th century, fell back on the idea of trying to hold the British Empire together by the intangible bonds of common culture. Language and education – which had originally been a supplement to military conquest – now became the chief issue. In Milner's view, the Afrikaners and British were to be united around British imperialism as a nucleus. Meanwhile, his policy of Anglicisation in schools made unaccountable progress; he had insisted that English was to be the medium of instruction in all public schools in the Orange Free State and the Transvaal. "And damn the consequences,"[87] he added arrogantly.

In the cities, it was oddly this air of pious irreverence that cast some Afrikaners with less self-assurance – men like General Louis Botha and General Jan Smuts – under the spell of Milnerism. But if Milner wasn't bothered, he also drew the attention of advocates of the new spirit of Afrikaner nationalism seeping across South Africa. In the countryside, economic uncertainty filled the air. The instinct of Afrikaners for land, wrote Dan O'Meara, was "shocked and revolted" by the arbitrariness of urbanisation

---

87 See https://en.wikisource.org/wiki/1922_Encyclop%C3%A6dia_Britannica/Milner,_Alfred_Milner,_
Viscount.

55

and proletarianisation.[88] Economically, Afrikaners appeared to be stricken, or dying, or convalescing from being thrust into a shrunken rural landscape that looked bleak and ominous.

To not a few Afrikaner nationalists, a permanent accommodation with Britain was unthinkable. Throughout the decade leading to the 1910 Union government, Afrikaner resentment grew stronger with the onslaught of Milnerism on their language, religion and culture. The squeeze on land saw increasing numbers of rural Afrikaners wandering into the petrifying abyss of acculturated, embourgeoised cities. They watched the flood of rural whites into lumbering factories, where once there was barren land, exacerbate the problem of poor whiteism.

As the Botha Cabinet plodded along, outwardly united but inwardly divided, the basis had been laid for a breach in the ranks of Afrikanerdom: on the one hand, pro-unionists; on the other, Afrikaner nationalists led by the Minister of Native Affairs, General JBM ('Barry') Hertzog. The 1910 compromise was thus a 'Union without unity' that soon faltered with the outbreak of the First World War in 1914, when Afrikaner nationalists in the ruling South African Party, led by General Louis Botha, broke ranks and rallied behind Germany. They were not satisfied with this arrangement of union; theirs was a more exclusive pastoral existence. The ideal of collective farming had, of course, not been alien to Afrikaners; the belief that land was the common good of those who tilled it – those who were white at any rate – had been deeply held.

Beneath the surface of things, a momentous gambit was under way: in January 1914, some 450 Afrikaner delegates gathered at a conference in Bloemfontein to establish the National Party. Its programme stated that the development of national life should be on 'Christian-national lines'; a phrase which, as will become evident in the next chapter, was to become as significant as the evangelism of the British mission schools. In a sense, this was "the real parting of ways" in South Africa's white political history, wrote John Vorster's biographer, John D'Oliveira. "Those who supported General Botha's conciliation with the British Empire went one way. Those who supported the Republican idea went the other."[89]

*

---

88 See O'Meara, D, *The Afrikaner Broederbond, 1927-1948: Class Vanguard of Afrikaner Nationalism* (nd) p. 10. Accessed at http://sas-space.sas.ac.uk/4037/1/Dan_O'Meara_-_The_afrikaner_broedberbond_1927-1948,_Class_vanguard_of_aflikaner_nationalism.pdf.
89 D'Oliveira, J, *Vorster – The Man* (Johannesburg: Ernest Stanton Publishers, 1978), p. 15.

One of the upshots Milner dismissed when he said "damn the consequences" was that a group of Afrikaners would go on to set up private schools and cultural organisations to teach the Afrikaans language and spread the tenets of Calvinist doctrine.[90] In the dying moments of the First World War, a group of men calling themselves Jong Suid-Afrika (Young South Africa) secretly gathered in May 1918 to take stock of things since the outbreak of the War and launch of the National Party in 1914: in Russia, the Bolshevik Revolution, led by a revolutionary Marxist named Vladimir Lenin, had just overthrown tsarism; in Versailles, a new world order was emerging from the ashes of Weimar Germany's capitulation to Allied forces after the First World War.

The men discussed an organisation they would later call the Afrikaner Broederbond (loosely translated, Afrikaner Brotherhood). The great concern of the founding generation of 'Broederbonders' (members of the Broederbond) – 14 railway clerks, policemen and clergymen – was the same concern as that of the 1914 generation of republicans led by Hertzog's National Party: spreading the basic tenets of Afrikaner-nationalist ideology. They concluded that reformists in the South African Party of Botha and Smuts had prostrated Afrikaners to English moneyed power. They even flirted with a racially exclusive variety of 'Bolshevism', Lenin's credo for socialist revolution, arguing that the socialist creed was natural to Afrikaners; it owed something to the anti-imperialist version of world-historical struggle on which so many Afrikaners had nursed their early years.

The Broederbond's own record of its early history advances in this atmosphere of ideological ferment, recounting the first 'Outsiders', or *Bittereinders* (those who fought to the end) as they came to be colloquially known, who refused to accept the authority and language of the British Crown. In this official version, declaimed by journalists Ivor Wilkins and Hans Strydom in their book, *The Super-Afrikaners: Inside the Afrikaner Broederbond*, based on classified Broederbond documents leaked to the pair sometime in 1977, the flame that stoked nationalist passion began in rebellion against the former Boer generals, Smuts and Botha, and the British-brokered Union government's support for England in the First World War.

Afrikaner nationalism, we now know, was skilfully mobilised by the Broederbond from the 1920s onwards in the theological, educational,

---

90 See Wilkins, I & Strydom, H, *The Super-Afrikaners: Inside the Afrikaner Broederbond* (Johannesburg: Jonathan Ball Publishers, 1980), p. 251.

cultural, economic, agricultural and industrial sectors as well as in government. A strategy of massive economic development was introduced to make South Africa less dependent on Britain and create thousands of job opportunities for poor Afrikaners. However, on the surface of this conceptualisation of Afrikanerdom, as former Broederbonder and retired Stellenbosch University historian, Willie Esterhuyse, articulated to me, was the questionable premise that all white Afrikaners instinctively shared traditional cultural values and were innately united as a Volk[91] against wealthy English-speaking South Africans. When I met him in December 2012, Esterhuyse questioned these assumptions. Only after their re-education and conscientisation as a Volk, he said to me, could they rise to power and satisfy their economic aspirations. What was needed was a common ideological platform that appealed to their ethnically exclusive unity as a Volk. In the Afrikaner cultural imagination, a timeless and somewhat idealised 'frontier tradition' – of a pastoral existence and ideology mythologised by allegoric reminiscences of the Great Trek and Boer wars – came to triumph over economic rationality. This mythologisation of the Volk chimes with Dan O'Meara's account in his seminal history of Afrikaner economic empowerment entitled *Volkskapitalisme*. In order to claim back a life lost to modernisation, wrote O'Meara, the idea of cultural unity was "imposed backwards in linear historical time as a core concept to reorganise aspects of South African history as far back as the Great Trek of 1836–38". In these terms, O'Meara argued, the past became "the inevitable movement to the present".[92]

These axioms were commonly held by first-generation Broederbonders. But in those tentative years, the Broederbond was far too young to take its place as the maker of Afrikaner history; and it was with this awareness that

---

91 Loosely translated, the word 'Volk' means 'people'. According to JJ Venter ('HF Verwoerd: The foundational aspects of his thought', *Koers*, Vol. 64, No.4, 1999, p. 417):

> The idea of an ethnic democratic republic was an invention of the French Revolution, moulded on the form of the ancient Western city state – it was surely not an invention for which Verwoerd has to be either credited or blamed. The eighteenth and nineteenth century moulded this ethnic nationalism in confrontation with British colonialism. Verwoerd worked for this ideal, and almost embodied it in his person. He was the man who realised this supreme good, and this alone goes a long way to explain the Verwoerd adoration in the last years of his reign. In this context he showed himself somewhat of a free thinker: he believed that Afrikaners and English-speaking South Africans could become one people – he used the word 'volk' for this unit. Blacks, however, could not join them.

As a Christian-Calvinist invention, it is, however, more deeply embedded in a religious Afrikaner movement bonded by a common culture and race.

92 Quoted in O'Meara (n 88 above), pp. 6-7.

the idea and language of cultural mobilisation that took hold in the minds of founding members in 1918 was soon replaced by the elitism of Afrikaner academics from the universities of Potchefstroom and Stellenbosch.

*

In the fight and heat of retreat and rebellion within Afrikanerdom, the Stellenbosch intellectuals were supremely confident. Professors LJ du Plessis, JC van Rooyen and HG Stoker, who by now operated as the Broederbond's ideologues,[93] had in a series of purges between 1919 and 1925 conveyed all the obsessive fascination of a semi-Masonic sect.[94]

In his account to me, Esterhuyse regarded 17 May 1921 as the first important milestone when the Broederbond committed categorically to strive for mother-tongue education in South Africa. For much of the 1920s, Esterhuyse said, the Broederbond for a while seemed to have modelled itself on the Freemasons, operating almost exclusively in the cultural field. The chronology of time certainly suggests its preoccupation with cultural mobilisation since its formation in 1918.[95]

Then came 1926, the year General Hertzog abandoned republicanism following the Balfour Declaration that same year, which granted South Africa dominion status. Wracked by dissension and division over Hertzog's 'betrayal', the Broederbond, still little more than a sect, ended its youthful flirtation with cultural mobilisation and started to "systematically infiltrate every arena of importance to the continued existence of the Afrikaner".[96]

By 1929/1930, the stock market crash and depression in the United States had its echo in a frenzy of economic and political realignments in South Africa. Within a year, South Africa's industrial and commercial sectors were shaken and weakened; mineral exports collapsed and the economy sank into prolonged depression. As the chaos deepened, the poverty and chain of social bonds seemed to tear apart rural Afrikanerdom. The links between town and country were loosened or broken; the channels of exchange shrank and became clogged; and the double burden of severe drought and falling export prices drove thousands of white farmers and sharecroppers off the

---

93 Ibid., p. 60.
94 Ibid.
95 Interview with the author, Stellenbosch, December 2011. Also see O'Meara (n 88 above); and Bloomberg, C, *Christian Nationalism and the Rise of the Afrikaner Broederbond, 1918-1948* (London: Macmillan, 1990), p. 90.
96 Ibid., p. 61.

land.[97] Angry Afrikaner workers grumbled that English-speaking capitalists had deliberately engineered the depression to drive down wages and employ low-paid blacks. Afrikaner nationalists shuddered at the sight of poor Afrikaners in spuriously urban centres of English-speaking cities – "nests of destitution, horror and degradation" was how one writer described it. "They were just as horrified," wrote Robert Massie, "to see white farm girls moving to cities to take jobs as maids for wealthy Indian families."[98]

Meanwhile, a moderate faction in the National Party, led by Hertzog, who was now Prime Minister, entered a coalition government with the South African Party of General Jan Smuts in 1933; a year later, the majority of each of the coalition parties fused to form the United Party. This was in many respects a strange assemblage of old foes; and it was not long before pro-imperialist English liberals and anti-imperialist Afrikaner hardliners in each of the coalition parties in turn drew back from fusion to organise themselves in the pro-British Dominion Party and pro-Afrikaner Purified National Party.

In the face of such pressures, ideas similar to those budding within fascist gangs orbiting Adolf Hitler in Germany began to take shape in South Africa. Afrikaner politicians, joined by Du Plessis, Van Rooyen and Stoker, who had insinuated the role of intellectual vanguard of Afrikanerdom, began articulating an ideology that drew on historical grievances – in a sense the crux of the Broederbond's intellectual combat – and now more clearly and energetically promoted racial purity as their theological and educational principles for Afrikaner empowerment.

But whatever the dissatisfaction with Hertzog's leadership of the Fusion government, both the class alliances underlying the National Party and Hertzog's enormous political stature meant the Broederbond intellectuals were in no position to mount an open challenge until Hertzog himself precipitated the break. In Esterhuyse's view, it was the long coalition/fusion government crisis of 1933/1934 that finally transformed the Broederbond. That fusion had yanked the Afrikaner middle class from its traditional political moorings gives some indication of the political vacuum following

---

97 In 1932, the Carnegie Commission sponsored a study of poverty in South Africa that focused exclusively on the white population and completely ignored the destitution facing other races. Of the 1.8 million white citizens of South Africa, 300 000 or almost 20 per cent, were considered extremely poor; the percentage of the Afrikaner population in poverty was between a quarter and a third. See Massie, RK, *Loosing the Bonds: The United States and South Africa in the Apartheid Years* (New York: Bantam Doubleday Bell, 1997), p. 7.
98 See Massie (n 97 above), p. 7.

the collapse of the National Party in the Transvaal around that time. As splits and fusions proceeded throughout the early 1930s, so, too, did the ideological organisation and consolidation of a new Afrikaner elite fall increasingly into the orbit of the Broederbond intellectuals: in the political vacuum, they progressively assumed the role of a 'war council' of Afrikaner nationalism.[99] An economic-empowerment movement was quietly asserting itself, with Bond leaders playing the role of a directing body. They alone now determined fields of action and their parameters, without themselves directly implementing policy.

For these ideologues, Afrikaner culture as a divine product, together with race history, the fatherland, and education distinguished the various 'nations' from one another only as a pretext for economic empowerment. They counterposed the individualistic evangelical doctrine of 'elective grace' as distinct from common grace. More than a genuine belief in 'God and Volk', such rhetorically overwrought blandishments were elaborate attempts by the Stellenbosch intellectuals to reinterpret the inexorable process of bourgeois revolution into new ideological forms that fitted the Afrikaner-nationalist mould. "We need economic influence, not just political power," declared Du Plessis in the Broederbond's theoretical journal, *Koers* (Directions).[100]

All this time, however, the Broederbond was trying to reconcile its elitist inclinations with the mass of Afrikaners.

IF THE MALAISE WAS PRINCIPALLY IN THE NATIONAL PARTY, THEN ALL THE 'ISMS' of collective salvation – economism, liberal capitalism, nationalism – now looked like various roads to hell. The pro-Hertzog leadership in the National Party had tried to leap from defeat and collaboration with pro-British forces in the Union government, right over South Africa's economic sovereignty, to modern, mostly imported dogmas of 'cooperative imperialism' by reconciling Afrikaners with the idea of the British Empire without enduring that profound rupture that guarantees the right to self-determination.

In an August 1933 analysis, published in *Koers*, Du Plessis asked, "Could it be possible that economic empowerment of the Afrikaner today in a South African political context is far less empowering than political power?" The

---

99 Quoted in O'Meara (n 88 above), p. 62.
100 Ibid.

question revolutionised South African politics and confirmed the theory
Willie Esterhuyse had begun to relate to me in the summer of 2012, which
was this: Afrikaner economic empowerment was not a product of Afrikaner
nationalism; the ideas of the Broederbond in the early 1930s weren't driven
by Afrikaner tradition. They were modern, and the ideology that held the
Afrikaner elite in its ecstatic grip had been produced by the Enlightenment, by
Voltaire – in fact, by Britain and Europe. This ideology had a name: capitalism. Its modern executors, Esterhuyse told me, were none other than Rhodes,
Beit, Stead, Milner and Hertzog. In Europe and Britain, its feverish mood had
long since broken by the end of the First World War; but, in South Africa,
where modernity failed successive generations of Afrikaners, the problem had
been spreading. Du Plessis, Esterhuyse suggested, was saying that imperialism
was a problem that Afrikaners should have been able to recognise – except
when they were blinded by a wishful belief in economic rationality.[101] Even
then, for some the urge not to see remained overpowering. Indeed, Du Plessis
probably had this in mind when he wrote that General Hertzog had "reconciled the great majority of Afrikaners with the idea of the British Empire".[102]

The shift at the high point of the National Party crisis in 1934 was subtle, but it would have large implications. Du Plessis' article, written in his
wearily elegant prose, was an incitement to Afrikaners to see economic
empowerment as part of the moral wreckage of Afrikaner nationalism. He
wanted his comrades to know that the 'economic collaboration' Hertzog
was advocating meant South Africa's monetary system, commercial and
banking policy, and industrial sector would remain 'imperialist-oriented',
and would grow increasingly so. "In place of the old political subjugation,"
he wrote, "we now enter a period of economic dependence. And the golden
chains so forged are much stronger and more dangerous than the old [politi-
cal] chains because they are more difficult to recognise, and once forged, are
not easily discarded."[103] He proposed that it was possible to redistribute the
wealth of South Africa "so that it would not just wind up in the hands of
Britain".[104] Du Plessis concluded with a clarion call: "Only a government
fully committed to South Africa's economic independence could escape this
octopus grip."[105]

---

101 Interview with the author, Stellenbosch, December 2011.
102 Quoted in O'Meara (n 88 above).
103 Ibid., p. 65.
104 Ibid.
105 Ibid.

From nowhere did the cry for unity come more naturally than the Broederbond.

*

"If we get our free republic it will not be from the hand of man, but the gift of God ... [b]ecause God, the Disposer of the lot of nations, has a future task laid away for our Volk."

So wrote the chairman of the Broederbond in a statement (discovered by Dan O'Meara) in the National Party mouthpiece, *Die Transvaler*. The Afrikaner Volk, the statement concludes, must "thus become conscious of their calling".[106]

This relation between divine circumstance and consciousness – between objective conditions and subjective awareness – seemed far-fetched but nevertheless alarming in 1933/1934 when the fusion government of Smuts and Hertzog had put a liberal plank in the National Party policy platform; and it expressed more than the chair of the Broederbond probably hoped to say. To judge from the context, what he had in mind was the ideological collaboration between Christianity and Afrikaner nationalism in a time of political crisis and economic depression when, the Broederbond's later secretary remarked, "The Afrikaner soul was sounding the depths of the abyss of despair."[107]

It was a time of confusion and bitterness among Afrikaners in the country's northern provinces of the Transvaal and Orange Free State: despite the fact that the Union of South Africa was, to all intents, now an 'independent'[108] country, Afrikaners were already divided between those who supported the first Prime Minister, General Louis Botha, and his policy of conciliation with Britain and economic expansion within the ambit of the British Empire, and those who saw the Union as the beginning of yet another battle to cast off the British Crown.

To large numbers of Afrikaners, including officials in the National Party, the rapid industrialisation and urbanisation taking place in South Africa during the 1920s and thirties meant putting the past behind them. At best, it meant embracing the liberal creed. In its mass, the emerging Afrikaner working class did not care much for inner cohesion and unity. They cared

---

106 Ibid., p. 70.
107 Ibid., p. 59.
108 'Independent', here, is not to be confused with a sovereign state. The Union of South Africa was to all intents and purposes a de facto British neo-colony.

even less for the hostility with which the Volk had confronted British impe-rialism in the past. Once the two former Boer republics were incorporated into the Union, the ardent pursuit of Christian-national ideals waned somewhat. Smuts and Hertzog variously pursued a policy of dual-medium instruction; the Anglican and Catholic churches sponsored a number of English schools, which attracted a large number of Afrikaner children; and many Afrikaans families, without sacrificing their own cultural and national identities, began to think that Afrikaans would always have lim-ited use. English was a lingua franca and, at the time, almost exclusively the language of business and politics in South Africa.

To the young Potchefstroom intellectuals were soon added four celebrated academics who had pursued their undergraduate studies at the University of Stellenbosch. To this emerging group of young Afrikaners , the 'abyss of despair' meant something far grander: confronting and defeating liberal-ism. By some accounts, the biggest developments on the road to cultural apartheid and educational insulation began when these men, with a reput-edly palpable air of frustrated ambition, entered the scene, setting the entire country on a course that would sunder from the historical record the cultural traditions and brave struggles by black people through a string of beguiling manoeuvres – from co-option and incorporation to repression – and inau-gurate a new era.

For them, the depths of despair was a mirror-imaging effect (in the Nietzschean sense). Now smarting from the abandonment of republican-ism since the Balfour Declaration and the latter's beatification of the British Crown, the whole calumny of the past, the full blast of that implacable hostility, was reflecting back with chilling dread in the innermost recesses of their being. Through a teleological rendering of the past, they evoked the era of the 1899–1902 Anglo-Boer War, when the smouldering embers of Afrikaner defeat and Lord Kitchener's scorched-earth policy fed grow-ing resentment among Afrikaners against everything British. Many of the survivors of the war were still alive and the horrific British concentration camps still fresh in their minds. On the eve of the Second World War, they grew beards and sported the rugged attire of Boer combatants in a re-enactment of the Great Trek. They lamented with horror the violent suppression by the Union government of the Boer Rebellion against South Africa's decision to go to war at Britain's side in 1914 and to invade South West Africa, then a German colony, and the execution of the rebellion's leader, Jopie Fourie, and the imprisonment of others for treason.[109]

Whatever their attire, these men were the rising intellectual vanguard of modern thinking in the stifling atmosphere of the 1930s. Out of personal inclination as well as strategic calculation, they brought back the idea of republicanism.

*

The crisis in the National Party brought to an abrupt end the multiclass unity of the fusion government that had flourished through nearly a decade of liberal capitalism. Despite deep social divisions since Union, it wasn't impossible yet, in the 1930s, to imagine a future that united the Volk against the fusion government. Such a policy would have required the pretext of divine providence in another sense as well: what the Broederbond chairman was telling his audience in his statement was that, in natural law, liberal notions of human equality should be implacably rejected; South Africa belonged to the Volk, and equality was their natural right.

If the heart of Afrikanerdom in the 1930s beat in the *platteland* (rural areas), wrote D'Oliveira, then its soul was to be found in the lecture rooms and corridors of the University of Stellenbosch, nestled among the lush vineyards and overshadowed by dark-blue mountains outside Cape Town. Nico Diederichs, PJ Meyer, Hendrik Verwoerd and Albert Hertzog (General Hertzog's son) were self-possessed, overpowering personalities who in the aftermath of the First World War had been strongly influenced by the university's reputation as the spiritual and intellectual centre of Afrikaner identity and white supremacy in South Africa. All had just returned from overseas study in the early 1930s, with Diederichs and Meyer, in particular, being strongly influenced by German fascism. With the Potchefstroom academics, they led the post-fusion ideological redefinition of Afrikaner nationalism.

For the four men, the Afrikaner sense of subjugation at the hands of British imperialism left little room for an Afrikaner Rhodes or Milner to emerge. Without denying the rationale of the economic empowerment cause, they began to feel that Afrikaners shouldn't regard it as the key to solving their problems – the elite no longer came first, either in time or in moral urgency. The crucial issue was no longer economic liberation but

---

109 O'Meara (n 88 above), p. 59.

political power based on self-determination and, more profoundly, the value of religious and cultural identity. Long after the split in the National Party and Broederbond, though, the stance of these new Afrikaner nationalists – the critics of home-grown elitism – still looked in many Afrikaner circles suspiciously like apostasy.

Many of these men had been interned in Germany, embracing the hawkish idealism of the Nazis. They had spent the early 1930s watching the Hertzog administration return to liberalism and the Broederbond founder from crisis to crisis, squandering opportunities. They had made their march through the great think tanks and policy journals of the world, honing their ideas and sharpening their strategies. Now they were coming back to South Africa as right-wing insurgents, scornful of the entrenched bureaucracy in the Broederbond, the more cautious moderates in their own party, and the tired, defeated National Party leadership. They were determined; all they needed was a mission.

Living a fairly marginal existence from South African politics after returning from overseas studies in 1927, the new generation of Afrikaner intellectuals saw real opportunity where the older generation of Afrikaner political leadership, formed in the early 20th century, grew battle-weary. They had not fought in the Anglo-Boer War and lived most of their lives in a unified South Africa. Given a chance of leadership, they would otherwise have had to wait a long time to bring a new vigour, ideas and perspectives to the Afrikaner nationalist cause.[110]

They were angry. Their chief foe was General Hertzog. LJ du Plessis, who assumed the role of Political Commissar, summed up their concerns in *Koers* in August 1933: "General Hertzog has achieved what neither General Botha nor General Smuts could accomplish. He has reconciled the great majority of Afrikaners with the idea of British Empire."

---

110 Ibid., p. 64.

CHAPTER 5

'Quiet influence'

THE AFRIKANER CULTURAL MOVEMENT

OF ALL THE SYMBOLS IN SOUTH AFRICA, THERE IS A TOWERING MONUMENT dedicated to the Voortrekkers on a hill just as you enter the capital city of Pretoria on the northbound highway. I remember my own first impressions of the place in the winter of 2010: a barren and lumbering hulk of grey bricks and stone overlooking the city's teaming landscape under a grey sky. The city I had come to know then was a picture of extremes, of black poverty and white wealth; but it also crackled with democratic dividends. The seat of government, the Union Buildings – within visible distance from the monument – was in the hands of the African National Congress (ANC); and Pretoria, for all its extremes, was no longer an apartheid garrison city.

It was a very different setting in 1937 that drew Hendrik Verwoerd's attention to a re-enactment by the *Federasie van Afrikaanse Kultuurvereninginge* (more commonly known by its acronym, 'FAK') (Federation of Afrikaans Cultural Societies) of the Great Trek. He was the Stellenbosch generation's most ardent disciple and zealous prophet. Bearded with a shaved upper lip, he had come all the way round to the view that the emerging Afrikaner economic elite's sins in the country were sins of omission, not commission. Through 1937 and 1938, wrote Dan O'Meara, commemorative ox-wagons rolled and bumped from town to town, ending in a festival of nationalist fervour. Old Boer attire became the rage. Women donned ankle-length chintz dresses and old-fashioned bonnets; men dug out their grandfathers' corduroy suits, colourful jerkins, and waistcoats.

By this time, the two former political opponents, Jan Smuts and Barry Hertzog, had joined forces in a fusion government; but as Europe moved inescapably toward war, tensions between them increased. Smuts saw Hitler as a despot feeding off popular rage; Hertzog viewed him as the legitimate voice of an oppressed people. Smuts shared Britain's view that Hitler's aggression

67

needed to be contained; Hertzog, under pressure from Daniel Malan, wanted South Africa to remain neutral. The fragile pact between Smuts and Hertzog held until September 1939, when war finally broke out between Germany and Britain. When the British government asked Hertzog to join the Allied forces against Hitler, the Prime Minister refused and Parliament voted him out of office. At Britain's request, Smuts stepped forward, and, after a 15-year hiatus, again became Prime Minister of South Africa.

Verwoerd and Malan, though scowling at South Africa's entry into the war, were delighted with Hertzog's abrupt exit from the government; if anything, it would heal the rift within the National Party. In December 1939, Hertzog's and Malan's supporters gathered at an emotional rally at the Voortrekker monument to mark the beginning of a newly unified National Party. From then on, Verwoerd fired up his Christian-nationalist republican course, chortling in print, when German bombers pounded English cities in preparation for invasion, that Britain had lost the war. "This is not only my opinion; it is my wish,"[111] he wrote.

For Verwoerd and his allies, the success of the centennial celebration implied an Afrikaner republic was no longer a pipe dream; the question now came down to a strategy for cultural mobilisation of the Volk in schools and universities.

*

Far from being an emerging force for unity and economic power, the empowerment flank of the Broederbond was ineffectual. One display of fecklessness after another had instead prepared Britain's proxy, the United Party, to believe that it could run South Africa with the force of an invisible hand. Afrikaner business, it was believed among Afrikaners, was a weak force in the country not because of what it was doing, but because of what it was failing to do. Their anger at the Afrikaner economic elite's complacency in the face of Barry Hertzog's betrayal was burning too high. Du Plessis' August 1933 article (we recall from the previous chapter) was not a gentle caveat but a cri de coeur. He sought to strip away Hertzog's apologia for imperialism and push his reader's face down into the stinking mess.

In this climate of perceived imperialist domination, the young intellectuals

---

111 Quoted in Siko, J, *Inside South Africa's Foreign Policy: Diplomacy in Africa from Smuts to Mbeki* (London: IB Tauris, 2014), p. 73.

strove to reinterpret the world and formulate a counter-narrative to the narrow elitism of the Broederbond intellectual vanguard. By 1934, the Afrikaner intellectuals had swung all the way round to the view that the older generation's sins – the Balfour Declaration which abandoned republicanism for imperialism, the fusion government, the subversion of Afrikaans as a language at schools – could be explained by Hertzogism's subjectivism and consequent ideological looseness, lack of ethnic consciousness and acceptance of 'foreign' notions of class divisions, all of which explained the general's 'sell-out' to 'imperialism'. If not to be repeated, such subjective criteria had to be replaced by objective ones. The entire conceptual apparatus and constituent elements of Afrikanerdom, together with social divisions, required extensive redefinition.

Not meshed in the cultural unity and loyalties of the Volk, such intellectuals were nonetheless susceptible to 'imperialist' blandishments. The Broederbond's new, ethnically inclusive delimitation of 'Afrikanerdom' thus involved the definition of what was peculiarly 'Afrikaans' about 'Afrikaners' – an intensive analysis of the interrelationships embracing the individual, the Volk, culture, God and the state. Through ideologues like Du Plessis, the Potchefstroom academics who dominated the Broederbond by this time had begun to elaborate an explicitly Calvinist doctrine of divine sovereignty. For these ideologues, culture was divine product; each 'volk' was a separate social sphere, each with a God-willed structure, purpose, calling and destiny.

The shift to this form of Christian nationalism was no longer about the right of Afrikaners to self-determination, but about divine rule based on Afrikaner culture and, more profoundly, the will of God. As a political gambit, cultural influence was seen as a key mobilising platform for reconciling Afrikaners with the idea of divine providence; political power was seen as the key to finally ending English hegemony. The ideological elaboration of Christian nationalism or discussion of policy on the so-called native question – the detailed development of the concept of apartheid – only began in the 1940s. At the moment, white supremacy was taken for granted. During the 1930s, this divinely created Afrikaner nation was politically divided, culturally atomised, and wracked by severe class divisions. Afrikaner workers, for their part, displayed scant interest in the culture and politics of the Volk, and behaved economically and politically in class terms. The huge poor-white problem and rapid denationalisation of urban Afrikaners squeezed off their pastoral lifestyles were the most glaring manifestations of these divisions. In the Cape, the divisions deepened along economic lines when a handful of Cape Town and Stellenbosch Afrikaner professionals formed Die Nasionale Pers (The National Press), or Naspers, and two insurance giants, Sanlam and Santam.[112]

In the young *broeders'* (brothers' i.e. Broederbonders') imagination, Afrikaner workers and businessmen had become lackeys of imperialism and foreign capitalism. And so they agreed on the major theme of the period as the overriding need for unity between Afrikaners of all classes, particularly the need to win workers to Afrikaner nationalism. As Nico Diederichs declared around the time, "If the worker is drawn away from our nation, we may as well write Ichabod on the door of the temple … . There must be no division or schism between class and class."[113]

Hankering after the idealised unity of the Great Trek and the republics in terms of whose mythology all were pastoralists united against external enemies, they decided that the actual translation of such ideological debates into a form of mass consciousness was to be achieved through a process of re-education and cultural assimilation.

Here lies the core of the break with the ideology of Hertzogism and the old National Party. Christian nationalism, or Afrikaner nationalism, was much more than a religious-ideological framework representing certain views of the world. The terms were moreover part of the cultural repertoire of a mass social and political economy focused on Christianity and language which emerged.

THE ORIGINS OF THE AFRIKANER CULTURAL MOVEMENT CAN BE FOUND in the struggle, between the empowerment flank of the Broederbond and the Potchefstroom intellectuals, for the hearts and minds of Afrikaners. By 1934, the latter were arguing that the policy of economic empowerment was destined to create an Afrikaner elite as a subsidiary force to English money power. Du Plessis authored a paper that year lambasting the Broederbond ("the Stellenbosch professors") for squandering the chance to help Afrikaners overcome class divisions. The essay had that fitful, inconclusive quality of a divided mind: Du Plessis wanted to get rid of capitalist impulses and divisions within the Volk, but he still accepted the rationale for not having

112 See O'Meara, D, *Volkskapitalisme, Class, Capital and Ideology in the Development of Afrikaner Nationalism* (Johannesburg: Ravan Press, 1983), p. 59.
113 Ibid., p. 71.

done so. He never quite came round to the position that elitism – which he equated with British imperialist designs for the co-option of Afrikaner leadership to its cause – was an aspiration of the very constituency at which his paper was targeted: the urban working class. Instead, he concluded that the unity of the Volk was to be achieved primarily in the realm of language, Christian-national education, and the development of cultural forms of organisation. In this process, he concluded, the Broederbond's control of organised Afrikaner culture through schools founded by the Broederbond was a potentially powerful weapon.

But well-off educated Afrikaners who formed these groupings were in a very different league from those in the north. By the late 1930s, power had already merged with wealth in the Cape to become the order of the day. And an obsession with betrayal and conspiracy – of plots, traps, subterfuge and high treason – became a pathology of the Afrikaner political mindset.

What all this represented was not just an elite coup against the poor but a grander historical shift. The post-Union consensus was all but over. The bitter words of a later anti-Cape survey of the formation of the Broederbond echoed an old conflict between north and south in Afrikaner-nationalist politics: "Compared with the acute stress raging in the northern provinces," wrote Du Plessis, "there was little need south of the Hex River."[114]

Yet their ideas and methods belonged to an epoch towards which the present moment, the period of industrialisation and urbanisation, was hostile; their desire for cohesion was being thwarted by industrialisation in a deeper sense as well: history had cut them off from chances of unity and action, and, because of their social atomisation, they did not have their desired impact. Their ideas and methods, wrote Dan O'Meara, were those formed in the atmosphere of military defeat and social dislocation, in which divisions between urban and rural Afrikaners were being nurtured.[115] This was a time when, in Karl Marx's famed words, "the idea pressed toward reality", but, as reality did not tend toward the idea, a gulf was set between them. Their whole existence was torn between the necessity and the impossibility of action.

As they contemplated a way out of the impasse, they decided that what the Afrikaner movement needed was not Voltaire, but its own Enlightenment to galvanise the Volk.

*

114 Ibid., pp. 59-60
115 See Ibid., 'Chapter 1: The Depression and the class basis of the Nationalist Party'.

That same year, 1934, Dr Piet Meyer, by then a rising star in the Broederbond, argued that Afrikaners had tried to leap right over the 18th century to modern, mostly imported dogmas, without enduring the profound rupture when legitimacy is separated from both might and faith, and the rights of the individual are enshrined as a basis of government. It was not capitalism Meyer had been railing against; it was the unequal terms of the social contract the English had negotiated with the National Party in the fusion government. Thus, in a letter to the Broederbond, Meyer asked, "Could it be possible that Christian-nationalism in a South African political context is far more revolutionary than, say, a Voltaire?"[116] English liberalism, for Meyer, now looked like the road to defeat. The crucial issue, he believed, was the Broederbond's founding principles of culture and education as levelling influences on deepening class divisions within the Volk.

Indeed, on university campuses, the argument that caused the final rift between English and Afrikaner students was over the role of language and culture in education. A year before, in 1933, the National Union of South African Students (NUSAS) was split along Afrikaans–English lines by 147 to 118 votes on a motion proposed by Meyer. The formation of the Afrikaanse Nasionale Studentebond (ANS) (Afrikaans National Student Union) was the result.

The following year, the first national congress of the ANS was chaired by Nico Diederichs just as he was studying Nazi methods in Germany. Diederichs was its impresario, with one degree of separation from everyone who mattered. More than anyone, he personified the young Afrikaner cultural insurgent clinging to decidedly dour views of mission schools and liberal universities. Having had a major influence on discussions at the founding congress of the ANS, the founding constitution (in which Diederichs had a firm hand) espoused a Protestant-Christian and cultural-nationalist creed and acknowledged the leadership of God in the sphere of culture as in every other sphere of life concerning the Afrikaner people's traditions embodied in history.[117]

Within this cultural repertoire, the Broederbond's chief organisation was the FAK. Formed in December 1929 in response to the Balfour Declaration and under the chairmanship of the Orange Free State National Party Member of Parliament (MP), Dr NG van der Merwe, the FAK was a broad

---

116 This quotation is attributed to Willie Esterhuyse, interview with the author, Stellenbosch, December 2011.
117 See O'Meara (n 112 above), pp. 70-71. For a fascinating account, see, also, Venter (n 91 above), pp. 430-431.

Broederbond front designed to provide central organisation and direction to the myriad Afrikaner cultural groupings that had mushroomed. The Broederbond's patronage of the FAK is indisputable. Its official history acknowledges that, as "a creation of the AB (Afrikaner Broederbond), the FAK is regarded by the mother organisation as its public arm".[118] The FAK was to become the most important and influential of the Broederbond's numerous public fronts. With some exceptions, the two bodies shared the same executives and officers, who publicly implemented FAK policies secretly decided in the Broederbond.

In this fashion, the Broederbond's early concern with routine cultural work was openly undertaken by the FAK, freeing the Broederbond to concentrate on other issues. In the words of its chairman in 1932,

> We find the Broederbond is slowly handing over the cultural work to its much bigger arm, the FAK ... . National culture and the welfare of the volk will only flourish if the South African people break all foreign bonds. After the cultural and economic needs the Afrikaner Broederbond will have to devote its attention to the political needs of our people.[119]

By 1937, at least 300 Broederbond front organisations in the cultural and educational fields suggested an immense informal network of influence sprinkled among all regions and sectors of the Afrikaner community where they could exercise "quiet influence".[120] In effect, then, the ideological debates in the Broederbond succeeded in the elaboration and development of the concept of a new historical subject – an organically united Afrikaner Volk. It was now defined in culturally exclusive terms, an exclusivity fired in past struggles and destined to be realised in a sort of republican nirvana. The organic Volk was now declared a divine product and assigned a divinely allotted calling. The real class divisions were to be overcome at the educational level through the ideological neutralisation of internal antagonisms and their replacement in thought by other antagonisms. Thus we find in the December 1942 edition of the Broederbond journal, *Koers*: "The Afrikaner Calvinist can only seek and find power in co-operation with Christian members of the volk because our existence was threatened in various ways by imperialists, Jews, Coloureds, Africans, Indians, Afrikaner renegades and

---

118 Ibid., p. 61.
119 Quoted in the *Rand Daily Mail*, 8 November 1935.
120 Quoted in O'Meara (n 112 above), p. 64.

so on."[121]

With an unsympathetic government in power, however, progress toward this aim was slow, until 6 July 1939 when the FAK convened a Christian-national education conference in Bloemfontein. Out of this conference an important agent in the fight for the Afrikaner education deal was born: the *Nasionale Instituut vir Opvoeding en Onderwys* (National Institute for Education and Teaching). Meanwhile, the campaign to secure an exclusively Afrikaans education system had been proceeding on a broad front.

The Dutch Reformed Church played a leading role in this move and many *predikante* (preachers) were active in school committees and the struggle for Christian-national education. Dr AP Treurnicht, who would later go on to become Deputy Minister of Education and Training under the National Party, reflected on the mood at the time in a speech at the Broederbond's 50th anniversary celebration in October 1968:

> For far too long, ... the Afrikaner had to suffer the insult of an alien culture being forced into the education of his children in the persistent Anglicisation process. It became the logical and compelling demand of his nationalism that his education should be in his own language and should form young lives for the Afrikaner community. And because the nation's origins and growth were so closely connected with the work, doctrine and activities of the church it was obvious that national life should be Christian in its education.[122]

Now the successful Afrikaner cultural movement lay directly in the path of that potent ideological force called Christian nationalism, composed in equal parts of God and Volk. A struggle by the new generation of Broederbond intellectuals and educationalists to emerge as the supreme cultural arbiters of all things Afrikaans had begun; and, through this process, to turn literary forms of Christian nationalism into divine myth and mass consciousness.[123]

As the 1930s wore on, the young *broeders*, as they came to be known, turned their attention to political power and its implications for the 'native

---

121 Ibid., p. 72.
122 Quoted in 'Afrikaner leadership experience', O Malley Archives. Accessed at https://www.nelsonmandela.org/omalley/index.php/site/q/03lv03445/04lv04015/05lv04154/06lv04196/07lv04198.htm.
123 See O'Meara (n 112 above), p. 74.

question'. All through that decade it was racial segregation, not British imperialism, that was the chief concern of party ideologues.

It was in Hendrik Verwoerd that the group was politically and intellectually invested to lead the way.

POSTERITY WILL REMEMBER HENDRIK FRENSCH VERWOERD – PSYCHOLOGIST, sociologist, journalist and statesman – as the chief architect of apartheid. The promise of this could be glimpsed in Verwoerd at a very early age. In 1917, Willem Verwoerd moved his family from Amsterdam thousands of kilometres south to the Orange Free State town of Brandfort. Their new hometown was already reeling from the impact of the effects of recent laws passed by the Union of South Africa. The Native Land Act of 1913 had introduced mandatory territorial segregation decreeing that thousands of independent black farmers and sharecroppers had no right to own land in areas now formally declared white, and restricting them to increasingly crowded and impoverished reserves.

Living for the first time in a predominantly Afrikaner environment, young Hendrik found himself in the midst of a broad social movement to increase the self-identity and pride of his adopted people; many had switched from Dutch to the simpler dialect of Afrikaans as the language of the Afrikaner Volk.

In 1918, he completed high school at the English-medium Milton High School in Bulawayo. The following year, 1919, he travelled to the Cape Province and enrolled at the University of Stellenbosch, just declared a *volksuniversiteit* (people's university) by Afrikaner nationalists. An avid reader of history, he became acutely aware of how the Anglo-Boer War of 1899–1902 had been stumbled into by Afrikaners, decimating its culture and leaving behind scarring images of muddy, blood-soaked trenches and the dead stillness of poisoned air in concentration camps. In 1921, he joined student debates on the suppression by the South African army of a revolt by white miners, known as the Rand Rebellion, and soon became head of the student movement. In 1924, at the age of 23, he became the first student in the country to write his doctoral dissertation in Afrikaans, a year before Afrikaans was proclaimed an official language; and then travelled to America and Europe, where he did postdoctoral studies on race at a number of universities, including Harvard, Hamburg and Berlin.

By this time, the march of history had taken Verwoerd from a young psychology student at the University of Stellenbosch in 1922 to the racist conclusion that 'primitive tribalism' was a low level in the hierarchy of culture.[124] By political affiliation, he identified with the national-socialist wing of the National Party. But as a psychologist living in the first half of the 20th century, his cause made him the disciple of a German intellectual current known as the Leipzig School. A few of the leading intellectuals at Leipzig University would eventually have the name of Adolf Hitler somewhere in their cortex, but most were likelier, in the mid-1920s, to cite Hans Volkelt, Otto Klemm and Karlfried Graf Eckbrecht von Dürckheim-Montmartin – who variously pioneered the schools of holistic and ethnopsychology – as their inspiration. The fit was imperfect. The advocates of holistic psychology saw human emotions as part of a complex of conditioning influences, impossible to decipher or control. Ethnopsychology emphasised human emotions in almost messianic terms as phenomena that could be isolated and evoked, making them measurable and open to manipulation.

In 1926, Verwoerd came under the influence of the Leipzig School. His doctoral thesis, entitled *The Blunting of the Emotions*, was submitted two years before his study tour to Germany; but Verwoerd's ideas on education and Afrikaner nationalism were clearly influenced by the Leipzig intellectuals. *The Blunting of Emotions* is obsessive; it dissects in relentless detail, using laboratory experiments, the psychological irrationality of reason by embedding it in an emotional environment, showing how much psychology encouraged both Volk ideologies and nationalist ones.

By the time Verwoerd arrived in Leipzig in 1926, development psychology and ethnopsychology, with their foci on human emotions and culture as closely interwoven with an ideological and political undercurrent that transcended the psychology of the individual, were crucial to the profile of the Leipzig School. It was a taciturn scholar named Hans Volkelt more than any other – having successfully linked development psychology to

---

124 For more on this, see Wolpe, H, 'Capitalism and cheap labour-power in South Africa: From segregation to apartheid', in *Economy and Society*, Vol. 1, No. 4 (1972), pp. 425-456; and Venter (n 91 above). According to Venter,

> [a]lthough [Verwoerd] did visit Germany during his formative years as an academic, he did not simply adopt romantic idealism like so many of his fellow Afrikaner leaders, who studied in Germany in the Weimar era. He tended towards totalitarian social planning on the basis of a few principles, which is reminiscent of the technocratic social engineering tradition related' to positivism. In his later years moderate idealistic traits surfaced. He derived his views on history and progress probably from this background of the eighteenth and nineteenth century philosophical spirit of the times.

ethnopsychology, social psychology and cultural psychology – who was a major influence on Verwoerd. Most records of Verwoerd's time at Leipzig were destroyed during air raids by Allied bombers in the Second World War, but traceable records salvaged from the ruins show Verwoerd by this time stirred by Volkelt's psychological field of education less than by ideological commitments. Of the courses he attended were Early Forms of Religion among Children and Primitive Peoples, which was closely related to his thinking in later years on the role of education for blacks in South Africa. Scrawls in Verwoerd's course calendar of the popular psychological maxim of 'misjudging children with the consciousness of adults' show his thoughts on black tribal communities as primitive and infantile – two characteristics he would later embroider in his deployment of Bantu education as a mirror of the cognitive process typical of children.

By the end of Verwoerd's thesis, a reader understood why its author had sought refuge behind education as an instrument of Afrikaner cultural hegemony. In the early 20th century, the impact of cultural-evolutionist stage theories in education was considerable. The theory drew a line between different civilisations and placed them in an evolutionary sequence. Thus, 'primitive tribal societies' appeared as the living remnants of former stages in the development of humanity as a whole. There was, in other words, a cultural hierarchy of nations. In this theoretical claim, education was to be both a function of Afrikaner intellectual enlightenment (*Volkdem*)[125] and child psychology for blacks.

In 1927, Verwoerd returned to South Africa and was appointed Professor of Applied Psychology and Sociology at the University of Stellenbosch. He was by this time, he once bluntly admitted in 1947, 'an extreme Afrikaner'; but he did not yet exhibit the focused interest in nationalist politics that would watermark his political career. He preferred to talk about the distinctive cultural traits of 'nationalities' rather than the innate biological differences among races. The Arab is fatalist; the southern Italian is emotionally unstable; the Japanese and French are philosophical; and the Scandinavian is boring, he once told students in his introductory lecture on sociology.

It was the plight of Afrikaners during a period of massive industrial transformation, with its constant threat of acculturation and unemployment,

---

125 Not to be conflated with 'Verligting', which, in the late 1960s, came to define the reformist wing of the National Party.

that galvanised Verwoerd's career. In 1932, a study of poverty in South Africa sponsored by the Carnegie Foundation found that 300 000 of the 1.8 million white citizens in South Africa were extremely poor; the percentage of Afrikaners in poverty was between a quarter and a third. This would become one of the most indelible marks on opinions, similar to those growing in Germany, in South Africa: politicians, joined by intellectuals, began articulating an ideology that harped on historical grievances, promoted cultural integrity and racial purity, and blamed the plight of Afrikaners on particular ethnic groups.

*

Through the 1930s and forties, Verwoerd's ambition would be to turn the poor-white question into a 'national question'. At the University of Stellenbosch, his interest in the problem hastened his intellectual shift to studies in racial purity. In 1932, he established the first sociology department in South Africa and, two years later, became a member of the Broederbond. That same year, popular displays of nationalist fervour were quickly followed by the Volkelt report on poverty in South Africa. Preparatory discussions ranged from how to mobilise Afrikaner capital and "people's banks", to the organisation of pro-nationalist and anti-communist trade unions and the promotion of Afrikaner investment corporations that would concentrate economic power in the hands of the Afrikaner middle class.

The gathering, known as the *Volkskongres* (People's Congress), had been convened six years later, in 1939, at the urging of the Broederbond. In front of the conference venue, a mixed crowd milled about; the stunned, the curious and the angry. A stenographer took notes as Verwoerd, who chaired the socio-economic committee, began addressing the arc of grave faces. At the root of the problem, he said, were the machinations of an English–Afrikaner collaboration which had failed to help most poor Afrikaners. Afrikaners were not focusing on the real source of white unemployment, he continued, which was excessive numbers of coloured and African workers competing for white jobs. Then, red with rage, he echoed his sentiments to an earlier *Volkskongres* held in 1934, proclaiming: "If someone should be unemployed, it should be the native."[126] At the end of his address, congress officials, who had been captivated by the young scholar, appointed him to

---

126 See Giliomee (n 74 above), p. 351.

a small committee created to implement the congress resolutions; within a short time he rose to chairman of the committee.

But, paradoxically, Verwoerd's very success at the congress was to create enduring problems for him in the Broederbond that would culminate in political difficulties he encountered in the early 1960s when he began to drive his policy of separate development and Bantu education. At some point during the conference, the thinking of Afrikaner businessmen, represented by Dr MS Louw, a leading Broederbonder and Managing Director of the Afrikaner life-insurance company, Sanlam, changed. In essence, the issue boiled down to economic empowerment; and in the Afrikaner politics of 1939 this minority view meant men like Louw pursued a tributary separate from the great swell of Afrikaner nationalism that had been surging since the outbreak of the Second World War. Afrikaner businessmen now understood what was expected of them; it was simple economics. As in the United States, the manufacturing demands of war snapped South Africa out of economic depression and into rapid economic growth. When white workers left factory jobs and boarded ships for the front in Europe and North Africa, plant managers desperate for labour recruited and trained thousands of Asian, Indian, coloured and African workers to fill vacancies.

By the time of the *Volkskongres*, businesses had already broken the job colour bar; urban Africans entered the cities more freely as police eased enforcement of the pass laws; and black families desperate for a place to live poured into the industrial heartland south of Johannesburg from the countryside, either cramming into the dense, ramshackle peri-urban black townships or building squatter camps without opposition from the state.

From a business perspective, the war signalled a dramatic turn from the Broederbond's initial focus on cultural unity and the mobilisation of social capital. In a bruising broadside, Louw fired the second salvo since the purges of the early to mid-1920s in the battle within the Broederbond for the soul of the National Party; this time it was across the bow of Verwoerd and his allies. Louw bluntly told the gathering in his address that the Afrikaner now intended to take the capitalist road: "If we want to achieve success," he said amid murmurs from his audience, "we must make use of the technique of capitalism, as it is employed in the most important industry of our country, the gold mining industry."[127] Louw, though a reputedly rock-ribbed nationalist of an extremely conservative political bent, had shown himself to be

127 Quoted in www.anc.org.za/books/reich14.htm.

flexibly pragmatic. With slow diction and great emphasis, he told his now silent, expectant audience that emerging Afrikaner business would not only have to compete with its English rivals, but also work within and with them; so, too, would white Afrikaners vis à vis black workers.

Louw went on to tell his audience, however obliquely, that the time for big moneyed power had come; and Afrikaner economic empowerment could no longer be presumed to be benign. "We must urgently establish a financial company," he said, "which will function in commerce and industry like the so-called 'finance houses' in Johannesburg."[128] The proposal Louw, who was given to tortured locutions, had set before the congress was artfully framed in the sweeping prose of Christian nationalism; but he more fundamentally envisioned recasting the economic landscape on a large scale. When Louw finished, a mild applause faded into silent consent. Economic reality had cast its shadow over them: the Stellenbosch Broederbond had found common ground with its English adversaries. Through a mixture of cajolery and flattery, the empowerment flank of the National Party proved, by general agreement, a tremendous success.

*

Inevitably, the question arises: what were the implications of this elite pact for labour and education policies? More important for our story than the question of Louw's fleeting victory is the broader pattern of acculturation in the Afrikaner community to which the *Volkskongres* points. Against this meshing of elite minds ranged extreme nationalists and poor Afrikaners who felt slighted. Their blueprint for segregation was contained in a critique (by a commission Verwoerd chaired on the race question) of the Fagan Report. To extreme nationalists like Verwoerd, what was happening in Europe was vital to South Africa; what was happening in business a minor distraction. The nature of power was changing because the territorial claim on power, traditionally demarcated by the colonial powers at the Berlin Conference in 1879, was declining. Europe and Britain were devastated by war and hardly lamented by the supreme victor, the United States, whose own modern history had begun in rebellion against the British Empire. Karl Marx, wrote Cold War historian, John Lewis Gaddis, "might have exaggerated

128 *'n Volk Staan Op*, compiled by Du Plessis, EP, for the Economic Institute of the FAK (South Africa: Human & Rousseau, 1964).

capitalism's contradictions, but the self-destructiveness of imperialism was plain for all to see".[129] Certainly, that was the National Party's hope.

The test for Verwoerd and his allies was whether Afrikaners were now willing to do the 'moral' thing: win back power that had been snatched by Britain in 1910, overthrow English liberalism, and establish a Christian-nationalist republic. For a man of his character, this was the promise of divine providence. Though wary of another rift among Afrikaner national-ists, he didn't pause; neither did the great majority of poorer Afrikaners for whom mystic appeals to the unity and economic well-being of the Volk were increasingly meaningless without political power.

The opportunity came in 1948, when men like Daniel F Malan were ascending the national stage and, as a member of the Senate, Verwoerd was expounding his own vision of Bantustans and Bantu education. Against them were liberal reformers of the opposition United Party, backed by Britain, who viewed nationalist policy as the first step toward a South African Gestapo and a radical black nationalist backlash. The United Party of Smuts and Hofmeyr went into the 1948 election committed to the Fagan Report's principle that African workers were a permanent part of South African society. Fagan concluded that migrant labour and native education were socially and economically undesirable. Urbanisation was an "economic phenomenon ... [which] can be guided and regulated, but not prevented".[130]

Favouring Malan and his National Party was an undercurrent of deep mistrust toward Britain, sentiments that grew as the vast majority of poor Afrikaners came to blame British imperialism for their plight. That spring in 1948, Verwoerd began his attack on the liberal opposition's motion of no confidence, in which the delay of the government to put the implica-tions and meaning of 'apartheid' clearly and unambiguously before the white population was lamented. For Verwoerd, British imperial designs on South Africa had discarded the Afrikaner working class in favour of cheap black labour and missionary education; his was an all-or-nothing proposi-tion. Just four years before, he began, the British-backed opposition had been demanding segregation. Now they stood opposed to apartheid and Afrikaner nationalism.

"What does it really mean?" he asked. "It means in the first place that a person who is, surely, a responsible and thinking person, addressed his

---

129 Quoted in Gaddis, JL, *The Cold War: A New History* (Penguin Books, 2006), p. 143.
130 Quoted in Lipton, M, *Capitalism and Apartheid: 1910-84* (Taylor & Francis, 1985), p. 22.

whole party openly in 1942 ... and, a few years after that, in the course of an important election, he then suddenly turned round and refused to carry out the policy for which he had gained ... support."

The point was well made. English liberals, Verwoerd said, were willing to discuss discriminatory measures against blacks "only in so far as their position is related to a series of economic matters", but not as political intervention by nationalists to defend poor Afrikaners. Then he concluded, "I want to state here unequivocally now the attitude of this side of the House, that South Africa is a white man's country and we are not prepared to allow the Natives to be the masters; we are not masters there. But within the European areas, we, the white people in South Africa, are and shall remain the masters."[131]

The rejection of the Fagan recommendations was a major plank in the National Party's election platform; instead, its Sauer Commission proposed a return to the Stallard principle that Africans should only be in white areas temporarily, and for a limited purpose; that they should retain their links with the reserves to which they eventually returned; and that the means of enforcing this was by stricter influx control and the extension of migrant labour.

On 27 May 1948, the National Party rose to power on an electoral promise of stricter enforcement of job reservation and education policies aimed at advancing the interests of the Afrikaner poor. By the early 1950s, however, increasing disgruntlement among the poor-Afrikaner electorate over government fecklessness increased pressure for more radical interventions and encouraged Verwoerd, who had been appointed Minister of Native Affairs, to more plainly set out his diagnosis of South Africa's ills and proposed remedies.

White capital, he once sneered, had become a problem for Afrikaners and a desirable residence for 'natives' who, under the combined impact of taxation and severe poverty, were flowing from rural reserves to urban areas looking for work. As a handful of wealthy businessmen loomed up in popular consciousness, the caricature of 'Hoggenheimer' (a reference to Anglo American corporation mining magnet, Sir Ernest Oppenheimer) in the Afrikaans press had become an increasingly recognisable target of Verwoerd. The solution, in Verwoerd's view, was a radical separation of the races in a new frontier. The cultural re-education of Afrikaners and blacks, generally, in Christian nationalism would thence bend an entire country to his will: apartheid.

---

131 Quoted in Siko (n 111 above), p. 50.

CHAPTER 6

'Good native, tribal native'

RETRIBALISATION

THE DRIVE FROM MOKOPANE TO THE LEBOWAKGOMO DISTRICT IN SOUTH Africa's Limpopo province takes you through dry scrubland over a large ridge of ancient volcanic rock. From the summit, where short tree stubs grow and the air is crisp, you descend along a winding road through a thicket of orange groves into a shallow valley. There is a petrol station on the left, a brick works, a sprawl of teeming settlements; and then miles and miles of nothing until the air turns to a faint, acrid whiff of smoke from coal-fired stoves and braziers.

It was a hot afternoon in early March 2000, and I was driving with a headman in the Ledwaba Tribal Council named Charlie Ledwaba to see one of the oldest surviving members of the community. I wanted to know how Bantu education had affected this former apartheid homeland.

Charlie believed himself to be something of an authority on the community's history. He relished sharing the odd fact about this fragile, barren land and boasted that he was able to trace the ancestry of the community back 200 years: a pocket-holed bed of sediment from an ancient lake here, a prehistoric volcanic eruption that caused the earth to swell here, a kimberlite pipe here.

On the way, our conversation kept turning to the year 1928. He leaned back in his seat, and wearing a small, proprietary smile told me that the Ledwaba had managed to escape the dissembling machinations of English mission schools through the early 19th and 20th centuries. That year, he said to me, the community was forced to vacate their ancestral land.

In Charlie's account, land dispossession and discriminatory labour policies were wedged in education policy. Having escaped colonial conquest for at least a century, the community occupied and farmed the valley, kept herds of cattle, goats and sheep, and tilled the surrounding land. There is evidence in a tattered ledger book in possession of the Tribal Council that the rivers and tributaries in the valley in the 19th century were panned for gold by villagers, with the gold being sold to white people until Afrikaners discovered gold on the farm Eersteling 17KS, immediately west of the royal kraal.

Tribal initiation schools were all the while conducted all over the valley. During the late 19th century, British mission stations were still a long way off from the northern parts of the country. "Afrikaner commandos were busy building a railway line from Johannesburg to the eastern Transvaal to transport minerals and farming product," Charlie said. "For a while they left us alone and even defended the area against the expansion of British missionaries." And, sure enough, the chronology of time does confirm the construction of a railway line during fierce battles between Afrikaners and the British in what roughly coincides with the Anglo-Boer War.

Here, then, was the brooding landscape that set the scene for the ideological conquest of the community. The earliest recorded existence of the occupation by the Ledwaba of land in the district under Chief Jack Eland is a war between Eland and the Voortrekkers, led by Louis Trichardt, from 1836 to 1838 in the vicinity of the Strydpoort Mountains. The Afrikaner military effort failed. But, if there was a nightmare of the colonial era, a place that captured the cumulative rot of a developing capitalism, it was in the realm of culture, labour and education.

*

After five kilometres of driving north along a tarred road, we turned onto a potholed dirt track and headed about two kilometres east. As the desolate settlement of Ga-Mashula came into view, Charlie shifted his gaze to the Martian-like rocky outcrops all across the village. "I grew up in the fields and valleys around here," he said, a nervous timber in his voice. It was here, in 1928, that some members of the Ledwaba community were disgorged from the farm Rietfontein by the government of the day before being banished to the Lebowa homeland, until the latter's reincorporation into South Africa in 1994.

It had been many decades since the Lebowakgomo district was able to support the communities settled throughout the valley through subsistence farming. In the four decades preceding 1990, forced removals and unemployment, exacerbated by mechanisation and drought, dramatically increased pressure on land availability. By the late 1980s, most villagers who lived in the valley were officially classified as 'not economically active'. In 1959, the government-sponsored Tomlinson Commission calculated that, generally, each farmer in black reserves would need to cultivate 45 hectares to survive. About two-thirds of the 200 000 Ledwaba had no access to land; an average of 67 people were squeezed onto each square kilometre of the valley; and a small number of chiefs and headmen took to subsistence farming to satisfy a small part of their needs. The majority of the community were forced to seek employment on white farms and in industry to survive.

*

The route to the only primary school in the area takes you up a rocky hill, off the main road, before you enter a terraced slope. There are no street lamps or basic sanitation amenities. Along the road, a modern, rectangular clay-brick building, about 50 metres in length, looms bizarrely over squat, modern one-room houses, mud huts and kraals of the village. In the afternoons, the shadows on the road are of slight schoolchildren and their mothers – walking, carrying, enduring. The school has its back to an entire history and racialised notion of tribal identity that, as author, Mark Gevisser, has written more generally of the homelands, had been "co-opted into one of the most formidable buttresses of white supremacism".[132]

When I visited the place for the second time in 2003, I mistook the school for an apartheid-era creation. It was built during the early 2000s from money donated to the Ga-Mashula Community Trust by the mining company, De Beers. In 2002/2003, the school had become the subject of media interest in a bruising battle between its donors and the Ledwaba community. The story, told to me by Charlie, is that the community's land claim had pitted them in a battle against De Beers. Running through the valley were rich diamond-bearing deposits discovered in 1996, with an estimated value of R40 billion. Nearby, the Marsfontein Mine, a joint venture between De Beers and the Canadian-listed Southern Era mining company, symbolised what was legally and economically possible in the early post-apartheid period. By 1997, delays in the resolution of the community's land-restitution claim left them with no choice but to bid for the mineral rights through a black-empowerment consortium. The application failed because the mineral rights still legally belonged to the heirs of Tom Naude, an Afrikaner politician

---

132 Gevisser, M, *Thabo Mbeki: The Dream Deferred* (Johannesburg: Jonathan Ball Publishers, 2009), p. 13.

who purchased a significant portion of Marsfontein in the Rietfontein area soon after the arrival of two attorneys in the area some time in 1927.

For a moment, Charlie turned a thought over in his mind, looking toward a clutch of youths in school uniforms ambling along the dusty track; and then he said softly, "It is a long distance from the graves of my ancestors on the other side of the valley." Bantu education, Charlie seemed to be saying, had not banished their heritage. I glanced at him and he met my look with a pained expression. I was about to ask him whether the apartheid strategy of 'retribalisation' and Bantu education was preferable to the liberal ethos of mission schools, then thought better. That his version was true didn't matter. I'd taken it for granted that detribalisation had been a major force in the subjugation of the community. This was one of the fixed ideas I had brought with me to the place.

*

I had been in the area a few hours and already began to realise that most of my ideas about the place were to be of no use. The school was not an apartheid relic. It had been built in the new racial dynamics of the post-apartheid order to haul tribal colleges into the 21st century. With the help of capital leveraged by the empowerment consortium, the community then struck a deal with Naude's 29 heirs to buy the mineral rights for R105 million. However, the heirs reneged and sold the rights to De Beers for a sum of R75 million. In 1998, the heirs told the community they "were no longer bound to sell the mineral rights to the Ledwaba community". De Beers then pushed ahead with the deal and created a shareholding structure in which it controlled 51 per cent of the mine and reserved a small portion for community-development projects. In a letter to the Gauteng Law Society written by Joe Maladji, an advocate in Pietersburg (now Polokwane) sympathetic to the plight of the community, the community roundly excoriated De Beers for riding roughshod over, and showing scant respect for, the rights and plight of the Ledwaba. "We were double-crossed by an unethical bunch of people,"[133] Maladji charged.

It was a perverse irony, Charlie told me, that this testimony to modern civilisation was donated by previous beneficiaries of Bantu education. "When the tribal colleges were encouraged by the apartheid government, it

---

133 Interview with the author, Pietersburg (Polokwane), April 2000.

was with one purpose: to turn us into homeland citizens and cheap labour for white farm owners outside the homeland," he said. After 1994, the bulk of the community's income came from remittances of contract workers outside the area. This was exactly as the apartheid architects intended. And so the era the community entered in 2000 had all the distinctive features of a surplus people: a tribal council, an under-resourced clinic, and a school; but with a difference: there were now theoretical rights to human dignity, education, and black advancement; but such rights were underscored by an entire legacy of colonial and Bantustan neglect.

"We drew the short straw and got a few miserable crumbs," Charlie told me. Those crumbs were the school.

As we entered the home of Ramadimetja Jacobina Ledwaba in the late afternoon, I found myself drawn to a painting of Chief Felix Eland – whom she had married during his chieftainship of the tribe in 1936 – hanging just above a wooden pedestal. There was another, more haunting, image. Her face clouded as we sat in the silence of her home, and with a faintly pained smile she drifted back to her experience as a 26-year-old petrified woman crawling through a dark tunnel of debris: the walls seemed about to collapse, to fold in on her; she was stuck, submerged, while all around her white Boer commandos on horseback demolished mud huts in the village.

She was 98 years old in March 2000 when she recalled the harrowing story for me. The Ledwaba had twice resisted Afrikaner encroachments on their land and lifestyle, but the arrival of two white attorneys named Brink and Haffner on horseback in 1927 would lead to their dispersal in the 1930s.

From her recollection, it is possible to trace the path eventually pursued by the Verwoerd government – which began with a frenzy of discriminatory laws immediately after the passing of the Native Land Act and then continued in fitful bursts, until Verwoerd's murder four decades later.

*

Economically, discriminatory measures were enacted against black farmers, traders and workers to prevent them from competing with whites and instead provide a large source of cheap labour for white farms and mines. The 1913 Land Act reserved almost 14 per cent of the land for Africans, who comprised 70 per cent of the population. Outside these 'reserves' – which would later become known as Bantustans, or homelands – in the 87 per cent of South Africa known as the 'white' areas, Africans could not own, or in most cases rent, land. The 1922 Stallard Commission laid down the principle that an African should only be in towns to "minister to the needs of the white man and should depart therefrom when he ceases to minister".[134] African men over 16 years old had to carry a 'pass' or reference book, which recorded the permission given to them to work and live in a particular white area. Official policy by this time discouraged African families and favoured the mining industry's system of migrant workers housed in all-male compounds while their families remained in the reserves, thus retaining their links with the 'tribal' areas.

After Union, the legal job bar, established on gold mines in the Transvaal Republic in 1893, was entrenched in the Mines and Works Act of 1911 and 1926, which barred Africans from more skilled mining jobs. In the state sector, the 1925 'civilised-labour' policy, designed to protect unskilled whites from undercutting by blacks, provided preferential employment in unskilled jobs for whites "at a level of pay at which the European employee can maintain his standard of living".[135]

In private manufacturing and services there was no statutory job colour bar during this period, but preference for whites was secured by the 1925 Customs Tariff Act, which made protection for local manufacturers conditional upon "satisfactory labour conditions including the employment of a reasonable proportion of civilised workers".[136] Higher expenditure on white education was another means of giving whites an advantage. Thus the Act restricted the right of an owner to allow natives to reside on or occupy land, except as servants or farm labourers.

When the two attorneys purchased the farm Rietfontein, they exerted pressure on Chief Jack Eland to either enter into contracts of employment with the owners or leave. Eland refused and his offer in a letter to the Chief Commissioner to provide a substitute employee was rejected. "It was the custom of the Ledwaba that the chief should not perform work as the employee of another since it does not befit his royal status," Ramadimetja recalled. It appears that more and more pressure was exerted on Eland to either enter into contracts of employment with the owners of Rietfontein,

---

134 Quoted in Lipton (n 130 above), pp. 17–18.
135 Ibid., p. 19.
136 Ibid.

ostensibly represented by attorneys Brink and Haffner, or to leave. Eland consistently refused. As a result, the farmers in the vicinity during 1928 forcefully removed Eland from the royal kraal, along with headmen and thousands of villagers who protested the move.

The looting and power vacuum that followed the removal of the community from Rietfontein shattered the cohesion of the community. Thereafter, most children were disgorged on farms and mines as wage labourers and tenants in what Merle Lipton described as the "brutal consummation of the emerging racial order".[137]

In 1936, Jack Eland was succeeded by Chief Felix, who married Ramadimetja Jacobina Ledwaba. She recalls that, some time in 1942, Felix made representations to the government to have his tribe resettled on ancestral land. The police then threatened him and he was much more cautious about exercising rights to the land.

Because the land was too small, thousands of villagers became part of the system of farm labourers at the time. Their expulsion and the relocation of millions more in urban black townships across the country to other designated urban areas would be yet another part of the grand-apartheid scheme. And so the Ledwaba found themselves pariahs in the land of their birth. It would set the political stage for the enactment of Bantu education and Verwoerd's grand-apartheid scheme.

Backtracking the unspoken tragedy of the community, I was led to a curious test case in the developing relationship between the apartheid doctrine of 'retribalisation' and the educational and labour requirements of the emerging apartheid economy. This was not crude racism; from their vantage point, the planners of the emerging industrial economy gradually began to see the relationship between land, labour and education as economically intertwined functions. The story describes the tragic drama of the ruthless destruction of a peasant economy by the apartheid state and the community's dissimulation and incorporation into the apartheid capitalist system.

*

With the industrial upheavals of the first four decades of the 20th century in South Africa, mining and manufacturing radically transformed rural agricultural economies into urban, industrial ones. The post-Second World War

---

137 Ibid., p. 17.

industrialisation phase heaved the South African economy into the industrial age, accomplishing in slightly more than a decade what in other countries had taken more than a century. Gigantic mining and manufacturing plants were carved out of barren land. The burst of industrialisation sucked labour from rural villages into the cities, leading to a massive movement of Africans into urban areas and an increase in the African workforce.

By the 1940s Smuts era, South Africa was becoming a major industrial power, but the great economic leaps forward were no longer possible without a relaxation of the job colour bar. The demands of a more complex economy made it especially difficult for businesses to expand without black labour. Two attempts by the United Party under Jan Smuts at reform – one in the labour market and the other in the education policy fields – during the early 1940s had the effect of assuaging some of the frustrations of the African middle classes by offering them privileges which encouraged integrationist hopes. The influence of new ideas and pressures of blacks, the liberal intelligentsia and urban businessmen were reflected in the publications of major official commissions, such as the Van Eck and Fagan reports. Smuts himself, then Prime Minister, famously said in 1942 that African urbanisation could not be stopped. "You might as well try to sweep the ocean back with a broom,"[138] he once remarked. Jan Hofmeyr, Smuts's second in command, went further, denouncing the "herrenvolk mentality" of whites and declaring in Parliament, "I take my stand for the ultimate removal of the colour bar from our Constitution."[139]

The job colour bar was eased and the training facilities for blacks were expanded to increase the supply of skilled workers. Occupational advancement and government pilot programmes, exercised though the Wage Board, led for the first time since the 1922–1925 'civilised-labour' policies to a narrowing of average black–white wage ratios. The 1945 National Education Finance Act freed African education from its constricting dependence on African taxes; Africans became eligible for old-age pensions and inclusion in the Unemployment Insurance Fund; and there was some easing of restrictions on black businessmen.

While the industrial colour bar restricted the occupational horizons of Africans in industrial sectors of the economy, the expansion of tertiary sectors in the post-war period opened up substantial new middle-class job

138 Smuts, J, *The Basis of Trusteeship in African Native Policy* (South African Institute of Race Relations, 1942).
139 Quoted in Lipton (n 130 above), p. 21.

opportunities for Africans. The net result was that Africans advanced into semi-skilled and, in some cases, skilled jobs.

The fact that there was at least some degree of concern about the control of black education for a role of subservience well before 1950 is indicated by the establishment of an Interdepartmental Committee on Native Education, known as the Welsh Committee, which reported in 1936. The main concern of the Committee was whether or not the state should assume responsibility for the administration and financing of black education. The Committee's recommendation that the state should intervene in these areas was not in fact adopted, but the Committee report provides valuable documentation of the ideology surrounding black education before 1953.

Considering the aims of black education from the standpoint of the average white South African, the Committee identified a lack of support for state provision of black schools: "From the evidence before the committee it seems clear that there still exists opposition to the education of the Native on the grounds that a) it makes him lazy and unfit for manual work; b) it makes him 'cheeky' and less docile as a servant; and c) it estranges him from his own people and often leads him to despise his own culture."[140]

Implicit in these segregationist comments was concern that blacks were more than workers and the assumption that appropriate attitudes would be acquired outside the schools. It would seem that whites feared that schooling would operate in the same way for blacks, and this impeded the continuous provision of the lowest level of workers.

The Welsh recommendations were a barely visible hairline fracture that over time developed into a profound break.

*

Perhaps, though, the most audacious consequence of Smuts's liberalisation phase was the growth in African traders. Whereas, in 1942, Africans in the Orange Free State were barred from all trade, by 1947 they were allowed to sell tea, coffee, sugar and tinned meat. Some idea of the size of the African trading class can be gauged from the rise of African retail businesses in South Africa. Between 1938 and 1948, the number of African businesses in the townships around Johannesburg alone increased from 192 to 1 683.

---

140 Quoted in Christie, P & Collins, C, 'Bantu education: Apartheid ideology and labour reproduction', in Kallaway (n ‡ above), p. 168.

This seemed to the National Party truly dangerous, for it undermined the tribal identity of black communities whose behaviour it (the National Party) might not have liked but whose survival was essential for the exercise of social control.

It was this challenge that Afrikaners, led by business, began to address with the government. What emerged during the mid-1940s was an awareness of the purchasing power of Africans. The government policy of encouraging African entrepreneurs to 'serve their own people in their own areas' came to be seen by Afrikaner businesses as being in conflict with their own desire to capture the major part of this spending.

These sentiments coincided with the halting and, in some respects, seemingly relentless trend towards apartheid, particularly in relation to labour and education policy. The emerging apartheid blueprint promised a step-by-step closure of every avenue of black advancement opened up by Smuts: exemption from pass and curfew laws, freehold property rights in urban areas, access to superior education through the liberal mission schools and 'open' universities, and the token representation of 'unqualified' voters in Parliament and provincial councils.

Unlike mission schools, which made a point of removing black students from their 'native environments', rural or tribal schools adapted their routines and curricula to the rhythms of the rural environments in which they were located. The schools only took children for the first five grades. Thereafter, they went to work on farms.

In the education field, the United Party model took twists and turns, vacillating between restrictions on schooling and greater provision of funding for the development of a skilled class of workers, but tending overwhelmingly toward the detribalisation of schooling and tertiary education.

During the years between the Act of Union in 1910 and the 1930s, missionary societies dominated the provision of black and coloured education; the colonial assimilationist approach reigned. By the 1930s, segregationist schooling patterns were already well established, and, throughout the 1930s and forties, operated to reproduce racial inequality. Black schooling provisions revealed no standardisation of administrative arrangements before Bantu education. Most of the schools, wrote Frank Molteno[141], operated under church or mission auspices, but there were also state schools and community or tribal schools.

---

141 Molteno (n 17 above), p. 92.

Whilst provinces were legally responsible for the control of black edu-cation, responsibility for funding resided in the central government. The funding arrangement in terms of the 1925 Act persisted until 1945: state expenditure was fixed, supplemented by a proportion of direct taxes paid by blacks. This proportion was increased a number of times between 1925 and 1945. Nevertheless, the principal feature of the funding arrangements throughout the period was their inadequacy: in 1930, white per capita expenditure was 22.12 pounds compared with 2.02 pounds for blacks. By 1945, per capita income for whites rose to 38 pounds compared with 3 pounds for blacks. As a result, educational provisions for blacks were far from adequate. The majority of black South Africans were schooled in crowded, makeshift classrooms.

In 1939, the Minister of Education in the United Party government admit-ted that two-thirds of black children had no schooling whatsoever. During the war years, the government improved the provision of education for blacks considerably, but, by 1950, less than half of black children between the ages of 7 and 16 were attending school, and only 2.6 per cent of black pupils were enrolled in post-primary standards. The average black child spent only four years in school.

There was also a shortage of teachers, many of whom were poorly qual-ified or not qualified at all. School facilities were limited: buildings were usually rudimentary and inadequate; and there were shortages of furniture, books and other equipment. In spite of the increased overall attendance of blacks, schooling remained concentrated at lower levels. In 1945, 75 per cent of blacks at school were in the first four years of schooling and only 3.4 per cent were in post-primary classes.[142]

The previous United Party government had also seen little need for the training of large numbers of black artisans for employment in the com-mon area. With the demand for education growing rapidly, schools had to take in far more children than they could teach effectively. The state helped by providing salaries for approved teaching posts, but overall state aid was insufficient in a modernising economy. School buildings were dilapidated and classes overcrowded.[143]

By the beginning of the 1940s, the South African education system was roughly comparable with that of the United States: The first two years

---

142 All data in Kallaway (n ‡ above), pp. 165-166.
143 See Gool, J, *The Crimes of Bantu Education in South Africa* (Unity Movement Publication, 1966). Accessed online at http://www.apdusa.org.za/wp-content/books/crimes.of.bantu.education.pdf.

were also known as the 'kindergarten period'. The next five years at school constituted the primary level, namely Standards 1, 2, 3, 4 and 5. However, even in those days, only about 1 in 200 African students actually completed Standard 5. The rest were material par excellence for the mines and farms. They could just about read a few simple sentences, count to 1 000, sign their names, and understand their white masters.

In the mid-1940s, both the United Party government and the Natives Representative Council, the main body for articulating black opinion, sensed that the system of black education was in need of drastic overhaul. The policy emphasised the training of whites for skilled labour in the so-called white areas. Blacks could only expect to do skilled work in the reserves. In terms very similar to those Verwoerd would use later, the Secretary of the Department of Native Affairs told the De Villiers Commission on Technical and Vocational Training in 1947 that "the unfolding of extensive government development schemes in the reserves would produce a large number of skilled posts".[144]

White supremacy was clearly incompatible with a steadily rising, better educated, urbanised black population moving up to strategic levels of the economy. Recognising this, JG Strijdom, the Transvaal National Party leader, warned DF Malan in 1946 that it would be impossible to maintain racial discrimination if the quality of education of the subordinate people was steadily improved, saying, "Our church ministers were far too eager to compete with other missionary societies in trying to provide the most education to blacks."[145] If the state in the future tried to withhold equal rights from educated people, he added, it would lead to "bloody clashes and revolutions".[146]

And therein lay a paradox, one that would be articulated by Verwoerd when he would reason that military might was only a quarter of the battle; the remaining battle would be fought not by soldiers, but through a process of social engineering. In this model, Nationalists proposed state control of black schooling within native reserves which would emphasise the training of communities in tribal culture and history.

It is here, in the evolving ideology and architecture of Bantustans and Bantu education, that the modern outline of our story begins.

144 Quoted in Kallaway (n ‡ above), pp. 165-166.
145 Quoted in Giliomee (n 74 above), p. 507.
146 Thom, HB, *D.F. Malan* (Cape Town: Tafelberg, 1980), p. 279.

CHAPTER 7

'An efficient force'

BANTU EDUCATION

Like all black South Africans who lived through that time, Ramadimetja Ledwaba never forgot how she heard that members of her community would, once again, have to relinquish their ancestral rights to land and heritage. It was a splendid summer's day – the kind of bright, crisp afternoon that makes a day full of promise. In Cape Town, Hendrik Verwoerd, who had been appointed Native Affairs Minister, had just emerged from Parliament ecstatic that his appointment of the Tomlinson Commission, headed by Richard Tomlinson, to conduct an inquiry into the transformation of the native reserves into permanent ethnic homelands for Africans had been approved.

History cracked open for South Africa on that day in 1950. But the abyss that opened for citizens of the new settlements was the deepest of all. Three years later, Verwoerd delivered his final blow: men, women and children would be uprooted in pre-dawn police raids on shanty towns, bundled into police vans, and "herded", in Verwoerd's penchant for Orwellian-speak, into heavily overpopulated rural reserves called 'homelands' in a manner reminiscent of Joseph Stalin's Gulags. Roughly 12 million, or 80 per cent of the population, were squeezed onto 13 per cent of the country's land. The next day, they had become non-citizens in their native land.

On that day, Ramadimetja recalled her community's second conquest. The construction of the Lebowa homeland, she said, entrenched tribal colleges as buttresses of the Bantustan policy. She, like other villagers, was not of Christian-missionary stock, which confirmed to me what Charlie Ledwaba had told me.

*

A year before, in January 1949, the National Party set up a commission on native education under the chairmanship of Dr Werner Eiselen, Verwoerd's Secretary of Bantu Affairs. Both Eiselen and Verwoerd himself firmly believed in mother-tongue schooling as the best form of education.

A Professor of Anthropology before becoming Chief Inspector of Native Education in the Transvaal, Eiselen had been studying the particularity of blacks and the preservation of African languages and cultures as a new model under apartheid. He was concerned that the education and labour market system were no longer controlled from the top; instead, the whole racial-planning system had become a never-ending, undisciplined liberal bazaar. To him there was little doubt that blacks would learn better through their own languages.

The main terms of reference of what became known as the Eiselen Commission were "the formulation of the principles and aims of education for 'Natives' as an independent race in which their past and present, their inherent racial qualities, their distinctive [characteristics] and aptitudes, and their needs under ever changing social conditions are taken into consideration".[147] In the main, Eiselen concluded that black education should be an integral part of a carefully planned policy of segregated socio-economic development for African people. He emphasised, above all, the functional value of schooling as an institution for the transmission and development of black cultural heritage. The Commission reported in 1951. It perceived a two-way relationship between schooling and reserves in the following terms:

> The reserves, being areas in which Bantu culture functions almost completely, have a special task to perform in the furtherance of the development of Bantu culture and schools. Many educated Bantu feel that the reserves are fast becoming economic and cultural slums; places to be avoided by the educated and enterprising ... . But if the reserves are to play their part they must be developed so that there can be a harmony between the schools and the way of life of the people; a way of life which will give scope for the expression of talent and ambition.

The report noted that finance had been pegged to a set figure, all teachers were to be trained in government colleges, and all syllabuses were to be

---

147 Quoted in Christie & Collins (n 140 above), p. 161.

those emanating from the government and imbued with the ideas of racial inferiority. The Christian ideal of an egalitarian and communal society in which everyone aspired to a universalist culture, which was both Western and Christian, was struck a severe blow.

The report formed the scaffolding for the Bantu Education Act in 1953, giving wide powers to the Minister of Native Affairs (at that time, Verwoerd) to bring into effect the major recommendations of the Commission. Black education was to be directed to white needs; it was to be centrally controlled and financed under the Ministry; syllabuses were to be adapted to the black way of life; and African languages were to be introduced into all black schools. Most importantly, however, control of the 5 000 mission-run schools at that time was to be gradually taken away from the missionary bodies and placed under the Department of Native Affairs.

When, in 1951, Eiselen announced his findings and recommendations, the report immediately caught Verwoerd's eye.

*

Verwoerd's first aim as Minister of Native Affairs was to institutionalise the provisions of the Bantu Education Act through the Department of Native Affairs.

The basis for Bantu education was laid by the 1950 Population Registration Act, and the Bantu Authorities Act a year later, which classified the whole population by race, based on appearance, descent and "general acceptance", and eventually converted blacks into foreigners in their land of birth. The parliamentary representatives and council created for them in 1936 were abolished; instead, each of the eight African ethnic groups, or 'nations', was to exercise its political rights in its own homeland.

On 4 March 1953, the Public Safety Act of 1953 and the Criminal Law Amendment Act 8 of 1953 were passed. Shortly after, in April 1953, the Reservation of Separate Amenities Act 49 of 1953 was passed. From this point forward, blacks would be denied public facilities in white areas and their right to protest restricted. Later that month, on 24 April, the President of the African National Congress, Chief Albert Luthuli, called off the Defiance Campaign, fearing arrests under the new Act.

Abroad, the sense of crisis signalled a change in attitude to South Africa and brought the first flickers of international opprobrium to apartheid into the open, marking the beginning of South Africa's long spell out in the cold a decade later. A rash of protests countrywide that thronged front pages of newspapers was to add revulsion to popular disapproval throughout the year.

Within a few months, Afrikaner nationalists had institutionalised apartheid. To liberals' ideas about power, Verwoerd added an efficient method of conquest. The victory of the National Party meant the ascendance to political power of a combination of white workers, middle-class professionals and farmers bound together by an Afrikaner-nationalist ideology. The principal differences between the National Party and its predecessors centred on the issue of urban black labour. The United Party, meanwhile, supported by manufacturing and diverse mining capital, appeared to be moving towards the phasing out of migrant labour and allowing certain blacks to settle in urban areas while still maintaining labour bureaus, pass laws and a policy of segregation in order to secure cheap black labour.

These apparently conflicting positions, articulated by historian Martin Legassick, saw the homeland base and the extension of migrant labour through the pass system and labour bureaus as extensions by extra-coercive methods of repressive measures of controlling labour and maintaining its supply at a cheap level. As Legassick remarked, "Both arguments were primarily concerned with the interests of capital and continued capital accumulation from an extra-economically coerced labour force; their differences were in the character, and to some extent the intensity of such extra-economic coercion."[148]

*

As 1950 dawned, the National Party, in power for two years, aimed firstly at taking control of the education of South African blacks by removing it from the hands of the missionary societies and churches. No one was in doubt as to the reasons. They were made plain in Parliament: the National Party took note of the "social environment in general" of black South Africans defined as rural, tribal and unskilled and said, "And so shall it remain."[149] Verwoerd made it clear that his intentions were ideological; his aim was to preserve the status quo and prevent black agitation. Mission education, for those who received it, was providing a base of confidence – unintentionally, it would

---

148 Quoted in Kallaway (n ‡ above), pp. 170-171.
149 Ibid., pp. 148-149.

appear, for political demands which were unacceptable to the nationalist and Afrikaner sense of what was right and divine. Government thinking was that control of the system of schooling, control of teacher training, and the removal of liberal influences could so shape black people's consciousness that they might accept a white ruling-class view of what the world was like and of their fitting and comfortable place within it.

The rise of apartheid education, from liberalism's perspective, meant the Afrikaner-nationalist victors would preside over an 'internal colony' of black subjects; but it also reversed the partial erosion of structural barriers to skills development and mobility that took place during the War and pushed back momentum towards the rise of the black middle and skilled classes.

And so, one of the National Party's first orders of business was the adaptation of the education system to the labour requirements of the apartheid order. The various forms of resistance which had arisen in and around mission and tribal schools by the time the National Party came to power, were repressed.

With such an audacious undertaking, the apartheid government faced, and in some ways didn't face, a paradox that was unavoidable. The government was trying to re-contour the country in a way that would allow black communities, for the first time since the colonial conquests, to cohere for self-government. But, if the system nested in a country racially divided into homelands, how would all the plans ever lead to success?

The means for reconciling business's need for African labour with the National Party's determination to limit African numbers and prevent their permanent urbanisation was migrant labour, which became a centrepiece of 'native' policy. "Migrant labour," Verwoerd told mining companies in 1952, "is the best ... system. Its strengthening and expansion ... to most of the other spheres of labour would be in the interests of the Bantu ... . Fully-fledged townships ... are not in accordance with government policy."[150]

Verwoerd also attempted to discourage the employment of Africans in urban areas by measures such as the 1952 Bantu Services Levy Act, which imposed monthly taxes on employers of urban Africans. Policy towards state control of black education extended to Africans already in urban areas was set out by the Eiselen Commission. "Cosmopolitan areas in industrial centres where people of many languages and customs are herded together

---

150 Quoted in Lipton (n 130 above), pp. 25-26.

provide particularly difficult conditions for the orderly and progressive development of Bantu cultures," the Commission noted.[151] "But if the reserves are to play their part they must be developed so that there can be a harmony between the schools and the way of life of the people."[152]

At the stroke of a pen, Verwoerd institutionalised the main plank of social engineering and control. To men like him, this was no mere quirk of temperament. To Cecil John Rhodes's philosophy of annexing land, not men, Verwoerd, after his return from studies in Nazi Germany, remarked: "If you want to control a people you must get hold of their education. You have to control minds." That's precisely what he set out to do.

In November 1950, the National Party Congress delivered its second blow: a motion that the country's education system should conform to the Party's version of Christian-national education. The policy had been prepared by a group of university professors and National Party politicians, including two Cabinet ministers, all members of the Broederbond.

*

It is in the interest of the bantu that he be educated in his own circle. He must not become a black Englishman in order to be used against the Afrikaner.

There is no place for [the native] in the European community above the level of certain forms of labour ... . Until now he has been subjected to a school system which drew him away from his own community and misled him by showing him the green pastures of European society in which he was not allowed to graze.

Native education should be controlled in such a way that it should be in accord with the policy of the state. If the Native is taught to expect that he will live his adult life under a policy of equal right with whites, he is making a big mistake. The Native that attends school must know that he will be the labourer in this country.[153]

This extract from a speech by Verwoerd during the introduction of the Bantu Education Bill to Parliament in 1953 echoed Paul Kruger in 1887,

151 Couper, S, 'At the expense of its own soul: Bantu education's threat of closure to Inanda Seminary', October 2010. Accessed at http://www.kznhass-history.net/files/seminars/Couper2010.pdf.
152 Ibid.
153 Molteno (n 17 above), pp. 92-93.

when he remarked, "The black man must be taught that he comes second and that he belongs to the inferior class which must obey and learn to serve as labourers."[154]

By and large, though, Verwoerd meant something more. Whereas Kruger viewed the 'native question' as detribalised labour, the policy of Bantu education was Verwoerd's answer to the 'native question' within a grand apartheid framework: Bantu education was nothing more than an artificial resuscitation of tribalism.

CR Swart, who at the time was President of South Africa, stressed the importance of retribalisation in the parliamentary debate on the Bill in a rhetorically overwrought performance: "Hon. members have mentioned that the Department of Native Affairs adopts the policy that natives should not be detribalised but should be educated in their own manner and should learn to be good natives as tribal natives, and should not be imitators of the white man."

The policy contained some strictly fundamentalist Calvinist doctrine. Wilkins and Strydom in their book, *The Super-Afrikaners*, quoted the following extract from the journal, *Blackout*: "Creation took place in six calendar days and fossils must be explained presumably ... as remnants of the [Biblical] flood."[155]

History and geography "were to be taught as divinely inspired in the narrow sense of the world. God had given to each people a country and a task. It was the Afrikaners' task to rule South Africa, and nobody had the right to question what was divinely ordained. Teachers who refused to subscribe to these doctrines would simply not be appointed."[156]

The principal effect of the Bantu Education Act of 1953 – and in this respect it was certainly a break with past practices – was that black education was brought under state control. Although this measure had been suggested by the 1936 Interdepartmental Committee, it was not adopted by the previous government. The Bantu Education Act stipulated that all black schools would have to be registered with the government. This measure enabled the government to close any educational programmes which did not support its aims. The administrative differences characteristic of black schooling in the

---

154 La Guma, A, *Apartheid: A Collection of Writings on South African Racism by South Africans* (New York: International Publishers, 1971), p. 35.
155 Wilkins & Strydom (n 90 above).
156 Quoted in Harvey, R, *The Fall of Apartheid: The Inside Story from Smuts to Mbeki* (Hampshire: Palgrave Macmillan, 2001), p. 68.

previous decades were to be replaced by a uniform system. Three types of schools could operate: community schools; government schools, and private state-aided schools, including mission schools, with schools falling into the last category only being allowed to operate with the necessary permission.

To promote tribal cultures, the Nationalists made vernacular education compulsory in African primary schools; in senior schools, both official languages, English and Afrikaans, were added. Verwoerd applied himself energetically to "sweeping back the ocean with a broom".[157]

*

In 1954, the state began taking over most coloured and black schools that had been under the control of missions and churches. That same year, the Bantu Education Act placed the supervision of black education under a special state department known as the Department of Native Affairs; funding and the administration of 'Native' education were to be transferred from mission schools to the state. The 5 000 or so mission schools produced, in Nationalist eyes, academic training with too much emphasis on English and "dangerous liberal ideas" that were seen as breeding grounds for an "African elite which could claim recognition in a common society". For other black sections of the population – the 2 million coloureds, 500 000 Indians, 50 000 Malays and 5 000 Chinese – similar departments had been formed, or were in the process of being formed.

A year later, in 1955, the government passed legislation that gave wide powers to the Minister of Bantu Education, including control over teachers' syllabuses and "any other matter relating to the establishment, maintenance, management and control over government Native schools".[158] In effect, the state showed itself prepared to reduce schooling provisions rather than allow them to operate outside its control. Whereas in 1953 there were over 5 000 state-aided mission schools, by 1965 there were 509 out of a total of 7 222 black schools. By 1959, virtually all black schools, including 700 Catholic schools, had been brought under the central control of the Department of Native Affairs led by Hendrik Verwoerd. Measures taken in 1955 also brought night schools, which had roughly 12 000 blacks enrolled in 1953/1954, under state control, leading to their closure in the years that followed.

---

157 Quoted in Lipton (n 130 above), pp. 25-26
158 Quoted in Christie & Collins (n 140 above), p. 171.

Within state schooling, the Bantu education schooling structure provided for lower-primary schools (Grades 1 to 4), higher-primary schools (Grades 5 to 7) and a series of post-primary schools. In the lower-primary schools, the curriculum was not unlike that of the 1930s and forties mission schools, being based on functional levels of communication, literacy and numeracy. According to this pattern of distribution, most schooled blacks would be prepared for subordinate positions in the workforce. Unlike mission schools, the new state-run black schools were poorly staffed and teacher qualifications were generally low.

If the 1910 Union government and 1913 Native Land Act camouflaged the War that had just been fought between the Afrikaners and British for resources and power with a smokescreen of race, South Africa would now be steered into a dizzyingly complex era in which the education of black people would be a devious route to a desirable goal: the development and brutal execution of grand apartheid.

It was the spark that lit the apartheid flame. The National Party, wrote *The Star*, now "steps into an era of apartheid with questionable premises ... . The Bantu Education Bill can only spell blood and revolution." It was not a classic case of media hysteria, of hype, as we shall see, that would shape reality and, in turn, mark the plight of black people beyond the end of apartheid. Every morning that year brought a story of South Africa's adoption of discriminatory legislation. The National Party government was pressing ahead with a lethal juggernaut of laws known as 'apartheid' which constricted every aspect of life for blacks to racially segregated, peri-urban dormitories called 'townships' and independent homelands known as 'Bantustans'.

IF ONE OF THE FUNCTIONS OF BANTU EDUCATION WAS TO BUILD THE HOMELAND system's blood and muscle, it clearly envisaged the separation of whites and blacks in political and economic structures, promoted ideologically through schooling and revealing a seamy side of destitution, neglect and squalor.

The Bantu Education Act therefore promoted the notion of political, cultural and economic segregation on broad terms. Verwoerd's notorious comments as Minister of Native Affairs in 1954 indicate a clear link between schooling and reserves:

More institutions for advanced education in urban areas are not desired. Deliberate attempts will be made to keep institutions for advanced education away from the urban environment and to establish them as far as possible in the Native reserve. It is the policy of my department that education would have its roots entirely in the Native areas and the Native environment and Native community. There Bantu education must be able to give itself complete expression and there it will perform its real service. The Bantu must be guided to serve his own community in all respects. There is no place for him in the European community above the level of certain forms of labour.[159]

But it was not until the passing of the Promotion of Bantu Self-Government Act in 1959, which provided for the establishment of separate black governments in the geographically fragmented homelands under the influence of the all-white South African government, that Bantu education would take on an institutional form and ideological character consistent with apartheid. Tied up with the National Party's push for the extension of migrant labour bureaus and other extra-economic coercive measures to control labour, the homeland policy would reduce the numbers of permanently settled blacks in urban areas and provide an alternative basis for the supply and control of black labour.

Verwoerd himself likened the process to cattle herded into a pen. The phenomenon of 'Bantustans' placed the process of 'proletarianisation' in the hands of the apartheid government; village chiefs and headman were the Paladins of the policy of 'retribalisation' through tribal colleges; and Bantustan administrations became shepherds of a class of non-citizens. The first half of Verwoerd's formulation in 1953 of course affirmed what was already the situation on the ground. Blacks had always been variously excluded from skilled or other advanced jobs and the central state bureaucracy. What distinguished Bantu education was Verwoerd's aim of creating new opportunities for blacks in the homelands – what he called "serving their own people".[160]

---

159 Ibid., p. 175.
160 Giliomee, H, 'Education in SA: Is Verwoerd to blame?', *Politicsweb*, 3 September 2012. Accessed at http://www.politicsweb.co.za/news-and-analysis/education-in-sa-is-verwoerd-to-blame.

Some of these areas were being readied for 'independence',[161] even though they lacked the physical cohesiveness and financial characteristics to make either political or economic independence viable. In his 1954 work, *Bantu Education: Policy for the Immediate Future*, Verwoerd wrote:

> [Bantu] education should stand with both feet in the reserves and have its roots in the spirit and being of Bantu society ... . [T]he basis of the provision and organisation of education in a Bantu Community should, where possible, be the tribal organisation ... . Their education should not clash with Government policy ... . If the native in South Africa today ... is being taught to expect that he will live his adult life under a policy of equal rights, he is making a big mistake.

In line with this policy, outlined in the 1950s but only developed in the 1960s, was the move to concentrate secondary schools as far as possible in the reserves. Similarly, the provisions in the Bantu education system for the separation of schools along linguistic and tribal lines bolstered retribalisation as part of the homeland policy.

Education became, in an official sense, part of a broad system of extending state control, which included strengthening and increasing repressive mechanisms such as labour bureaus, pass laws, and restrictions on urbanisation. Whereas these latter measures were largely geared towards physical coercion, schooling was a less repressive means of reproducing labour in a stable form.

*

The last remaining members of the Ledwaba were given notice to vacate Rietfontein by 6 January 1955. The community was accorded the status of a tribal authority in the area, which became the Lebowa homeland in which the Lebowakgomo township was developed.

The years that followed brought more decline in black communities as the apartheid regime careened toward its objectives. Overall, there was a

---

161 In reality, these areas, known as the TBVC states – Transkei, Venda, Bophuthatswana and Ciskei (as well as Lebowa) – were independent in name only. They were, in effect, self-governing provinces that relied on the Republic of South Africa for their revenue and so-called foreign aid, and they were dependent on the earnings of migrant workers in the Republic. Moreover, they were recognised as independent states only by one another and by South Africa.

marked deterioration in the qualification levels of teachers and the quality of education, which would perpetuate the ideology of inferiority in state schools, including tribal colleges. All international science textbooks were forbidden in Bantustan schools. About 20 000 international books, some of classical "Western Culture", were banned;[162] special textbooks, written in six pseudo-African languages developed by civil servants in the Department of Native Affairs called "vernacular, were used for African pupils"[163]; and English and Afrikaans were gradually removed from the school curriculum, making it virtually impossible for African matriculants to enter white universities or pursue studies abroad.

Although the number of pupils in the first five grades had increased 10 times in the decade since 1953, the number of schools and teachers remained roughly the same. Pupils now only attended school for two-and-a-half hours daily.

By 1966, a national survey by *The Star* reported approximately 7 000 African schools in the whole of South Africa. Many of them were halls, tents, steps, ramshackle buildings; in fact, any structure with a shelter where children could be accommodated. Out of these schools, only 169 were government schools; the rest were state-aided on a rand-for-rand basis, staffed by 28 000 teachers. The general average in every class was 70 children.

On 10 April 1965, the *Rand Daily Mail* reported that only 968 out of 200 000 children enrolled in Sub A reached Form 5; and 362 matriculated. In other words, only 1 in 500 children passed matric and was ready to enter university. A month later, on 23 May, the *Sunday Times* ran an education survey on Bantu education which revealed that the actual percentage of passes in matriculation had dropped to 0.06 per cent – that is, 6 out of every 10 000 children enrolled passed matric.[164]

But there was another outcome, besides the statistical legerdemain, that changed the lives of communities like the Ledwaba in a deeper sense. If Bantustans gave apartheid its physical anatomy, Bantu education would give the new racial frontier its blood and muscle. With his ambition and imperious sense of cultural exclusivity, Hendrik Verwoerd had risen to power confident that he could take charge of the country's black population and put it at the service of the Afrikaner cause.

162 Quoted in Gool (n 143 above).
163 Lee, FJT, 'Bantu education', in *International Socialist Review*, Vol. 27, No 4, Fall 1996, pp. 153-156. Accessed at https://www.marxists.org/history/etol/newspape/isr/vol27/no04/lee.html.
164 Quoted in *The Star*, 26 February 1962.

CHAPTER 8

The assault on academic freedom

UNIVERSITIES

FROM A NEWS POINT OF VIEW, THE YEAR 1959 DAWNED SLOWLY. IN CAPE Town, wisps of mist drifted across Table Mountain, tempering the summer heat, and residents began their routines with unhurried complacency – the humdrum of suburban neighbourhoods, the morning newspaper, the school run, the journey to work. The city (and country) was deceptively ordinary. It was as if the run of events since the apartheid-policy juggernaut in 1953 had been steadily gathering impetus – from slow news days to increasingly worrisome headlines.

On 1 March 1953, a leading liberal politician named Alan Paton was putting the finishing touches to his imminent announcement of the launch of the Liberal Party of South Africa in Cape Town. In Johannesburg, a 42-year-old black lawyer named Nelson Mandela was drafting the 'M-Plan' to organise black people on a street/block basis. Several thousand kilometres north, his comrades, Walter Sisulu and Duma Nokwe, were hopscotching across West Africa. From there, they would travel to Bucharest, Romania, to attend the communist-sponsored World Festival of Youth and Students for Peace and Friendship before taking an extensive tour of countries behind the Iron Curtain as guests of Czechoslovakia, Poland and Russia.

On 15 April that same year, the all-white South African general election consolidated the position of the National Party around the nationalist pro-gramme of apartheid under Prime Minister Daniel Malan, who had just won an absolute majority of 156 seats in the House of Assembly. The United Party, under JGN Strauss, lost several seats, and suffered several splits after the election. Another seat was taken by a communist named Sam Kahn, who gained the seat from an Independent. The Communist Party of South Africa, banned by the National Party government in 1950, had relaunched itself underground as the South African Communist Party (SACP).

Meanwhile, mounting crises kept the African National Congress (ANC) reeling from internal faction fights. One of the first signs came in May 1954, with a notification by the ANC National Executive Committee that a leading Youth League member named Potlako Leballo was being expelled from the organisation and his Orlando branch committee suspended pending an investigation. He had been arguing for the ANC to break ties with the Communist Party and denounced as "eastern [communist] functionaries" the Youth League leaders who accepted invitations to the communist-sponsored World Youth Festival in Bucharest in 1953.[165] Leballo would soon go on to launch the Pan Africanist Congress along with Robert Sobukwe.

A year later, in the country's industrial heartland of the Transvaal, every possible political reporter was thrown into round-the-clock coverage of the Congress of the People. Hundreds of people gathered in Kliptown, Soweto, to draft the Freedom Charter. All through that year the National Party government had been calling for a whites-only referendum to decide whether the Union of South Africa under the British Crown should become a republic.

Virtually every morning of January 1956 brought a story of the government's plans to press ahead with laws which would constrict every aspect of life for blacks to racially segregated peri-urban dormitories called 'townships' and 'independent homelands'. On Tuesday evening of 2 February, opposition-party liberals had been dreading the coming of the next day. Beneath the veneer of mundanity, change was in the air on the morning of 3 February. Its winds began blowing from the south-east, rustling up dust and leaves on the cobbled boulevard of Parliament; and the sun rose in a sky that was to become spuriously cloudless, bathing the city in a golden glow. But the climate, not to mention the tranquillity, was incongruous to the mood inside Parliament.

*

That afternoon, Hendrik Verwoerd entered the large panelled chamber in Parliament. His inner circle was hardening around a group of Nationalists that had risen to prominence on a battery of draconian laws that would form the legal framework for grand apartheid, with Verwoerd at the centre. He had just won a fight at the National Party Congress against liberal

---

165 Gerhart, G, *Black Power in South Africa: The Evolution of an Ideology* (University of California Press, 1979), p. 140.

establishment forces of Afrikaner business, led by business mogul, Anton Rupert, to put a republican plank in the party's policy platform. To not a few Afrikaners, including extreme right-wingers, Verwoerdian apartheid meant defeating black radicalism through the agency of 'soft power'. And, although he had lost the succession battle in 1953 to JG Strijdom, following the retirement of Prime Minister Daniel Malan, Verwoerd won the war for his party's soul.

Now he was restless. He walked to the lectern, briskly adjusted the microphone, glanced over at his audience, and with an almost imperceptible shrug warmly welcomed his audience in his lilting Afrikaner accent. Before him were rows of green leather seats lined with South Africa's all-white Cabinet – a largely male political SWAT team that would tear apart the country in its drive for a model solution to the continuation of white supremacy.

In opposition quarters, an air of taut expectation hung over the Senate chamber that Verwoerd would say something which could be interpreted as state control of universities. A handful of opposition party members of Parliament (MPs) blanched as they listened.

As Verwoerd sidled up to the climax of his performance, claiming he had a duty to speak frankly, liberal MPs cringed. They had heard rumours that he was up to something like this, but nothing prepared them for *this*. The message Verwoerd was delivering was "stunning and yet utterly predictable" in the choking atmosphere of the National Party victory at the polls in 1953, opposition MP, Helen Suzman, recalled when she spoke to me in 2009.

Verwoerd's speech was an eloquent work of demagogy whose soaring rhetoric reduced the subtleties and complexities of the times to their lowest common denominator: the racial segregation of institutions of higher learning. Barely three years after defeating the United Party of JN Strauss at the polls, South Africa's mainly white English-speaking universities were being asked to prostrate themselves to the government's Christian-nationalist policy. Verwoerd declared pointedly that the Extension of University Education Act was to become an integral part of the Bantustan scheme of retribalising African communities within self-governing homelands.

If the scheme was intended to drive the National Party's carefully manufactured ideological enterprise in the second half of the 20th century, it would also revive an old rivalry between liberals and Afrikaner conservatives over South Africa. It began with a climatic confrontation more than half a century earlier in the Anglo-Boer War, reaching its denouement in a precarious covenant between Afrikaans- and English-speaking whites in 1910 to the exclusion of blacks from economic and political life, and ending in what later formally became known as apartheid in 1948, when the National Party rose to power. "South Africa and Britain," wrote the London *Daily Telegraph*, "now step into an old war."

WHEN CECIL JOHN RHODES BEQUEATHED IN HIS WILL LAND AT THE FOOT OF Table Mountain for the construction of a university, his thoughts might have strayed. He meant to exclude blacks from the benefits of higher learning; it was his wish that the university would provide a 'collegiate environment' for an English and Afrikaner elite to bond against blacks. Here Verwoerd and Rhodes held a profound, shared view.

By the late 1940s, the University of Cape Town's (UCT) position, high on the slopes of Table Mountain, suggested the image of an ivory tower, which, in a sense, it was. It belonged to a different generation from that of Rhodes, a different century even; this institution of blacks and whites. Although the particular grandeur of the campus and liberal ethos which characterised human relations still gave it a British colonial flavour, by 1957 UCT was no longer just a fine Anglo-Saxon university; it was attracting people from many walks of life. As Margaret Ballinger, a Liberal Party MP, recalled in her memoir *From Union to Apartheid: A Trek to Isolation*:

> While racially separate schools were the established practice in the lower educational levels, on the upper levels there had been a marked trend towards a measure of multi-racialism. While the University College of Fort Hare, established in 1916 for non-European students, had come to provide higher education for a small number of black students, increasing numbers of blacks had sought entry into white universities, many of whom had been accepted in the English medium campuses of UCT, Wits and Natal.[166]

And so, in the power struggles of the first four decades since 1910, UCT had become an institution open to all racial groups, albeit of the idiosyncratic sort conditioned by the country's curious circumstances. In reality, senior staff and students remained overwhelmingly white and English; UCT was

---

166 Ballinger, M, *From Union to Apartheid: A Trek to Isolation* (Cape Town: Juta, 1969), pp. 349-350.

still a segregated institution in a segregated society where blacks were prohibited by law from mingling with whites. While the university espoused liberal rights, blacks were still servants in all-white dormitories housed in magnificent antebellum mansions. Within this bizarre landscape came liberal gentlemen and scions of the English landed elite. There were new kinds of people – advocates of change, serious intellectuals, radicals, and even some communists and blacks.

But there was another, deeper reason – often unspoken but clearly evident – why Verwoerd was driven by urgency. Liberal campuses had been a central, defining source of ideological opposition to the National Party. The government had initially turned its attention to radical black leadership in the ANC and SACP that liberal campuses had been producing. A survey of middle-class Africans in the late 1950s by the South African Institute of Race Relations found a majority of black students prepared to accept violence as a method of political action; and almost half believed that the use of force was inevitable.

Verwoerd believed that the government could not put university apartheid on hold for the years it would take to sweep back the tide of black radicalism emerging from these institutions. More than black opposition, he was haunted by the spectre of liberalism and its potential consequences for his vision of separate ethnic homelands. He was acutely aware of how a liberal education could lead to radical ideas and felt that the Public Safety Act and Criminal Law Amendment Act were not enough to break the support of many white liberals for the ANC-led Defiance Campaign of 1952 and the loyalty they felt to the Liberal Party.[167] With its constant threat of 'black Englishmen', which during the late 1950s Cold War had already begun to fissure into two competing intellectual and ideological versions of apartheid, black radicalisation confirmed for Verwoerd the ultimate danger of open universities.

The launch of the Liberal Party in 1953 by Alan Paton, initially for white liberals of the old Cape multiracial tradition, albeit on a programme of qualified franchise for blacks, was a more immediate threat to the emerging doctrine and institutional architecture of Bantustans. "I think that Verwoerd came to see that Anglicised blacks in the Cold War era was unthinkable," said Allister Sparks, contemplating his days as a journalist in

---

167 Driver, CJ, *Patrick Duncan: South African and Pan-African* (Cape Town: David Philip, 1980), p. 120.

the Verwoerd years.[168] "He felt the policy of liberalism was political suicide. He felt that time was not on the side of Afrikaner nationalism if universities were allowed to become brain trusts of subversion."[169] Above all, Verwoerd knew that Bantustans could not function without destroying the mindset of millions of black South Africans who would know no other political or economic life other than what they would experience in the homelands.

Here was the "forcing ground of Western ideas"[170] and the greatest encouragement to Africans to abandon their people and culture in favour of the green pastures of white society.[171] It was here, in the liberal ethos of detribalisation, that Verwoerd was ready to grasp the nettle.[172]

*

Paradoxically, the vision Rhodes had for UCT produced results that liberals wanted to avoid. They were not happy with the direction the ANC-led Congress Alliance seemed to be taking since the Defiance Campaign. Even at the ANC Conference at Queenstown in December 1953, Patrick Duncan, a founding member of the Liberal Party and leading proponent of open universities, who was a guest, felt that communist influence was increasing: "The whole atmosphere of the conference," Duncan wrote in a letter to the left-wing University of Witwatersrand historian, Professor Julius Lewin, some time in 1955, "was dominated by the [Communist] Party line. The UK [was] lined up as the [bogeyman]; the USSR, etc., as liberators from colonialism."[173]

Duncan was himself a product of Rhodes's scholarship programme at Balliol, Oxford, and an ideological scion of Rhodes's mentor, John Ruskin; he disliked state control and talk of nationalisation in the ANC's Freedom Charter and considered himself an 'anti-communist'. He approved of America and Britain, his biographer, CJ Driver, wrote of him, "and so [he] was – in one terminology – an 'imperialist' who applauded the end of colonialism".[174]

---

168 Interview with the author, Johannesburg, May 2011.
169 Interview with the author, Johannesburg, June 2012.
170 See Ballinger (n 166 above), p. 350.
171 See Alexander, N, *One Azania, One Nation: The National Question in South Africa* (London: Zed Press, 1979), p. 108.
172 Ibid.
173 See Driver (n 167 above), p. 122.
174 Ibid., p. 131.

In the same letter, Duncan questioned the rationale for the Congress of the People in 1955 at which organisations allied to the ANC gathered to draft the Freedom Charter. One of the most basic tenets of the Freedom Charter was opening the doors of learning and culture to all. But so, too, were the nationalisation of the mines and socialisation of all land and mineral resources. Concerned about the Freedom Charter's 'socialist leanings', Duncan was convinced that the strategy of the SACP was embedded in the Charter; it was the same as the popular-front strategy of the Communist International in Europe of the 1930s, which communist parties would use for their own political ends. He went on to question the reconstitution of the Communist Party of South Africa in 1953 as a clandestine current in the Congress Movement. Among liberals like Duncan, the longer Afrikaner nationalists survived, the more chance of communism. Radical opposition from liberals and the embrace of a universal franchise were, in their calculations, the only defence against black radicalism. Thus, in March 1955, after an awkward exchange of letters between himself and ANC President, Chief Albert Luthuli, Duncan told Alan Paton that student opposition to Bantu education had to become a mobilising platform for liberal campuses and the Liberal Party programme. Both Duncan and Paton believed that university apartheid was akin to revolution; it would strengthen the Afrikaner right and black left, and doom any chance of liberal reform.

*

The following year, in 1956, both the UCT and Wits (University of the Witwatersrand) student representative councils (SRCs) formed academic-freedom committees to mobilise all university constituencies against the government's announcement that year that it was going to proceed with the enforcement of university apartheid. In its newsletter of that year, the Wits SRC noted, "In this endeavour, the SRC was greatly assisted by the Senate after a famous debate in 1954 had endorsed the maintenance of open admission to Wits."[175]

Liberal opposition to encroachments on academic freedom continued through the 1950s, reaching a high mark in a 1957 protest march of some 2 000 white students, academics and university management at Wits. At

---

175 Quoted in Moss, G, *The New Radicals: A Generational Memoir of the 1970s* (Johannesburg: Jacana Media, 2014), p. 61.

UCT, students organised similar demonstrations. Early one morning, a small group of students staged a protest outside the campus's Jameson Hall. The next morning they returned with a few hundred supporters. Thus began the first campus protests that would spark a national movement.

But if the protests were a provocation, they were also a miscalculation. "It didn't help that whites often used 'liberal' to mean 'non-racial'," Martin Legassick told me; and since white communists too were non-racialists, 'communist' and 'liberal' became synonymous.[176] Legassick had been a student activist in the liberal National Union of South African Students (NUSAS) during the 1950s and a strong advocate of direct student action by NUSAS instead of symbolic protests. Sensing rising student antipathy to rigid authority and the vacuum left by the 1950s clampdown on both black liberation and liberal political organisations, white radicals came to see NUSAS as the leading cause championed by students on campuses.

In those terms, student protests against university apartheid immediately drew the attention of the government. Not only had the Liberal Party and NUSAS misjudged the government, which had become more recalcitrant; in their fear of communism, liberals had given the far right of the National Party a rationale for total repression and the left justification for revolt.

THE SECOND BLOW SINCE THE BANTU EDUCATION ACT CAME IN 1958, WHEN Verwoerd characteristically turned his election campaign into an intense crusade against liberal institutions of higher learning. In the months before the enactment of higher education legislation, he alone had begun to craft the principles and rationale for a new Bill that would champion more radical measures toward university apartheid. Cerebral with a proclivity for logical argumentation, Verwoerd ruled by policy rather than emotion; he liked the certitude and simple directness of structure and was infected with an enthusiasm for legislative interventions that would haul the National Party government closer to his vision of apartheid. He alone understood the full scale and complexity of the mission he was embarking on; he had set out to accomplish nothing less than wreck the entire complex of planning, thinking and behaviour inherited from the United Party on liberal campuses. Until this point, Verwoerd felt that the thrust and parry of debate on Bantu

---

176 Interview with the author, Cape Town, 6 December 2011.

education in Parliament was too abstract. He was convinced that the whole fate of apartheid as a political and economic system lay in whether universities would be more effective in conditioning the thinking and behaviour not only of the black population, but also of whites generally.

During early 1958, Verwoerd began drawing up the details of a proposal for a new Bill with the help of Eiselen. In Ballinger's account, "the proposal was to stamp on the field of higher education the pattern of apartheid which the Bantu Education Act had applied in the fields of primary and secondary education."[177] Here, she recalled, "the situation to be met was somewhat different in character from that in schools. The Minister of Education, Arts and Science, with whom the responsibility for higher education lay, was persuaded to introduce a Bill which set out to provide a spate of university colleges for Africans, Coloureds and Indians." With Verwoerd's astute guidance, the Minister allowed the Bill to go to a Select Committee after a second reading, thus establishing the principle of separate institutions.[178]

Since the session was nearing its conclusion, the Committee was turned into a socio-economic commission to enable it to carry on with what was to prove an extensive programme of evidence-taking during the recess. No sooner was the taking of evidence completed, Ballinger recalled, "than the obviously departmentally prepared report began to emerge not from the Department of Education, but from the Department of Bantu Administration and Development, headed by Verwoerd".[179] "It significantly contained Dr Verwoerd's ideas logically developed to include the amazing proposition that each new institution should be governed not by a (University) Senate composed of senior teaching staff and a Council representing all the parties interested in promoting the institution according to the familiar and established pattern of university institutions, but by a Senate and an Advisory Senate and a Council and an Advisory Council."[180] The line of differentiation was race. "The actual membership of each body," Ballinger recalled, "was to be in the control of the Minister himself as indeed was to be the case in respect of all the organisations and activities of the proposed new institutions."[181]

However, this huge accomplishment was enormously divisive. Ballinger

---

177 Ballinger (n 166 above), p. 349.
178 Ibid., pp. 349-350.
179 Ibid., p. 351.
180 Ibid.
181 Ibid.

remembered the Committee being divided from the beginning: "… the government on one side, the opposition parties on the other".[182] Opponents who felt the Bill would tear down so many entrenched interests were guarded and wary of its impact.

*

For a time, a group of Afrikaner academics at the University of Stellenbosch – descendants of the Cape Afrikaner liberal elite – while known generally to be supporters of the government, were as determined as backers of open universities in the socio-economic commission that there should be no legislative interference with the right of universities generally to decide whom they would admit. When it became clear, according to Ballinger, that, despite the weight of evidence against segregation, the majority report was to maintain, and in fact extend, the pattern of the original Bill, at least one report was inevitable.

The rising popularity of Verwoerd in 1958 placed pressure on the Commission and sparked anxiety among some Afrikaner academics, who, until then, had sided with the liberal opposition. Verwoerd, we remember, viewed the Stellenbosch academics with deep suspicion. The liberal elite, he felt, was wedded to big business and, therefore, an internal threat to Afrikanerdom and a leading cause of the poor-white problem which had begun to develop in the 1950s. Their anxiety found expression at a meeting of the Broederbond front, the South African Bureau for Racial Affairs (SABRA), in Durban in December 1958. SABRA was founded in 1948 by a group which included such prominent Broederbonders as Dr JE Donges, Dr W Eiselen, Dr MC de Wet Nel, and Dr Nico Diederichs. Between them and the Federasie van Afrikaanse Kultuurvereniginge (FAK), SABRA campaigned categorically to win the minds of Afrikaner youth over to nationalist ideology. At the December meeting, universities and their appropriate line of development were the major subject of discussion. Not surprisingly, the result was the return of Verwoerd's plan, this time, under the grand new title of the Extension of University Education Bill, for the development of ethnic colleges, with the contingent liquidation of Fort Hare and "the substitution for it of a college for the Xhosa people".[183]

The dominant academic voice in SABRA was that whatever liberal

---

182 Ibid.
183 Ibid., p. 350.

academics might think and feel about their own profession, it was for the government to decide what should be done. The push for control of the education of black people at all levels was for Verwoerd only the formal aspect of a process of cultural insulation which the objective of apartheid and separate development demanded. Verwoerd's character, his comfort with the plain Afrikaner idiom of "good neighbourliness", former apartheid Minister of Foreign Affairs, Pik Botha, recalled when speaking to me, gave his confrontational world view a benign face that suggested something higher than grim combat. Educational indoctrination, Verwoerd believed, was a more efficient force for sweeping back the permanence of blacks in white areas and keeping races apart.

Promising tougher measures against the business elite, Verwoerd gradually gained popularity with the Afrikaner electorate through 1958 and continued to expand his political support, eventually winning an overwhelming constituency victory after the death of Prime Minister JG Strijdom in September that year. He now contemplated his opponents: along with the English-speaking liberal opposition, the Cape Afrikaner intelligentsia and a group of powerful financiers were the plutocrats who had emerged from the Afrikaner Bond of Hofmeyr during the 1930s and forties. Most notable among them was Anton Rupert. He was a man who with mixed perplexity had swung all the way round from support for apartheid to liberal labour and education policies.

The swashbuckling entrepreneur had cut his teeth in the tobacco business under Broederbond auspices and built a mighty empire called Rembrandt Tobacco. Older Broederbond members remembered how Voorbrand Tobacco Corporation – Rembrandt's predecessor – distributed its products at Broederbond meetings. "We were asked to smoke and cough for the Volk and Vaderland," one of them once told journalist Ivor Wilkins with a chuckle.[184] In 1958, Rembrandt was spread all over the world. By the time of Verwoerd's presidency, Rupert wanted to resign from the Broederbond. He thought the Bond's narrow Afrikaans image and single-minded focus on apartheid education would dent his labour requirements and damage his business image internationally.

There thus emerged a divergence between Afrikaner nationalism and liberalism that solidified in 1958, the first year of Verwoerd's presidency, when he addressed the National Party Congress, arguing that the government shouldn't simply oppose liberalism; it should also underscore the National

---

184 Quoted in Wilkins & Strydom (n 90 above), p. 425.

Party's creed by promoting Afrikaner economic empowerment.[185] It was, to all intents, a backhanded swipe at English mining magnates who had gone on to amass vertiginous wealth, despite the National Party's 1948 victory over the United Party. The speech was deliberately calculated to challenge the idea that had been gaining ground in moderate English and Afrikaner business circles of promoting an all-white liberal coalition of pro-capitalist forces against Verwoerd.

And that was the real rub. In a sense, what Verwoerd had said accorded with the old Cape franchise, done away with in 1936, with one fundamental difference: he wanted separate voters rolls for blacks in separate homelands where, as he put it, blacks could realise their ambitions "without grazing in the green pastures of white civilisation".[186]

*

In *Bantu Education: Policy for the Immediate Future*, Verwoerd's visionary text for Bantustans in 1954, he had described the key role universities would play in the new racial order. Echoing his plans for schools, tertiary institutions were to become the guiding nucleus of apartheid's success, with their roots "entirely in the native areas and the native environment and native community".[187] He proposed that "advanced education in black reserves would be given ... complete [cultural] expression, and there it will perform its real service".

> The Bantu must be guided to serve his own community in all respects.
> For this reason it is of no avail for him to receive a training which has as
> its aim absorption in the European community. Until now he has been
> subjected to a school system which drew him from his own community
> and misled him by showing him the green pastures of European society in
> which he was not allowed to graze. This attitude is not only uneconomic
> ... it is abundantly clear that unplanned education creates many prob-
> lems, disrupting the community life of the Bantu and endangering the
> community life of the Europeans.[188]

---

185 See Clark, NL & Worger, WH, *South Africa: The Rise and Fall of Apartheid* (London & New York: Routledge, 2013), p. 55.
186 See Alexander (n 171 above), p. 108.
187 See Clark & Worger (n 185 above), p. 55.
188 Ibid., p. 173.

University apartheid was, in the sense conveyed by Verwoerd, a psychological and social weapon of control. As a political gambit, one of Verwoerd's first orders of business as Prime Minister in 1959 was the extension of state measures to bring universities under his direction. State control of education would be used to prop up the homeland bureaucracies as well as the hegemonic functions of Afrikaner economic empowerment more specifically geared to fulfilling the labour needs of capital in general, both in respect of skills and attitudes and values appropriate to apartheid social relations.

Part of those relations would come to depend on the existence of a black elite in the homelands that would both support the Bantustan structures politically and legitimise them economically.

AS VERWOERD CONCLUDED HIS SPEECH THAT AFTERNOON, IN 1959, THE liberal press, which had been hoping for a mild politeness, was disturbed. Few in the liberal establishment felt reassured. There was talk of anarchy, black majority rule and communist dictatorship. Anything seemed possible.

What no one could know that afternoon was that one theatre of Verwoerd's apartheid strategy would in fact involve state repression of a different kind on South African soil. Universities would become the battleground in a silent war fought not by soldiers, not by violence as a first line of attack, but by ideas. It would be fought across a vast swath (as we shall see later in this book), beginning in the Central Intelligence Agency (CIA) headquarters at Langley, Virginia, before engulfing black protest movements in South Africa, trade unions, dust-bowl mines, and the Afrikaner political establishment. In this new era, black students would take the lead. All that was in the future, however. At the moment, the National Party was primarily concerned with banishing the liberal image of higher education and replacing it with a vigorous new conservative muscularity.

By the close of the 1950s, the entire edifice of apartheid education ranged from cultural and religious indoctrination to racial and ethnic stereotypes. Between the National Party, the FAK, SABRA and the education department, the government energetically campaigned to win the minds of the youth to the concepts of nationalist philosophy among whites and a life of inferiority among blacks.

Here was the crux of apartheid education policy. It had its origins in a policy statement by the Broederbond in 1935. "In our efforts to find a morally defensible Christian way of co-existence between white and non-white in our country," the statement read, "and on our borders, the Broederbond came in direct contact with two biggest and most dangerous present-day forces of the dark bedevilling relations, namely communism and liberalism."[189]

But communism was only really a pretext; the ideological justification for a system of race indoctrination and domination. The primary purpose of the Extension of University Education Act, as Ivor Wilkins and Hans Strydom have noted,[190] was acceptance of the Bantustan system through social engineering rather than violent repression. In the wake of the 1976 youth uprising, a document drafted by the Broederbond, entitled 'The strategy aimed at the private sector and the general population of the white country', was a powerful testimony of the threads running through the thinking on education policy:

> In the strategic planning of South Africa, it is accepted that in the defence of the country only 20 percent can be achieved by military preparedness; the other 80 percent depends on spiritual and psychological preparedness ... . A popular movement fed and supported by an organisation with the means and manpower to give effective leadership throughout the country, on the one hand, to establish a positive climate for the execution of the masterplan, and on the other hand, to play a direct part in combating radical ideas, must be created immediately. Just as radicalism has abandoned the use of political methods to achieve its goals, so will a counter-action have to parallel politics so as to be less dependent on politics. In practice, politics will have to rely on and exploit the climate that the counter-action establishes to enable it to achieve its objectives.[191]

Just the fact that there was acknowledgement that "an unwilling and unmotivated public opinion that is constantly urged to make concessions and change"[192] would eventually become such a hindrance to the government that it would not achieve its objectives, reflected the primary role of education. "Such an effective counter-action," the document went on, "will of necessity have to be defensive, disseminating knowledge about the objectives and methods of radicalism in South Africa and about its specific characteristics.

---

189 Quoted in Wilkins & Strydom (n 90 above), pp. 198-199.
190 Ibid., pp. 261-262.
191 Ibid., p. 281.
192 Ibid.

Radical action will have to be stigmatised in the same way that actions to put it in jeopardy are currently stigmatised."[193]

This is precisely what Verwoerd had in mind when he announced that a central body of education would be established for every homeland and ethnic group "to help form public opinions in favour of the policy".[194] Although Verwoerd's economic ideas were modern and capitalist, one of the most basic tenets of the new Act was the inculcation of ethnic nationalisms in black groups with a Christian-national outlook.

Thus was the Broederbond blueprint for blacks – buttressed by the Group Areas Act of 1950; the Resettlement of Natives Act of 1954, which empowered the government to remove 100 000 blacks from squatter settlements in western Johannesburg to Meadowlands; the Population Registration Act of 1950, enabling government to draw up race registers; the Reservation of Separate Amenities Act of 1953, keeping the races apart in public spaces; and the Bantu Self-Government Act of 1959 – nestled in a system of segregated education on which apartheid largely depended for psychological control.

*

By the end of 1959, the separation-of-universities process had begun in earnest. The passing of the Extension of University Education Act effectively ended the enrolment of 'non-whites' at the universities of Witwatersrand, Cape Town and Natal, and began to establish separate tertiary institutions for blacks in the homelands.

Here, most clearly, the rights of blacks were to be restricted to lower forms of learning. Those who proceeded to tertiary institutions were to be trained in institutions in which the state could control both administrative structures and curriculums in preparation for Bantustan bureaucrats with inferior tertiary qualifications, but just enough to enable these areas to function administratively and economically.

Within 'bush colleges', Broederbond rectors were appointed until they were gradually replaced by blacks in accordance with the concept of 'evolving autonomy' for the homelands.

In 1959, the Broederbond appointed an education task team under the

---

193 Ibid.
194 Ibid., p. 261.

chairmanship of Professor HJJ Bingle, Rector of Potchefstroom University (then the Potchefstroom University for Christian Higher Education [PU for CHE] and now the North-West University).

During the following two years, members of the Broederbond held two major conferences to thrash out the details of its policy. Bingle was a techno-crat, a stickler for detail. For months he had insisted on trying to accomplish realistic steps rather than risk extreme leaps that would not stand a chance. Some Broederbond members had suggested scrapping the idea of black higher education altogether, but Bingle knocked down the idea as too radi-cal; instead he suggested a new structure. By 1963, the task team's report was ready and some members were delegated to present their national edu-cation policy blueprint to Broederbond members in Cabinet. The blueprint of the organisation's education policy, entitled 'Urgent tasks', directed the organisation to "help ensure that the Department of Education, Arts and Science be divided so that education could exist as an independent depart-ment. Under this department should fall the universities, including technical training and teacher training."[195] While this meant that teacher training would be removed from provincial jurisdiction, provincial governments would still be involved via the National Advisory Board and the professional Education Council.

So sweeping was the policy that, by the early 1960s, the guardians of Christian nationalism were instituted within and throughout the country's educational structure. Two universities in South Africa owed their exist-ence largely to the Broederbond's efforts. In Johannesburg, a need was felt to counter the liberal traditions of the English-medium University of the Witwatersrand, where, in the 1960s, NUSAS was at the height of its aca-demic-freedom campaign. In the early 1960s, the Executive Council of the Broederbond started working in earnest on the creation of an Afrikaner university in the city. Thus one finds in the minutes of a Broederbond Executive Council meeting held at the Volkskas building in Johannesburg on 1 December 1965, representations by the chairman, Dr Piet Meyer, for "the establishment of an Afrikaans university on the Rand".[196] The close involvement of the Broederbond in the establishment of the Rand Afrikaans University (later to become the University of Johannesburg), situated in the Broederbond stronghold of Auckland Park, Johannesburg, was reflected in

---

195 Ibid., p. 258.
196 Ibid., p. 262.

the university's hierarchy.

Meanwhile Rhodes University in Grahamstown, a traditionally English-speaking campus, had decided to establish a satellite campus in Port Elizabeth. To counter the spread of English-speaking influence, the Broederbond initiated moves to establish a university it could control in the seaport. As a result, the University of Port Elizabeth came into being under the rectorship of a senior Broederbonder named Professor EJ Marais. Having established the university as a bilingual campus, the Broederbond made strenuous efforts to ensure that the bias of the campus was towards Afrikaans. It launched a campaign to "fill the university as far as possible with Afrikaners". An instruction was sent to members in a monthly circular on 2 June 1964:[197] "With the establishment of a university in Port Elizabeth in mind it is cordially requested that in particular friends (members) in the area will use their influence to ensure that as many Afrikaner students as possible register there. Friends across the whole country can naturally assist in this matter."[198]

Similarly, the universities of the Western Cape and Durban-Westville incorporated coloured and Indian students into ethnically separate institutions in the context of an elaborate restructuring of the political system.

The Act exemplified the ambivalence in the government, involving some expansion of participation in education to black universities but on an ethically separate basis and in a form so complex and bizarre that it was difficult to gauge its effect and workability.

A final function of the Act was hegemony. The original Christian-national education policy, drafted by the Broederbond in 1948, dealt with African education:

> We believe that the role of white South Africa with respect to the native is to Christianise him and help him on culturally, and this vocation and duty had found its immediate application and task in the principles of trusteeship, distinguishing the native status from that of the white, and in segregation ... that instruction and education for the natives must lead to the development of the native community on Christian-National lines, which is self-supporting and provides for itself in every respect.[199]

---

197 Broederbond letter number 4/64/65, in Wilkins & Strydom (n 90 above), p. 262.
198 Ibid.
199 Ibid., pp. 262-263.

Stressing cultural differences between white and black, the Bantu education system would thus prepare blacks to accept differences as part of the unchallenged order. The Eiselen Commission stated:

> The Bantu child comes to school with a basic physical and psychological endowment which differs from that of the European child ... . But educational practice should recognise that it has to deal with [the] Bantu child, i.e., a child trained and conditioned in Bantu culture endowed with a knowledge of a Bantu language and imbued with values, interests and behaviour patterns at the knee of a Bantu mother. These facts must dictate to a very large extent the content and methods of his early education.[200]

The policy was refined in the Education Advisory Council Act of 1960 and the National Education Policy Act of 1967, in which the Broederbond's perverse hand played a leading role.

*

In the chaotic dawn of the 1960s clampdown on black liberation organisations and white liberal opposition, all of this confirmed for Verwoerd that history was on his side. He had hoped for a dreamy romanticism, where repression would be replaced by softer methods of educational indoctrination and segregated homelands. As the homelands became independent, Africans belonging to the relevant ethnic groups became foreigners in South Africa. It was as simple as that: classic 'Volk and Vaderland [Fatherland]' theory.

But the reality would prove not so elegant. Bingle and his hardy band of technocrats left a dangerous vacuum: "This assimilationist view," the Columbia-trained Afrikaner educationist, Ernest Malherbe, observed in his dense assessment of the policy soon after the Soweto uprising by the youth in 1976, "ignored the fact that South Africa was a multilingual country and that its children, no matter what their home language, might be destined to associate with one another when they became adults in every kind of political, social and economic activity."[201] As this view gained ground, the state

---

200 Quoted in Kallaway (n ‡ above), p. 175.
201 Frankel, P et al. (eds), *State Resistance and Change in South Africa* (Johannesburg: Southern Book Publishers, 1988).

school, instead of being regarded as virtually a replica of the South African community in miniature, became the preservation of the identity of the Afrikaner majority and thus served to consolidate its political power. This exclusiveness of the school (and university) in the course of time served to generate stereotyped attitudes not only in regard to English–Afrikaans relationships but also on ideological issues involving black–white relationships.

In 1977, Malherbe assessed the effect of the system in these terms:

> The Broederbond knew that, by separation, the future of Nationalist policies would be assured. The fact that young people during the most impressionable years of their lives were by deliberate segregation deprived of the normal opportunities of rubbing shoulders with persons, building different views from their own, tended to make them less adaptable in meeting new challenges due to changing circumstances. The same would also to a large extent apply to the teachers in these separate institutions.
>
> It is therefore no surprise that a national survey conducted in 1974 by professor Lawrence Schlemmer, Director of the Institute of Social Research at the University of Natal, revealed that the political opinions of Afrikaners under 25 years of age "offered scant encouragement to those who hoped for more enlightened and forward-looking policies. Their apathetic attitude showed no sense of urgency to come to terms with our basic racial conflict and it differs little from that of their elders".[202]

All through the 1960s it was apartheid's future, rather than liberalism's, that hung in the balance. The year 1948 brought a change in the ruling bloc, which in 1949 set about creating a social formation more consonant with its needs. Apartheid was the mask and Bantu education was the most efficient weapon for reproducing labour in the form the ruling party desired.

The maintenance of the system would involve the largest enterprise aimed at reinforcing the racial structure of the economy. It was a daring enterprise, but there was just one problem that would show itself later: from institutions of control, black universities and schools would become hotbeds of rebellion. To not a few English-speaking white South Africans, including some Afrikaner businessmen, apartheid would no longer mean minding your own business – English business at any rate. It would soon mean potentially dangerous impulses by a new militant generation of black students to

---

202 Wilkins & Strydom (n 90 above), pp. 264-265.

revolution. Before long, changed circumstances would add Afrikaner academic liberals, moderate intellectuals, and civil servants who increasingly came to see the educational apparatus as part of the ideological repertoire of liberalism's battle for hearts and minds in the 'Cultural Cold War'.

PART III

Nusas and the Liberal Agenda

1959–1968

CHAPTER 9

The United States in South Africa

THE 'CULTURAL COLD WAR'

IT WAS LATE 1959 AND THE SIX-FOOT TALL SLENDER FIGURE WALKED CASUALLY up the stairs, as if he'd done this before. The awaiting Pan American aircraft was flying to West Africa beneath the vast canopy of an African sky toward its final destination, New York. For nearly two months, Hans Beukes had been secretly holed up, just across the South African border in the British Protectorate of Bechuanaland, in the home of Seretse Khama and his British wife. On that evening, Beukes was finally escaping his native land on an American travel visa for a foreign country. "A sense of almost physical relief" from the mental straightjacket of apartheid is how Beukes later described the moment in testimony to the United Nations General Assembly.[203]

The scene had more of the hallmarks of a quixotic Hollywood thriller, as well it should have, than a single event. Unclear as to just who Beukes was, the American authorities didn't bother. Yet, if Washington had not heard the name Hans Beukes before, there were many in South Africa – and for that matter a handful of men at Langley, Virginia, headquarters of the Central Intelligence Agency (CIA) – who had. 'Hans' was by then something of a household name in South Africa – an accidental hero within cloistered, white, liberal student circles and across middle-class suburban dinner tables – whose plight had alternately evoked revulsion and sympathy.

Paradoxically, politics beguiled the young man. As a descendent of the Herero community and son of conservative coloured parents in Rehoboth, his driving ambition was a professional career, and maybe a life abroad.

South West Africa was, in those days, carved into two halves. The southern half was a vast and fortified zone, comprised of arable farmland and inhabited by whites who generally made a comfortable living as farmers.

---

203 See Lowenstein, A, *Brutal Mandate: A Journey to South-West Africa* (Macmillan, 1962).

The South African authorities referred to it by a name that seemed to have come straight out of Aleksandr Solzhenitsyn's *The First Circle*. They called it the 'Police Zone'.[204] Just across the northern boundary was another country – a hot, desolate, and windswept dust bowl of non-citizens inhabited by mainly Herero, Nama and Ovambo communities. The fate of the two halves remained enmeshed with cruel disappointment, humiliation, and ruin. All this was on the northern side.

Every morning, before the sun grew dangerously hot, large crowds of men and women gathered at the entrance of the quasi-official South West Africa Native Labour Association. While some were children who had no education at all, most were unemployed farm labourers. Only a few lucky enough to be signed up for menial jobs could enter the Police Zone. Because of the heavy security presence, they called the northern boundary, more prosaically, the 'Red Line'. In this country hardly anyone noticed.

Hans Beukes was among a handful of 'non-citizens' to cross the Red Line into South Africa, where he enrolled as an undergraduate student at a coloured teachers training college in Cape Town, with funds raised by the Rehoboth Community Council. But his early resolve to stay out of politics was suddenly shattered when he gained notoriety with the South African government as a sort of radical malcontent.

Earlier that year, 1959, government authorities ransacked his luggage and seized his passport at the South African port city of Port Elizabeth, where he was about to board a passenger ship for a long journey to Oslo, Norway, on a student scholarship donated to the National Union of South African Students (NUSAS) by the Norwegian Union of Students. "Commie propaganda," spat out a security agent, waving American Democratic Party Congressman Adlai Stevenson's book, *Call to Greatness,* at a colleague.[205] This account, relayed to me by 'Jan',[206] a South African intelligence operative stationed in South West Africa around that time, was confirmed by newspaper reports of the incident. Adlai Stevenson was, of course, considerably more 'liberal' and pro-capitalist than his Afrikaner detractors had made him out to be.

No matter. What Beukes probably did not know when he tried to leave South Africa was that he had challenged – with bold swiftness and dismaying

---

204 Swanepoel, PC, *Really Inside BOSS: A Tale about South Africa's Late Intelligence Service (And Something about the CIA)* (Self-published, 2007), pp. 28-29.
205 See Lowenstein (n 203 above), p. 46.
206 Not his real name.

arrogance in the view of the South African authorities – that which lay at the core of the apartheid stratagem of keeping its black citizens pliant and uneducated. They had reason to be worried. The impact of the Beukes affair among Western liberals and liberal activists was considerable. Until 1959, apartheid lay hidden in the shadows of the Cold War. While the administration of US President Dwight D Eisenhower on occasion publicly condemned apartheid, Western nations were generally happy to maintain quiet diplomatic and economic ties with the National Party government.

In the wake of the Port Elizabeth incident, the media in South Africa and abroad was fawning over the story. Articles, editorials and letters filled inches and inches of newspaper columns. Because of the Beukes affair, conservative white South African students who had been critical of the more liberal NUSAS were now squarely behind the organisation, having been swayed by inflammatory charges made against it by the government. Student protests were organised at the University of Cape Town (UCT), Parliament was picketed and a 'Hans Beukes Fund' was set up.[207] So flagrant was the ensuing furore, Richard Cummings, a former CIA operative turned author told me, that almost overnight Beukes had become an international sensation and cause célèbre for South African liberals.[208]

Jan recalled in speaking to me that the South African intelligence community, by then a ramshackle "bunch of amateurs", was unaware of what the Beukes incident truly represented. "At that time," he said, "they saw spies in every corner, but few of us saw the deeper agenda behind the Beukes affair. Intelligence gathering and analysis, you have to understand, was still developing into what it would become in later years."[209]

As it turned out, Washington's officialdom was also none the wiser. Either by sheer coincidence or cunning design, a secret battle to influence the student movement in South Africa had begun.

How Hans Beukes came into NUSAS's orbit follows a sinuous path leading to a group of 'international liberal interventionists' – a ubiquitous cabal of American anti-communists commonly known by the moniker 'Cold Warriors'.

The story is convoluted; but let's start half a world away.

*

---

207 Cummings, R, *The Pied Piper: Allard K. Lowenstein and the Liberal Dream* (New York: Inprint. com, 1985), p. 85.
208 Ibid., p. 85.
209 Interview with the author, Johannesburg, August 2012.

On 17 February 1958, a young University of North Carolina graduate named Allard Lowenstein wrote a letter to US Senator Hubert Humphrey, accompanied by a flattering editorial about Humphrey in the *Durham Morning Herald*. The story related by Lowenstein's biographer, Richard Cummings, was that Lowenstein hoped the Senator might find the article flattering and suggested he (Lowenstein) might be of some use to the Senator.[210]

On 27 February, Humphrey wrote back to Lowenstein thanking him for his letter and for his "helpfulness" during his (Humphrey's) visit to Chapel Hill. A follow-up letter from Lowenstein on 12 March enclosed an analysis of US efforts in the psychological realm of African countries.[211]

Lowenstein saw in Humphrey a way out of the rut in which he (Lowenstein) found himself – a "restless ruin", but "determined and ambitious" was how Cummings described Lowenstein. Born during the 1929 Great Depression into a wealthy Jewish immigrant household in the upmarket community of Harrison, New York, Lowenstein had all the appurtenances of the New York elite – the very best of a private-school education and liberal upbringing. His father, Gabriel, a cerebral Lithuanian immigrant who gave up a career in medicine for the restaurant business in New York, may have had strong roots in Eastern Europe, but it was precisely Allard Lowenstein's generational disconnect, wrote Cummings, that strengthened his elective affinity for everything American.[212] His sister, Dorothy Di Cintio, called it "the old syndrome of the [Jewish] immigrant".[213] An avid reader of history from boyhood, Lowenstein was acutely aware of how the unsuggestive surface of collective grievance in Eastern Europe and Germany could quickly morph into the menacing spectre of Stalinism, Nazism and racism.[214] Those who knew the young Lowenstein have recalled, in speaking to Cummings, that he already enjoyed in his late teens the reputation of a virulent "anti-communist".[215] By the time he went to the University of North Carolina at Chapel Hill, Lowenstein was, in his close friend Sandy Friedman's words, "the stereotype of a liberal" intellectual.[216] Lowenstein was certain, Friedman told Cummings, that "America was in peril, and that if it was to be spared

210 See Cummings (n 207 above), pp. 67-68.
211 Ibid., p. 68.
212 Ibid., pp. 9-10.
213 Ibid., p. 15.
214 Ibid., p. 10.
215 Ibid., p. 120.
216 Ibid., p. 15.

from radical impulses in the Third World it would not be from the right or the left but from the centre".[217] "His own warnings," wrote Cummings, "were expressed in *Brutal Mandate* [Lowenstein's book] of the potential for a cycle of violence ... until all European liberals have fled Africa." If that were allowed to happen, Lowenstein observed, it would lead to the rise of "communists, black racists, gangsters, religious fanatics, political opportunists, and countless individuals angling for power".[218]

A graduate of the prestigious Yale University, Lowenstein's whole appearance was fashioned "as a kind of caricature", as Cummings described him; "the tardiness of dress, a [wash and wear] slacks kind of guy, stocky and compact with a bull neck and torso which made his head seem a little too small for his body, a crop of wiry black hair, and harassed look behind coke bottle glasses".[219] More than his "cartoon physicality" was the infectious urgency of his presence, a voluble, confident personality, a former acquaintance, Hendrik Hertzberg, told Cummings, "from the intensity and, always, the secrecy".[220]

Lowenstein first stumbled into national consciousness in a blaze of applause at a National Student Association (NSA) annual convention in 1948 as a nominee for the vice-presidency. There, his explosive delivery of movement and speech from the floor on racism in America had delegates shooting to their feet, spellbound, cheering lustily.[221]

His persuasive performance also caught the eye of an influential assemblage of American liberalism – among them the widow of Franklin Delano Roosevelt, Eleanor Roosevelt, Averell Harriman, and labour lawyer, Joseph Rauh – opposed to both Marxism on the extreme left and anti-New Deal-style conservatism on the right. This 'intellectual vanguard' of the New York non-communist left, faithful to the legacy of Franklin Roosevelt, had a name. They called themselves the Americans for Democratic Action (ADA). Launched in January 1947, in New York, the ADA and Lowenstein were a natural fit: he was young and ambitious, brilliant, pugnacious, a fearsome polemicist known for his implacable performances of logical argumentation.

The group had come to realise soon after Roosevelt's death in April 1945, and his replacement by a scowling, mid-Western anti-communist named

---

217 Email correspondence with the author, 10 August 2011.
218 Quoted in Cummings (n 207 above), p. 167.
219 Ibid.
220 Ibid.
221 Ibid., p. 37.

Harry Truman, that confrontation with the Soviet Union in a nuclear age was apocalyptic. With Germany vanquished, the Truman administration had blundered into the Cold War none the wiser as to how to deal with the West's former communist ally in the war against Nazism: the Soviet Union. And so, having embraced the soft edge of George Kennan's front tactic, Lowenstein and his comrades in the ADA became associated with the so-called liberal internationalist wing of the Washington set.

In author Hugh Wilford's outstanding book, *The Mighty Wurlitzer: How the CIA Played America*, we find a detailed account of the genesis of Washington's post-war covert programmes and its clandestine efforts to aid and influence the non-communist left and 'friendly', covert student movements in hostile states using front organisations. Kennan had watched for years from his post at the American mission in Moscow the Soviet leader, Joseph Stalin, and his despotic regime get away with murder. In early 1946, he wrote a policy memorandum famously advocating a strategy of covert operations and 'black' psychological war known as 'containment'. A major plank of the strategy was the use of student movements linked to the United States in Soviet satellite countries in Eastern Europe to help bring down the Soviet Empire; the other was "support of indigenous anti-communist [student movements] in threatened countries of the world ... a covert operation utilising private intermediaries".[222]

A few months later the 'Truman Doctrine', wrote Wilford, "committed the United States to a global policy of saving 'free peoples' from communist aggression".[223]

The formation of the CIA soon after the Second World War was to be the prime strategic instrument. At just that moment, new legislation enacted by the Truman administration cloaked the CIA in secrecy, giving sweeping powers to the agency director to spend funds covertly and conceal information from the public as well as Congress.[224] All that was needed now was for recruits in the newly launched agency to turn this plan for covert warfare into action.

*

222 Quoted in Wilford, H, *The Mighty Wurlitzer: How the CIA Played America* (Harvard University Press, 2008), p. 21.
223 Ibid., p. 22.
224 Ibid., p. 35.

From his anonymous quarters in Washington, Frank Wisner, tall, with piercing eyes, plunged headlong into his new assignment. The following year, in June 1950, Wisner's Office of Policy Coordination (OPC) would embark on one of its boldest gambits: it would fund an anti-communist rally in West Berlin, out of which was to emerge the CIA's principal front operation, the Paris-based Congress for Cultural Freedom (CCF), which would have a hidden hand in the affairs of intellectual, student and labour movements through a vast network of fronts in Eastern Europe. Wilford declares that, over the course of the next decade, the CCF would become one of the West's main defences against the ideological appeal of communism and a dominant institutional force in American intellectual life.[225]

As well as being inveterate anti-communists, men like Wisner thought in liberal terms, advocating a foreign-policy posture always on the prowl for a 'third force' to mediate revolutions from Vietnam to South Africa. Wisner worked for these ends through the formation of "student and cultural associations which make up democratic society", as journalist Andrew Kopkind put it in his 1986 essay, 'Neglect of the left'.[226]

In late 1958, two developments took place that made the need for a reorientation of the CCF's activities to the developing world all the more urgent. The first were serious challenges to racial segregation in the US South. The other development was half a world away: the continuing retreat of European powers from their colonial dominions in Africa and the ensuing contest between the two superpowers for the political allegiance of the 'emerging nations'.

Unfortunately, the same developments that had suddenly made winning the battle for African hearts and minds so crucial were also producing a new generation of more radical black American leaders who shared the CCF's anti-Soviet agenda in Africa, but not its imperialist ambitions. Images of white police officers turning dogs and fire hoses on non-violent black protestors in the US South played particularly badly in post-colonial Africa, a region of growing geopolitical and economic importance where Cold War propagandists had to compete for ideological influence with new currents of black nationalism.

---

225 See Scott, C, *Competing Visions: The CIA, the Congress for Cultural Freedom and the Non-Communist European Left, 1950-1967*, honours thesis submitted to the Western Michigan University, May 2008. Accessed at http://scholarworks.wmich.edu/cgi/viewcontent. cgi?article=1943&context=honors_theses.

226 Kopkind, A, 'Neglect of the left: Allard Lowenstein', in *Grand Street*, Vol. 5, No.3 (Ben Sonnenberg Publishers, Spring 1986), p. 230. Accessed at http://www.jstor.org/stable/5006887 on 9/11/1.

In this atmosphere, wrote Wilford, US government agencies, including the CIA, began casting around for intellectual and student leaders in the United States who might be called on to paint a positive image of the country and help steer newly independent African regions away from communism. Among them was John A Davis, a black Columbia University-educated social scientist and Professor of Government, and self-confessed member of WEB Du Bois' 'Talented Ten' (the great writer's explicitly elitist plan for creating an African-American intelligentsia), who had later rebelled against his mentor's influence.

Archival evidence, discovered by Wilford, indicated that, at a meeting in 1954 at the Connecticut home of former Executive Secretary of the National Association for the Advancement of Colored People (NAACP), Walter White, attended by Eleanor Roosevelt, Davis had been placed in charge of a two-year research project investigating foreign attitudes to civil rights and race problems in the United States. With funds channelled through the American Information Committee on Race and Caste by the CCF, Davis's project embodied a new approach to African affairs, one that began fashioning an agenda for promoting cultural exchange between the United States and African nations and downplaying socialist anti-colonialism in favour of liberal anti-communism.[227]

Beyond elite liberal circles in the United States, however, this tendency lacked any tangible ideological buy-in. By 1949, the rise of Cold War anti-communism had pushed the African-American intelligentsia beyond the pale just as they helped move the NAACP toward the Truman administration.[228] Clearly, the US government would have to look elsewhere for allies.

IT WAS ON A SUN-DECKED SHIP CALLED THE *GEORGE WASHINGTON* IN 1946 that a group of American students travelling on diplomatic passports from a communist-dominated international student conference in Prague plotted the idea of an American student organisation.[229] As with so many other groups whose identity transcended territorial boundaries, the end of the Second World War saw the mobilisation of student organisations from all over the world around the creation of global bodies meant to overcome

---

227 See Wilford (n 222 above), p. 199.
228 Ibid., p. 204.
229 Cummings (n 207 above).

the destructive rivalries of traditional international relations. The World Federation of Democratic Youth was a Soviet front launched at a conference in London in 1945, and the International Union of Students was formed the following year in Prague. Neither organisation, however, was independent of power politics; both rapidly succumbed to domination by communist bureaucrats, who harnessed sincere youthful hopes for world peace to the cause of defending the Soviet Union against perceived American aggression.

Within the group, two individuals stood out for the important part they would play on the African continent. One was a genial man named Jimmy Wallace who immediately involved Lowenstein, then still an undergraduate student at Chapel Hill.

In December 1946, the Harvard International Affairs Committee helped organise a meeting in Chicago to counter the International Union of Students at global events. This initiative, which grew out of discussions among 25 US delegates who attended the founding congress of the International Union of Students in Prague earlier that year, led to the first meeting of the US National Students Association (NSA) in the summer of 1947 in Madison, Wisconsin.

Three years later, in 1950, Lowenstein won the presidential nomination at the NSA convention. He knew where liberalism's advantage lay. Lowenstein's first order of business, only a few months after his presidential election, was to travel to an international student convention in Helsinki. There, on a frosty afternoon in August 1951, a diverse audience of students met for the International Union of Students World Youth Festival sponsored by the World Federation of Democratic Youth. To the American liberal delegation present at the gathering, it was the most startling provocation of the Cold War. Among the Americans present, Lowenstein, as President of the NSA, was incensed by the dominant influence of communist countries over Third World students. "He took the position that it was a waste of time debating with communists at communist-run youth festivals," recalled Lowenstein's successor as President of the NSA, William Dentzer, in an interview with Richard Cummings.[230] Similar Soviet-sponsored efforts, wrote Cummings, to appeal to intellectuals' and students' dread of another world war were eliciting a strong response in Western Europe.

The battle at Helsinki signalled the opening salvo in a battle that had come to be known as the 'Cultural Cold War' – the Soviet–American contest

---

230 Ibid., p. 41.

for the allegiance of the world's intellectuals and students.

But it was the Hungarian fiasco six years later, in 1956, that confirmed the ultimate absurdity of the administration of Dwight Eisenhower's predilection for hard power, and allied Lowenstein to Senator Hubert Humphrey. In October that year, fighting broke out in the streets of Budapest, provoked by Frank Wisner's Radio Free Europe's and the Voice of Free Hungary's (both propaganda fronts of the CIA and CCF) call to people to back the installation of the moderate Imre Nagy as head of government. When Nagy announced his intention of taking Hungary out of the Warsaw Pact (the Soviet compact with East European satellite states), Soviet tanks rolled into the Hungarian capital, Budapest. In the bloody fight that followed, thousands of Hungarians were killed, along with 669 Russian troops. Later, 3 000 resistance leaders, including Nagy, were executed.

The CIA/CCF intervention was exposed as a failure; and it was Frank Wisner who, in a strange twist of fate, became a casualty of George Kennan's psychological warfare. Wisner's behaviour grew manic and erratic. He took to drinking alcohol heavily, and three years later was eased out of his post and shipped off to the largely ceremonial position of CIA Station Chief in London. In 1965, at age 56, Wisner committed suicide.

As well as effectively finishing off Wisner, the Hungarian tragedy signalled the final abandonment by Washington of both the main strategic goal identified by Kennan in the late 1940s – the covert use of Eastern bloc emigres to destabilise the Soviet Union – and the embrace of student fronts in newly decolonised countries on the African continent. In fact, a very underrated aspect of global hegemony that the US established by this time was the normative role of culture and education in influencing and nurturing large elements of the ruling classes in the Third World, directly through its own institutions on US soil and indirectly through the supply of teachers, syllabi, grants, research equipment, and libraries to 'national' institutions located in African countries themselves.

It was up to a new generation – the liberal, so-called 'good wing' of the CIA – to pursue its softer edge.

*

By 1958, Allard Lowenstein and Senator Hubert Humphrey were part of a cultural and ideological nexus, wrote Kopkind, that sanctioned covert operations and mounted public movements against radicalism in the United

States and abroad. "While maintaining a rhetorical respect for civil liberties, they drove the left out of the labour movement, out of the Democratic Party, out of academia, government, and out of the civil liberties field itself."[231]

In the age of McCarthyism, according to Cummings, it might have been the rabble-rousers who created the climate for those expulsions, but it was liberals who did the expelling.[232] It was in fact the liberal Humphrey, not the pouting anti-communist, Senator Joe McCarthy, as is commonly thought, who wrote the Bill to outlaw the American Communist Party. By neglecting the left, Kopkind noted, the liberal international interventionists sought a new legitimacy within the right, a vital centre, a new political reality.[233]

With the dying embers of the Second World War receding into the icy tundra of the Cold War, Humphrey and his liberal campaigners now stepped into a new battle, a battle where virulent anti-communism was to form the domestic campaign platform for Lowenstein's mission abroad. From that moment on, the fate of the colonies became a matter of economic control and ideological influence as the two superpowers vied for power. Europe and Britain were devastated by war and hardly lamented by the supreme victor, the United States, whose own modern history had begun in rebellion against the British Empire.

In South Africa, that put decolonisation in an entirely new context: the rise of apartheid in 1948, from Washington's perspective, was in one sense a vindication of Woodrow Wilson's advocacy during the first quarter of the 20th century of self-determination in European and British colonies. But to allow a relatively developed African country with an emerging industrial–military capacity to fall under black nationalist and communist control could shake self-confidence throughout the African continent and non-communist world.

Paradoxically, when President Woodrow Wilson made the principle of self-determination one of his Fourteen Points, he had meant to staunch the appeal of Bolshevism, but the effect was to excite opponents of imperialism throughout Asia, the Middle East and Africa. Among those incited was a diminutive pacifist in British India named Mohandas Ghandi, a communist guerrilla leader named Ho Chi Minh in French Indochina, an obscure young librarian in China named Mao Zedong, and an Afrikaner nationalist in South Africa named Hendrik Verwoerd.

---

231 Quoted in Wilford (n 222 above), p. 238.
232 See Cummings (n 213 above), p. 44.
233 See Kopkind (n 226 above), p. 230.

What set South Africa apart from other non-aligned countries was the re-emergence of a new rival that had challenged both the effects of British colonialism and threatened the preservation of the post-Second World War order in which the United States was the pre-eminent power across the globe.

The United States had feared precisely this. Both colonialism and author-itarianism, Washington believed, were antiquated institutions that could only discredit the West in its new spheres of influence around the world. To US neoconservatives' ideas about US power, what all this meant was that the choices of newly independent, 'non-aligned' African states could yet tip the balance of power in the Cold War. In US Secretary of State, Allen Dulles's, view, it was South Africa that was a peculiar test case. The problem in the second half of the 20th century, as far as he was concerned, was whether non-aligned states in the British Commonwealth would, under the terms of the emerging, new post-war deal, be drawn to communism in the struggles against colonialism, or the Free World.

Yet the policy of apartheid also meant the Afrikaner nationalist victors would preside over an 'internal colony' of black subjects for whom com-munism was potentially an attractive alternative. In other words, the risk that black nationalists, radicalised by the decolonisation wave sweeping through the African continent, would associate US support for Afrikaner self-determination with imperialism was too high. In this policy perspective, the tendency of black radicals to undermine the US's friends and leave the way open to its enemies turned both grand imperial strategy and morality on their heads. ("Our friends might be nasty, but our enemies worse."[234])

The debate on US Cold War foreign policy is beside the point of our story, but the question of its conduct in student movements in South Africa may shed some light on the frontiers that continued to hobble the student move-ment. This was where Allard Lowenstein came in. Lowenstein, we recall, belonged to a generation of US citizens mainly to the right of such organisa-tions as the NAACP, which espoused a mixture of socialist economic ideals and a diasporic cultural consciousness known as 'Afrocentrism'. Now in his early thirties, he had a restless, devouring mind that leaped from enthusiasm to enthusiasm, giving ideas (the brilliant and the feeble) an equal hearing.

In 1958, Humphrey's floundering democratic campaign for the US Senate needed a boost. With the American civil rights movement stirring,

---

234 For more insight into this strategic moment, see Mokoena, K (ed), *South Africa and the United States: The Declassified History* (New York: The New Press, 1993); and Cummings (n 207 above).

Humphrey, urged by Lowenstein, cast an uneasy eye on the possibilities in South Africa. Although Lowenstein did not officially work in Humphrey's office, he had managed to convince the Senator in his letter of February 1958 that the South African question was not just cheap political theatre; he genuinely believed that, if US officials continued to support a repressive regime in South Africa, they would not only drive Africans "into the arms of Peking and the Soviets",[235] they would also help forge a domestic alliance between communists and black nationalists. A more humane face of the United States in South Africa, he felt, would help turn the tide of revolutionary consciousness away from the Soviet Union to the West, and thus staunch the rising tide of communism in the United States. South Africa would be Humphrey's campaign ticket; and Lowenstein, gregarious and charming, turned out to be a smash choice for the job to pioneer the new role of covert action in South Africa.

*

In 1959, Lowenstein was an academic who taught courses on the politics of southern Africa. Academics in such situations had been routinely recruited by the CIA. While such persons were typically used as analysts, they also performed 'operations', including the provision of funds for political organisations.

The suspicion that Lowenstein was acting at the behest of the CIA to mobilise student support in South Africa in the battle to weaken radical impulses in the African National Congress–South African Communist Party alliance and neutralise the Verwoerd government has clung to his reputation. Critics (such as Cummings and Wilford) of his legacy have speculated that he was already a CIA agent in 1950 and that his presidency of the NSA was crucial in bringing about closer relations between the student movements and the Agency.[236]

In early 2011, I contacted Richard Cummings in the United States to find out whether Lowenstein had worked for the CIA. Cummings claimed he had documentary evidence, accessed via the Freedom of Information Act, which confirmed that Lowenstein was working for the CIA when he visited South Africa in 1958. And sure enough, the document, titled 'Document No. 10' in

---

235 Quoted in Wilford (n 228 above), p. 218.
236 See, for instance, Wilford pp. xix-xx and p. 45.

Lowenstein's 'CIA file', was emailed to me by the Curator of the University of Pittsburgh archive. Dated 19 February 1962, it was one of those routine bureaucratic memos addressed to the Chief of Personnel, Security Division, from the Chief of the Contact Division. The document stated:

> It is requested that priority security checks be procured on Subject as described in the attachment. Our deadline is 23 February, 1962, for approval to contact Subject on an ad hoc basis. Subject reportedly has stated that he had done some work for CIA. If he were used in a [WHITED-OUT] capacity, then this is an indiscretion regarding which our field representative would like to know something about the background before contact is made.

In other words, Lowenstein was not a CIA 'agent', which is a term of art (according to Cummings) referring usually to individuals under contract with the Agency for specific periods of time and for specific purposes; but rather a 'consultant' to be used on an 'ad hoc' basis. Such people, I was told by a retired CIA station chief,[237] "were generally older than normal recruits to the Agency". Evidence suggests that Lowenstein had been recruited while still a student and President of the NSA in 1952. The authenticity of the document, Cummings said to me, was confirmed to him by two former CIA station chiefs in Moscow and Saigon as a 'recruitment document'.

Years later, in 1967, a powerful expose of the CIA's covert operations by *Ramparts* magazine revealed that the Agency, vested with broad, unspecified powers of covert operation by its legislative charter, the National Security Act of 1947, had already begun making secret subsidies to the NSA (founded in the same year), first through wealthy individuals posing as private donors, then, more systemically, via fake charitable foundations created especially to act as funding 'pass-throughs'.

More important than the question of Allard Lowenstein's CIA connection was the broader pattern of CIA activity in liberal student organisations on campuses, to which the Beukes affair points.

"The 'work' for the CIA to which the document was referring," Cummings confirmed to me, "was clearly the smuggling of Hans Beukes out of South Africa."

---

237 Interview with the author on condition of anonymity.

CHAPTER 10

Insurgent liberals

HOW THE CIA PLAYED NUSAS

THE NATIONAL STUDENT ASSOCIATION (NSA) AND NATIONAL UNION OF SOUTH African Students (NUSAS) seemed tailor-made for each other. If the NSA was among the Central Intelligence Agency's (CIA) principal fronts for ideological influence among students, NUSAS was the organisational expression of its liberal offensive in South Africa. NUSAS had been founded in 1924 in an attempt to unify white English- and Afrikaans-language campuses in South Africa. By 1936, four Afrikaans colleges split from NUSAS and joined the rival Afrikaanse Nasionale Studentebond (Afrikaans National Student Union), a strongly Christian-national organisation promoting racial segregation. At the end of the Second Word War, NUSAS finally admitted its first black university member – Fort Hare – although there had been nothing that prevented this being done earlier. The black section of the University of Natal followed Fort Hare into NUSAS in 1947.

By 1959, NUSAS had staged a fight against the segregation of universities along ethnic lines under the campaign banner of 'academic freedom'. It was the high-point of liberal protest for both NUSAS and English-language universities, particularly the University of Cape Town (UCT) and the University of the Witwatersrand (Wits). Throughout the campaign, NUSAS expressed outrage over government harassment of its members. In one-time NUSAS President Glenn Moss's recollection, "the government had withdrawn passports from NUSAS leaders and, in a few cases, banned them". [238] Offices were also raided, emails opened, and documents confiscated by the police because the government regarded the non-racialism of the organisation as subversive. [239]

---

238 Quoted in Moss (n 175 above), p. 48.
239 See Cummings (n 207 above), p. 85.

In Allard Lowenstein's own experience, this differed only in degree from what the hawkish Federal Bureau of Investigation in the United States had done to the NSA when it monitored its activities and placed informers at its congresses.[240] Having received news in the United States of the NUSAS campaign in 1958, Lowenstein began cultivating relations with white South African liberal students. He had been in touch with the President of NUSAS, Neville Rubin, and arranged to stay with him during a visit to Cape Town that year. In Richard Cummings' account,[241] the NUSAS campaign, as far as Lowenstein was concerned, was fit for purpose; and when Rubin invited him to give a greeting to the annual NUSAS congress in Johannesburg, Lowenstein grabbed the opportunity. The South African student movement in 1958, wrote Cummings, was a fantastic opportunity, not just for attracting students to the liberal cause, but galvanising an offensive that would launch the CIA-sponsored NSA student enterprise on South African soil.[242]

The aim was to create a cultural link between a segment of foreign students and the United States. Post-war reconstruction programmes designed to aid European recovery had undoubtedly demonstrated the superiority of the US way of life, but they had failed to swing the cultural balance in favour of the United States. The need, therefore, was to demonstrate to young students "that America had cultural traditions and values worthy of their affiliation and, in so doing, create nuclei of understanding of the true values of democracy and resistance to communism".[243]

*

In 1958, Lowenstein, accompanied by two Princeton students, Emory Bundy and Sherman Bull, travelled to Johannesburg – bounding with energy – via a circuitous route under the auspices of an exchange programme. In reality, Lowenstein had already been Humphrey's 'foreign-policy adviser', Bundy later confirmed to Cummings.[244]

Just how spontaneous were the events that would follow is hard to gauge. If Lowenstein had stumbled into the Beukes affair purely by chance soon after his arrival in Johannesburg, why was Hans Beukes found in possession

240 Ibid.
241 Ibid.
242 Ibid.
243 Quoted in Wilford (n 222 above), p. 124.
244 Cummings (n 207 above), p. 69.

of a book by Adlai Stevenson, a mentor and close associate of Lowenstein, Eleanor Roosevelt and Democratic Party Senator Hubert Humphrey – and all members of the New York-based liberal-internationalist Americans for Democratic Action?

Whether Beukes was part of the CIA's, and therefore Lowenstein's, mission from the moment he crossed the Red Line into South Africa as part of the CIA's strategy of covert operations remains to be confirmed. What is true, we now know, is the CIA's reach could be long and deadly. If Lowenstein was among a liberal cabal of 'Cold Warriors' determined to take the 'deadly' out of right-wing US foreign policy in South Africa (and Africa), he was almost certainly part of a carefully choreographed plan.

There are, the records show, different versions of what happened. That spring in 1958, Lowenstein, Bundy and Bull had been lounging around a Johannesburg hotel when Lowenstein received word from the US Consulate in Johannesburg. Inside the gloomy pile of brown bricks of the Consulate, its outer perimeter bristling with cast-iron railings, were the offices of the US Vice-Consul in Johannesburg, Frank Carlucci.

Carlucci told Cummings that he could hardly remember Lowenstein in the Consulate in Johannesburg. But publicly at least, Carlucci kept a low profile in US foreign affairs, feigning a grab bag of diplomatic duties at the Consulate and avoiding controversial issues and media attention. Providing such congenial cover was among his least-demanding duties. As Cummings tells it, temperamentally he was a far shrewder and tougher player "than his bland exterior" suggested.[245] A staunch anti-communist with a visceral conviction that all wars in the second half of the 20th century were Cold Wars, there was a steel underneath the bland sheath of patrician geniality. John Stockwell, a former CIA operative in southern Africa during that time, who worked with Carlucci, in his tell-all tale of the CIA's role in the region wrote that Carlucci gave "a carefully measured appearance of dishevelled urbanity". He was, Stockwell recalled, "a gentleman willing to employ the tactics of a street fighter".

What few knew then, what no one *could* know, was that Frank Carlucci happened to be a US intelligence operative working under diplomatic cover in southern Africa during the 1950s and sixties; a charge he would, not surprisingly, later deny, but which has since been confirmed by numerous documented sources. "I was in South Africa in the late fifties, but was a

---

245 Cummings (n 207 above), p. 158.

minor functionary," is all he told Cummings, who in the early 1980s had been working on his biographical account of Lowenstein's involvement in the CIA. But those who had been associated with the CIA, Cummings later reflected of his own experience as a CIA agent, "could neither confirm nor deny any kind of association with it".[246] Two sensitively placed Agency men during that time revealed how US embassies of major cities, such as the one Carlucci ran in Johannesburg, usually housed CIA stations and bases around the world and served as the principal headquarters of covert activity.[247] Carlucci was something of a 'freelance buccaneer' in the late 1950s, a retired agent stationed in the Middle East and Africa about that time, working within the interstices of the ever-shifting alliances and labyrinthine conspiracies produced by Europe's retreat from its colonies.

There is no documented evidence, but, by some accounts, the message from Carlucci was simple and urgent: Lowenstein and his associates were to smuggle Hans Beukes out of South Africa to New York. If this is true, history, it would seem, had bequeathed Lowenstein the circumstances and opportunities that would have far-reaching implications for our story. For if the clubby Washington set failed to see the importance of Beukes, their swashbuckling brethren at CIA headquarters in Langley, Virginia, certainly did not.

Notwithstanding the friendly posture of the United States toward apartheid South Africa around that time, the men at Langley did have a concealed objective, a more benign form of racial coexistence than Hendrik Verwoerd had in mind; a form of apartheid in all but name. They had launched a two-pronged enterprise backed by secret funds. The first prong of the strategy was to soften the appearance of support for a vile regime in the anti-communist cause by discrediting radical left-wing organisations. The second prong was a clandestinely staged operation of 'building assets', in intelligence parlance – a process of seeking out 'allies' willing to cooperate with the CIA, preferably organisations and individuals who could be manipulated into belief in the goals of the Agency.

Both tactics were designed to have a singular effect: staunching the march of communism. All that year, 1958, it was in fact communism, not apartheid, that was on trial in what would become the boldest foreign-intelligence gambit in South Africa since the end of the Second World War. However, if

---

246 Ibid., p. 60.
247 See Marchetti, V & Marks, JD, *The CIA and the Cult of Intelligence* (New York: Dell, 1974), p. 71.

apartheid gave voice to an instinctive sense of black anger, and an obsessive, even apocalyptic intensity and belief in communism, there could be no permanent rapprochement – as far as Carlucci was concerned – with the Verwoerd government. But neither was the type of regime change orchestrated through violent coups such as in the Congo around that time possible in a country such as South Africa, where the National Party government already had at its disposal a formidable military apparatus managed by people whose experience and skill were presumably without parallel in African countries.

It was against this background of intensified statutory racism by Verwoerd and the emotionally overwrought radical ideological impulses this threatened to unleash among black people that the Beukes affair was conjured into being. Frank Carlucci is not around to verify this version, but a declassified CIA memorandum on the situation in southern Africa I found while sifting through correspondence between the Johannesburg embassy and Washington around that time, dated December 1959, reveals that a campaign in the region had in fact been carefully choreographed in advance by Langley. There is no explicit reference to Carlucci's involvement in the CIA's 'black operations'. As is customary in the Agency, highly sensitive information in declassified files is whited out. But, by applying the method of placing the person in a place and time, it seems Carlucci had been moving in that direction since Britain's withdrawal from the Gold Coast – now Ghana – years earlier and before Belgium's declaration of its intention to withdraw from the Congo. Unknown until quite recently was that he had been instrumental, behind the scenes, along with CIA Katanga Station Chief Lawrence 'Larry' Devlin in the Congo and an obscure New York diamond broker with close ties to Washington named Maurice Tempelsman, in plotting the execution of the Congolese liberation fighter and Soviet sympathiser, Patrice Lumumba, and orchestrating the coup that eventually led to the rise to power of the US proxy and kleptomaniac, Mobutu Sese Seko.

Could it be that what genuinely engaged Carlucci in South Africa, instigated no doubt by his spymasters at Langley, was what drew him to the Belgian Congo: the spectre of a communist backlash against colonialism and racism? There is circumstantial evidence that Carlucci's presence at the US embassy in Johannesburg during the late 1950s provided the diplomatic rationale for the overt dimensions of US Cold War foreign policy. If the accounts of Cummings and Stockwell are to be believed, unlike the Congo, South Africa – the white Afrikaner security establishment at any rate – was a formidable power, and Carlucci was determined to use whatever he could to show up the apartheid government and present the United States as a sympathetic do-gooder in African affairs in the face of rising Soviet support for black liberation struggles. To men like him, the settlement of the 'South African question' was not simply something to be based on cold military calculations, but a highly complex matter that required sustained international pressure and covert influence.

FRANK CARLUCCI'S IDEA, LOWENSTEIN DECIDED, WAS BRILLIANT. AS A foreign-policy aide to Senator Humphrey, Lowenstein's mission to gather data on the effects of apartheid in South West Africa appeared to have had a dual purpose: he also had to smuggle Beukes, who it turns out was a member of the predominantly anti-SWAPO Herero community from Rehoboth, out of South Africa. In the process, he was to rally NUSAS support for Beukes in a context of liberal resistance to university apartheid.

The CIA's two-step on the Beukes affair therefore contained a certain geopolitical logic – it was intended to restrain Pretoria's apartheid and sub-imperialist ambitions and thus defuse left-wing pressures in South Africa, stopping short of toppling the government. In Cummings, we find clear evidence that Lowenstein's plan gradually took shape in the fall of 1958, as he met Hardin and Leslie Boyd in Cape Town and picked up a Volkswagen that somebody wanted driven to Johannesburg. With Hardin at the wheel most of the time, they took a dangerous drive into the late night to University College of Fort Hare in the Eastern Cape, then the only institution of higher education for blacks in South Africa.[248]

One evening in 1958, Lowenstein met a group of black student leaders, many of them from South West Africa, at the campus for a free-ranging conversation on the South African situation that lasted till dawn. Lowenstein then briefly returned to the United States and, in mid-1959, travelled to South Africa for the second time with NSA Vice-President Curtis Gans' financial endorsement. (We may recall at this point that the NSA was created as a CIA front and conduit for funds to non-communist causes abroad.) In Johannesburg, he addressed the NUSAS congress of some 300 delegates. "There may be moments when you feel alone and isolated, but it is your tormentors, not yourselves, who are alone and isolated," he told his audience.

248 Cummings (n 207 above), p. 85.

"Your cause is the cause of men of goodwill everywhere, and your behaviour is their inspiration."[249]

The cause célèbre of the congress was Hans Beukes, who had been offered a scholarship to study in Norway and had been given a passport which was subsequently revoked "in the best interests of the state".[250] Lowenstein wanted Beukes at the very least to register a protest as an individual to the United Nations (UN) by sending a cable. But weeks before the NUSAS congress he found the tall, unhappy man unresponsive. Beukes, Lowenstein's associate, Emory Bundy, told Cummings, was conservative, saying, "It had been impressed on him by his family." Although he was, in Lowenstein's opinion, a perfect candidate for the task at hand, Beukes's opportunity for higher education "required him to be entirely free from politics, and he believed that a cable would jeopardise his chances of getting to Norway".[251]

Then Beukes addressed the NUSAS congress himself, electrifying the audience with his simplicity as he spoke of his life in South West Africa. Inspired by the response he got after his address, Beukes had finally sidled up to Lowenstein's scheme. Soon after the congress, Lowenstein set about cementing his plans for Beukes's escape. With Beukes safely en route to New York, Lowenstein's first order of business upon returning to the United States in the summer of 1959 was to place the 'South Africa–South West African question' on the UN General Assembly agenda.

As quickly and suddenly as Hans Beukes entered the spotlight, before fleeing South Africa, the rapid progression of events would reveal the Lowenstein plan as only the tip of a very large iceberg. The Beukes affair was a provocation. Just as the South African authorities dithered over press reports of the Port Elizabeth incident, when Beukes's travel documents were revoked by the security police, Frank Carlucci saw an opportunity for his two-pronged propaganda coup that would wrench apartheid out of the shadows into the international spotlight and bring the United States a giant step closer to an alliance with moderate, white student groups opposed to communism in South Africa.

That possibility appeared only too credible while South Africa maintained occupancy of South West Africa.

*

---

249 Ibid.
250 Ibid.
251 Ibid., p. 86.

On 25 April 1945, practically the eve of the Allied forces' declaration of victory, a glittering event half the earth away in San Francisco, resplendent with long black limousines, red carpets, exploding flashbulbs and expensive champagne, had all the razzmatazz of a Hollywood theatrical than a diplomatic gathering of powerful men and women attempting to alter the future. "Welcome United Nations", proclaimed the bright neon marquee of a downtown cinema.[252]

If the occasion was more suited to a Hollywood theatrical, it was probably because it *was* a US production. Despite the grand appearance of 50 flag-bearing countries packed into the San Francisco Opera House to haggle over the terms of a new post-war and post-colonial world order, the birth of the UN was the grandest professionalised anti-communist front of a rising US imperialism.

At the end of the First World War, the victorious Allies decided that the colonies of their recent enemies would not be distributed among the victors. Instead, those colonies would become annexes of developed nations through the machinery of the League of Nations, eventually leading to some form of self-government within a Western frame. The exception, of course, was South West Africa, previously a German colony until its defeat by Allied forces in the First World War. Responsibility for administering the territory was awarded to Britain, which, in turn, delegated the actual governing authority to the Union of South Africa, then part of the British Empire.[253]

At about the time that South Africa achieved sovereignty, after the Second World War, the Afrikaner National Party government alone refused to recognise the jurisdiction of the reconstituted United Nations over South West Africa. Instead, the government announced its intention of incorporating South West Africa into the Union, and to this end 10 seats were added to the Union Parliament in 1949 to be filled by whites of the territory. South Africa stubbornly maintained that the UN's international obligations in South West Africa expired with the UN's forerunner, the League of Nations, a contention that had been rejected repeatedly by the UN General Assembly and by advisory opinions of the International Court of Justice (ICJ).

It is in the interstices of diplomatic and administrative bungles in the evolving context of post-war decolonisation that Lowenstein and Frank Carlucci pulled off their master stroke that could well have aided US designs on South

---

252 Quoted in Bamford, J, *Body of Secrets: How America's NSA and Britain's GCHQ Eavesdrop on the World* (London: Random House, 2002), pp. 21-22.
253 See Lowenstein (n 203 above).

Africa for decades to come. In 1953, the UN set up a Special Committee on South West Africa that issued yearly reports on conditions in the territory based on information collected from statements by petitioners, who the World Court (the ICJ) had ruled "may submit written or oral evidence".[254]

In Lowenstein's own account, documented in his book *Brutal Mandate: A Journey to South West Africa*, if the UN General Assembly provided the legal rationale for disputing South Africa's occupation of South West Africa, Hans Beukes seemed to offer just the opportunity the United States needed to draw the UN's teeth over South West Africa and entrench its interests in the region. The Beukes affair therefore contained a certain zeitgeist – what was happening in South Africa was vital, strategically and economically, to the United States in the region; what was happening in South West Africa a useful rallying point within the UN General Assembly. Seen from this perspective, the prohibition by the apartheid authorities on Hans Beukes's movements in 1958 was viewed in some foreign-intelligence quarters as a tangible barrier and constant reminder of South West Africa's colonisation by South Africa and the latter's separation from the rest of the world.

It is only recently, with the release of declassified US State Administration documents by former president Bill Clinton, that historians have come to appreciate the extent to which the Kennan-esque definition of 'containment' foreshadowed a more aggressive strategy of economic expansion. The first significant revelation came in a 1957 meeting of the US National Security Council (NSC). A top-secret NSC directive arising from that meeting confirmed the US's reputation as an imperialist power and its ambivalent attitude to black majority rule in South Africa: "To a considerable extent, the African is still immature and unsophisticated with respect to his attitudes towards the issues that divide the world today. The African mind is not made up, and he is being subjected to a number of contradictory forces. The African is a target for the advocates of communism." [255]

Beneath its smiling liberal face, then, Lowenstein's Beukes mission pretty much fitted the old imperialist mould. Despite his own public avowals, proclaiming freedom and democracy as the only just cause, Lowenstein knew this.

*

---

254 Ibid.
255 Quoted in 'The NSC memorandum 5719/1: The continuation of 19th century colonialism is harmful to our interests'. For an interpretation of NSC 5719, also see White, G Jr, *Holding the Line: Race, Racism and American Foreign Policy toward Africa, 1953-1961* (United States: Rowman & Littlefield, 2005), p. 31.

In October 1961, the British Empire had shrunk from an expansive dominion into the sharp, piercing menace of a white Afrikaner republic. If Britain
and European colonialism represented what the United States had rebelled
against, in South Africa, beginning with the Anglo-Boer War of 1899–1902,
it was always with the Afrikaner cause for self-determination that the
United States sided against British rule. So striking was antipathy towards
Britain that the future head of the US formal wartime espionage service,
John Foster Dulles, would famously write a high-school essay venerating the
bravery of the Boers during the 1899–1902 Anglo-Boer War.[256]

The Washington brass knew this. So did Lowenstein, and he was all too
willing to coddle their racial prejudices. What Lowenstein knew, but was
not about to reveal, was that South Africa faced no serious threat of internal subversion by communists. In 1926, the Soviet Union, under Joseph
Stalin, had specifically ordered the then Communist Party of South Africa
(CPSA) not to pursue a revolutionary socialist programme. No mass insurrection under the tutelage of the CPSA against the Union government was
to be mobilised and no private properties in the Union were to be attacked,
even though the Union, and later the apartheid government, was the Soviet
Union's ideological enemy. Under the popular-front tactic – broadly, a coalition of anti-fascist forces pursued in Western Europe during the 1930s
– Stalin wanted no anti-Soviet provocations that could upset the precarious
balance of power between East and West that would come to be known
years later as détente.

The United States wanted just the opposite. If the success of the US system was, to recall Fromkin's words, indeed "a matter of economy", the end
of colonialism would signal not the end of Afrikanerdom's historic conflict
with imperialism but the first battle of a new war. Democracy was only
ever really a pretext. The point, from Washington's point of view, was not
a universal franchise, but a moderate coalition of white and black elites. In
other words, if Verwoerdian apartheid was in part a response to the British
Empire and black majority rule, the solution to the economic quandary
would have to come not from Verwoerd, not the African National Congress
(ANC), but from Washington. NUSAS was the leading cause; Hans Beukes
was the catalyst.

*

---

256 For more on this, see Mosley, L, *Dulles: A Biography of Eleanor, Allen and John Foster Dulles and
Their Family Network* (New York: The Dial Press, 1978).

In *Brutal Mandate*, Lowenstein's travelogue published in 1961 on his South Africa–South West Africa mission, the author had shown a keen interest in the models and values that shaped US liberal thinking about the Cold War and apartheid. The gambit worked. Soon after Beukes's testimony, the United States voted for a resolution calling on the government of South Africa to enter into negotiations with the UN in order to place the territory under the UN trusteeship system.

In an effort to keep the momentum going, Lowenstein worked diligently to organise student involvement between the NSA and NUSAS. In early 1961, NSA officers expressed interest in an 'educational campaign' in which funds raised on American campuses would be channelled to NUSAS through the World University Service, later revealed to be a CIA conduit that student spies such as Craig Williamson would use for their nefarious ends. At the moment, Lowenstein, who had been working with Hans Beukes, offered to coordinate the disbursement of the funds for "general educational defence and welfare purposes" in South Africa with NUSAS President, Neville Rubin.[257] It was arranged that the banking facilities of the American Committee on Africa would be used to receive funds from the NSA. In this way, wrote Cummings, a "voluntary" fundraising effort was used to bolster CIA-financed student programmes in South Africa of the International Commission of the NSA.[258]

In a memorandum, dated 22 October 1959, Ann Morrissett wrote that funds were "to be treated as the test of our special funds, with some part of them used for administrative and promotional expenses".[259] In the spring of 1961, Ernest Wentzel, chairman of the Transvaal region of the Liberal Party in Johannesburg and past president of NUSAS, with whom Lowenstein stayed during his 1959 trip, wrote to Lowenstein via his chief assistant, Ethel Grossman, in New York: "There is an ideological battle in South Africa between communism, nationalism and liberalism. If liberalism is to prevail, we must be able to compete powerfully with our adversaries."[260]

The most specific form of help, Wentzel wrote, that could be provided was financial. Later, Adrian Leftwich, the new president of NUSAS, made a similar appeal to Grossman in a letter bearing the NUSAS insignia. NUSAS, Leftwich wrote, had passed resolutions "condemning outright the

---

257 Cummings (n 207 above), p. 97.
258 Ibid.
259 Ibid.
260 Ibid., p. 118.

government's policy of apartheid … and consequent upon this adopted a resolution outlining a campaign against educational apartheid".[261]

The closeness of Allard Lowenstein to South African liberals who were promoting the programmes of NUSAS explains his influence in shaping these programmes. He was modelling his own experiences with the NSA on South African campuses.

---

261 Ibid.

CHAPTER 11

Gentlemen accomplices

THE US–SOUTH AFRICA LEADER EXCHANGE PROGRAM

THE BUCOLIC SETTING OF ATHENS WAS AN IMPROBABLE PLACE FOR A TAWDRY South African drama. On summer mornings, a tranquil light washes over the labyrinthine alleyways and streets and then fans out along a winding road into the hills and valleys north of the city. On the crest of a hill over-looking the plains of Attica outside Athens is the towering Mont Parnes Hotel. There, an unlikely cast of characters gathered in late June, 1966, for a three-day conference.

It was 11 years since an edgier group of eminent US academics, led by an avuncular sociology professor named Frank Loescher, had gathered at Haverford College in the spring of 1955. Troubled by an emerging post-colonial era that had signalled the start of the Soviet–American contest for the allegiance of national liberation movements in the Third World, the assemblage of academics, politicians, businessmen and church leaders dis-cussed the implications for the United States of growing United Nations (UN) pressure on South Africa to end apartheid.

They concluded that Afrikaner and black nationalism was bound to result in a clash "full of violence and ruthlessness with worldwide repercussions". "Because it is difficult for outsiders to have a direct and constructive influ-ence on the way of life of another country," Loescher told the gathering, "influencing the course of events would be best left to the umbrella influence of a cultural and leader exchange programme involving private agencies, civil servants, academics, students and journalists from both countries."[262]

Two years later, the United States–South Africa Leader Exchange Program, or USSALEP as it became commonly known, was launched at a

---

262 African-American Institute, United States–South Africa Leader Exchange Programme, briefing document, 1958. Available from Wits Historical Papers USSALEP Collection.

gathering in Wingspread, Wisconsin, as a privately organised and supported institute. It arose first under the aegis of the African-American Institute, and shortly after as a privately incorporated Delaware corporation – America's murky equivalent of the Bahamas or Cayman Islands – headquartered in Philadelphia. In the tense atmosphere of détente (the Cold War truce between the two superpowers), the group lost no time formulating a messianic justification for two-way cultural exchanges aimed at strengthening mutual relations between the two countries.

This time, there were some finer shadings with the Athens entourage. A group of 14, mainly white Afrikaner academics, civil servants, theologians and newspaper editors on the South African side took their places beside their 12 American counterparts to discuss more serious matters of South Africa's race policy. Among the South Africans present were very influential men, some of whom the Verwoerd government had chosen to run enormous companies and powerful portfolios in the state. In those heady days, it seemed the group shared almost regal ambitions for moderate change that placed them on the same side in the face of the threat of South Africa falling to radicals opposed to everything liberalism represented and wished to retain – an illusion, as we shall see, that did not endure.

Modelled after the Wingspread gathering, the Athens conference was intended to rally white Afrikaner academics against the more severe racial policies of their government, which just two years before had passed a juggernaut of repressive legislation, including the Extension of University Education Act.

Whether or not the South Africans knew of the parallel streams coursing through USSALEP is not clear. They had come to the gathering at the urging of Frank Loescher, then in his twenties and USSALEP's Programme Director and General Secretary. Outwardly, Loescher remained stiff and correct. He looked every bit the scholar – urbane and bespectacled. But deep inside, he was scowling at the new and youthful White House. He had been sold on the liberal policy of the Kennedy administration and suddenly felt out of place and out of time in a hawkish culture built around the botched Cuban invasion that seemed suddenly to have turned its back on the liberal internationalists, the dovish Cold Warriors.

The South Africans were led by an Afrikaner businessman named Hendrik van Eck. Almost immediately, Loescher and Van Eck became, in the clinical sense, paranoid; they regarded each other with a taut wariness.

On the first day of the gathering, Van Eck had given an oratorical performance laced with spurious grandiloquence about the virtues of a "centuries-old record of racial peace and genuine goodwill second to none among communities anywhere in the world" that sent a frisson through the gathering.[263]

"Given the time to do it in our own way and without due haste," he said, "we may yet, in spite of all the criticism levelled at us now, produce in South Africa a showpiece of how peoples of different colour can not only live side by side in peace and harmony, but assist one another towards attaining … that which is within their reach."[264] He had in mind the segregation of universities along ethnic lines.

With his poker face and boastful manner, Van Eck had a twin message to convey. Reciting turgid economic data and comparative statistics to show how the country had blossomed under apartheid, he told his US counterparts that South Africa was open for business, pragmatic and reliable, despite doubts in the West about its commitment to democracy and genuinely free markets. In her record of the event, Loescher's wife, who had been scribe for the gathering, noted that the US party was startled.

Having upended his audience's settled categories, the second part of Van Eck's delivery was tougher. "We realise we cannot escape the impact of change that has taken place, and is taking place, in the world and more particularly in Africa," he coyly said, leaning forward with an apologetic smile. "What we do not intend to do is let the wind steer us off our course and into the hands of communists," he told his audience, in obvious reference to British Prime Minister Harold MacMillan's 'Wind of Change' speech three years earlier.[265]

On the surface, Van Eck's speech was clever diplomatic footwork. It was also a shrewd effort to align South Africa's racial policies with the broader fight against communism. Van Eck designated South Africa and the United States as allies in the war against different manifestations of the same enemy – Soviet expansion steered by Moscow. If the detailed record by Loescher's wife, right down to the physical dimensions and tenor of the event, is to be believed, Van Eck had prepared the ground well.

"In the United States and in Britain you make it a criminal offence for people to display their race-consciousness," he said, his voice growing stronger as he squared off. There was silence in the room. He had everyone's attention.

---

263 Ibid., see minutes.
264 Ibid.
265 Quoted in the *Evening Post*, 27 June 1996, in USSALEP Collection, Wits Historical Papers.

"In the communist world it is being exploited for ulterior purposes. In South Africa, we are trying to live with race-consciousness, to accept it as a fact of life and to accommodate it in a system of peaceful co-existence."[266]

Of the three options – at least while he accustomed himself to the trappings of power – Van Eck was batting for the latter. His language was indistinguishable from the rhetoric of 'peace' and 'human progress' that had become commonplace in the United States and Britain since the end of the Second World War. Yet, for all the optimism, Van Eck's US audience knew better. Most crucially, and again inextricably bound with their other affinities, the group was bound by rhetoric: a hatred of communism. No one in the room bothered to pursue the obvious contradiction between this common goal and the more fundamental problem of apartheid – a worrying trait given the project for which they had signed up.

*

Perhaps the most telling moment was not anything said publicly, or even in private dinner conversations at the classy Mont-Parnes Hotel as phalanxes of waiters and waitresses arrived with successive courses. It came in a letter I found while sifting, 50 years later, through piles of USSALEP conference papers, minutes of meetings and correspondence at the University of the Witwatersrand Historical Papers research archive. Marked 'Private and personal', Harold Hochschild, who was Honorary Chairman of the Board of American Metal Climax Inc. in New York (which had been doing a brisk trade with South Africa) and a guest of honour at the gathering, had written to Alan Pifer, the USSALEP Convenor and Executive Associate at the Carnegie Corporation of New York, shortly after the gathering. Dated August 1966, the letter conveyed his impressions of the exchange programme. Phrased in cautious and even obfuscatory terms, it was largely critical of USSALEP, and in retrospect appears to have been a tactical warning to Pifer that there was little chance of winning the allegiance of Afrikaner participants, even as they were trying to build a moderate coalition. The implicit message to Pifer was to expose the "mutual fallacies" surrounding prospects of "moderating Nationalist racial policies" in South Africa. "In my mind there is no question that the exchange program is barely tolerated by the South African government for the sake of relations with the United States, that

266 Wits Historical Papers USSALEP Collection; see minutes.

the said government expects Dr van Eck to keep the program from becoming a nuisance to it while this sufferance continues and that he accepts this responsibility."[267]

Van Eck ranked as leader of an elite group of Afrikaner nationalists within the National Party, drawn from a different background; they were men of power with strong roots in business who clustered around and controlled the state's businesses. He had been chosen to represent South Africa at the gathering because of his confident, non-threatening manner. Only he seemed able to control the direction of USSALEP. Although Loescher suspected it, he did not know that Van Eck, now working for the state-owned Industrial Development Corporation, had been secretly sent to Athens by the Verwoerd government.

Months later, Hochschild had predicted in a letter to Pifer that apartheid was a precursor to the real conflict in South Africa against communism. "In the ultimate showdown," he wrote, "which only the Africans themselves can force, whether by physical or economic pressure – and one cannot yet see any sign of that on the horizon – moderate influences on both sides will probably be hopelessly submerged until times change and new educated African and Afrikaner leaders emerge."[268]

Two weeks later, Pifer wrote back. "If USSALEP can serve as a channel of communication to the moderate university professors, it may just possibly turn out to be highly important at some critical point in the future," he noted, in an oblique reference to Hochschild's discordant note of an extremist threat.[269]

Washington, Pifer seemed to be saying, had the Verwoerd government in its sights; but first USSALEP had to win over Afrikaner moderates to the liberal cause. With a fresh bout of international pressure on South Africa, and diplomacy ongoing at the UN, what was the point of pressing ahead with rigid race policies? What was needed, Pifer believed, was the allegiance of Afrikaners themselves; and that was extraordinarily difficult.

In the ideological battle, the test both Pifer and Loescher had set was whether those in powerful positions in South Africa were willing to do the practical thing: reform South Africa's rigid race laws and establish a moderate coalition.

*

267 Quoted in USSALEP memorandum, 1 August 1963. In USSALEP Collection, Wits Historical Papers.
268 Hochschild's typed letter to Pifer, August 1966, in Wits Historical Papers USSALEP Collection.
269 Quoted in USSALEP memorandum, 15 August 1963, in Wits Historical Papers USSALEP Collection.

On the surface, USSALEP gave the impression of being a united, tight-knit group; but beneath the pomp and ceremony of Athens lay an audacious gambit by Washington to challenge the power of the National Party government. Their chief foe close at hand was Verwoerd, and he knew them better. USSALEP was not a united group. The great question of the day was whether or not to support Verwoerd and his apartheid doctrine; and this question divided them. On the one hand, there were those who hoped for an alliance with Verwoerd. But there were other, pragmatic, reasons for opposing Verwoerd. There was the business elite – especially the US and South African mining houses – which increasingly chafed under the restrictions imposed by the government. Verwoerd's aggressive efforts at apartheid had failed to improve the living conditions of black people, and a gathering political storm loomed over the economy.

The biggest difference between South Africa and its Western interlocutors, which the US delegation to Athens seemed reluctant to publicly acknowledge, lay in their most basic views of trade. In 1961, the immediate strategic interest in South Africa was gold and uranium. South Africa was a major gold producer, and, to stabilise prices, the United States was forced to import minerals. Internal US State Department documents suggest that the dependent relationship was all too evident.

In truth, however, Pretoria was pursuing hostile policies in South Africa that Washington found increasingly hard to defend in the ensuing melee of the Sharpeville massacre in March 1961. That year, the United States became the focal point of international pressure in the UN to disinvest from South Africa after the banning of liberation organisations. The Sharpeville massacre witnessed a sharp outflow of private capital and a USD1.4 billion decline in stock values. Disinvestment also had the potential to throttle the diamond- and gold-mining industries and so, as the mining magnate, Harry Oppenheimer, argued in Parliament around that time, "The continuation of trade between the United States and South Africa was the only way to keep the industry on its feet and prevent job losses."

We must at this point admit the hypothesis that highly particular interests were effectively represented behind the scenes by a powerful or well-connected person or group. In this fashion, the relationship between the United States and South Africa had been uniquely awkward.

The suggestion that Washington fielded a liberal-Afrikaner front group in its turn to covertly exert cultural influence among South African academics and Afrikaner politicians is less implausible than it might seem at first. The thinking that reformists in South Africa and corporate America could do business, and that a moderate coalition – as opposed to a rigid apartheid doctrine – could lead the way to reorienting the country toward America and the West certainly ran high up the policy chain in Washington. There is no record of how the USSALEP agenda churned into gear, but let's start with the year 1957, two years after the launch of the USSALEP at a gathering of US and South African academics at Wingspread, Virginia.

UNTIL THE SOVIET BLOCKADE OF BERLIN IN 1960, THE ADMINISTRATION of President Dwight Eisenhower had shown no sign of wanting to deal with South Africa. The 'apartheid question' was on the cards but had never been in Eisenhower's heart. And so South Africa became the liberals' leading cause because the Eisenhower policy of quiet diplomacy seemed to be failing, but for a larger reason, too: they saw South Africa as a test case for their ideas about US power and world leadership. South Africa represented the worst failing of the Cold War and the first opportunity for an American policy on Africa.

Four years earlier, in 1957, Richard Nixon fired a warning shot in a National Security Council (NSC) memo. It was a frank exposition of the themes of his recent travels through Africa to find out what was happening in the process of decolonisation. Nixon's memo dripped scorn, claiming that hawkish conservatives like US Secretary of State John Foster Dulles had misjudged the posture of newly independent African states.

With Eisenhower in the chair of an NSC meeting in 1957, Dulles and Nixon made their arguments. A swaggering, hard-edged Cold Warrior who had embraced the hawkish realism of the Republicans, Dulles told Eisenhower to get ready for fierce competition for power and influence in Africa between the Soviet Union and United States. He proposed that independence was premature and that the grafting of Western-style parliamentary democracy onto an African culture that still believed in "Paramount Chiefs and Animism" would mean "ethnic strife, rampant corruption, and extensive violence" ripe for Soviet manipulation. "There is no middle ground," he said. "Africans must be told to decide whether they are with us or against us."[270]

---

270 Memorandum of discussion at the 314th meeting of the National Security Council, Washington, 28 February 1957, in *Foreign Relations of the United States, 1955-1957*, National Security Policy, Vol. xix. Accessed at https://history.state.gov/historicaldocuments/frus1955-57v19/d110.

As an assiduous proponent of Afrikaner nationalism in South Africa, he then floated plans for an aggressive campaign against black nationalism. Then it was Nixon's turn. He interpreted the same set of facts from a different perspective. The driving force within the newly enthroned independent regimes, he said, would be "nationalism".[271] He then presented his strategy of intellectual combat as an extension of politics. Looking through his Cold War prism, he proposed the reorganisation of African nationalism within a Western frame – as a force for Western domination. "As a first course ... we should tell the Africans that we support a continuation of independent national neutralism," he said.[272] Nixon's carefully crafted argument – having the advantage of a recent National Intelligence Estimate that indicated the Soviets would fail because of the 'nationalism factor' – was far more convincing, an on-the-other-hand rejoinder which skilfully applied the principles of the Cold War strategist George Kennan's strategy of containment to South Africa. This was, Nixon believed with good reason, the only certain way of taming nationalist forces short of brinkmanship and "boom and bang" – in Halpern's dismissive phrase – adventurous coup schemes involving pro-Western black leaders.[273]

The words drew Eisenhower's attention. "Africa has strategic importance, but do not seek military bases," he began. Then he added his own council to the Nixon proposal: "We must first work through educational and cultural relations. We must win the minds of the people."[274]

Apparently, this was not the only brazen enterprise. Nor was it the only scheme involving USSALEP.

*

Browsing through the USSALEP archive at the University of the Witwatersrand (Wits) in Johannesburg, I came across a draft NSC memo, dated 1 November 1963, to President John F Kennedy. The memo was one of those secret bureaucratic briefs on how to handle "the economic risk of investment in South Africa" at a UN Security Council meeting later that month.[275]

---

271 Ibid.
272 Ibid.
273 Ibid.
274 Quoted in Cohen, HJ, 'A perspective on fifty years of US-Africa policy: The Nixon legacy', in *American Foreign Policy Interests*, 2010, pp. 209-210. doi: 10.1080/10803920.2010.501201.
275 National Security Council memorandum, 1 November 1963, in Wits Historical Papers USSALEP Collection.

Kennedy arrived in the White House at a time when the political climate had become increasingly unstable. In Washington, an air of suspense hung over the US Senate chamber as news spread of the possibility of 200 Soviet divisions attacking West Germany. Communist parties in Western Europe, especially France and Italy, were garnering as much as 25 per cent of votes in democratic elections. Some of the more radical elements in those Soviet-financed parties were speculating about being 'liberated' by the Soviet Red Army. Communist insurgencies in South-East Asia were on the move. And the arrival in the international community of 30 or more newly independent African countries falling under Soviet influence was a real possibility.

By this time, the UN had begun to take up issues of human rights, and the problem of apartheid became an important agenda item. Washington itself was hesitant, and if there was a consensus among others, Eisenhower's ideological crusaders were taking a cautious line: openly condemning apartheid while quietly doing nothing to remove it.

By 1961, South Africa had become the focus of two power struggles; one was between a business elite and Verwoerd over the latter's determination to press ahead with apartheid, even as South Africa faced international isolation; the other was the turn to arms by the African National Congress (ANC) in a context of the expansionist policies of the Soviet Union. Even though the Soviet Union was a distant place, Kennedy found the ANC in South Africa more immediately troubling.

By this time Nelson Mandela was becoming something of a cult figure with enormous appeal among mainly young black militants. Mandela believed the abandonment of non-violence and the introduction of the use of force to be justified because, as he told a journalist, "No leader is going out to say we want peaceful discussions because the government is making that kind of talk senseless. Instead of getting a favourable response, the government is more arrogant. The African reaction can only be a show of force."[276]

As the days and months dwindled down to 16 December 1961, the day the banned ANC officially declared guerrilla warfare against apartheid, the skies were ominous; threats loomed on the horizon as Verwoerd passed a battery of racist laws. And what were the new threats? They were everyone and everywhere: American imperialism, British neo-colonialism, African

---

276 Quoted in Cummings, R, 'A diamond is forever: Mandela triumphs, Buthelezi and De Klerk survive, and ANC on the US payroll, in *International Journal of Intelligence and Counter-intelligence*, Summer 1995. Accessed at http://www.namebase.net/diamond.html.

nationalism, resurgent communism, right-wing Afrikaners, sanctions.

The heart of the Kennedy memo was a 'long-range proposal' for a set of modest reforms by the South African government in return for which the United States and Britain would give categorical support to Verwoerd. But there was more than a little chicanery to the document. Washington seemed fully aware in which direction Verwoerd was tilting. "While the proposed reforms are modest and gradual," it noted, "... the South African government would have openly to scrap apartheid – a complete admission of defeat for its present policy."[277]

It seems the authors were determined to call Verwoerd's bluff, and even urged a 'Plan B': "Even if it has practical interest, there's serious doubt whether South Africa is yet ripe for such a proposal ... . The scheme may, therefore, be a starter in two ways – first as a serious proposal to the South Africans; second, if they refuse, as a public US gambit which would seriously split Verwoerd's near-monolithic present white support." Because a militantly hostile posture by the West toward Verwoerd ran the risk of "driving even liberal white South Africans into the Verwoerd camp," more covert measures were needed.

And there you have it. The plan was a perfect political storm for Verwoerd, a dangerous convergence of his most avid enemies coming together from the worlds of liberalism, US imperialism, and the Afrikaner business elite. There is no linear narrative between the Nixon and Kennedy memos and the USSALEP plan, but it seems hardly coincidental that less than a year later the overriding goal for the United States would be to transform the Athens summit into concrete gains that might pre-empt a radical backlash in South Africa by both black nationalists and right-wing Afrikaners and alleviate the economic burden of Verwoerdian apartheid on vital US national interests.

It was in this hardening atmosphere of deepening international tension and perceived crisis in South Africa that a powerful group of opinion makers in Washington and South Africa had begun to think that the longer Verwoerd remained in office, the greater the risk, in Hochschild's words, that "white and black nationalist movements in South Africa would pass increasingly to extremists".[278]

*

277 National Security Council, 1963.
278 Correspondence from Harold Hochschild to Frank Loescher, USSALEP Collection, Wits Historical Papers.

The crucial issue in South Africa, as far as the Kennedy administration was concerned, was no longer national liberation but a limited form of democracy based on a qualified franchise, and, more profoundly, minority-group rights. Their ideological patron was none other than the doyen of American Cold War foreign policy, George Kennan, who years later would visit South Africa as a USSALEP trustee. Arranged through friend, Harold Hochschild, and sponsored by Pifer's African-American Institute, USSALEP had curiously drawn on help from the US State Department – a marker, if there ever was one, of strong links with Washington – to arrange Kennan's arduous schedule of tours, luncheons, receptions, dinners, press interviews, and meetings with public figures. That Kennan had no objection 'in principle' to the idea of separate development, having long believed that race shaped culture, was a sure sign of USSALEP's political posture. Recent US efforts to pretend otherwise, he confessed to Marion Dönhoff in 1965, had even left him "sympathetic to apartheid".[279] Like Hochschild, he nonetheless felt that apartheid had to be reformed if extremism was to be averted. Apartheid, Kennan wrote to the President of the African-American Institute shortly after returning to Princeton University, was "not only offensive to our sensibilities, but clearly inadequate to South Africa's own needs and doomed to eventual failure".[280] Any quick shift to majority rule there or elsewhere, though, would be "a disaster for all concerned". "Blacks were not ready for it, and whites were determined to fight rather than yield. So did it make sense for the United States to be supporting 'national liberation' movements?"[281] he mused.

The shift in thinking would have large implications. If an unqualified democracy was not the immediate goal, national liberation looked suspiciously like apostasy, especially when it was carried to its logical conclusion. In 1966, that conclusion was a bone of contention among members of the USSALEP Board at the Athens gathering that brought the tempestuous marriage between American liberals and Afrikaner nationalists to a head. But for others in South Africa, such as Van Eck, USSALEP stood for different things – an opportunity to present the gentler face of Afrikaner nationalism, foreign trade, and ideological legitimacy. At the moment, the area of overlap was what mattered.

In hindsight, this was only one part of the story. For, after all, who, or

---

279 See Davis, JL, *George Kennan: An American Life* (New York: Penguin Books, 2011), p. 633.
280 Ibid., pp. 604-605.
281 Ibid., p. 605.

what, was behind USSALEP? The first suggestion of an answer had arrived, quite literally, at the door of USSALEP.

CHAPTER 12

Dummy foundations and funding pass-throughs

THE USSALEP PLOT THICKENS

IN THE EARLY SUNLIT HOURS OF A SEPTEMBER MORNING IN 1965, A MAN named Richard Parry paid USSALEP's (United States–South Africa Leader Exchange Program) Jim Brewer a visit. Brewer would later recall that encounter as a worrying potentate, given the project for which he and other USSALEP executives had signed up.

An enthusiastic proponent of covert intervention as a foreign-policy tool, Parry was assigned to the Central Intelligence Agency's (CIA) covert-action unit. Officially, he was an Agency bureaucrat, a desk-bound paper analyst at the Agency's headquarters in Langley, Virginia. His 'deniable' role, however, included overseeing the deployment of secret funds to educational and leader exchange programmes designed to influence the political direction of Third World countries. Vociferously anti-communist, Parry was one of those swaggering cloak-and-dagger hardliners who assigned historic blame to liberals in the Kennedy administration for losing their nerve in the Cold War. Brewer might well have counted himself among those liberals, along with Frank Loescher and Alan Pifer.

On the morning of September 1965, Parry called on Brewer to look at reports US exchangees had written since his last visit in December 1963. As Brewer rummaged through filing cabinets for USSALEP exchangee files, Parry questioned the selection process for exchangees. "I knew the answer he expected," Brewer would later recall, "but I answered in standard bureaucratic procedure. I said, 'They were nominated usually by people on the management committees and had to be approved by the management committees in South Africa and the United States.'"[282]

---

282 USSALEP correspondence, in Wits Historical Papers USSALEP Collection.

That wasn't good enough. As Parry paged through the files, he grew visibly agitated. Brewer recalled that he found Parry strangely persistent. "He suddenly went into a dialogue that he thought all the American exchangees were too liberal, and asked, 'Don't you send over conservatives?'" Then Parry lobbed an even more explosive question: "Are you doing a service to the USSALEP program by focusing on liberals?"[283]

Unsure of where exactly Parry was heading with his line of inquiry, Brewer shrugged. He had one question: What did Parry mean by 'liberal'? By this time Parry was finding his own sentiments on the subject harder to contain. "This is just rubbish," he fumed, flipping through the list of American exchangees. "It seems to me that many of the people were Quakers, etc., and radicals like Judge Maris. I think the selection of Henry Nichols, for one, was appalling!"[284]

Brewer recalled dismissing the remark with almost studied indifference and leaving Parry to pour over the files in his office before heading off to a meeting with two US exchangees. A week later, Brewer wrote a two-page account of the meeting under the plain title, 'Visit of Richard Parry, CIA': "Although he [Parry] inferred he had little knowledge of the exchangees," Brewer noted, "it became quite clear that he knew who the exchangees were before he entered our offices. Towards the end, he also asked to whom the reports were sent and the size of the office staff."[285]

Brewer knew that he was being asked to account to USSALEP's handlers at Langley. He might even have added that he, too, was 'witting' of the CIA's involvement in USSALEP. Some conspiracy researchers have long speculated whether some USSALEP management committee members were already familiar with the CIA. Among them, Brewer would certainly have been just the type of 'independent operator' to whom the CIA would have subcontracted its covert operations. In any case, it is clear from Brewer's account how indisputably entwined USSALEP and the CIA had become. But it is equally obvious that Brewer was likely in the know.

There is a curious 'endnote' to the Parry encounter that provides an important key to our understanding of USSALEP. If the CIA connection to USSALEP was one of the most closely guarded secrets of the time, here finally was the most stunning revelation of the dark workings of US power in South Africa. It also helps explain why some conspiracy

283 Ibid.
284 Ibid.
285 Ibid.

researchers cast their suspicions of USSALEP immediately to an anti-Verwoerd underworld.

*

A year after Richard Parry's visit to USSALEP's offices, revelations by the left-wing San Francisco-based magazine, *Ramparts*, of CIA-funded covert operations greatly contributed to the fog of suspicion floating around the leader exchange programme.

By 1966, a student named W Eugene Groves was preparing to launch his campaign to run for President of the National Student Association (NSA), a post, we recall, that had offered several previous holders such as Allard Lowenstein a stepping stone to higher public office. By the age of 23, Groves had won a Rhodes scholarship to Oxford in 1965 and had just returned home to run for president when he learnt a secret about the organisation that would change his life. In Hugh Wilford's exposé of US front organisations during that period,[286] we find evidence that, despite its appearance as a free and voluntary centre for US student groups, the Association, its sitting President, Philip Sherburne, informed him, was secretly funded by the CIA. This arrangement, Groves learnt, dated back to the infamous National Security Act of 1947 which gave unspecified powers of covert action to the Agency in its propaganda war with the Soviet Union.[287] That same year, 1947, the CIA, we recall, began making secret subsidies to the NSA, which had just been founded, first through wealthy individuals posing as private donors and then, more systematically, via fake charitable foundations created especially to act as funding "pass-throughs".

Students in the NSA's International Affairs Division who had been groomed by undercover intelligence officers attending NSA summer seminars and who were sworn to official secrecy, then helped channel the money abroad, where 'friendly' liberal student organisations spent it on various activities intended to combat the influence of radical ideas. By the time Eugene Groves was let in on the secret in 1966, the CIA's covert programme extended beyond Europe to liberal student organisations in South Africa such as the National Union of South African Students (NUSAS); it also expanded to academic and leader exchange programmes such as USSALEP.

---

286 See Wilford (n 222 above), p. 1.
287 Ibid., pp. 1-2.

Groves was profoundly disturbed by what he perceived as "terrible errors" in recent American foreign policy, particularly the war in Vietnam; his instinct, therefore, was to reveal all. As he mulled over the situation, he feared attacks from both the left and the right of US politics. The liberal cause, he felt, would be the casualty.[288]

It was a tip-off from a disgruntled NSA official in charge of fundraising named Michael Wood to a spirited and idealistic Berkley graduate named Sol Stern that set the ball rolling. Wood, who knew about CIA foundation grants, decided to break ties with the Agency. But when he could not explain the sudden loss of funds to NSA members, the executive of the organisation fired him for incompetence. That's when he told Stern what he knew. Still in his twenties, Stern ran an explosive piece which told of the CIA's secret penetration and financing of the NSA through tax-exempt foundations.

At the same time, *The New York Times* published a pre-emptive advertisement and a statement by the NSA. But if the matter was intended to staunch the flow of revelations, it failed miserably. To the horror of Groves and others, the *Times* went on in the weeks that followed to run a series of stories revealing covert CIA sponsorship of an astounding variety of other organisations engaged in Cold War propaganda. Soon, media heavyweights in the United States followed the money trail from the CIA-connected foundations – growing from about 2 200 in 1955 to more than 18 000 in 1967 – named in *Ramparts*, in what was described by one CIA operative as the biggest security leak in the Cold War.[289] The story blew the whistle on an elaborate web of citizen front groups covertly supported, and sometimes even created, by the spy agency since the early days of the Cold War. Among the organisations which had been exposed as conduits of funds to USSALEP were the African-American Institute, the Carnegie Institute – where USSALEP's Alan Pifer was a director – and the Farfield Foundation.

High-ranking officials in the educational and labour movements had worked secretly with the CIA to spread the principles of anti-communism around the world. Liberal and anti-communist academics, students, intellectuals, writers, artists, journalists and politicians were the recipients of secret government largesse.

The effect of the revelations was shattering. A fusillade of articles in South Africa on the USSALEP angle soon exploded into public view, starting that

---

288 Ibid., p. 2.
289 Ibid., p. 8.

January when the *Sunday Times*, a weekly Johannesburg-based newspaper popular with white liberals for its racy exposés, ran a front-page story under the banner headline, 'US super-secret spy agency wants to control SA revolts', in which George Moir, USSALEP's South African Secretary, denied any connection between USSALEP and the Farfield Foundation. Raymond Heard, the *Sunday Times* Washington correspondent, reported a week before: "The USSALEP programme, while denying it originally got cash from CIA channels, has turned to the Farfield Foundation, a CIA front, to sponsor at least two non-white journalists – Lewis Nkosi and Nat Nakasa – as Niemen Fellows."[290]

On 2 February that year, the *Sunday Times* ran another front-page piece by Heard under the headline, 'Dollar-aid alleged for anti-apartheid groups'. In his piece, Heard wrote that the CIA had sponsored a wide range of student and potentially subversive anti-apartheid groups through "dummy" private foundations. Among them, the American Committee on Africa, which coordinated most anti-apartheid efforts, received generous aid from CIA-backed foundations, Heard wrote. But it was Heard's revelation of funding links between the Farfield Foundation, a CIA front, and USSALEP that sent a shudder through the government. "The CIA," Heard wrote, "through its fronts has got into the anti-apartheid business for two reasons – it wants to have some control over the education and leadership of any future revolution which may break out; and it also feels that if it does not aid groups, they would become the stooges of the communists."

As the media dug deeper into the swaths of anti-Verwoerdian intrigue in South Africa during those years, the government was stunned by the intricate web that linked the CIA, academics, business and USSALEP. There were more layers, honeycombed with bizarre people.

BY THE TIME OF THE ATHENS GATHERING IN 1966 (DISCUSSED IN THE PREVIOUS chapters), the arc of history had taken USSALEP from leader exchanges to an explicitly political belief that human rights, not nationalism or communism, was the only true guarantor of capitalism in non-aligned countries of the Third World. Its US leadership – men like Frank Loescher, who had

---

290 *Sunday Times*, 'Dollar-aid alleged for anti-apartheid groups', in Wits Historical Papers USSALEP Collection newspaper clippings, 2 February 1966.

previously directed the Philadelphia Commission on Human Relations – identified with the liberal wing of the Democratic Party. But as liberal interventionists and US patriots living in the second half of the 20th century, their cause also allied them to the conservative side of US power.

These Cold Warriors in Washington saw American power in almost messianic terms – they were inveterate nationalists, or 'neoconservatives' as they came to be known. Loescher, in particular, was interested only in what US power could achieve in South Africa on behalf of liberal ideals.

The USSALEP records show that, in the first half of 1955, Loescher made frequent trips to South Africa, funded in all likelihood by the African-American Institute (AAI), where he met University of Stellenbosch scholar Nic Olivier, Frederick van Wyk, an assistant director of the South African Institute of Race Relations who had just completed a six-month study of US and Canadian intergroup tensions on a Carnegie Corporation travel grant, and Hendrik van Eck.

Emory Ross, another significant name in the USSALEP leadership circle and a consultant on Africa, and Loescher met with South Africa's Ambassador Holloway in Washington in June 1955 to report on the discussions of the Haverford conference. Holloway was prudent and industrious, a character trait Loescher and Ross found favourable. In the summer of 1956, Loescher visited South Africa for the second time and discussed the exchange scheme with CB Brink, then Moderator of the Dutch Reformed Church in the Transvaal, Hendrik van Eck, who was Director of the South African state-run Industrial Development Corporation, Nic Olivier and JL Sadie of the University of Stellenbosch, and Leo Marquard and Quintin Whyte of the South African Institute of Race Relations.[291]

In all these engagements, Loescher and his Afrikaner counterparts were courting each other and sussing each other out. Loescher wanted the imprimatur of South Africa's leading Afrikaner intellectuals and business and religious leaders on US policy on South Africa; and he wanted to know whether the United States could count on the commitment of moderate Afrikaners to a course of gradual change. He said what his South African counterparts wanted to hear. As a group, they were confident; all they needed was a higher purpose, a statement of values that would unite them.

Unlike hawkish conservatives in the US State Department, liberals like Loescher seemed to feel passionately that South Africa could be transformed

---

291 USSALEP, AAI Prospectus, 1958, Wits Historical Papers USSALEP Collection.

by democracy. They had their reasons for wanting to believe this, reasons that the South Africans didn't entirely share. For Loescher, the prime mover was what South Africa represented: "A microcosm of what would soon confront America and Europe, beyond colonialism, in their relations with the rest of the world," he would later recall.[292]

In this grim world view, liberal human rights do-gooders might not have liked the tendency to undermine the great moral questions of the day, but the survival of friendly regimes like the National Party government in South Africa was essential for resistance to black majoritarianism and communism. There the two sides converged.

Interviewed by a journalist months after the Athens gathering, Loescher, by then Programme Director and General Secretary of USSALEP, scoffed at the notion of black majority rule. "Black Africans are not ready for liberalism," he once remarked.[293]

And therein lay the rub. The marriage between US liberals and Afrikaner nationalists was an unnatural one – of Washington and Pretoria, hawkish Cold Warriors and liberal internationalists, Afrikaner nationalism and liberal capitalism – that only the strange circumstances of the Cold War could have brought into being. The diplomacy of combatting communism offered both sides a pretext – a common cause based on a vague idea of democracy that wasn't majority rule, an idea that was about individual and group rights and, above all, minority rule. They also converged on a strategic objective: Verwoerd had to go.

They were likely right. All the drama, the intense heat of argument, may have carried a special thrill for Washington insiders, but there is no known record that liberals like Loescher were aware of the dark undercurrents coursing through USSALEP.

*

If Loescher was USSALEP's impresario, with one degree of separation from everyone who mattered in South Africa, it was Alan Pifer who helped carry the fight into South Africa to 'modify' its rigid apartheid policies, funding the 1957 USSALEP founding conference at Wingspread and corralling the boundaries of what was, in effect, a foreign-intervention programme in

---

292 Ibid., Loescher memorandum.
293 Ibid.

Athens. If one thought of South Africa then as a limited diplomatic venture for the United States, as opposed to a covert political–military undertaking, Pifer certainly had the right stuff.

More than anyone, he personified the Cold War liberal insurgent, staging frequent educational and cultural exchanges between the United States and South Africa, preparing to groom a generation of new Cold Warriors to build a new axis of power in the West. There emerged then, in 1963, a dominant current of liberals, backed by Kennedy – albeit divided among themselves between militant anti-communists in Eleanor Roosevelt's Americans for Democratic Action group, who advocated aggressive sanctions and United Nations (UN) intervention, and Kennedy who felt that the Verwoerd government could be overthrown neither by violent internal revolution nor by military force from outside the country.

On 22 July that year, Pifer, a dyed-in-the-wool Kennedy loyalist, told a gathering of USSALEP Joint Management Committee members at Wingspread that he "could not visualise confrontation with South Africa"; neither could he imagine sanctions against South Africa that would prove effective. "During the past six years you from South Africa have been obliged to witness a steady hardening of world opinion toward your country. The Republic, sad to say, has become something of a pariah among nations, vilified and condemned ... But can we seriously contemplate an embargo on this trade or, on the other hand, a refusal of the nations of the world to buy South African producers, especially gold?" he asked.[294]

By the time of the Athens gathering a year later, Pifer and Loescher were the closest thing to soft-boiled liberals who would lead the liberal cause and, Kennedy thought, just the means he needed to shift the White House from the rigid confrontational Cold War regimen in non-aligned countries of the Eisenhower era. Kennedy was not against gradual reform in South Africa if it brought the kind of stability that would help ease trade relations with the United States. But he stood firmly against the mad delusions of regime change that his hard-line opponents in Washington seemed to nurture.

*

By 1966, the liberal consensus that saw education and culture as primary weapons in the Cultural Cold War was breaking down. Whether Loescher

---

294 USSALEP minutes, 22 July 1963, Wits Historical Papers USSALEP Collection.

was aware of it or not, the USSALEP gambit had become a philosophical brief for Richard Nixon's emerging doctrine of US unilateralism: the expansion of the national interest by exporting US values to the Third World, beginning in South Africa.

There was a little blinkered partisanship in this thinking, but there was also an ideological disposition, for it drew on a powerful set of ideas that came out of a marriage between one of the 20th century's greatest movements, the movement for human rights and US nationalism, or 'neo-conservatism' as it came to be known. This new kind of war would later be known as 'humanitarian intervention', and in the United States its advocates acquired the militant moniker 'liberal interventionists' or, in shorthand, 'liberal hawks'. Until that moment, most liberals' preferred institution for doing the intervening was the UN.

By the close of the 1950s, scenes of repression in South Africa – of raids on white liberal students' and black nationalist leaders' homes, arrests and bannings, and, moreover, the illegal occupation of South West Africa by Pretoria – had shown that the UN wasn't up to the task. Nor was it given the necessary push by the powers that sat on the Security Council, especially the United States.

Through the 1950s and early sixties, the UN provided an anti-colonial Soviet Union with a platform for solidarity with the Third World, and the apartheid regime was an obvious target. Moreover, the Soviet–Third World alliance was instrumental in persuading the UN General Assembly to pass a series of covenants and declarations on human rights issues. South Africa provided a crucial benchmark in this context: the country was perceived as the last outpost of a decaying colonialism, given the concentration of political power in the hands of the white minority and the dependence of the latter on the oppression of the black majority for the production of wealth in a capitalist economy.

Yet, efforts to cast South Africa as a pariah state notwithstanding, there was very little the UN did to force change in Pretoria. For US liberals like Loescher and Pifer, ongoing repression in South Africa demanded a swift response; and if it wasn't going to come from the UN it would have to come from the United States.

In the tense atmosphere of the Cold War, humanitarian intervention carried the odour of 'vital strategic interest' that tended to dissolve in a mist of high purpose. There emerged in US foreign policy terms like 'nation-building' as a kind of existential choice between Western-style democracy and authoritarianism. Loescher was the smiling, humanitarian face of US covert action. Unlike Pifer, he did not want to know about Washington's dark side; he certainly did not look hard enough, he later admitted, because the CIA's covert operations were "hard to imagine" only where it was ideologically suspect and politically inconvenient. After all, this was the secret 'hard' core of Washington, the inner sanctum to which only a few top officials, whose service dated back to the 1940s, had access.[295] CIA Director, Richard Helms, in his own patronising way, tried to explain this during his appearance before the Church Committee investigation years later into the Cuban invasion. "When you establish a clandestine service [like] the Central Intelligence Agency," he enlightened them, "you establish something that was totally different from anything else in the United States government. Whether it's right that you should have it, or wrong that you should have it, it works under different rules ... than any other part of the government."[296] The statement was an eerily prescient description of the limits of democratic power.

Here, then, was the heart of the USSALEP plan laid bare. With its language about US dominance, moderate coalitions, and new spheres of influence, the Eisenhower administration poured the foundation for what became known as the Cultural Cold War, and its first test in Africa: apartheid. The Kennedy administration built the intellectual scaffolding for the conduct of this war.

USSALEP may have been born of a desire by US liberals for educational and cultural exchanges between South Africa and the United States, but the operation was the CIA's from beginning to end.

---

295 Tablot, D, *Brothers: The Hidden History of the Kennedy Years* (London: Pocket Books, 2007), p. 112.
296 Ibid.

PART IV

The Black Student Movement

1968–1976

CHAPTER 13

Psychological liberation

THE RISE OF BLACK CONSCIOUSNESS

He knows
he must carry a pass
He don't care for politics
He don't go to church
He knows Sobukwe
He knows Mandela
They in Robben Island
So what? That's not my business

THESE LINES, PRINTED IN 'THE DETRIBALISED' SOME TIME IN THE EARLY
1970s (recounted by Lynn Maree),[297] are about the indignity of a black man
who can barely write. In Maree's own declamation of the excerpt, the man
is accosted by stories about murder, rape and robbery in newspapers and
comes to believe that black proponents of national liberation are violent and
godless, a barb clearly meant to parody the inferiority complex that Bantu
education gave black people. The man seems convinced that subversion of
the apartheid system is no business of his; so he defers to white domination.

Here we have the egregious legacy of Bantu education. In the National
Party's drive to shape black consciousness, liberated somehow from personal
ambition and collective redemption, the apartheid authorities had devoted
enormous effort to wiping out black self-worth and the spirit of liberation
that had been growing since the 1940s. The system sought to eliminate all
progressive political and ideological influences and cultural practices beyond
the control of the state. Black students were instead prepared for a realistic place as "hewers of wood and drawers of water" in white-dominated

---

297 See Maree, L, 'The hearts and minds of the people', in Kallaway (n ‡ above), p. 158.

society. Years later, Steve Biko would recall how basic humanity came to define black self-awareness in the bosom of the official system. "Black people under the Smuts government were oppressed but they were still men," he wrote in September 1970. "But the type of black man we have today has lost his manhood. Reduced to an obliging shell, he looks with awe at the white power structure and accepts what he regards as the 'inevitable position'."[298]

The whole atmosphere, reinforced by indoctrination and penalties, shrouded the apartheid system in paternalistic garb. The official orthodoxy was strict and severe: people went to gaol, or worse, for seeking greener pastures beyond the Bantustans, or daring to challenge their subordinate station in white society.

To the world, these projects might have seemed like preposterous delusions. But, for its architects, there was some value in maintaining the segregated education system, and even fewer radical ways of imagining the future. The writer Gail Gerhart, who spent several years during the 1970s researching the impact of the education system on black student politics, recalled that the African problem during the 1960s might always have been "identity-confusion, fear and a resigned apathy about the future, but at no time had these problems been more starkly apparent than from the great silence and obscurity of the post-Sharpeville clampdown on black opposition, when all black initiatives and voices of dissent had been forcibly stilled".[299] "The National Party strategy," Gerhart went on, "aimed at conditioning and coercing blacks into acceptance of apartheid policies, appeared to be at least achieving the desired effects."[300]

Even so, the basic human instinct for dignity and fairness survived in this hostile climate. By the mid-1960s, some black students had begun to brush with another consciousness. To this generation, the psychological liberation of black people was necessary because Bantu education had failed. It had created so many wants and repressive apparatuses that people had to find a way out of the cult of psychological demolition before liberating themselves from the economic trappings of the system. And when they looked around for a way to think about the uncharted era that began since the institutionalisation of apartheid, there was one available.

*

298 Quoted in Gerhart, G, *Black Power in South Africa: The Evolution of an Ideology* (University of California Press, 1979), p. 286.
299 Ibid.
300 Ibid.

The role black consciousness came to play on university campuses was nei-ther inevitable, nor was it merely an ephemeral thing. It started as a war of ideas that bears a startling resemblance to the present. To understand how and why it came to be such a potent force among students, we have to trace its origins.

The year 1960 found white liberals brooding over the decline of the Liberal Party in the face of an ascendant, virulent Afrikaner nationalism. In the 13 years since the National Party's victory in 1948, white South Africa – both Afrikaners and English – benefited from probably unrepeatable cir-cumstances. A kind of social contract was struck: the two factions of the white ruling establishment were joined by opposition to black majority rule and the spectre of communism. Overnight, they were part of a new order in which the National Party became the visible superstructure of the Verwoerd regime. But, in 1960, old antagonisms, long subdued by the unifying ethos of economic privilege, began to resurface. It seemed to start as a pragmatic political response by English-speaking white liberals to a hardening of Afrikaner-nationalist attitudes to the race question.

The government was at the moment pressing ahead with discriminatory laws which would constrict every aspect of life for blacks to independent homelands,[301] even though they lacked the physical cohesiveness to make political or economic independence a viable or believable concept. The expulsion and relocation of thousands of black dwellers in urban 'black spots' to other designated, racially segregated, peri-urban dormitories called 'townships' was yet another part of the grand-apartheid scheme. Hundreds more, including Nelson Mandela, were banned along with their organisations.

Emboldened, at least partially, by English liberal diffidence in the face of an emerging global consensus on apartheid, Verwoerd won a fight that year against liberal opposition forces of the United Party to put a 'republican' seal on his government's foreign-policy goals. In October 1960, a whites-only referendum decided that the Union of South Africa, consummated in 1910 when the Afrikaner republics of the Orange Free State and Transvaal and the British protectorates of Natal and the Cape united under the Union of South Africa, would thence become a republic. Verwoerd now had permis-sion to change the country's status from a constitutional monarchy under the British Crown to a republic with its own head of state. The government,

---

301 See n 161 above.

in effect, was given a mandate to tighten the screws of apartheid on the country's 12 million black citizens. In May 1961, a date that marked the signing of the Treaty of Vereeniging that had brought the Anglo-Boer War to an end in 1902, South Africa became a republic.

Abroad, it also signalled a change in attitude to South Africa and brought international opprobrium to apartheid into the open, marking the beginning of South Africa's long spell out in the cold. A rash of protests countrywide that thronged front pages of newspapers was to add revulsion to the disapproval through 1960, including international trade sanctions.

For English-speaking whites, the country they had known – the land of milk and honey, of gold and diamonds, of empire – had vanished, destroyed as utterly as if wiped out by a foreign enemy's bullets.

There were bullets alright. But they would come from within the country.

IT WAS A TRANQUIL DAY ON 21 MARCH 1960 WHEN THE FIRST LIGHT OF DAY began to shine on a black township near Johannesburg called Sharpeville; but the mood that morning was hushed and anxious. Bus drivers did not report for work; and people were urged by the Pan Africanist Congress (PAC), which had earlier split from the African National Congress (ANC), to march on the local police station and demand arrest in an act of defiance against the country's Bantustan system and pass laws. At midday, hundreds of police reinforcements carrying semi-automatic rifles arrived in Saracen armoured vehicles. Shortly afterwards, a scuffle broke out at the gate which breached the wire fence of the station.[302] The day ended with 67 black demonstrators killed and 187 wounded by police in a shooting spree that lasted 30 seconds. Graphic photos of the dead and the ensuing chaos were flashed around the world in media reports. The editors of *Newsweek* magazine ran the story on the cover and coupled it with a long feature on the political and social status of Afro-Americans and the burgeoning civil-rights movement that had been sparked by a sit-in by black US students at a Woolworths cafeteria on 1 February that year.

All that March, stories of massive clampdowns on black protest organisations and of escalating state repression thronged newspapers. Beginning with the PAC, security police stormed into a dozen high-profile cases, for

---

302 See Tom Lodge's account as quoted in Swanepoel (n 204 above), p. 25.

the first time finding themselves involved in intelligence work that had an anti-communist profile.

The year 1960 alone brought 27 major cases, by far more than the number reported in any previous year. The clampdown prompted the liberal *Rand Daily Mail* to begin charting the arrests in a periodic column. As word spread of South Africa facing utter isolation, the prospect within the ANC of overthrowing the state grew for the first time since earlier acts of petition aimed at reaching an accommodation with the country's all-white rulers.

In this new political melee, black nationalism and communism were becoming wedged in an underground movement fomenting armed revolution. On 16 December 1961, the day of the republic, the ANC launched Umkhonto we Sizwe (Spear of the Nation) and set the exiled liberation movement on a collision course with apartheid. This was something new. The decade that followed Sharpeville scrambled everything and knocked something ajar in the liberal world view. Black people were challenging not only their oppression but also the liberal idea of their accommodation to symbolic protests. Though blacks were free to join the Liberal and Progressive parties until 1968, it was whites in these organisations who for the most part arrogated to themselves the task of articulating African demands. In the wake of Sharpeville, African students loyal to the ANC had formed the African Students Association (ASA); PAC students had formed the African Students' Union of South Africa (ASUSA); and students loyal to the Trotskyite Non-European Unity Movement had formed other teacher organisations in the Western Cape and Natal. None of these organisations, however, had survived since identification with banned movements was hazardous, university authorities were hostile to student political groups, and the groups themselves were divided. And so, for want of other political outlets, many black students had, in the period 1961 to 1964, begun focusing attention on the National Union of South African Students (NUSAS), a multiracial liberal organisation with membership drawn from white English-speaking universities.

The combination of the government's secession from the British Commonwealth of Nations, the banning of liberation organisations, and the arrest of prominent black political leaders made it possible for a group of liberals in NUSAS and the Liberal Party to contemplate, and even advocate, the use of force for the first time. There was more than a little brinkmanship in this thinking as the relative silence that followed the state's clampdown created a leadership vacuum. There was also idealism; for it drew on an idea that came straight out of the 20th century's movement for human rights.

*

The white student rebellion of the 1960s was a slow-moving but threatening tide for liberalism, often expressed in later years in acts of sabotage that fell just short of frontal confrontation with the state. Glenn Moss, a NUSAS student leader in the late 1960s who later became a 'New Left' activist and academic at the University of the Witwatersrand (Wits), has chronicled the 'white radicals', a group of young NUSAS student activists during the 1960s and early seventies, and how they adapted to the leadership vacuum created by the banning of liberation organisations – while in most cases cynically rejecting the more radical ideological inclinations of black nationalism and communism. They were, Moss recalled, essentially liberal insurgents who feared that, unless they demonstrated active opposition to apartheid, the field of opposition would be open to communists.[303]

By 1963/1964, sporadic acts of sabotage had drawn some prominent NUSAS leaders away from middle-of-the-road liberalism of white rank-and-file members into the illegal African Resistance Movement; they began responding instead to the mood of the black majority that was angry and impatient for meaningful action. Addressing a gathering he believed was a closed NUSAS seminar at Botha's Hill in April 1964, NUSAS President Jonty Driver called on students to turn from symbolic protest to real action for liberation. In effect, recalled Moss,[304] Driver was asking students to accept a proposal to radically transform NUSAS into an extra-legal revolutionary organisation. Reports of the speech reached the media and were soon followed by negative reactions from the authorities and not a handful of white students. Excoriating the oppositional role NUSAS had begun to play by 1963, then Minister of Justice, John Vorster, in a speech in May that year described the organisation as a "cancer in the life of the nation".[305] Threats of disaffiliation by students followed; Driver was censured at the July 1964 NUSAS annual conference; and the organisation began a firm swing toward the right, largely confining itself for several years to symbolic multiracial activities and protests against government infringements on the

303 See Moss (n 175 above), 'Chapter 2: Radical changes to liberal politics'.
304 Ibid.
305 Quoted in Gerhart (n 298 above), pp. 257-258.

right of universities to admit black students without ministerial permission. Organised under the umbrella of NUSAS, liberal English-speaking universities like Wits and the University of Cape Town (UCT) had confined oppositional voices to issues of academic freedom, arguing that the passage of the Extension of University Education Act through Parliament in 1959 struck at the core of the right of universities to admit and reach whomever they deemed appropriate regardless of race, creed or religion and without state interference.

In the restraint and relative silence of state repression, NUSAS protests rarely linked apartheid education to broader sociopolitical issues, although some students and academics worked tirelessly to do this through the 1960s. As the doors for black expression and activism closed, a new breed of black students had begun to see that NUSAS's timidity failed to provide them with a political home. For liberal whites, verbal protests and symbolic racial mixing were seen, in Gerhart's recording of her interviews with black student leaders during that period, as the "outer limit of action, disguising an unconscious attachment to the status quo".[306]

The real action was elsewhere; 'bush colleges', as they came to be known, would be the next promising wave of black student protests against apartheid education.

*

In 1967, as rumours of black student opposition inside NUSAS were making the pro-forma rounds on white campuses, a small group of black students had swung round to the idea that racially separate universities were not such a bad thing. They were breeding grounds for anti-state criticism and potential mobilising platforms for something better. They were now willing to turn their energies to the system of Bantustans, urban Bantu councils, and government-created institutions of state planning.

Many of them, originating in the liberal ethos of NUSAS during the 1960s, watched the Cold War era unfold in African countries as a battle for hearts and minds, the civil rights and subsequent rise of the black-power movements in the United States, and the student revolutions in Germany and France. They watched in fascination, and, while NUSAS leaders were turning to the right, they swung sharply to the left.

---

306 Ibid., pp. 258-259.

The great ideological concern of first-generation black consciousness student leaders was the same concern as that of the apartheid government – liberalism. They had been studying at segregated universities since the mid-1960s, but were critically aware of being manipulated and therefore cynical of what was being taught. From their vantage point, they saw that student politics and organisation was increasingly conservative. The years of state repression had not only emptied student politics of the big picture; they had also left black students and universities bereft of leadership. It was also a time when black students saw the necessity to free themselves from white liberal paternalism. But within the prevailing politics of NUSAS they had as yet only a faint notion of their collective power.

Moreover, they argued that the clampdown on NUSAS during the early 1960s did not teach liberals the lesson that NUSAS had tragically over-reached and needed to know the limits of white student leadership. They concluded instead that NUSAS had embraced "a liberal orthodoxy linked to privilege and hypocrisy".[307] There was, of course, no single liberal orthodoxy, Moss remarked in his account of the period. There was a common assumption among white liberal students, he recalled, that "Afrikaners were responsible for apartheid and that the civilising tendencies of English-speakers – the assimilation of blacks into English culture – might slowly erode the worst tendencies of racial inequality and prejudice".[308] Most white liberal students, Moss went on to argue, attending the almost exclusively white English-medium universities in the 1960s "understood apartheid as a consequence of racial ideology imposed on the society by Afrikaner nationalism".[309] Part of the ideological challenge by the young black activists to liberalism was their rejection of this assumption – in particular, the assumption that English-speaking whites derived no real benefit from racial domination and the token incorporation of small numbers of black people into organisations and events. "Our unwillingness to fight," they tended to say, "only encouraged black subservience."

As the 1960s stumbled along – the institutionalisation of university apartheid, the unilateral declaration of the republic, the banning of political organisations, the turn to armed struggle by Umkhonto we Sizwe, the Sharpeville massacre – they began a daring attempt, perhaps far more audacious than many of them could have imagined at the time, to challenge not

---

307 Quoted in Moss (n 175 above), p. 36.
308 Ibid.
309 Ibid.

only apartheid education but its liberal cover, too. By 1967, the group gradually began to take shape as a loose caucus in NUSAS. In statements released
by the group, they warned that black student activism had grown provoca-
tively weak. Accommodating themselves to white leadership was therefore
a sign of defeatism.

These warnings were laced with anger at soft-headed 'liberal do-gooders'
who had lost their nerve. The tone was personal and, in a sense, natural; it
owed something to the Fanonian version of 'psychological revolution' on
which so many black-consciousness activists had nursed. In their radical
world view, there wasn't much room for human rights within the white liberal
bloc, especially when NUSAS put talk of 'equality', as an abstract typo-
logy, at the centre of its campaigns. The sentiment of black students within
NUSAS, as one participant later recalled, was "complete disillusionment".[310]

This frustration among black students found little focus or articulation,
however, until 1968 when a few students in NUSAS began to seriously analyse and reflect on their political predicament. Although never a member of
NUSAS, a key figure of the group was a student named Sathasivan 'Saths'
Cooper. After matriculating from Sastri College, one of the better-heeled
Indian high schools in Durban, in 1967, Cooper enrolled a year later for
a Bachelor of Arts degree at the University College on Salisbury Island in
Durban. As a young firebrand, Cooper was against the government motion
for the imminent renaming of the College to the University of Durban-
Westville. He saw this as yet another plank in the emerging edifice of
apartheid state planning, he recalled in speaking to me, "where black ghettos were becoming breeding grounds for mental ghettos".

Politics gained the upper hand in the young Cooper's life at an early stage.
In the repressive world of apartheid, Sastri College was something of an
incubator for anti-apartheid activism. Cooper tolerated no slight, no insult,
and was already rebellious by the time he entered the campus, recalled his
younger brother, Kumarasen. In his first year at university, Cooper knew the
ways of the system. Brimming with resentment, he came to the place on the
official form for racial classification. He could enter either the nationality
of his grandparents, who came to South Africa from India, or his parents,
who, as far as he was concerned, were 'black South Africans'. Cooper wrote
'black', and the entry deepened his woes. It was a strange twist of fate. The
surname 'Cooper' was an Anglicised version of 'Kapoor'. Cooper recalled

---

310 Interview with the author, Johannesburg, May 2015.

that his father had changed the name to gain greater acceptance and opportunity in white South Africa. And yet, here was Saths Cooper, his career path already limited as a South African of Indian ancestry, now in the firing line of the state and, to all intents, excluded by the system from almost any prospect of upward social mobility for writing 'black'. "After that, the die was cast," Cooper told me with a wry smile. "The state didn't like jokes."

It was no joke. By the time Cooper began his first year of studies, the University College was designated an Indian campus. He soon found himself engaging students from various black campuses and playing a leading role in the formation of the Student Representative Council (SRC) at the college. When I met Cooper in January 2016 for one of our regular breakfasts at a restaurant in Killarney, Johannesburg, he told me that being black, no matter what the government had designated various ethnic groups in its grand-apartheid blueprint, was a state of mind. "In South Africa," he once recalled, "black consciousness was a way of identifying subjectively with the conditions we found ourselves in objectively at the time. We rose above any narrow ethnic or tribal definition because the apartheid state was busy increasing the Bantustans in our country ... to further remove people from collective action and collective identification. So black consciousness in fact comes in as a cleavage during the incipient stages of 'Bantustanisation'."[311]

The dawn of 1969 found Cooper at a dead end. Suspended and eventually expelled from the university for his political beliefs, his rebellious instincts were now circumscribed by a court order prohibiting expelled students from active involvement in liberation politics. The following year, 1970, the South African government denied him a passport to study overseas, where he had received a scholarship.[312] "The state created conditions that blocked all avenues," he later said to me, his eyes still burning from the memory. "I couldn't study abroad. I couldn't earn a living. In fact, there wasn't much I *could* do in the stifling atmosphere of the time."

All doors but one were closed: underground resistance. And so, his bitterness deepening further, Cooper plunged headlong into full-time political activities. Through campus politics he had already been meeting frequently with fellow activists Harry Nengwekhulu, Strini Moodley and Barney Pityana; and it was through their discussions that the philosophy of black consciousness emerged. It was also this group that had been urging a move

---

311 Interview with Cooper, 14 April 2003.
312 For more on this, see http://www.sahistory.org.za/people/dr-sathasivan-saths-cooper#sthash.
   BcLdZtzR.dpuf.

by black universities away from the liberal NUSAS. The most notable figure within the group was a young University of Natal student named Stephen Bantu 'Steve' Biko.

*

In Biko, black students found their champion. Born in 1946 in the small town of King William's Town in the Eastern Cape, Biko's baptism into revolutionary politics had come as a teenager when, in 1963, his older brother, a student at Lovedale High School, was arrested as a suspected Poqo activist and gaoled for nine months. Interrogated by the police and expelled from Lovedale, where he himself had been a student for only three months because of his brother's activities, Biko cultivated a strong resentment to white authority. It was an attitude he carried with him in 1964 when he entered St Francis College, a Catholic boarding school at Mariannhill in Natal and one of the few remaining private high schools open to Africans in South Africa.[313]

Even in the liberal atmosphere of St Francis, it seemed to Biko that thought-control was the norm. Christian principles had impressed the young man, as did the ideal of an eventual integrated society. But he was not satisfied, Gail Gerhart recalled of her interview with Biko in the early 1970s, "to have any white try to influence his thinking about the precise detail of either ends or means when it came to the future of Africans".[314]

In 1966, Biko enrolled for a degree in medicine at the University of Natal 'non-white' medical school, familiarly known as Wentworth. This was a rare feat for blacks generally. For decades, teaching was the main profession open to African university graduates, given the restrictions placed on black entrance into technical, scientific, civil service or business careers. Starting in the 1940s, however, limited opportunities for entrance into medicine and law began to open up. Until the mid-1960s, almost all older African doctors and lawyers had been educated abroad; but the road to success in these professions was arduous and the number who managed to earn degrees was still very small. For the few who did qualify, the rewards were great.

More important for Biko than any measure of class distinction or education were psychological differences – the relative detachment from the

---

313 See Gerhart's interview with Biko (n 298 above), pp. 259-260.
314 Ibid.

ideological and institutional reach of the state that medicine offered – which distinguished himself from the calibre of men (and they were all men) in control of the ANC. Not only did medicine and law bring more prestige and significantly higher income than teaching; they also brought independence. For, unlike teachers, who held their positions at the pleasure of the apartheid government, doctors and lawyers had the option of self-employment. To paraphrase Gerhart, black youths like Biko were determined to assert the intellectual profile of blacks not as an annexure to white civilisation but as an act of demolishing the stereotype of Africans as perpetual 'trustees' of 'superior' races.

Biko was soon elected to the SRC at Wentworth, and, through the SRC, became active in NUSAS. For black students like Biko, the main reason to join NUSAS was a cynical pragmatism: without it, there was no reasonable prospect of engagement with discriminatory laws and practices on liberal campuses. In July 1966, he attended the NUSAS annual conference as an observer, and a year later as a Wentworth delegate at the July annual conference in Grahamstown, which saw bitter reactions from black students when the host institution, Rhodes University, prohibited mixed accommodation or eating facilities at the conference. There were other issues besides: by this time, we recall, NUSAS had come to symbolise the same tired slogans as those of the Liberal Party. Its white members were widely viewed by black students as 'ladder-climbing careerists' and beneficiaries of apartheid with a certain 'paternalistic' disposition to blacks.

Cooper, who had later become a close friend and comrade of Biko's, remembered a fiery polemicist, undogmatic but highly disciplined in his thinking. He once told me that Biko increasingly began to question the allure of what he saw as "the artificial integration of student politics". In those early days, as with South African politics generally, African students were hanging back, resentful but reticent, "hiding behind white spokesmen who had been defining black grievances and goals".[315] For liberal whites, apartheid was defined as the problem; non-racialism was the scattershot antidote; and liberalism meant speaking up for black students. Repeated over and over in words and symbolism, this liberal approach, and in fact the entire liberal discourse, had to Biko's way of thinking become not an inspiration to constructive action but a defence of the status quo.

Against NUSAS's paternalism and timidity, Biko and his black-conscious-

---

315 Ibid.

ness comrades meant something far grander: confronting and defeating apartheid through psychological revolution. At the NUSAS congress in July 1967, Biko championed a battle to put a radical plank in the organisation's politics. Though he failed to convince the NUSAS leadership to focus on conscientising white students who benefited from the privileges of the apartheid system, he won the war for a new student organisation. And so it was at the NUSAS congress that Biko and some fellow medical students began to draw black students into a candid discussion of their role as second-class citizens within NUSAS.

Soon after the Grahamstown conference, Biko and a group of black students travelled to nearby Stutterheim, where a conference of the multi-racial University Christian Movement (UCM) was convened. It was at this gathering that Biko first began canvassing support for an all-black student movement that would open the floodgates of black intellectual expression and stage an open rebellion against the dominant liberal orthodoxy of NUSAS.

Out of those early engagements a new black student movement blossomed. It had begun in rebellion against NUSAS, but would soon take on an ideological form and character called 'black consciousness'.

CHAPTER 14

'A movement of blacks for blacks'

THE SOUTH AFRICAN STUDENTS' ORGANISATION

DURING THE CHRISTMAS RECESS IN DECEMBER 1968, ABOUT 30 MEMBERS of black university student representative councils (SRCs) met at a forested slope in Mariannhill just outside Durban in Natal. The place was one of the country's most placid sceneries, and also one of the tragic settings of liberal politician Alan Paton's novel, *Cry, the Beloved Country*. There was both tragedy and hope when the students gathered there: they were young men and women in their early twenties, self-confident, hopeful; but their ambitions were even younger, far beyond their experience and capacity for the task they were being called upon to accomplish. They had come to the meeting at the urging of the University Christian Movement (UCM) and Steve Biko who worried that black students dealt with politics as a 'privilege'.

The UCM, led by a Protestant minister, named Basil Moore, and Colin Collins, a Catholic priest, had by this time already lured many black students to its ranks since its founding in 1966, and had begun to show a strong interest in 'Black Theology', an African-American intellectual movement with obvious applicability in black South African churches. A number of Africans within the UCM reacted enthusiastically to Biko's oratorical performance at the Stutterheim gathering. Buoyed by the response he was getting, Biko decided to let his medical studies slide in order to organise a formal meeting of black student leaders to discuss the launch of a new organisation.

Except at the University of Natal's Wentworth medical campus, university authorities on all African campuses had refused students permission to formally affiliate to NUSAS; and so the goal of 'getting into NUSAS' had retained a certain allure for many black student leaders. A number of student leaders from Turfloop University (now the University of Limpopo) were present who had loyalties to the Pan Africanist Congress (PAC) and

African Student Union of South Africa, a student organisation formed by the PAC after Sharpeville. Their antipathies to NUSAS had always been strong, and they needed little persuasion to accept the idea of an exclusively black organisation. Asked to examine carefully the rationale for this attitude, however, pro-NUSAS students present were quickly swayed by Biko's arguments. In this group, Biko found an encouraging receptiveness to his idea of an all-black organisation.

As they gathered in the Mariannhill conference venue, they were confronted with a task far beyond their practical capabilities. In theory, some of them were already familiar with the works of Franz Fanon, Julius Nyerere, Malcolm X and WEB du Bois. But now they were being called to fire the first salvo in a psychological war for black self-assertion. They were summonsed not to rescue NUSAS but to take the radical measures NUSAS had never made. "There was no room for prevarication," recalled Saths Cooper. "What was needed was an independent organisation of black students *for* black students."[316]

At some point during the conference, Biko met privately with some young student leaders to begin drawing up the details of the new organisation. The name of SASO, the South African Students' Organisation, was chosen and plans were laid for a formal inaugural conference. When that conference met at Turfloop in July 1969, Biko was the logical choice for the position of president. Other leading figures from the outset were Barney Pityana, an ex-Fort Hare student from Port Elizabeth, Harry Nengwekhulu, Hendrik Musi, Petrus Machaka and Manana Kgware of Turfloop, Aubrey Mokoape, a medical student, and J Goolam, Saths Cooper and Strini Moodley, Indian comrades of Biko's, the former a medical student and the latter an ex-student at the Indian University College of Durban-Westville.

*

It was at the Turfloop conference that the SASO strategy rapidly took shape. Biko was, as all who knew him agree, an original thinker and trailblazing intellect; but he could also be resolute and uncompromising. He set out to accomplish nothing less than the transformation of the new organisation from a blunt abstraction into a sharp instrument for psychological liberation.

---

316 Hereinafter, all direct references to Cooper are from interviews with the author, Johannesburg, January–May 2015.

Because of lingering loyalties among many black students to NUSAS, and initial suspicions some harboured about the motives and origins of SASO, Biko and his comrades decided that an open break with NUSAS and a frontal assault on its ideology would be advisable until SASO found its feet as an organisation.

The first SASO constitution, adopted in July 1969, was accordingly his singular, huge contribution. It stated the purpose of SASO as the promotion of "contact and practical cooperation among black students studying at the affiliated centres". SASO, it stated, would "represent the non-white students nationally", noting that, "owing to circumstances beyond their control, students at some non-white centres are unable to participate in the national student organisation of this country".[317] Still, the constitution recognised NUSAS as the mother body of students generally.

By July, when SASO convened its first General Students Council at the University of Natal, this somewhat diffident stance was replaced by a harder line. Contact between SASO and such multiracial organisations as the UCM and the Institute of Race Relations was mooted, but recognition of NUSAS as a 'true' national union of students was withdrawn. SASO, declared a carefully worded resolution, was "aware that in the principles and makeup of NUSAS the black student can never find expression for the aspirations foremost in their minds".[318] Instead, the conference resolved SASO would now act "in accordance with its belief that the emancipation of the black people in this country depends entirely on the role black people themselves are prepared to play". Self-reliance was the new imprimatur. "Blacks are tired of standing at the touchlines to witness the game that they should be playing," a policy declaration stated earlier in 1970. "They want to do things for themselves and all by themselves."[319] The phrasing of these words, direct and self-assured, was Biko's.

For Biko and his SASO comrades, the task was to turn the word 'consciousness' from a listless noun into the operative verb, 'conscientise'. To students of this persuasion, the clampdown on black opposition organisations and psychological impact of decades of colonial and apartheid indoctrination wasn't an occasion for SASO to mobilise in direct action in a frontal offensive against the apartheid system. By 1970, the ideological glue which bound most students to NUSAS began weakening on NUSAS

317 Quoted in Gerhart (n 298 above), p. 262.
318 Ibid.
319 Ibid.

campuses. "Changes in attitudes," Glenn Moss recalled, "criticism of white liberals from the side of black consciousness and the growing radicalism of student action led considerable numbers of students to question their positions of relative privilege."[320] In his recollection of the times, former NUSAS activist, Martin Legassick, records that a group of white students (himself included) in NUSAS began flirting with the New Left politics of the European Marxist, Georg Lukács, just as criticism of symbolic protest politics intensified on both NUSAS and SASO campuses by the late 1960s. Moss recalled a period of heightened ferment. The new challenges to the existing order, he wrote, began developing with surprising force, despite the political defeats of the 1960s.[321]

During the years between the launch of SASO and the close of the 1960s, the accusation that SASO was 'racist' came from all directions, both from hardened liberals with a sincere commitment to non-racialism and from other opponents of the government who found it convenient to blame the new SASO 'menace' on Afrikaner nationalists. The liberal media tended to highlight the same apparent congruence of black consciousness with the apartheid philosophy and drew equally deluded conclusions. The emergence of SASO, wrote the East London *Daily Dispatch*, "is one of the sad manifestations of racist policy at Government level".[322]

At the same time, the new radicals on NUSAS campuses, including Martin Legassick, Glenn Moss, Eddie Webster, and Halton Cheadle, launched a sustained attack on the ideology of liberalism that dominated opposition politics. Most students attending the almost exclusively white English-speaking universities at the beginning of the 1970s would have understood apartheid as the consequence of racial ideology imposed on society by Afrikaner nationalism. The new radicalism insisted that talk of white society – in particular English-speaking business – derived benefit from racial discrimination and so had a stake in its survival.[323]

These students argued that apartheid liberal orthodoxy was based on a value system that included adherence to the rule of law, a belief that charity to the less fortunate was politically progressive, and that politically motivated violence should always be condemned and rejected. Additionally, here was an insistence on multiracialism as an act of faith even when this was

---

320 See Moss (n 175 above), 'Chapter 2: Radical challenges to liberal politics'.
321 Ibid.
322 Ibid.
323 See Moss (n 175 above), pp. 37-38.

based on the token incorporation of small numbers of black people into organisations and events. Multiracial activity was viewed as a political act of opposition in and of itself. Not even the vast disparities in wealth, access to resources, skills, experience and confidence, coupled with geographical separation and differences in language use, were sufficient to challenge this liberal world view.

Ideologically and materially, students from white NUSAS-affiliated campuses had every reason to limit their generational rebellions and association with a new radicalism. They were linked to the interests of the ruling elite of society through family, opportunity, ideology and the expectation of a privileged future. Sustained and radical opposition to apartheid threatened their career paths.[324] For others, campus-based opposition to apartheid in the 1960s had consequences for some of NUSAS's leadership. The government had withdrawn passports from NUSAS leaders and, in a few cases, banned them.

More than a little irony pervaded this moment. The SASO break from NUSAS was such that it had punctured the thin membrane of liberal manipulation, but which had produced results liberals wanted to avoid – a politics of left-wing radicalism. In the tense atmosphere of 1961, when liberal insurgents like John Lang were ascending the national stage, liberals, who had become known as communist 'fellow travellers', were the bogeymen for white Afrikaners. Lang's behaviour may have been more perverted anti-communism than deliberate treason, but the outcome was the same. It was cause for concern because it upset the balance of power.

The mainstream of SASO and the student movement was dedicated to conscientising black people by building self-awareness. They disliked talk of human rights and democracy by radical liberals in NUSAS who had taken to acts of sabotage in the 1960s as cases for expending blood. To SASO leaders, these were dangerous fantasies. During the initial years of the 1970s, this view pushed SASO closer to a cohesive philosophy and programme of action.

But for all the hype about SASO, the young student leaders orbiting Biko's sun may have brought certain shared assumptions, forged in opposition to NUSAS's liberalism, yet their ideas were untested. How could SASO possibly realise its mission of student mobilisation if there was no coherent idea of what psychological liberation meant? And so, in the heady onrush

---

324 Ibid., p. 48.

of events following SASO's launch came the development of certain ideas about the philosophy of black consciousness.

THE TERM 'BLACK CONSCIOUSNESS' WILL ALWAYS BE LINKED WITH OPPOSI-tion to what SASO called 'common-society liberalism'.[325] The connection is so tight that we've forgotten the history of the term.

The pivotal place black consciousness, as both a body of ideas and diasporic social movement, occupied within black protest politics rested on a particular convergence of the withdrawal of formal colonialism from Africa and the rise of liberal hegemony in anti-apartheid circles on university campuses.

When Biko countered NUSAS's multiracialism by appealing instead to the concept of an all-black organisation, he was speaking to a distant intellectual tradition in the US black-power movement. Within the United States itself, an ideology of African-American identity politics called 'Afrocentrism' gained an echo in the 1920s among a coterie of African and African-American intellectuals including WEB du Bois, who had famously declared that "the problem of the twentieth century was the colour line".[326]

Although riven by internal conflicts of one sort or another, this group of intellectuals was united by strong social bonds. One of these was a shared sense of alienation from the dominant, liberal political culture of the 1930s. Most crucially, and inextricably tied up with their other affinities, the group was bound together by its hatred of Stalinism. Converging in the retreat of British and European colonialism from the African continent were the underpinnings of a post-war US global governance architecture that sup-planted New Deal-style liberalism with an international order of ideology and culture in which ideas of decolonisation were to become universal to anti-colonial liberation movements in Africa.

Like Du Bois, whom most African-American intellectuals had passed through, several of them tried hard to invent new forms of radicalism in the United States by embracing the class politics of the anti-Stalinist left. During the civil-rights protests in the United States after the 1950s, their peculiar

---

325 Gerhart (n 298 above), p. 271.
326 See 'Du Bois and the question of the color line: Race and class in the age of globalisation', *Socialism and Democracy Online*, 19 April 2011. Accessed at http://sdonline.org/33/du-bois-and-the-question-of-the-color-line-race-and-class-in-the-age-of-globalization/.

combination of fervent anti-Stalinism and cultural elitism wedded the African-American intellectuals with radical intellectuals emerging in Africa in the midst of the decolonisation movements sweeping the continent. These movements were by this time constituted (on the one hand) by anachronistic hierarchies of their own societies and foreign rule, which was itself much too complicit with those hierarchies. On the other hand, they were inspired by the radical side of European modernity: the Enlightenment ideas of secular reason and the right of every social entity to emancipate itself through the exercise of that reason; the ideas of the Bolshevik Revolution which had exploded upon the world just as these mass movements were emerging.

Within this determinate repertoire of 'progressiveness' was the American Society of African Culture (AMSAC), formed in June 1957 with the aid of Richard Davis. Although the old form of radical leftist engagement with African affairs by Pan Africanists like Du Bois in the United States and George Padmore in the Caribbean was by now more or less squelched, a new kind of 'cultural nationalism' amidst the general outbreak of national liberation movements across large areas of the former colonies and semi-colonies was rising in the United States on a wave of civil-rights protests – one that celebrated black identity, not to achieve integration into Western culture but in defiance of it.[327] Identified after the mid-1960s by the slogan 'Black Power', this new mood was most powerfully expressed in the United States during the early years of the decade by the radical black nationalist Malcolm X.

Gradually accreting out of these gatherings were incipient black consciousness forms of organised agitation to colonialism around very real possibilities for sorting through the twin correlates of tactics and strategy.

*

"A time had come when blacks had to formulate their own thinking," Biko mused at one point, "unpolluted by ideas emanating from a group with lots at stake in the status quo."[328] The black-consciousness slogan had been to heighten the confidence of black students in themselves; and indeed the idea had touched thousands. But without an organised formation, the relative merits of such ideas would remain mere exhortations crafted out of

---

327 For more on this, see Wilford (n 222 above).
328 Quoted in Stubbs, A, *Steve Biko, 1946–77 – I Write What I Like* (Johannesburg: Heinemann Educational Publishers, 1979), p. 10.

University of Cape Town student, Chumani Maxwele, on the concrete plinth that used to house Cecil Rhodes's statue. 11 April 2015.
©Gallo/Sunday Times/Esa Alexander

Cecil John Rhodes. ©Shutterstock/Everett Historical

The Cecil John Rhodes statue is removed at the University of Cape Town on 9 April 2015.
©Gallo/Roger Sedres

PW Botha (left) and Prime Minister, Dr HF Verwoerd (right), 14 December 1959.
©Gallo/Die Burger/Media24

Drum magazine covers celebrating black consciousness at an Arts on Main gallery in Maboneng, Johannesburg. (Left to right) Kwame Nkrumah, Muhammed Ali and Steve Biko. ©Shutterstock/nicolasdecorte

A rally at Curries Fountain Stadium in Durban,
25 September 1974. ©Saths Cooper

Jay Naidoo at the University of California,
Los Angeles, 8 October 2013. ©Shutterstock/s_bukley

Saths Cooper (left) on 20 December 1982, the day of his release from Robben Island, accompanied
by *The World* journalist, Farook Khan. ©Saths Cooper

Student occupation
of Senate House,
University of the
Witwatersrand,
21 October 2015.
©WitsFeesMustFall

Shaeera Kalla
(left) with Wits
student leadership,
21 October 2015.
©WitsFeesMustFall

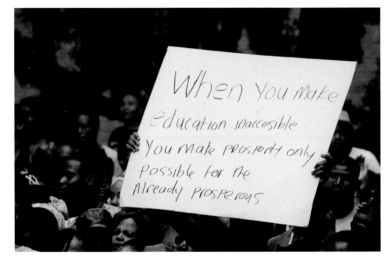

Protest poster,
University of the
Witwatersrand,
21 October 2015.
©WitsFeesMustFall

Students unfurl a
banner remembering
Marikana, Senate
House, University of
the Witwatersrand,
21 October 2015.
©WitsFeesMustFall

Protest poster,
University of the
Witwatersrand,
21 October 2015.
©WitsFeesMustFall

Wits students
block traffic in
Braamfontein,
Johannesburg,
21 October 2015.
©WitsFeesMustFall

Student–Worker
alliance over
outsourcing,
University of the
Witwatersrand,
21 October 2015.
©WitsFeesMustFall

Poster calling for
the fall of Blade
Nzimande at the
University of
Johannesburg,
21 October 2015.
©WitsFeesMustFall

Demonstration
at the University
of Johannesburg,
24 October 2015.
©WitsFeesMustFall

Demonstration at the University of   Protest poster, 24 October 2015. ©WitsFeesMustFall
Johannesburg, 24 October 2015. ©WitsFeesMustFall

Protestors at the University of the Witwatersrand, 29 October 2015. ©WitsFeesMustFall

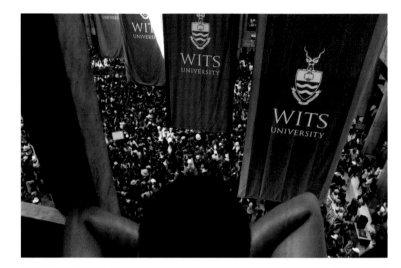

Occupation of
Senate House,
University of the
Witwatersrand,
29 October 2015.
©WitsFeesMustFall

Another poster
addressing higher
education minister,
Blade Nzimande,
University of the
Witwatersrand,
29 October 2015.
©WitsFeesMustFall

Students join
workers in a picket
against outsourcing,
University of the
Witwatersrand,
29 October 2015.
©WitsFeesMustFall

a rhetoric of 'identity' and typical of the indeterminate 'placelessness' of amorphous 'movements' rather than practical codes, norms and institutions upon which a more identifiable black consciousness could be built.

The inauguration of SASO in July 1969 was a direct response to this challenge: an expression of both the desire for black leadership and the organisational capacity for coordinated action against the psychological condition of colonialism. They had come to the realisation that opposition to liberalism was not enough; no movement could be based solely on a negative platform. Just as the PAC a decade earlier had turned to the ideological formulations of Ghana's first post-independence president Kwame Nkrumah and the December 1958 All African Peoples' Conference in Accra, Ghana, so SASO, too, in its efforts to construct a positive ideology of militant self-reliance began to actively shop for ideas in the black world outside South Africa. At SASO's inception, this voyage of self-discovery was already practically underway, and by 1970 it had resulted in the identification of SASO with the well-articulated ideology of black consciousness.

Where, though, to find the raw material for the developing philosophy?

In the 1960s, Cooper said to me, radical literature was a premium for blacks in South Africa. "But some of us in SASO had already encountered these African writings and turned naturally to them as a source of ideas," he said. Cooper recalled several individuals standing out for the important part they played in the decolonisation movement. Particularly influential in lending both content and method to the ideology of black consciousness were the writings of the Algerian revolutionary and psychologist, Franz Fanon. Fanon was the archetypal intellectual: among the brightest of his generation. Some of his work had become available in South Africa by 1968. Most widely read was *The Wretched of the Earth* in which he analyses settler colonialism and the psychological consequences for rulers and ruled. Having rejected as 'neocolonial' the class politics of New Left European Marxism, led by Nicos Poulantzas and Louis Althusser, Fanon's major contribution to African politics was in the realm of black 'psychological liberation' as a condition for violent revolution. Most influential, perhaps, may have been Fanon's cynical views on political morality, which he regarded in the colonial context of the times as wholly determined by self-interest. The need to dispense with self-serving definitions of good and evil; the desirability of destroying pretence and popularising racial conflict as a prelude to radical change; the rejection of gradual solutions designed by the powerful to blunt the anger of the oppressed; a dismissal of petty bourgeois blacks anxious to step into the shoes of the exploiter as an act of 'social treason' – all these features of Fanon's canon also enter into the writings of SASO leaders on black consciousness.

Less visible, but arguably as influential on Biko and his comrades, were the literature and political writings of Cheikh Anta Diop and Léopold Senghor on Negritude, Kenneth Kaunda on African humanism, and Julius Nyerere on self-reliance and *Ujamaa,* or African socialism. Nyerere's 1967 Arusha Declaration on self-reliance rang true, wrote Barney Pityana in 1971, when it stated, "We have been oppressed a great deal; we have been exploited a great deal; and we have been disregarded a great deal. It is our weakness being oppressed, exploited and disregarded. Now we want a revolution – a revolution which brings to an end our weakness [so] that we are never again exploited, oppressed or humiliated."[329]

Men like Biko, Pityana and Cooper had daring and smarts. To the emerging ideas on Negritude and self-reliance, they added a quality of their own. To the extent that there had been a conceptual void in the general articulation of liberation in the ideological debate, it is best conceived as Biko saw the challenge of the second half of the 20th century: 'psychological liberation'. Accordingly, Biko felt that conscientisation was the first step towards physical liberation at a time when Verwoerdian apartheid had been institutionalised in universities.

At various times, SASO leaders met secretly in the stultifying political conditions of the time to discuss the concept of psychological liberation. As state repression intensified, the idea grew more ambitious. For a long time they debated, often into the early hours of the morning, whether the liberation cause could be advanced by such Eurocentric concepts as class consciousness, which meant acceptance of the very bourgeois order in which the black working class was invested. Later, they concluded that class consciousness, following Fanon's analysis, was a bourgeois concept. Still later, they spent many days contemplating the prospect of psychological liberation. They had been nurtured by Fanon's ideas, but they had other sources of inspiration as well. They had access to radical texts, the dog-eared or mimeographed manuscripts that were officially prohibited but secretly distributed from hand to hand. "We would receive a copy and read it overnight in safe settings," Cooper recalled, "and in the morning we'd give it back."

---

329 The Arusha Declaration, 5 February 1967. Accessed at https://www.marxists.org/subject/africa/nyerere/1967/arusha-declaration.htm.

Then came a sudden bolt of inspiration. They were profoundly influenced by the Latin American writer Paulo Freire's 'Dialectical Humanism' in his work, *The Pedagogy of the Oppressed,* published in 1970, and his concept of 'conscientisation'. The banning of Freire by the National Party government during this time failed to prevent covert circulation of the book by SASO comrades at 'bush colleges'.

The Pedagogy of the Oppressed, more than any other text, offered insight into what Freire called "the cultural invasion of oppressors as actors" on the oppressed as "objects". "The term 'conscientisation'," wrote Freire, "refers to learning to perceive social, political and economic contradictions, and to take action against the oppressed elements of reality."[330]

South Africa had long been the object of Christian nationalism, and Freire's groundbreaking work was almost entirely based on his observation of systems like apartheid. For young militants around Biko, the work opened a window as no other study had done on why Fanon's 'psychological liberation' as opposed to Marx's 'class consciousness' made more sense in black South Africa and how the process of conscientisation functioned.

The book first arrived in Durban as smuggled photocopies and instantly became a craze, recalled Cooper. "We had ideas but the book was a way forward, a credo for our movement. I remember the starting point for engagement between comrades: '*Have you read Freire?*'"

Having adapted Freire to South African conditions, Biko began work on his own definition and elaboration of the concept as a mobilising tool. "Conscientisation," he wrote, "is a process whereby individuals or groups living within a given social and political setting are made aware of their situation. The operative attitude here is not so much awareness of the physical sense of their situation, but much more their ability to assess and improve their own influence over themselves and their environment ... to free themselves from a situation of bondage."[331]

Seen from this perspective, the liberal approach could never provide a solution because it failed to take into account the psychological dimension of the African plight, most importantly the need to cast off mental complexes of dependence and deference towards whites. In SASO's analysis, the greatest check on black self-assertion was the black inferiority complex instilled over centuries of European colonialism. If this check was to be removed,

---

330 Quoted in O'Neill, E, 'Paulo Friere: Revolutionary thinker', in *Socialist Voice*, January 2016. Accessed at http://www.communistpartyofireland.ie/sv2016-01/09-freire.html.
331 Quoted in Woods, D, *Biko* (London: Penguin Books, 1968), p. 145.

blacks had to create a convincing new identity and pride which could liberate them from subservient attitudes. Like African nationalism before, SASO had arrived anew at the diagnoses and cure originally devised by African National Congress (ANC) Youth League militant Anton Lembede in the 1940s under the rubric of Africanism. Against the individualistic and capitalist traits of white liberalism, the communalist and socialist traditions of African society were to be shown as equally valid, even superior, in the African setting.

In most SASO propaganda during the late 1960s and early seventies, however, long-range goals were pointedly left vague, and black consciousness was defined primarily as an orientation towards the present. Black consciousness, declared the SASO Manifesto adopted in July 1971 was "an attitude of mind, a way of life" in which "the black man saw himself as self-defined and not as defined by others". It required, above all, "group cohesion and solidarity" so that blacks could be made aware of their collective economic and political power.[332]

Speaking before the first General Students Council of SASO in July 1970, Biko presented his vision of black consciousness. In August 1970, *SASO News* ran an article entitled 'Black souls in white skins?' containing Biko's address. The article was a blistering critique of white liberalism. It was also an unofficial policy statement that outlined the 'race problem'. Its intellectual ambition confirmed Biko's reputation as an intellectual trailblazer. "Basically the South African white community is a homogenous community," the article declared at the outset.[333] "All whites enjoy privileges and have to try to justify their privileged positions to themselves. The National Party ideologues offer the theories of 'separate development' as a rationale. But these are not the people we are concerned with," Biko wrote.[334] "We are concerned with that curious bunch of non-conformists ... that bunch of do-gooders that goes under all sorts of names – liberals, leftists, etc. These are the people who argue that they are not responsible for white racism ... . In short, these are the people who say that they have black souls wrapped up in white skins."[335] Liberals, he went on, "arrogantly presume that the country's problems require integration as a means to an end: hence the

---

332 Quoted in Sellström, T, 'Sweden and national liberation in Southern Africa', *Vol II: Solidarity and Assistance, 1970–1994* (Stockholm: Nordiska Afrikainstitutet, 2002), p. 548.
333 Biko, S, 'White skins, black souls?' Accessed at https://franknatter.wordpress.com/2010/08/09/white-skins-black-souls-highly-recommended-critique-of-white-liberals-steve-biko/.
334 Ibid.
335 Ibid.

multiracial political organisations and parties and the 'non-racial' student organisations".[336] Because of the influence of whites on blacks, he argued that

> this prescription had come to be taken in all seriousness as the *modus operandi* in South Africa by all those who claim they would like a change in the status quo. Yet the integration ... is artificial ... [because] the process of forming the integrated complex has been extracted from various segregated societies with their in-built complexes of superiority and inferiority, and these continue to manifest themselves even in the 'non-racial' set-up of the integrated complex.[337]

He concluded with a simple and direct caveat. "As a result, the integration so achieved is a one-way course, with the whites doing all the talking and the blacks the listening. However sincere the whites in such situations imagine themselves to be, they can't escape the hypocrisy inherent in their position as privileged members of society." [338]

'Black souls in white skins?' was one of those philosophical oeuvres that foretold a grand historic shift. Inspired by the ideas of African-Americans and Pan Africanists, the piece showed black students that black consciousness could lead to power, and that power required ideas that would lead to a new collective consciousness. This was not a lesson that came suddenly. Their earlier lives in NUSAS in the 1960s had been studies in political futility, all the more intense for their impotence, carried on as if moral statements on non-racialism and liberalism were natural bedfellows. But the experience at least taught the black students to take themselves and their ideas very seriously, to treat intellectual combat as an extension of the political kind.

In 'Black souls in white skins?', Biko helped pour the philosophical foundations for a new black-consciousness movement, and its first test: the conscientisation of black students on SASO campuses.

TOWARDS THE END OF 1972, THE CLEAVAGE BETWEEN NEW LEFT RADICALS and liberals in NUSAS became accentuated. The minority Left, led by Eddie

---

336 Ibid.
337 Ibid.
338 Ibid.

Webster, a student at the University of the Witwatersrand (Wits), was more and more emphatically dissociating itself from pacifist liberals and centrists who tried to hold a middle position. In his autobiography, Moss describes the evolution towards New Left Marxism as a process in which, of their own accord, the NUSAS radicals were drawing closer and closer to the anti-Stalinist politics of the European neo-Marxists Nicos Poulantzas and Louis Althusser, and he does no justice to the impact of black consciousness and SASO's break from NUSAS on them.[339] The deeper truth emerging from the pages of Moss's account is that the white Left was prodded and pushed that way by the radicalism of black-consciousness militants, who were quicker in grasping the trend of NUSAS's liberal hypocrisy and urged white students to abandon paternalism. In practice, the New Left radicals looked less inspiring on SASO campuses than the white ivory towers of NUSAS. Their policy on student leadership, race and class was not so different from NUSAS's homage to non-racialism in the name of democracy, even though this neglected the reality that blacks experienced class exploitation first as a disenfranchised group and then as an exploited class.

In the minds of young black student leaders like Cooper, the ideas and language of European Marxism were half a world away; the other half was psychological, a belief, Cooper said to me, in the "transformational power of self-awareness".

At the end of the 1960s, after Verwoerd's assassination and his replacement by John Vorster, NUSAS drifted to the right; in 1971, the NUSAS leadership retreated from direct action; and, in 1972, Cooper watched them drop their former commitment to political action under pressure of changed circumstances or their own shifting views – until the only one standing to challenge apartheid education on black campuses was SASO. Everywhere Cooper looked, both in the realm of politics and student opposition to encroachments on academic freedom, liberals were in tired retreat. Without black students to focus its mind, NUSAS had wandered back into conservatism.

Against this, Cooper, in his position as Publicity Secretary of SASO, launched a powerful attack. The end of Verwoerd, he began to argue, was precisely the moment not to withdraw but to extend. NUSAS shouldn't mourn the loss of the balance of power but instead use its roots in white student communities to conscientise white students. For Biko, the struggle for democracy and student access was as much about non-racialism as black

---

339 See Moss (n 175 above), Chapter 2.

exceptionalism. The values of non-racialism might be universal, but only black people could secure them.

Cooper recalled "thinking that those hippie counter-culture Lefties were a little insensitive to the black condition. The sixties were my formative experience in the broadest sense, because then it was a question of a struggle for awareness and leadership of student struggles and broader social and political struggles."

And so, in their early twenties, Cooper and a battalion of black youths became soldiers in the black-consciousness revolution.

*

A revolutionary moment occurs, wrote Karl Marx, when philosophy grips the masses. SASO's challenge in the early 1970s was to burrow deep into the interstices of black consciousness and reach a wide black audience. 'To speak the language of the people', however, required more than abstractions like 'consciousness' and 'value systems'. To rural blacks, such concepts were wholly foreign; to urban workers, they could easily have seemed obscure when measured against tangible problems like wages, crowded trains and pass laws. Biko himself was acutely aware of the problem. "To take part in the African revolution it is not enough to write a revolutionary song," he wrote in 1970, and, quoting Sékou Touré, he said, "you must fashion the revolution with the people. And if you fashion it with the people, the songs will come by themselves."[340]

But over and above problems of rephrasing the tenets of black-consciousness philosophy in everyday language, "there were very practical organisational problems arising out of the student situation", recalled Cooper. Outreach into urban townships and rural reserves required resources and strong organisational coordination. Participation in voluntary community projects in which Cooper was involved represented a genuine sacrifice for students whose families were already facing financial hardship. Time, too, was a constraint during the academic year. But perhaps most intractable of all, wrote Gail Gerhart in her book *Black Power*, was the problem created by the generational gap in African society: whatever the economic and social changes wrought by city life and formal education, the youth were still expected in all situations to defer to age. Students might be regarded as

---

340 Quoted in Gerhart (n 298 above), p. 291.

leaders of the future, but no one – at least until the lessons of 1976 began to come home – ever seriously considered the possibility that they might be leaders of the present.

Recognising the difficulties of trying to build a national movement when student leadership after their graduation from university – and from SASO – would have no congenial arena into which to move, SASO leaders started in early 1971 to explore the possibility of launching an 'adult' wing of the black-consciousness movement. They met in Bloemfontein in April with representatives of six other organisations to discuss the idea of establishing a nationwide 'umbrella' organisation of black groups. A follow-up conference in August, addressed by Biko, drew together representatives of 27 organisations and elected an interim committee under the chairmanship of MT Moerane, the editor of *The World* and President of the Association for Educational and Cultural Advancement of the African People of South Africa, to consider drawing up a constitution. When this committee reported at yet another conference held in December 1971, SASO's efforts to steer the evolving movement in the direction of bold political initiatives met resistance from older delegates, including Moerane and Dr William Nkomo – two founding members of the ANC Youth League who over 30 years had mellowed from 'rebels' to 'realists'. They favoured greater emphasis on cultural and economic causes, at least initially. Most present supported the general principles of black self-assertion as broadly popularised by SASO. A majority favoured defining 'black' to include Indians and coloureds. What older participants seemed to fear was the 'gloves-off' militancy of SASO, which appeared likely to lead the organisation and anyone involved with it into an early clash with white authority. After fierce debate, a vote showed proponents of the SASO view to be in the majority. The overtly political Black People's Convention (BPC) was formally launched in Pietermaritzburg in July 1971 under the leadership of Cooper, Drake Kokam, Mthuli Shezi, and Reverend A Mayatulam. Its constitution and statement of purpose strongly echoed the language of SASO.

As it turned out, the clash which moderates had feared was not long in coming. In early 1973, the government launched an offensive against SASO and the BPC leadership, including serving banning orders on its leaders. By 1973, the defiant new tenor of SASO's stance and its mocking attitude towards prominent Africans who, Cooper recalled, "continued to behave like so-called 'non-whites'" had noticeably altered the vocabulary of the cautious politics of the older generation.

While links with worker organisations were weak, SASO and the BPC drew strong support from the black clergy, resulting in the launch of the Black Renaissance Convention at an all-in conference in December 1974, which brought together a cross section of black leaders and intellectuals at St Peters Seminary in Hammanskraal north of Pretoria.

The diffusion of SASO's new mood into the high-school generation was given tremendous impetus in mid-1972 by campus revolts which followed the expulsion of Abram Tiro, a SASO leader, and two others from Turfloop. Their expulsion was prompted by Tiro's stinging attack on black education in a graduation address at Turfloop on 29 April. When students organised a boycott of classes to protest the expulsion, the authorities closed down the university and announced that all students would have to apply for readmission. Student boycotts soon spread to other black campuses. By June, a nationwide student rebellion was under way. One result was the expulsion of a large number of students from black universities, many of whom had transferred their energies to political activities outside the campuses.

In a situation of developing black–white confrontation in which mere talk had been the main activity, the younger school students were highly impressed by the action of older students who had put political commitment above their own careers. To the high-school generation, SASO leaders became heroes who had been bloodied in an actual clash with white authority. One consequence was heightened political consciousness by the end of 1972 among high-school students, leading to a welter of political youth organisations across the country. The most notable of these, which were to provide the organisational impetus behind the township youth uprisings of 1976, were the South African Students Movement formed in Soweto high schools and the National Youth Organisation, a federation of youth groups in Natal, the Transvaal and the Eastern Cape.

One day, after the mid-1972 state clampdown, Cooper found himself sitting across the table from Biko. Ever the cynic, Cooper looked at Biko and asked point-blank, "What now?" Biko, who had a strong sense of mission, replied, "It's time to bury apartheid."[341] Cooper was speechless, because what Biko said was both breathtaking and scary.

---

341 Interview with the author, Johannesburg, May 2015.

CHAPTER 15

The road to Soweto

APRIL 1974 – OCTOBER 1975

THE SPARK THAT LIT THE SOWETO FLAME ON 16 JUNE 1976 FLASHED IN an unlikely corner of the world. Exactly five years to the day, in June 1971, the leaders of the national liberation movement in Mozambique, known as FRELIMO, pulled off a public relations coup when they received an audience from Pope John Paul VI. The Pope's sympathetic response to their grievances shook the centurions of Portugal's military, which by then had one of the highest percentages of armed forces in the world. Many of them had been deployed to three distant colonies of Mozambique, Angola and Guinea Bissau, where for more than a decade they had waged a costly and futile battle to vanquish nationalist rebel movements.

By January 1974, discontent within Portugal's military command was approaching boiling point. The professional officer corps, smarting from real and imagined indignities, had begun to meet secretly to discuss their grievances. In February, General António de Spinola, a mentor of many of the army officers, openly challenged his superiors by publishing a slim volume entitled, *Portugal and the Future*. Spinola, a heavily decorated and immensely popular leader and one of António de Salazar's closest advisers, had tried privately to move the government toward a negotiated settlement with FRELIMO. Having been rebuffed, he repeated his argument in print, urging that the government should admit that the conflicts in Africa could not be won by military means. Instead, he proposed a negotiated political settlement and referendum in the colonies. Though the book was moderate in tone, it electrified the country, selling 50 000 copies in a matter of days. Prime Minister Marcel Caetano, who had replaced Salazar in 1968, read it in one go until the early hours of the morning and instantly realised that he was facing a possible coup. Trying to head it off, he fired Spinola, deployed his protégés throughout the country and extracted an oath of loyalty from his top 100 generals and admirals. A few weeks later, the army suppressed a spontaneous mutiny by the Fifth Infantry Regiment.

Unbeknownst to Caetano and his advisers, a group of Spinola loyalists had already drafted a political programme calling for the democratisation of Portugal and the decolonisation of the three African territories occupied by Portugal. A few hours later, 'Grândola' had played on the radio waves, and converging regiments surrounded the capital city of Lisbon and encircled the barracks to which Caetano had fled. On the evening of 26 April 1974, after Caetano capitulated and fled into exile, Spinola entered the capital to public acclaim. At a press conference, the general declared that he was the head of a 'junta of national salvation' and promised respect for all of Portugal's international treaties, and free elections.

On the morning after the coup, thousands of Portuguese citizens filled the streets of Lisbon to celebrate the end of colonialism. Some placed carnations on the barrels of guns and pinned these flowers on military uniforms.[342] It became known as the Carnation Revolution.

*

The coup caught many of Portugal's former allies by surprise. Just a few days before, the state-run South African Broadcasting Corporation described South Africa and Portugal as the two most stable governments in the southern African region. No one feared the implications of the new Portuguese government's transfer of power to liberation movements in its former colonies more than Prime Minister John Vorster, who watched in astonishment as two bulwarks of white supremacy collapsed overnight. South Africa had an immediate neighbour, Mozambique, which was regarded as a vital buffer against military incursions by the African National Congress (ANC) into South Africa as well as a vital port for shipping South African goods abroad.

Although the Portuguese conquistador, Vasco da Gama, in 1498 visited Quelimane and Mozambique, it was in the latter part of the 16th century that the Portuguese colonial presence became more permanent,[343] with Eduardo Mondlane as its founding president. The Mozambique Liberation Front, or FRELIMO, founded in 1962, had successfully waged a liberation struggle against Portuguese colonialism and by the time of Mondlane's

---

342 Accessed at http://www.en.wikipedia.org/wiki/Carnation_Revolution.
343 Accessed at http://www.infoplease.com/encyclopedia/world/mozambique-country-africa-history.
    html.

assassination in Dar es Salaam, Tanzania, on 3 February 1969, controlled some 20 per cent of the country.

In September 1974, FRELIMO and Portuguese representatives reached agreement on the independence of Mozambique. In the minds of many white South Africans, particularly supporters of the apartheid regime, the collapse of the Portuguese military dictatorship meant that there were now two hostile neighbours, Mozambique and Angola. In the Vorster government, the task of securing the country's borders fell directly on two men, PW Botha and Pik Botha. "Domestic policy on a settlement with the South African liberation movements was always going to be determined by favourable settlements in the frontline states," Pik Botha told me over a cup of tea at his smallholding north of Pretoria.[344]

In both countries, South Africa backed third-force groups in destabilisation campaigns. In January 1974, reports in the press – largely pro-apartheid – raised grave concerns about the consequences for South Africa of FRELIMO's assumption of power in Mozambique. "We were worried because Mozambique was now a rear base for guerrilla incursions into South Africa by the ANC," Botha said.

But Botha's first test came not from the ANC or its military wing Umkhonto we Sizwe, but an unlikely quarter. Stirred by news that FRELIMO and the Portuguese had reached agreement on Mozambican independence, Muntu Myeza, the Secretary General of the South African Students' Organisation (SASO), and Saths Cooper met at the SASO offices in Beatrice Street, Durban, around the middle of September 1974. The two men agreed that this was a marvellous opportunity to build solidarity with FRELIMO for exactly the reasons the apartheid regime feared. They settled on mobilising support, especially on university campuses where SASO had a significant presence, and urban centres where the Black People's Convention (BPC) had strong branches. They chose Wednesday, 25 September, the 10th anniversary of FRELIMO's armed struggle against Portugal, as the day to publicly launch the solidarity campaign. Because Cooper was banned and could not make public statements, Muntu agreed to be the official spokesperson for both organisations and the chief organiser of what would become known as *Viva FRELIMO* rallies nationwide. Cooper recalled the pair calling a meeting in Durban of the key leadership of both SASO and the BPC where they

---

344 Hereinafter, all direct references to Botha are from an interview with the author, Pretoria, November 2011.

put forward their ideas. "There was enthusiastic support and full agreement with our declared position, and steps were taken to disseminate the information to the relevant branch leadership of the organisations," Cooper told me. "As timing was critical, and there needed to be an element of surprise for the apartheid regime, we decided to inform the Sunday newspapers about the rallies which were to be held that Wednesday."[345]

When the announcement was made on Sunday, 22 September, a ripple of mixed excitement and fear spread across the country. Pik Botha was stunned. Most of white South Africa was expectant, he recalled to me, if not wary of the consequences. Most young black people, though, were exhilarated by the announcement. The media had also reported that a FRELIMO representative would be one of the speakers at the main rally at the Curries Fountain stadium in Durban.

Rallies were scheduled for all black university campuses or nearby venues. In Johannesburg, the rally was planned for the Donaldson Orlando Community Centre and a host of other regions.

Nkwenkwe Nkomo, who was the national organiser of the BPC, was dispatched to Maputo to consult with the FRELIMO leadership and return with a statement which would be read at the various rallies. Hari Singh, who was the adopted son of the late activist, Debi Singh, reappeared on the scene after an absence of over two years, smelling that adventure was afoot.

Cooper recalled Hari volunteering to drive Nkwenkwe to Maputo. "This was an offer that we could not refuse as we had few other options. Coastal Govender's car was unlikely to survive the trip, but Coastal gamely took the car to a mechanic to convince us that it was up to the task," he said. So it was that Nkwenkwe, Hari and Coastal went to Mozambique.

That Monday, Jimmy Kruger, who held the portfolios of Justice, Police and Prisons, announced that the *Viva FRELIMO* rallies had been banned, but there was a legal loophole, Cooper said. "We checked the *Government Gazette* and when we saw that the banning was not promulgated we issued a press statement which read: 'We are not aware of any banning. Even if there were, we couldn't care less. The will of the people shall not be suppressed by a foreign settler minority regime.'"

The statement was published on Tuesday, a day before the rallies were scheduled to be held. The following morning, Kruger, realising his oversight,

---

345 Hereinafter, all direct references to Cooper are from interviews with the author, Johannesburg, January–May 2015.

hastily pushed through the promulgation just as black youths and workers began gathering at Curries Fountain Stadium. That morning, newspapers carried reports quoting Kruger's warning of a "revolutionary communist onslaught" that FRELIMO portended. He also alluded to the need to avoid racial hostility and violence in South Africa. However, Cornelius Koekemoer, a National Party figure in Vryheid, had been threatening that, if the regime was unable to put a stop to the rally, "hundreds of whites" would converge on Curries Fountain.

"We were in a bind," Cooper recalled. "The regime was busy cordoning off Curries Fountain with police and military personnel. Most of the people who were keen to attend the rally would not have heard of the banning and we had no access to radio. There was no television because Hertzog, an apartheid minister, refused to countenance such a vile phenomenon which would signal miscegenation and the end of apartheid," Cooper told me, saying: "The only option was for one of us in leadership to approach the police at Curries Fountain and ask them to allow an announcement calling on those who had gathered to depart as the rally had been banned."

At their meeting, held at the doctors' quarters at King Edward Hospital where Aubrey Mokoape was an intern, they discussed who would under-take this task. There was silence in the room; the risk was clear: arrest by the police. Finally, Cooper volunteered. Nkwenkwe and Aubrey then raised Cooper's banning, which precluded him from attending any gathering, as a concern. The police, they said, were certain to arrest Cooper. Cooper pointed out that "it would probably save anybody else being arrested". After batting the issue back and forth, they decided that Muntu, as the offi-cial organiser of the event, should go to Curries Fountain and approach the police to make an announcement asking those assembled to disperse.

The trio from Mozambique had meanwhile arrived prior to the meeting and reported their interaction with Monteiro at the government offices in Maputo. They had to effectively craft a statement that Monteiro reluctantly agreed could be read.

*

Tensions rose as thousands of people gathered outside Curries Fountain Stadium on Wednesday morning, 25 September. They filled every avail-able nook and cranny, including the grounds of Mansfield High School opposite the entrance to Curries Fountain, which had been blockaded by a

212

heavily armed police and military presence. From there, spread out before the armed wall of police and military just beyond the open clearing in the stadium, the crowd was in a buoyant mood, pressing shoulder to shoulder, singing freedom songs and dancing. The scheduled time of the rally had come and gone. Muntu eventually arrived and tottered through the throng from the eastern side, past the entrance, to Sastri College. When some in the crowd saw Muntu, a parade of applause and chanting broke out, the singing growing louder as he approached the stadium. "It was an outpouring of enthusiasm unheard of in those times," recalled Cooper. At just that moment, a chasm of approaching police separated Muntu from the crowd. People surged, pushed and shoved their way into the bright sunshine where Muntu had joined the singing. Then, just as the crowd turned, still shoulder to shoulder, toward the stadium, instinct and years of struggle took over. The approaching police rubbed their emotions raw. Something dramatic, they knew, was about to happen.

In later evidence in the SASO/BPC trial at the Palace of Justice in Pretoria the following year, the police painted a picture of the crowd being led in a pincer formation. They used the description of the horns of an ox, an allusion to how King Shaka led his troops, with Muntu at the leadership of one of the pincers/horns converging on the police to surround them. "The impression one got was of this poor (but highly armed) police force being overwhelmed by a peaceful crowd in a horned pincer-like formation of aggressors," recalled Cooper.

The police charged the crowd with batons, tear gas and rubber bullets and let loose scores of vicious dogs. During his detention, Cooper remembered seeing some of the footage and photographs "which showed that a jolly crowd was set upon by an eagerly aggressive police force". In their haste to escape the police onslaught, the crowd littered the Mansfield High sports grounds with shoes, bags and various other possessions. Scores of people were arrested and charged with attending an illegal gathering, fomenting racial hostility, and other crimes.

Those known SASO/BPC members in the crowd were arrested and raids were conducted on various premises, including the SASO offices in Beatrice Street where some members like Patrick 'Terror' Lekota were arrested.

Cooper remembered being in his flat in the suburb of Sydenham where he was confined between 6 p.m. and 6 a.m. daily, and between 2 p.m. on Saturdays and 6 a.m. on Mondays. The police arrived at his door "a couple of times" that night, he said to me, but he did not let them in. It was close to midnight when he heard his attorney's voice outside that he let the police in. "By now the head of the security police, Francois Steenkamp, and the Regional Commissioner of Police, who was in uniform, and numerous other policemen were at my door," he said. When Cooper opened the door, he encountered a furious Steenkamp who informed him that he had been forced to bring the Regional Commissioner, as his men were about to break down the door. He informed Cooper that he was under arrest and, in the presence of his attorney, his men would search the flat and seize whatever they deemed fit. "I was held at the Rossburgh Police cells under the Criminal Procedure Act and ought to have been given access to my attorney thereafter but wasn't," he said. On Friday, 27 September, Cooper was to appear in the Durban Magistrate's Court, but the detention was converted to another 14 days' detention. He was being held under section 6 of the notorious Terrorism Act was all he was told.

The very next day, Cooper was signed out of Rossburgh Police Station by two security policemen and escorted to the parking lot. There he discovered that there was already another detainee in the car. Lindelwe Mabandla was married to Brigitte Mabandla, who was to become Minister of Justice under Thabo Mbeki. In the seemingly eternal interim, the journey to Pretoria's local prison, and then on to Robben Island, was long.

By late 1974, at least 20 activists in SASO and the BPC had been restricted by banning orders, and police had decided that enough evidence of illegal activity could be marshalled to obtain court convictions against key figures in the movement. By mid-November, at least 35 activists were being held under a variety of security laws that denied them contact with families or lawyers. In January 1975, 13 *Viva FRELIMO* detainees were charged with offences under the Terrorism Act. The case of *the State v Cooper and eight others* – sometimes called 'the SASO 9' – opened in Pretoria in August 1975, and lasted 16 months. Their eventual incarceration on Robben Island in 1976 was to inspire a generation of black youths who had become politically conscious during the SASO student rebellion in 1971.

With the SASO leadership routed and the ANC leadership exiled, it fell on this new generation of school-going youths to rally to the SASO cause.

The black-consciousness movement was nearing its nadir.

*

Shortly after the *Viva FRELIMO* arrests in September 1974, Mapetla

Mohapi and Malusi Mpumlwana were dispatched from King William's Town to Durban to keep the SASO headquarters operating. But once a new leadership was in place, SASO returned to its autonomous course, which, in practice, meant the cultivation of ever-closer relations with the ANC's underground in Natal.

In 1975, the ANC and Pan Africanist Congress (PAC) were gradually assembling rudimentary underground networks of veteran members and prisoners released from Robben Island. Both movements were fishing for new recruits in the pool of young militants harvested by the black-consciousness movement.

The pressure to work out a modus vivendi between black-consciousness groups and older liberation movements was acutely felt by Biko and his circle in King William's Town. In spite of its outwardly fortuitous character, this rift had set in motion an irreversible process of differentiation, in the course of which African nationalism was to become a tributary separate from the current of black consciousness. In the ANC leadership, some of the most radical elements were already describing themselves as African nationalists, opposed to insurrectionists and the pure class politics of Marxist orthodoxy and socialist revolution. This, even more than the objective circumstances of the division, concealed its true nature. The division assumed an irrational, bewildering aspect. What Biko saw in 1975 were several groups professing the same principles and objectives. On the face of things, this was quite true, Cooper mused to me. "The objective was liberation." So far, the protagonists were divided only by a difference in temper and strategic orientation to race, although this difference would eventually be rationalised into a deeper controversy over the very concept of liberation.

In 1975, Biko had shown that he was prepared to subordinate differences to the higher cause of defeating apartheid. He saw an urgent need for a unified resistance movement in which minor differences over ideology and tactics would not detract from the pursuit of common goals. As one means of building links, Biko and his comrades established the Zimele Trust Fund to raise money for projects to employ released political prisoners, dozens of whom lived in dire poverty in the Eastern Cape. By this time, Biko's authority in the affairs of the movement as a whole was only an informal one. SASO, the BPC, and the plethora of black consciousness-oriented youth, and high school and cultural organisations now functioned almost entirely independently of one another.

In a clandestine meeting with Robert Sobukwe in May 1975, Biko was able to get assurances of Sobukwe's full support for efforts to reunite the ANC and PAC. Working mainly through Mpumlwana and Mohapi, Biko began an indirect dialogue with Griffiths Mxenge and Harry Gwala, two high-ranking ANC underground leaders in Natal, Zeph Mothopeng and other leading PAC figures in Johannesburg, and an array of older leaders in the Cape and elsewhere. Plans to hold a secret unity meeting just after Christmas had to be aborted, but Biko's cautious efforts to broker dialogue and cooperation continued.

In mid-December, over 1 000 people gathered at the Fourth National Conference of the BPC in King William's Town. Knowledge of secret unity talks was limited to a handful of Biko's close confidants. Through this core group, the BPC conference was steered toward·discussion of major issues on which the unity negotiators hoped to build a consensus. A conference state-ment refining the definition of black consciousness aligned the movement with the ANC's multiracialism by stating that the aim of black conscious-ness was not "Black Power" but rather the creation of "a truly open, plural society". In a gesture conciliatory to the PAC, the document used the name 'Azania' for South Africa.[346]

Almost immediately after the conference, Biko and his confidants, who now included Kenneth Rachidi, the newly elected BPC President, and Mxolisi Mvovo, Biko's brother-in-law, who had been elected Vice-President, drew up additional draft papers in preparation for a national symposium to produce a major policy document on black communalism as a basis for unity.

In reality, however, most ANC and PAC leaders felt threatened by these young, fiery and highly articulate leaders who did not formally subordinate themselves to the older organisations. From inside the black-consciousness movement, it seemed to Biko and others that the older organisations were largely made up of ineffectual has-beens, people far away and out of touch with contemporary realities. Some might have seen armed struggle – and, therefore, the movements pursuing it – as the key to liberation, but Biko believed it was political struggle within South Africa's borders that would eventually turn the tide. Among many hard-core activists of the black-consciousness movement, these strategic and ideological issues loomed increasingly large as the dominance of the younger movement began to be

---

346 See 'The origins of the anti-apartheid movement', *O'Malley Archives*. Accessed at https://www. nelsonmandela.org/omalley/index.php/site/q/03lv03445/04lv04015/05lv04154/06lv04157.htm.

challenged by the older liberation organisations.

Biko's choice was clear, although it was a choice for which he would one day pay the ultimate price. It is no wonder, however, that the symptomatic significance of this difference, so obvious in retrospect, was not in plain view to many, if not from most of the actors. Both the ANC and PAC did not yet perceive the revolutionary frame of mind behind Biko's black-consciousness ideology.

In preparation for the national symposium, Biko, not yet cooled off by the heat and clash of engagements with older-generation leaders and organisations, began to express the contradictions in his attitude to the dogma of ANC and PAC policies in his preparatory papers. There were moments of somnolence, new whispers among SASO comrades of betrayal. But the thought that he, or any of his comrades, should assume titles of ANC commissars seemed incongruous to Biko. Several more years were to elapse before these ideological tendencies would emerge. But first white and black South Africa had to face a fateful trial by fire.

THE FORCE OF SASO'S BLACK-CONSCIOUSNESS IDEOLOGY, THE TOUGH language and idealistic principles of SASO's new credo, was felt far beyond university campuses by 1971. Biko already had in mind black high-school students who would be brought into the orbit of SASO's activities. At its 1972 annual conference, SASO resolved to build links with school-age youths and to extend SASO's leadership-training methods to include them. When the Trio incident at Turfloop resulted in mass walkouts by black university students in mid-1972, dozens of SASO activists found work as teachers in understaffed secondary schools, carrying the contagion of black consciousness out of one set of classrooms into another.

In Johannesburg, where *The World* and the *Rand Daily Mail* periodically carried reports and statements by SASO leaders on the university crisis, high-school students became avid consumers of news on their new idols. In the Eastern Cape, the East London *Daily Dispatch* played a similar role after Biko's restriction to King William's Town in March 1973. The growing popularity of Afro dress, music, poetry and township theatre with a black-consciousness message broadened SASO's appeal even further, wrote Gail Gerhart, until 'thinking black' had become an 'in thing' among literate young Africans in the townships of the Witwatersrand and the Eastern Cape.

As Biko and his comrades watched the new wave of consciousness grip the masses, their minds may have flashed back to the SASO conference in December 1971 when Biko prematurely declared a programme of direct action. How similar in a way these two moments appeared: the leading men were the same; most of the recriminations of the 1971 conference echoed in the surge of consciousness in black townships. But how different was the scale of mobilisation and intensity of consciousness. "The rising black consciousness," Cooper recalled Biko declaring, "needs no justification." What he implied, although never quite expressed in so many words, was that 'Phase Two' of SASO's programme of action had begun.

In reaching out to a youth constituency, SASO's aim was to lay the broadest possible foundation for future political mobilisation. High-school students who might one day become university students formed a pool of potential recruits; young school leavers, employed and unemployed, formed another. Criss-crossing the country to meet church and YMCA (Young Men's Christian Association) groups, youth clubs, student societies and informal township social gatherings, Biko (who by this time had taken up full employment as the BPC's Youth Coordinator), Harry Nengwekhulu, Bennie Khoapa, Tebogo Mafole and other movement organisers fought for the formation of regional youth structures which could draw existing groups together into larger umbrella bodies of principally school leavers.

In August 1972, the Natal Youth Organisation was launched at the Edendale Lay Ecumenical Centre near Pietermaritzburg, followed in a matter of months by the formation of the Transvaal Youth Organisation (TRAYO), the Eastern Cape Border Youth Union and the Western Cape Youth Organisation. In early June 1973, representatives of these bodies met for four days in King William's Town and launched the National Youth Organisation (NAYO). NAYO reflected the strong guiding influence of SASO's ideology and personnel as well as its programmatic focus on spreading political awareness through cultural activities, literacy projects and propaganda against homeland and system collaborators.

By the time NAYO moved onto the political stage, however, this repertoire of low-risk tactics was steadily losing appeal. The authorities were banning high-profile black-consciousness leaders and intimidating outspoken activists by rounding them up for questioning and gratuitous beatings at local police stations. One result of the ever-harsher political climate was that NAYO and its constituent bodies tended to attract only those who were already highly politicised and had moved on to thinking about 'Phase Two', the physical liberation that was to follow 'psychological liberation'.

Preoccupation with 'Phase One' had dimmed the enthusiasm of youthful recruits for the patient tactics designed a few years earlier to spread the philosophy of black consciousness. Planning for armed revolt now seemed much more urgent, especially after Mozambique's independence in June 1975 opened up new prospects for guerrilla infiltration across South Africa's north-eastern border. Within a year of NAYO's founding, some if its members were organising secret cells and trying to re-establish contact with the older liberation movements in the hope of forcing those organisations to the left and preparing the ground for armed combat. Some had already fled to neighbouring states to try to link up with the ANC or PAC, or Botswana representatives of the black-consciousness movement.

Between June and October 1975, police swooped on dozens of young people suspected of subversive activities under cover of NAYO and its affiliates. Seven of those arrested were tried for terrorism in what became known as the 'NAYO trial', beginning in Johannesburg in late 1975. The trial shows that, although the prospect of insurrection by young Africans looked less promising than many assumed, the number of people who were prepared to undertake high-risk political action was appreciably growing. Events in Mozambique had imbued blacks with optimism and the white security forces with a new ruthlessness. Brutal police-interrogation methods were becoming a fact of life. At the NAYO trial, the atmosphere among spectators became so charged that on 18 March 1976, a violent confrontation between police and a large crowd gathered in the street outside the court building grabbed news headlines. Taut emotions were ready to burst forth from beneath Johannesburg's surface calm.

*

Even with heightened consciousness, it would have taken time before a revolutionary movement (to borrow Lenin's famous axiom on the eve of the Russian Revolution in 1916) 'for itself' replaced the one 'in itself'. Before that happened, so elementary a process as the continuation of Bantu education – the precondition for youth unrest – had to be disrupted.

In reaching for the generation immediately junior to themselves, SASO's strategists targeted senior secondary-school students. Dropout rates at every stage of schooling were high, with the result that Africans enrolled in the last two years of high school in the early 1970s comprised less than 2 per cent of their age cohort. These students, though predominantly working-class, formed an incipient intellectual and economic elite by virtue of their education. As potential university students, they were SASO's constituency-to-be and the social group most at risk of falling foul politically of the apartheid state's long-term co-option strategies. The physical concentration of high-school students in institutional settings made them relatively easy to reach compared with the working or unemployed youth. Their level of literacy also made them recruitable through written propaganda and verbal persuasion. The only barriers to their rapid politicisation were fears by parents and the hostility of some government-employed teachers and school principals to anything exuding the faintest whiff of politics.

By December 1975, contacts with older siblings, the circulation of black-consciousness publications, and the popularity of younger teachers infected with the SASO virus all ensured the fairly speedy dissemination of the new consciousness among high-school students. Within two years of SASO's birth, high-school students had begun here and there to form small political clubs, often at the instigation of former SASO students expelled from colleges who went on to become school teachers. Organising themselves as debating societies or community clubs, the associations came and went as the friendship groups on which they were based formed or dissolved.

The most important of these high-school groups was the Soweto-based African Students' Movement (ASM), which, in January 1972, changed its name to the South African Students Movement (SASM) as part of an ambitious plan by SASO to build a national organisation. The revolutionary cycle, which the Portuguese coup had set in motion, was coming to a close.

CHAPTER 16

'Year of fire'

1976

IN THE EARLY MINING DAYS OF 1897, A COVETOUS PROPERTY SPECULATOR named Hermann Tobiansky bought more than 200 acres of prime land to the west of the city of Johannesburg on a trough in the market. His intention was to cash in on soaring residential prices as white workers poured into the city. After pegging out 1 700 small stands and streets, Tobiansky ran afoul of the city's municipal regulations. Unable to sell the plots to whites, he sold them to blacks instead, well before the enactment of the Native Land Act of 1913 made such transactions impossible. Thus emerged a vibrant black freehold area, known in the apartheid nomenclature as a 'black spot' in a white area, that became a legendary cultural hub and epicentre of black politics. Tobiansky named the place 'Sophiatown', after his wife Sophia.[347]

To the Afrikaners in power, Sophiatown was an abomination, the epitome of all the travails of mishmash cohabitation. On 9 February 1955, 2 000 policemen, armed with handguns, rifles and clubs forcefully moved its black residents out of the area. Government trucks transported its 60 000 inhabitants a sanitary distance out of town to what would become a sprawling conglomeration of dormitory units known simply as the 'South Western Townships', or 'Soweto'. Over the next eight years, bulldozers rolled in. Sophiatown was flattened, and then removed from the map of Johannesburg.[348] This social devastation on an appalling scale was wrought in pursuit of the theoretical objective that South Africa was not one country but multiple 'nations', and that therefore no melting pot could be allowed and black roots put down in white areas. Blacks may have been needed as workers, but a sense of impermanence had to be preserved and a social and

---

347 Accessed at https://en.wikipedia.org/wiki/Sophiatown. For a good account of this, see Sparks, A, *The Mind of South Africa: The Rise and Fall of Apartheid* (Ballantine Books, 1991), pp. 188-189.
348 Ibid.

physical distance maintained. It was not enough simply to segregate living areas: a law of 1954 required that there should be a buffer strip at least 500 yards between the nations.

It was here, on a bare, windblown veld, that the African Students' Movement (ASM) took shape in the late 1960s around weekend and vacation study groups of Soweto students preparing for matriculation exams with the assistance of Tom Manthata, a young teacher at Sekano Ntoane High School who was also involved in the organisation of church-based youth clubs. Manthata was a Catholic seminary dropout disaffected with the church, but drawn to the unconventional theology of the University Christian Movement (UCM) in which his cousin, Justice Moloto, was a leading activist. Through Moloto and the UCM, Manthata became a friend of South African Students' Organisation (SASO) leaders and an adherent of SASO's emerging philosophy. The ASM organised a handful of school debating societies that were nurtured by Manthata and several like-minded Soweto teachers, sometimes using the occasion of sports tournaments to arrange interschool debates on topics likely to stimulate political discussion.

In July 1971, the ASM made its first tentative foray into public consciousness by staging a noisy demonstration to protest the excessive time students were required to spend practising for choir competitions at the expense of their studies. The day after, placard-waving ASM members disrupted a national choir competition of 4 000 participants in Springs outside Johannesburg. The tabloid headlines of *The World* warned that children were "running wild".[349] The ASM's message on this occasion was ostensibly not political, but the protest was an effort by the organisation to thrust itself into the spotlight as a voice for student complaints. Peter Lenkoe, a student at Madibane High School and President of the ASM, reported to a SASO national executive committee meeting in Pietermaritzburg five months later that the organisation was attracting between 700 and 800 active participants to its meetings.

When the ASM reorganised itself as the South African Students Movement (SASM) in January 1972, it aimed to build a national movement of high-school students but found the task more formidable than anticipated. After about a year, branches were functioning at nine Johannesburg schools and

---

349 Gerhart, G, 'The 1976 Soweto uprising', University of Witwatersrand Institute for Advanced Social Research seminar paper presented on 2 May 1994. Accessed at https://core.ac.uk/download/files/979/39667638.pdf.

a roughly equivalent number of schools scattered throughout the country. Branches would be established only to fall dormant within a semester or two. Travelling beyond the area of the Reef in Johannesburg required money and mobility that SASM organisers did not have. Channels of communication, the lifeblood of any organisation, shrank and became clogged; the old manner of mobilising door-to-door support was impossible in the repressive atmosphere of the time.

More favourable opportunities were to be found in inviting outside speakers to give lectures to school clubs; and university students prominent in SASO found themselves frequently invited to address high-school debating societies. Cultural activities like concerts and plays were another way for SASM to draw audiences and potential supporters. The most interested students would then be invited to participate in weekend seminars at Wilgespruit outside Johannesburg or church centres in Roodepoort, where facilities were made available for student meetings. "The choice of churches was also a way in which to legally gather," Cooper told me.[350]

Here, again, Cooper recalled, the leaders of SASO usually made the principal input, organising political discussions and workshops on techniques of organisation, how to raise funds, and adult literacy using Paulo Freire's method of conscientisation.

But in the course of March 1973, a state of affairs came to prevail under which SASM, like National Youth Organisation (NAYO), was dealt a severe blow. The banning of its top leadership, along with SASO's, shook and weakened the organisation, until a new leadership corps was assembled in mid-1974 with the encouragement of SASO and the Black People's Convention (BPC). In the meantime, Biko and his lieutenants in King William's Town's Ginsberg location had helped form SASM branches in several nearby high schools in the Eastern Cape.

The rejuvenated SASM, arriving on the scene after the Lisbon coup of April 1974, was increasingly driven by the growing appetite among the black youth for armed struggle. The African National Congress's (ANC) Radio Freedom was now broadcasting illegally into South Africa on short wave, and Umkhonto we Sizwe leaflets and literature were circulating more widely than ever. It was a time, we remember, when some students drawn to SASM were determined to become guerrilla fighters and fled

---

350 Hereinafter, all direct references to Cooper are from interviews with the author, Johannesburg, January–May 2015.

South Africa by hazardous routes. Some succeeded, others were captured, and more than a few turned back when discretion became the better part of valour.

*

On a cold Easter weekend in 1975, a group of SASM leaders gathered at a conference in King William's Town. Never before had any assemblage of youths assumed so prodigious a burden of responsibility as that which the SASM leaders shouldered. The spectre of revolt stalked the halls of the venue. Nemesis was only beginning her work.

The students had come to the gathering at the urging of SASO and organisers of the Black Community Programmes in King William's Town against a backdrop of intense debate and disagreement that increasingly strained relations between older and younger activists. Some youths, impatient to join the guerrilla armies in exile, Poqo (the Pan Africanist Congress's [PAC] armed wing) and Umkhonto we Sizwe, took issue with their older comrades, who argued that guerrilla warfare would be fruitless until a stronger political foundation for revolution had been laid inside South Africa. They pressed home the need to build the SASM as a body that would politicise high-school students as agitators for the radicalisation of adult society in the future. A document prepared for the conference by Malusi Mpumlwana, of the BPC, outlined behavioural do's and don'ts for a growing cadre of political agitators working circumspectly "within the law but outside the system". It was still official policy in senior black-consciousness organisations to shun any identification with the banned exiled movements, even if individual members chose to associate with them privately and – in spite of Steve Biko's stance – in ongoing engagement in protracted secret talks with underground representatives of the ANC and PAC in the hope of building a united front.

In the SASM, would-be fighters outnumbered talkers, and counsels of caution from older activists often provoked resentment. "When we asked questions concerning the future programme of the people," Daniel Montsitsi, a militant SASM leader at Sekano Ntoane High School in Soweto, later recalled, "we were told, 'We have to conscientise the black masses as this will ensure understanding and support, for only then shall we be able to bargain from a position of strength.' Unfortunately we were not in the mood to bargain or negotiate; we were impatient and militant and rebellious toward the black consciousness leadership."[351]

While abstract debates about the alternative merits of guerrilla warfare and mass insurrection continued unresolved, SASM, through SASO, received two donations from the International University Exchange Fund in Europe, one in late 1975 and the other in May 1976, totalling USD7 000. This made it possible to finance travel expenses and employ a full-time SASM organiser named Zweli Sizani. Participation picked up in Soweto, and, in early 1976, several SASM branches were launched, or were in the process of being formed in schools in Mamelodi, Mabopane and Atteridgeville in Pretoria, as well as KwaThema in Springs, Kagiso in Krugersdorp, Tembisa in Kempton Park, Thaba 'Nchu in the Orange Free State, KwaMashu in Durban, and Athlone High School in Cape Town.

During the last weekend of May, the organisation held a three-day conference in Roodepoort where a range of topics related to student and national life were debated. Three senior black-consciousness figures addressed the meeting along with SASM's outgoing president, Vusi Tshabalala, who called on his members to brace for further harassment from the state. A new executive was elected, while Sizani continued as full-time organising secretary. Some of SASM's activists had acquired substantial organising experience and had a clear vision of SASM as a vehicle for the national mobilisation of students; although, even as late as May 1976, it could not be anticipated how such a mobilisation might be triggered or what its outcome might be.

THE CONFLAGRATION THAT WOULD HEAVE SASM INTO NATIONAL PROMInence came from the government's imposition of Afrikaans as a medium of instruction in African schools on a 50-50 basis alongside English.

On 21 March 1968, the Executive Council of the secretive and highly influential Afrikaner Broederbond noted that Afrikaans as spoken word was being neglected in Bantu education. "Broeders in responsible circles of Cabinet," the minutes of that meeting reflect, "have confirmed that much has already been done to give Afrikaans its rightful place but that there were many problems." They recommended that the Executive refer the matter to Broeders in the Department of Education "with the request that serious attention should be paid continuously to the use of Afrikaans in Bantu

---

351 Quoted in Gerhart (n 298 above), p. 162.

education".[352]

In September that same year, the Broederbond, in a secret circular headed 'Afrikaans as a second language for the Bantu', set out its policy of "getting more blacks to use Afrikaans": The circular stated: "Two years ago in our monthly circular we drew the attention of members to the importance of using Afrikaans [in speaking] to the Bantu. That idea, and the hints with it, created widespread interest and [has] borne fruit. As a result, most right-thinking Afrikaans speakers today concentrate on addressing the Bantu in Afrikaans wherever they meet them."[353]

The contention, the circular went on, "is that the Bantu must learn one of the official languages as a second language. The other official language can be a third language which he does not necessarily have to know as well as the second language. The second language must be Afrikaans... ."[354]

The circular then listed progress already made towards establishing Afrikaans as a second language among blacks: "According to available figures, about 3.5 million Bantu live on white farms," the circular noted. "It can be accepted that a minimum of 3 million ... use Afrikaans in contact with their employers."[355]

In early 1971, the Broederbond once again urged its members to make Afrikaans a second language for blacks. The following year, a call went out to all members to donate Afrikaans textbooks.

Dual-medium instruction had officially been prescribed since the mid-1950s, but educationists had been critical of the policy, and their objections, plus a dearth of African teachers proficient in Afrikaans, had resulted in most African schools being granted annual exemptions from the formal requirement through to 1974. During that year, the Department of Bantu Education sent out a circular stating that half the subjects in black high schools had to be taught in Afrikaans. The circular, issued by Bantu Education's Regional Director in the Southern Transvaal, WC Ackerman, was unambiguous: arithmetic, mathematics and social studies had to be taught in Afrikaans; and science, woodwork, and arts and crafts in English, starting in Standard 5 (Grade 7).[356]

Ackerman's circular provoked a series of protests. The African Teachers'

---

352 Quoted in Wilkins & Strydom (n 90 above), p. 215.
353 Ibid.
354 Ibid., p. 238.
355 Ibid.
356 Ibid., p. 217.

Association protested to the Minister of Bantu Education that "it is cruel and short-sighted".[357] The Joint School and Committee Boards of the Southern and Northern Transvaal regions met officials from Bantu Education. But government remained unbending. The Deputy Minister, Punt Jansen, told Parliament that year he had not consulted blacks, "and I am not going to consult them" on the language issue.[358]

On 20 January 1976, at a meeting of the Meadowlands Tswana Board at the Moruta-Thuto Lower Primary School called by the Circuit Inspector representing the Department of Bantu Education, the Circuit Inspector told the Board that all direct taxes paid by the black population of South Africa were being sent to the various homelands for educational purposes. "In urban areas the education of a black child is being paid for by the white population, that is English- and Afrikaans-speaking groups. Therefore the Secretary of Bantu Education has the responsibility towards satisfying the English- and Afrikaans-speaking people."[359]

African teachers and community school boards raised strong objections, but department officials were unyielding. Students affected by the new policy obtained poor exam results at the end of 1975. Fears of failure joined with political distaste as the next school year began. Adding insult to injury, just as the 1976 school year opened, Prime Minister John Vorster announced in January that Dr Andries Treurnicht, the hard-line leader of the *verkrampte* (right-wing) faction of the National Party, would become the new Deputy Minister of Bantu Education.

In early February 1976, two members of the Meadowlands Tswana School Board were dismissed. The Regional Director gave no reasons for the dismissals, but it was believed that they were due to the Board's refusal to use Afrikaans as a medium of instruction in its schools. On 8 February, the remaining seven members of the Board resigned in protest.

*

The first reported student action began on 25 February, when Junior Certificate students at Thomas Mofolo Secondary School in Soweto verbally clashed with their principal over the medium of instruction and police were called in. On 17 May, students at Orlando West Junior Secondary School

---

357 Ibid., p. 215.
358 Ibid.
359 Ibid., p. 216.

boycotted classes. They demanded to see the inspector, but he refused to meet the pupils. Two days later, a committee of students at the school presented a five-point memorandum to their principal protesting the use of Afrikaans as a medium of instruction. After several meetings with the principal and staff, the students drafted a letter, stating their grievances, to the Regional Director. The day after, students at Belle Higher Primary, Emthonjeni Higher Primary and Thulasizwe Higher Primary schools joined the boycott. On 24 May, Pimville Higher Primary and Khulangolwazi Primary schools joined in.

Soweto was now convulsed by protest action. On 24 May, the Director of the South African Institute of Race Relations sent an urgent telegram to R de Villiers, an MP and executive member of the Institute: "Deeply concerned Afrikaans medium controversy black schools x Position Soweto very serious x Could you discuss matter with Minister concerned."[360]

A day later, Treurnicht tersely wrote back, "We will determine what the contributory factors are, but at the moment it is said that the pupils are striking because the teachers are not capable of teaching Afrikaans."[361]

Government's dismissive stance was a provocation. At SASM's May 1976 conference, the subject of Afrikaans as a medium of instruction was hotly debated. The conference noted the context of the imposition of Afrikaans with grave concern. Between 1970 and 1975, the number of African pupils admitted to Form 1, the first year of secondary school, shot up from 49 504 to 149 251. One result was that thousands of African teenagers began to reach levels of schooling far beyond those of their parents.

But there the optimism stopped. African schools, delegates argued, ranked the lowest on state expenditure per pupil, the number of trained teachers and quality of school facilities. Schools for Indians and coloureds fared somewhat better, while the system for whites consumed public resources out of all proportion to the number of pupils serviced. These inequalities in no way reflected the level of demand for education in the respective communities. Educational achievement was one of the few paths out of poverty for Africans, and working-class parents struggled over many years to meet the costs of books, uniforms and fees necessary to keep their children in school.

The general mood was a deep sense of foreboding about Afrikaans as a medium of instruction. That the youth were being forced to adjust to new

---

360 Ibid., p. 219.
361 Ibid.

levels of economic insecurity deepened an already widespread sense of despair.

*

"Do you want to make us really desperate," asked Desmond Tutu, the Anglican Dean of Johannesburg, in a statement carried on the front page of the *Rand Daily Mail* on 1 May 1976. A week later, in an emotional letter to Prime Minister Vorster, Tutu tried again to warn that African patience was running out. "I am frightened," he wrote, "... that we may soon reach a point of no return, when events will generate a momentum of their own, when nothing will stop their reaching a bloody denouement."[362]

Tutu's passing reference in his letter to the collapse of Portuguese colonialism only hinted at powerful hopes and expectations that events in Mozambique and Angola had kindled among Africans. In addressing all blacks, especially young African students, he later warned that the sudden and unexpected turn of events in Mozambique and Angola had transformed the idea of liberation from something distant and abstract into "something real, something possible".[363]

As the 1976 school year began in January 1976, overcrowding in African schools reached new levels nationwide. To reduce the number of school years from 13 to 12, the Department of Bantu Education had decided in 1975 to abolish Standard 6 (Grade 8) from the following year, enabling students to proceed directly from Standard 5 into the five years of secondary school leading to matriculation. Although this change promised eventually to relieve pressure on classroom space, it meant that, in 1976, pupils finishing both Standard 5 and Standard 6 proceeded together into the first year of high school, creating an unwieldy bulge that meant yet more overcrowding and double shifts, and more shortages of textbooks and qualified teachers. In the Transvaal, however, protests by teachers and a few African school boards had failed to roll back the ruling that "Afrikaans instruction in half of all subjects be phased in, starting at junior secondary level".[364] The language ruling most immediately affected the very students caught in the bulge. For schoolchildren in their teens, the injustices of gutter education suddenly seemed utterly unbearable.

From this point on, events would move rapidly to 16 June that would

---

362 See Gerhart (n 349 above).
363 Ibid.
364 Ibid.

mark 1976, to borrow the left-wing historian Baruch Hirson's title of his book on the subject, as a "year of fire and ashes".

*

Before the middle of January 1976, came the first signs of student tensions over the imposition of Afrikaans as a language of instruction in Soweto high schools. Because of slow communication, the media did not pay much attention to the SASM's renewed efforts to build a national following. But already in mid-January, Steve Biko was writing in *SASO News*, "We are witnessing the beginning of revolt." A fever of excitement was taking hold of students; and several meetings of the SASM were followed by minor skirmishes with the apartheid-education authorities. How Biko received the revolution can be seen in the rapid procession of events.

On the morning of 27 May, the first violent incident was recorded when a teacher of Afrikaans at Pimville Higher Primary School named K Tshabalala was stabbed with a screwdriver by a student. Students then stoned police who had tried to arrest pupils responsible for the stabbing.

Within the fortnight between the incident and 3 June, students at five schools in Soweto boycotted classes. Two days later, on 5 June, students at Belle Higher Primary School stoned school buildings and other pupils who had returned to classes. On 8 June, students at Naledi High School stoned police and burnt their car. Fifteen students were detained but were released after questioning.

At all its meetings, wrote historians Tom Karis and Gail Gerhart in their recording of the period, the SASM concentrated its efforts on senior students, whereas the language problem directly affected only students in Forms 1 and 2 (Grades 8 and 9). As mid-year exams approached, a class boycott over Afrikaans erupted among Form 1 and 2 students at Orlando West Junior Secondary School. Within a fortnight, the boycotts had spread to seven other schools.

It now seemed possible for students that the apartheid educational structure, built of racism and delusion, should soon collapse. The first tremor shook the system after the conference of the SASM from 28 to 30 May. Seeing an opportunity to take a leadership role, several members of the SASM's national executive called a meeting at the Orlando YMCA (Young Men's Christian Association) in Soweto on the afternoon of Sunday, 13 June, ostensibly to form a SASM regional branch. Standing before an unexpectedly large number of students, Tsietsi Mashinini, a final-year student who was a leader in the SASM branch at Morris Isaacson High School in the Jabavu section of Soweto and a regional executive committee member, asked students to stage a mass demonstration the following Wednesday.

After a heated discussion on the Afrikaans issue, Mashinini's proposal was greeted with loud applause. One after another, the students voted in an action committee to organise the protest. The committee would consist of two representatives from each school under a leadership structure headed by Mashinini and Seth Mazibuko, a Form 2 student who had led the initial boycott at Orlando West Junior Secondary School.

At about 9 a.m. on the morning of Wednesday, 16 June, Vilakazi Street in Soweto was seized by 100 000 students marching toward Orlando Stadium. They converged from every corner of Soweto, waving placards denouncing compulsory Afrikaans instruction. Then followed the first volley of tear-gas canisters fired on marching students near the Orlando West Stadium. Both sides confronted each other: the police with tear gas; the demonstrators with stones.

THE FERVOUR OF STUDENTS, HOT AND IMPULSIVE, REACHED ITS CLIMAX moments later when the police shot live bullets into the crowd, killing 12-year old Zolile Hector Pieterson and wounding several other children. The students, inflamed by this provocation, stampeded into action. The Soweto revolt had begun; thousands of demonstrators began to rampage through the township, smashing windows and using petrol to set fire to schools, vehicles, the West Rand Administration Board, municipal beer halls and other government buildings. By dusk, Soweto looked like a prologue to revolution. Battalions of youths roamed the township, torching apartheid symbols.

The following day saw more fighting squads in the township. As dawn broke, the Soweto virus had become a contagion, spreading to Krugersdorp on the West Rand and downtown Johannesburg, where police and white thugs broke up a protest march by students from the University of the Witwatersrand (Wits). On that morning, newspapers around the world ran a photo of two crying teenagers carrying the limp body of Hector Pieterson that was to become the face of 'June 16' and an inspiration for future student struggles.

The uprising had with such breathtaking rapidity become a national movement, eventually affecting more than 100 urban areas of South Africa over a year. Even as police clamped down on demonstrations, students dammed up the raging torrent of the revolt by drawing in adult participants and broadening the protest against the entire system of Bantu education. The government's Regional Administration Boards remained targets throughout, along with black collaborators in the Urban Bantu Councils and homeland governments. In August, students tried to use stay-aways and consumer boycotts to weaken the state through blows directed at white business.

When all the weaknesses under which the revolt laboured are considered, the tactic of intersectional alliances, designed to damage business without engaging in a general strike, appears almost faultless; and its results must be judged impressive. During the intervening months, the student movement had become a publicity disaster for the apartheid government. By the end of February 1977, unrest deaths stood officially at 575.

*

"It happened at Angola – Why not here?" proclaimed a large banner hanging in a classroom at Orlando West Junior Secondary School on 16 June. Further nourishing the demand for respect and recognition was a sense of expectation that a successful revolution might soon occur in South Africa.

It was not hard for the SASM students who constituted the core of the Soweto Action Committee to think back to a time before 16 June when building a constituency had been an uphill battle. Suddenly a constituency, even a potential national following, was standing ready; retreat would have been both ignoble and inconsistent with the precepts of the black-consciousness movement which had strongly impressed upon young people their responsibility to analyse, organise and act as if the future of the country was in their hands. In the uncharted terrain of confrontation with the state, the black-consciousness slogan, "Black man, you're on your own" had become "Black student, you're on your own".

The reopening of schools in the last week of July was marked by high absenteeism and outbreaks of arson at schools around the country. During the July winter recess, the Soweto Action Committee had realised that nothing could be organised until students returned to school. Burning schools was no solution. Political awareness was at fever pitch, but constructive action required the strengthening of communication networks that could only operate if students were congregating at schools on a daily basis.

Moreover, the Soweto Action Committee itself needed to be expanded from its original complement of about a dozen students into a body representing every Soweto secondary school, not just the ones that had been represented at the meeting on 13 June.

On Sunday, 1 August, Soweto's Urban Bantu Council held a public meeting at the Jabulani Amphitheatre to report on their consultations with the government around student grievances. There was a high turnout of students who jeered the councillors' appeals for moderation and called for the release of detainees and a continued offensive against Bantu education. That afternoon, a smaller meeting of several hundred parents and students at the Regina Mundi Church made appeals for students to return to school. Tsietsi Mashinini addressed the meeting and endorsed the call for a return to school. He announced that student leaders would meet the following morning at the Morris Isaacson High School. When that meeting in turn convened on 2 August, the Soweto Action Committee renamed itself the Soweto Students Representative Council (SSRC), re-elected Mashinini as chairman, and resolved that each of Soweto's 40 junior- and senior-secondary schools should be represented on the SSRC by two students. Murphy Morobe, another senior student at Morris Isaacson, became vice-chairman, replacing Seth Mazibuko who had been detained. It was agreed that a list of demands regarding Bantu education would be compiled and forwarded to the government though the SSRC. On Wednesday, 4 August, students would march to John Vorster Square, the headquarters of the Security Police, in downtown Johannesburg to demand the release of detained students and other leaders. Parents were to be urged to support student demands by not going to work between Wednesday and Friday.

Thus began a new confrontational phase of the student revolt. Just when black students in Johannesburg began successfully drawing older generations into the uprising, unrest was spreading spontaneously to new regions of the country. The 1976 stay-aways were primarily a demonstration of resolve and a vague threat that there could be worse to come if black demands were not met.

WITH THE SASO 9 BEHIND BARS ON ROBBEN ISLAND, OF THE EMINENT black-consciousness student leaders who helped create SASO and the black-consciousness movement it was Steve Biko whom the police targeted in the aftermath of the Soweto revolt. Since his 1973 banning and restriction to King

William's Town, Biko had continued to promote black consciousness and self-help through local Black Community Programmes. As far as the government was concerned, the philosophy of black consciousness had gripped the youth and was now moving into a dangerous phase, Saths Cooper recalled, "of mobilising a frontal assault on the state". Indeed, Biko believed, as Robert Massie once put it, "that the ideas of black consciousness were catching on and hoped that this would mark the beginning of significant change".[365]

When Biko emerged from gaol, he found the South African government in a funk. In late September, the police opened fire during the funeral of a 20-year-old man, killing several mourners. The SSRC, still the major political force in the township, had managed to organise a third stay-away, this time with the assistance of hostel dwellers; but a fourth one in early November failed. The SSRC members then tried to redirect their attention to the township. They launched campaigns to clean up the festering mounds of garbage that had piled up since the government had stopped collecting it in June; they demanded the closure of hundreds of shebeens; and they organised a partially successful Christmas boycott by black consumers of white stores. A few months later, at the height of its power, the SSRC successfully fought a large rent increase in Soweto.

It was in this atmosphere of rising militancy – a sense for the first time since the 1950s among the youth, Cooper told me, "that the regime could be shaken and maybe overthrown" – that the student movement suffered constant assaults by the government on their leaders and supporters. In 11 months, the SSRC went through no less than four presidents; one was arrested and three fled to Botswana.

Meanwhile, official harassment of Biko by the security police became an occupational hazard. During one of the police swoops in August 1976, Biko was arrested and imprisoned without charge. "On the day of his detention he seemed sure he would be back soon and did not appear unduly worried," his wife, Ntsiki, recalled to Massie "but we became extremely worried and his mother actually feared for his life."[366]

Much to Ntsiki's relief, Biko was released after 101 days of solitary confinement in prison; but her fears would soon prove prophetic.

*

365 Quoted in Massie (n 97 above).
366 Ibid., p. 419.

On 18 August 1977, Biko and a friend had strayed far outside the limits of his banning restriction into a roadblock near Grahamstown in the Eastern Cape. He was captured and transported to police headquarters in Port Elizabeth, stripped naked and confined to a dark, dank cell without contact with his family or water and soap to wash. He was fed only bread and water.[367]

On Tuesday morning, 1 September, after nearly three weeks in solitary confinement, prison guards interrogated Biko for several hours, handing him pamphlets from informants that they wanted him to acknowledge as his own. Biko was no stranger to interrogation; he could be defiant and reticent under duress. In the early hours of Wednesday morning, 2 September 1977, Biko's interrogators decided that, if he would not cooperate, they would use everything within their arsenal to break him.

When the morning team arrived, they found Biko unconscious and shackled to a grille on the floor. Several hours passed before a doctor revived him. During the next 24 hours, Biko, shackled in the interrogation room, neither ate nor urinated. Colonel Pieter Goosen, the blustery head of the Port Elizabeth Security Police, testified later that he was not alarmed by this because he believed that Biko, a medical student, was capable of faking these symptoms through "the use of yoga".[368] The next day, the police summoned a specialist who discovered that he had lost the extensor planar reflex in his foot, a sure sign of neurological impairment. When Goosen finally ordered Biko's transfer to the Sydenham Prison infirmary to determine whether there was cerebral bleeding, a spinal tap showed red cells. Still, the authorities concluded that the sample had been contaminated during the procedure and could not be interpreted as proof of injury to the brain.[369]

On Sunday, 11 September, the doctors informed Goosen that Biko urgently needed to be transferred to a hospital in Port Elizabeth. Instead, two police officers heaved Biko's limp body, still naked, into the back of a Land Rover, chained him inside and drove more than 1 500 kilometres north through the night to the fortified police hospital outside Pretoria. When they arrived, they dragged him into a filthy cell and left his battered body writhing on the cold concrete floor. A few hours later, wounded, naked and alone, Stephen Bantu Biko died.

His legacy, as we shall see, would become an inspiration to future battalions of black youths – well into the period beyond liberation.

---

367 Ibid., p. 421.
368 Ibid., p. 422.
369 Ibid.

PART V

The Apartheid-Skills Quandary

1977–1993

CHAPTER 17

A courtship of favours

BUSINESS AND APARTHEID

THE SMOULDERING EMBERS OF 16 JUNE 1976 FOUND THE BUSINESS
establishment brooding in a desperate dead end. Just a year earlier, the
government of John Vorster had rescued business from the massive show
of force by black-consciousness students. With the student movement's
organisational structures routed, business and government forged a sort of
unofficial pact – despite their differences, the continued accumulation of
wealth was harnessed to government's exercise of force over revolutionary
impulses among black students.

Now business was anxious again. The paroxysm of anger that had erupted
in that vast township, just a 20-minute drive from the manicured lawns and
posh villas of white suburbia in Johannesburg, shook the centurions of the
apartheid order and brought home the spectre of revolution for the first time
since the 1950s, when black mobilisation was at its peak.

To a small group within the elite establishment, the reaction of Soweto
students to some of the more egregious features of Bantu education – principally Afrikaans as a medium of instruction – and the state's violent reaction
were deeply unsettling. With the eyes of the world increasingly on graphic
images of young unarmed schoolchildren felled by heavily armed policemen, the country seemed adrift – South Africa presented a scene without
precedent since the Anglo-Boer War at the turn of the 20th century; a land
without order or purpose; "a surrealist tableaux of ruins", in author Ian
Sayer's expressive depiction of war-torn Germany during the early 1940s.[370]
Their prime concern was that apartheid was spawning radical ideas among
black students who, in the wake of the Soweto uprising, had cast a younger

---

370 Quoted in Sayer, I & Botting, D, *Nazi Gold: The Sensational Story of the World's Greatest Robbery*
(Britain: Mainstream Publishing, 1998).

generation of school-going youths as the standard-bearers of the coming revolution.

It may have crossed the minds of a few in elite circles that time was running out, and, in that connection, that the economy might plunge, in a manner of speaking, into free fall. That, at any rate, seems to have been the line of thought of a wealthy Johannesburg socialite named Irene Menell. As the student protests spread to other townships in the Transvaal in the spring of 1976, it was Irene Menell who took the initiative and turned her impressive network of social contacts to more progressive use.[371] As a Progressive Party liberal whose husband, Clive Menell, was Chairman of Anglo Transvaal Mines Consolidated, better known as Anglovaal, she included within her social set both government ministers and South African corporate leaders. Her idea was initially modest – to build a network of do-gooders in business. But they would become, in effect, a shadow administration, a 'corporate government' of influential individuals committed to saving capitalism.

*

At just that moment, on a wintry morning in December 1976, a small audience gathered at Amherst College in Massachusetts, in the United States, to hear a speech on an academic and cultural boycott of American corporations doing business in South Africa. The speaker, Karl Seidman, was Co-Chairman of the Amherst South African Support Committee. He had shot to prominence as one of the prime movers behind a campaign to urge the Board of Trustees of the college to commit to a student resolution on the withdrawal from South Africa by those US corporations in which the college owned stock. For several months, the committee Seidman helped create had been petitioning the Amherst College Board to urge US corporations to divest their holdings in South Africa. Twice their resolutions were defeated. Seidman reported to the gathering that the trustees had argued in their October decision that the continued participation of US corporations working to implement progressive policies in the South African economy "would be the best way to reform the system of apartheid in that country".[372] The college trustees, Seidman went on to report, maintained a sudden

371 See Pallister, D & Lepper, I (eds), *South Africa Inc.: The Oppenheimer Empire* (Simon & Schuster, 1987), p. 103.
372 Choragos, 'Colleges take different stands on South Africa', 8 December 1977, in USSALEP Collection, Wits Historical Papers.

exodus of US business from the country would do more harm than good to black South Africans. He then read out extracts from a statement issued by the trustees setting out Amherst's stand on the matter: "The Trustees will expect corporations active in South Africa to take positive steps to eliminate educational segregation, job segregation, unequal pay among the races and other practices which sustain apartheid."[373]

Then, in a radical break with college policy, Seidman roused his listeners by launching into a furious tirade against the college trustees. Amherst College was sanctioning "America's friendship with a regime that systematically discriminated against black races," he thundered. "I'd say that American companies are happy to ignore race laws in South Africa as long as they stand to profit. They are by implication helping to maintain the system of apartheid."[374] The audience erupted in cheers. Many students and academics present knew better.

By the early 1970s, the US economy was a huge flotilla of businesses floating on a sea of capital, international banking insurance and stock portfolios. Over the years, this environment had bred certain understandings about the way the stock market should work. The most important was known as the 'Wall Street Rule'. This widespread convention dictated that shareholders should hold on to their stock as long as they were happy with the performance of fund managers. Corporate managers liked this understanding because it meant that the infinite galaxy of industries, managers, companies and strategies could be reduced to a single measurement – the stock price. Like an omniscient deity, the market thus allotted merit and demerit with each shudder of the ticker tape. To transform the shareholder resolution system into a mechanism for influencing corporate policy, Seidman and his student associates at Amherst knew that they had to exert pressure on shareholders to exercise their democratic right to divest their stocks from South African businesses. As such, a repudiation of the Wall Street Rule also meant a rejection of the tradition of 'blind investor support'; it meant challenging the proxy universities had signed over to the fund managers. If public attention could be focused not only on investment returns but also on the morality of investment decisions, they realised, then the trustees of universities could be prevailed on.

Seidman concluded by denouncing apartheid and calling on students to

---

373 Ibid.
374 Ibid.

take urgent action. "Our petitions have been defeated," he said. "It is time to stage demonstrations to force the college to review its decision."[375]

The anti-apartheid US–South Africa Student Solidarity Movement marked something of a turning point in the US struggle for hearts and minds in South Africa. The media prominence of the campaign signalled the final attempt by the South African government to reform state policy on Bantu education and business.

What is probably true is that the agenda-setting circumstances of Irene Menell and her business network started with two parallel dramas that began to unfold in 1961/1962 and slowly converged a few years later. One was a bold political gambit by an elite network of somewhat incongruous forces in South Africa bonded by a common goal to reform apartheid while maintaining its essential features. The other was global in scope – hatched not in South Africa, but in the United States.

To understand why the Amherst initiative was so important to the work of Menell, it is first necessary to reach back to the developing relationship between business and apartheid that made a response to the education crisis all the more urgent and the two men who would become major forces behind the initiative: Harry Oppenheimer and Charles Engelhard.

A HARD RAIN PELTED THE STREETS OF NEW YORK ONE AFTERNOON IN EARLY 1960, sluicing down the gutters. Harry Oppenheimer, who had recently been crowned prince of the Anglo American Corporation empire, trotted through the dim light of the swanky Carlyle Hotel lobby to an ornate private dining room.

He shook the rain from his overcoat and with a broad smile waved hello to his host. A young Massachusetts senator, clean-cut with boyish good looks, named John F Kennedy sat alongside a beautiful brunette woman named Jackie. Seated opposite the Kennedys was a nebbish man named Charles Engelhard.

In public appearances, Harry Oppenheimer's manner was polished and self-confident, a harbinger of the change the United States sought to midwife from the South African quandary of the 1960s. Physically, he was of medium height, neatly turned out with a round face and a fine moustache. He was the

---

375 Ibid.

archetypal mining oligarch: rapacious, pugnacious, a modern-day Rhodes. As a well-connected German Jew who had become a naturalised Briton, his father, Ernest Oppenheimer, was destined for great things in South Africa. He had all the characteristics likely to cause resentment and envy among the white Afrikaner population. He arrived on the diamond fields of Kimberley in November 1902, five months after the end of the bitterly fought South African war which brought the Afrikaner republics of the Orange Free State and the Transvaal into the British Empire.[376] At the age of 22, the silk-hatted, bloated character of Hoggenheimer, wrote David Pallister and others in their history of the Anglo American empire, "with strong Semitic features soon came over the years to personify the hated capitalist in both communist and later Afrikaner nationalist propaganda".[377]

With money borrowed from the US company Consolidated Mines Selection (CMS) in 1915, Ernest Oppenheimer set up what was initially known as the African American Corporation in 1917. Those in the United States disliked the name because, as William Honnold, Managing Director at CMS, commented around that time, it "would suggest [on the US side] our dark-skinned fellow countrymen and possibly result in ridicule".[378] The name Anglo American Corporation of South Africa was eventually agreed on and the company was incorporated in September 1917 with an issued capital of £1 million.[379] From then on, Anglo, as it came to be known, forged strong relations with the United States while drawing hostility from Afrikaner nationalists since 1948 toward Anglo's 'imperialist leanings'.

The Oppenheimers were quick to see crisis in the developing relationship between apartheid and business. One of Harry's broadsides took direct aim at the indulgence Verwoerd had extended to territorial segregation. "What good was an apartheid order if it didn't bring prosperity?" he once asked.[380]

Within days of the Sharpeville massacre in March 1960, he and a group of businessmen had requested an urgent meeting with Verwoerd to discuss the relaxation of the country's pass and education laws and wider group participation in the country's politics, but Verwoerd did not oblige. All the while Oppenheimer saw the Christian Calvinist fanaticism and emotional frenzy of Afrikaner rallies in the build-up to the referendum on a republic

---

376 Pallister & Lepper (n 371 above), p. 48.
377 Ibid.
378 Ibid., p. 54.
379 Ibid.
380 Ibid.

and found them worrisome rituals reminiscent of the torchlight marches and pagan parades in Nazi Germany. But it was, above all, the threat to his business interests of an Afrikaner nationalist government and the spectre of communist retribution that bothered him. Sir Ernest Oppenheimer, wrote David Pallister in his account of Anglo, pressed two lessons on his son: "He being of Jewish decent would have to excel to survive and then constantly engage those in power. Harry Oppenheimer seemed to add two lessons of his own. One was his already deep and abiding anti-communism."[381] The other was a view of what business and political alliances would do for his business interests. A few businessmen were troubled, they admitted – but for Oppenheimer it was always a question of what could they do. He being a first-generation South African of German–Jewish descent knew better. Anglo, to be sure, had no qualms about secretly trading with both the Nazis and Soviets, and even conspiring with the apartheid government when it suited the company. But the nationalist upsurge sweeping the African continent and recalcitrance of Verwoerd to reform the apartheid system threatened to turn South Africa into a dark, brooding sense of dread.

He had assumed control of the Anglo American empire on his father's death in 1957 and retired from Parliament. By 1961, he had skilfully combined the art of politics with his family's shrewdness for business. He had bankrolled the liberal opposition in South Africa and, along with his late father, diversified into just about every sector of the South African and global economy.

The group controlled 40 per cent of South Africa's gold, 80 per cent of the world's diamonds, a sixth of the world's copper, and it was the country's largest producer of coal.[382] The family home, a sprawling estate in Johannesburg called Brenthurst, was an emblem. I had twice visited the estate in the mid-1990s and early 2000s after Harry Oppenheimer's death. The old appurtenances and signatures of the family's fortunes were well maintained: impressionist paintings, antique silver, Louis XV furniture.[383]

Harry Oppenheimer was no less meticulous to a fault on the day he met Kennedy. Having benefited from cheap, unskilled black labour during the early mining days and experienced first-hand the problem posed by apartheid for industry's demand for a more mobile and skilled black labour force,

381 Ibid.
382 Ibid., p. 93.
383 Ibid.

Anglo found a loophole in the system: if the export of unprocessed minerals to the United States could be secured, the problem of skills and black mobility could be subverted.

Kennedy knew that Oppenheimer's tight control over the supply and demand of diamonds through the London-based Central Selling Organisation was necessary to maintain the industry's viability. According to Pallister, he also knew that the US Justice Department had received information that the "De Beers organisation was a large contributor to both political parties and should this investigation get to a stage where cases were actually filed, the anti-trust division would probably receive much political pressure".[384] This raised the possibility that the diamond cartel and its allies might have found some way of intervening in the anti-trust division.

Pretoria was viewed as an important Cold War ally in Washington, Kennedy knew, but South Africa was also strategic in other respects that made Oppenheimer a valuable resource. Thus were the two men linked by a common interest and affinity.

But as Kennedy cast an uneasy eye over Oppenheimer's violation of American anti-trust laws, not to mention Oppenheimer's public denunciation of black majority rule, he found the Verwoerd government in South Africa more immediately troubling. In 1960, the United States was the focal point of international pressure in the United Nations (UN) to disinvest from South Africa after the bannings of liberation organisations and the Sharpeville massacre in March 1961. Disinvestment also had the potential to throttle the diamond- and gold-mining industries. Oppenheimer felt the continuation of trade between the United States and South Africa was the only way to keep the industry on its feet.

And so when news of Sharpeville spread across the world and the UN began discussing the imposition of sanctions on South Africa, it was to Charles Engelhard that Oppenheimer turned for an introduction to Washington's high society.

*

For a while, US student activists focused on Engelhard as a tangible target for their sanctions campaign after discovering that the New Jersey Regional Office of the National Conference of Christians and Jews intended to give

---

384 Ibid.

Engelhard the group's annual Brotherhood Award at a special dinner in his honour.[385] The leader of the activist group, George Houser, protested sharply on the grounds that Engelhard was a major supporter and beneficiary of the apartheid economy "on the back of a Bantu education and cheap labour system".[386] On the day of the award, five hundred chanting demonstrators – mainly students – from the American Committee on Africa and local churches and universities picketed the dinner. In Robert Massie's account, Engelhard, red-faced and angry, and , surrounded by a police escort, pressed through the barrier of people and received the award for 'building human understanding'.[387]

In this milieu, he was a master of exploiting the wildly profitable frontiers of US trade with polecat governments. Around the world, Engelhard moved in the shadows of opportunities. These advantages, combined with his awareness of his own entrepreneurial talents, rapidly gave Engelhard a brash sense of self-assurance that made him a commanding presence.

He had led a colourful life in the Cold War as a sanctions-buster and brought the same entrepreneurial gusto to South Africa, combining overseas financial exploits with cloak-and-dagger intrigue. With a coveted place in Washington high society and an impressive list of contacts across the business world, Engelhard was one of those elusive oddballs orbiting Oppenheimer's world; a predatory capitalist; a shrewd law-skirting buccaneer who took his business opportunities and his partners where he found them. He was the last US member of the board of Anglo and a liberal contributor to political campaigns according to the purest capitalist principles. He was in favour of the winner, whoever that might be.

The protest against Engelhard produced no results, however, leaving Houser and the anti-apartheid activists pondering where to focus next. The answer came with the efforts of two students at the Union Theological Seminary, Charles Powers and David Hornbeck. The two young men, who had been enrolled in a special one-year intensive programme at Columbia University's School of International Relations,[388] decided to spend part of their academic year studying US trading practices with, and bank lending to, the apartheid regime.

Their target was Engelhard's empire, Engelhard Minerals and Chemicals

---

385 See Cummings (n 207 above), p. 175.
386 Ibid.
387 See Massie (n 97 above), p. 215.
388 Ibid., p. 215.

Inc., a diversified company based in New York City he built from a small metal-fabricating company he inherited from his father and incorporated in Delaware, the swashbuckling tax haven for Washington's financial elite. In the late 1940s, he had journeyed to South Africa to make his fortune from a surplus of gold in the mines, but government regulations prohibited the export of gold bullion from South Africa without permits from the central bank. Britain, which still controlled the financial affairs of South Africa, wanted to retain as much gold as possible within the sterling bloc. Engelhard found a legal loophole through that regulation: while it was illegal to export gold bars, it was legal to export objects d'art made of gold. And so, through a form of financial alchemy, he formed a company called Precious Metals Development that bought gold from the mines and cast it in statues and other religious items. He exported these religious objects d'art to Hong Kong, where they were melted down and turned back into gold bullion, which could then be sold on the free market.[389]

When Engelhard first crossed paths with Harry Oppenheimer in Johannesburg, there was an instant bond. As Pallister notes, "Both men shared much in common: Jewish roots, a passion for racehorses, and on occasions brilliant raconteurs."[390] They were also approximately the same age and fabulously wealthy. Oppenheimer invited Engelhard to join the board of Anglo, and, for his part, Engelhard invited Oppenheimer to participate in a number of mutually profitable joint ventures.

Oppenheimer relied on Engelhard Minerals and Chemicals Inc. to provide the services, credit terms, and contacts necessary to keep its US clients from buying their synthetic diamond grit from General Electric.[391] Powers and Hornbeck later concluded that Oppenheimer turned to Engelhard to take up the General Electric challenge.[392] Their discoveries were wide-ranging, including the claim that Oppenheimer had constructed a labyrinth of corporate camouflage to evade US anti-trust regulations. The Justice Department investigators theorised that, before General Electric began mass-producing synthetic industrial diamonds, De Beers had been able to manipulate diamond prices from its offshore bases in London and Johannesburg. Now, however, with General Electric pouring out a virtually unlimited supply of

---

389 Ibid., p. 217.
390 Pallister & Lepper (n 371 above), pp. 118-119.
391 See Epstein, EJ, 'Chapter 18: The American conspiracy', in *The Diamond Invention: The American Conspiracy* (Hutchinson, 1982). Accessed at http://edwardjayepstein.com/diamond/chap18_print. htm; also see Pallister et al, pp. 151-154.
392 See Massie's account (n 97 above), pp. 214-215.

industrial diamond abrasives, major users of industrial diamonds were no longer dependent on De Beers. The De Beers cartel then decided to intervene directly in the United States by covertly buying control of companies that distributed diamond grit and diamond drill stones. Through these companies, it guaranteed itself a share of the US market.

Specifically, Oppenheimer had arranged for Engelhard's holding company, Engelhard Hanover, to become the US distributor for De Beers' abrasive grits. "The idea was that grit sales needed a new 'American look', with the old De Beers monopoly image less exposed," the lawyers noted. They concluded that the entire scheme was intended by De Beers to avoid "exposing gem monopoly to anti-trust sanctions".[393]

After months of research, Powers and Hornbeck concluded that the two banks that had shown the most initiative in extending financial services to Engelhard were Chase Manhattan and First National City Bank (later Citibank), both of which owned and operated their own branches in South Africa. Citibank, they found, had been secretly building up a cache of 'black gold' looted by Germany during the Second World War and appropriated by the United States after Germany's defeat. It seemed likely, they surmised, that the bank had been playing a role in laundering apartheid gold in similar fashion, with Engelhard and Oppenheimer the principal protagonists.

In reconstructing this complicated arrangement, the US Justice Department investigators later found that it was based on a quid pro quo. In return for acting as an intermediary for De Beers, Engelhard received all the costs for setting up a Swiss company called Prometco, plus a guaranteed profit of 100 000 English pounds a year. It was a fairly lucrative deal for Engelhard, and it also accommodated his friend Oppenheimer. Armed with their study, Powers and Hornbeck visited student groups in nearby schools to enlist their support of a boycott of First National's and Citibank's branches in Morningside Heights near the seminary. Quickly, the Amherst Solidarity Committee, the Student Cabinet of Union Seminary, the Columbia University Student Council, the Executive Committee of Government at the Theological Seminary, and the Managing Board of the newspaper at Barnard College all signed on. Soon afterwards, other groups from outside academia offered their support, including the American Committee on Africa and the Southern Africa Council of the National Student Christian Federation, which later became the University Christian Movement (UCM)

393 See Epstein (n 371 above), pp. 151-154.

and a major force behind the formation of Steve Biko's South African Students' Organisation (SASO) and the Black People's Convention (BPC) in South Africa.

*

After a preliminary investigation into the trade, US authorities later filed a lawsuit accusing Oppenheimer of flouting anti-trust legislation. But it was a strange convergence of ideas, interests and affections between Oppenheimer and Engelhard that was one of the more curious subplots that intrigued Kennedy. If Engelhard was in a way the US's North Star in its project of securing African resources, Oppenheimer was the driving force on the ground.

Meanwhile, faced with these challenges in South Africa, John Vorster, who had struggled to be faithful to the doctrine of his dead master and to bring Verwoerd's gauzy vision of the future into the gritty present, had swung round to an outward-looking foreign-policy dispensation and the need for foreign investment. In the United States, Engelhard worked his special brand of alchemy to front the sale of US diamonds to the diamond cartel. In this fashion, the relationship between Oppenheimer and Engelhard – and thus the United States and South Africa – had been uniquely awkward.

By then, various heads of state were indebted to Engelhard, who had better connections in Africa than most of their ambassadors. Engelhard wanted to convince Kennedy that Oppenheimer was a worthy interlocutor and a man with whom to do business.

The risks taken on behalf of the United States, Kennedy must have felt, had earned the men at least an hour of his time at the Carlyle Hotel in New York. The men immediately warmed to each other and they cast protocol aside and spent over an hour talking on all manner of subjects: on apartheid, on the African National Congress (ANC) and on the prospects for peaceful change in South Africa. But there was one subject they touched upon about which Kennedy was uncharacteristically coy: sanctions.[394]

*

Soon after the Amherst gathering in 1977, General Motors (GM), which had been heavily invested in South Africa and eager to staunch pressure to

---

394 Ibid.

disinvest, appointed a committee of five outside directors to develop ideas to release the pressure. The challenge, GM knew, was to find someone to lead the team who had sufficient standing in the black community to neutralise criticisms of the corporation, yet could be counted on to understand and support the basic principles of capitalism. GM eventually settled on the Reverend Leon Sullivan, a 49-year-old pastor of the Zion Baptist Church in North Philadelphia and a national advocate of remedial and vocational training for the inner-city poor.

Born in 1922 in a clapboard house in Charleston, West Virginia, Sullivan had been raised by his deeply religious grandmother. At the age of 10 he was thrown out of a store in downtown Charleston after unwittingly trying to buy a Coca-Cola at a whites-only counter. Demonstrating precocious resolve, Sullivan immediately embarked on a personal crusade against racial injustice. For years he persisted without encouragement or success.[395]

When he graduated from high school, Sullivan attended West Virginia State College, an all-black institution, on a basketball scholarship. In his undergraduate year, his grandmother, whose health was rapidly failing and who couldn't afford medical care, exhorted him from her sickbed: "Leonie, help your people," she told him. "And don't let this kind of thing happen to anybody else."[396] A few days later Sullivan decided to become a clergyman. While still at College, he met Adam Clayton Powell, who had been a member of the National Association for the Advancement of Colored People (NAACP). Powell liked him and soon became his patron.

At the same time as the Sullivan principles were being adopted, the first ripples of activity were surfacing. Other universities followed suit – Harvard and then Yale. Outside Washington, the growing community of activist investors had responded to the Soweto uprising with a new burst of support for sanctions of various kinds. Corporate executives also began feeling more pressure to articulate a plausible policy with which to respond to public inquiries. The surge of interest convinced some executives to back Sullivan's efforts to draft a statement of principles. During the summer of 1976, as the media debated the role of the US government and business in South Africa, calls for decisive action increased. Tim Smith and the Interfaith Center on Corporate Responsibility stung GM by publishing a full-page advertisement that had been purchased for GM dealers in South Africa declaring their

395 See Massie (n 97 above), p. 287.
396 Ibid.

support for the South African Defence Force. In August 1976, Vernon Jordan of the National Urban League publicly demanded that US corporations in South Africa declare a moratorium on all new investments and become more active in ending apartheid. By the fall, the external pressure on corporations had eased and Sullivan's efforts to advance the principles faltered. Sullivan's campaign received a boost with the election of Jimmy Carter, who indicated his intention to redirect US foreign policy. Carter's foreign-policy team faced the gargantuan task of altering the policies established over eight years by Henry Kissinger. The new president had announced that the cornerstone of his foreign policy would be a commitment to re-evaluate the US's relations with dozens of countries. His new ambassador to the UN, Andrew Young, was quick to extend the new approach to southern Africa in January 1977. Even before he had assumed the post, he told reporters that he thought the new administration would have "an aggressive policy to move towards majority rule in southern Africa". "I don't see sanctions," Young continued, "because sanctions very seldom have worked. I think what we have got to do is find ways to use the tremendous influence we have to move towards majority rule."[397]

Carter, while agreeing with Young's sentiments, spent the first months searching for a balance between the tacit cooperation of the past and an outright break with Pretoria. Within weeks of the inauguration, the United States began proposing that the members of the UN security Council approve a Declaration of Principles opposing racism in southern Africa. The State Department then drew up a secret list of additional steps – from withdrawing US military attachés in Pretoria and ending the exchange of intelligence information to reducing loan guarantees and refusing visas to South Africans – that the US government could take. Leon Sullivan's effort – a privately sponsored, religiously guided effort to induce change within key sectors of the South African economy – seemed the perfect corollary.[398]

Young worked actively to shape and promote the endorsement of the corporate statement of principles. Despite the many statements they had made about their commitment to equality after the uprising in Soweto and a full year of private discussions, several executives were still uncertain whether they should sign Sullivan's statement.

On 1 March 1977, after 18 months of private pushing, debating and

---

397 Ibid., pp. 407-408.
398 Ibid.

cajoling, Sullivan finally announced the "statement of principles of US firms with affiliates in the Republic of South Africa", in which he called for non-segregation, equal and fair employment, the development of training programmes for blacks, an increase in blacks in management positions, and improved schooling for blacks.[399]

The South African government responded with cautious approval. "This … is a very laudable stand to take as opposed to the one you first advocated," wrote the South African counsel to Sullivan. The Urban Foundation similarly welcomed the codes as a moderate way to balance its growth imperatives with change. Anti-apartheid groups were less enthusiastic. George Houser of the American Committee on Africa immediately attacked the principles as "an exercise in triviality". "There is no demand for any change in the fundamental structure of apartheid, no demand for black political rights and equal education," wrote Houser a month after the announcement. As a result, "there is no way that a continued US corporate presence in South Africa can serve any purpose except to reinforce white rule".[400]

Meanwhile, similar student efforts to those of Amherst were eliciting a strong response on other US campuses: A few days later, an Ad Hoc Committee for Divestment Now of Wellesley College had begun actively campaigning on campus, calling for the divestment before 20 December that year of an estimated USD38 million worth of shares which Wellesley held in corporations with holdings in South Africa.[401] The group sponsored a rally and circulated fact sheets on the role of multinational corporations in South Africa as well as petitions advocating divestment. At about noon on a day in early April the following year, students at Wesleyan University began a four-day sit-in at the Board of Trustees offices. They refused to leave the offices unless the Chair of the Board, Colin Campbell, agreed to reconstitute the Board and withdraw the university's investments in US banks that provided finance for South African businesses. Around the same time, students on the campus of Yale University peacefully protested the issue of South African racial policy. A Special Yale Committee demanded that Yale divest about USD200 million invested in companies and banks dealing with South Africa.[402] Another Yale student group staged a demonstration on a Saturday morning in early April calling for more direct action – 'complete and

399 Ibid., p. 408.
400 Ibid., p. 409.
401 *Greenwich Times*, 'Wesleyan students protest college South Africa policy', 17 April 1978.
402 Ibid.

immediate divestment' from all companies doing business in South Africa.

By late 1977, Harvard and Yale university students had joined Amherst in their opposition to the Sullivan codes. In South Africa, the black-consciousness-inspired SASO and the South African Students Movement (SASM) leadership reacted with irritation and anger, arguing that the Sullivan principles had no programme except the furtherance of the US system. The issue, they argued, came down to attempts by business and government to salvage the apartheid economy without overhauling its racial underpinnings: Bantu education and Bantustans.

They knew that time was not on their side. In the final months of 1976, the country was sliding into utter economic chaos. The apartheid legacy was formidable.

HARD TIMES MEANT DESPERATE MEASURES, AND, THOUGH IRENE MENELL might not have had 'stakeholder capitalism' in mind when she turned her social network into a philanthropic endeavour, she recalled the idea "blossoming" into an audacious gambit: to save capitalism.[403]

The story, relayed by David Pallister et al., is that, some time in August 1976, Clive and Irene Menell met Freddie van Wyk, a Director at the South African Institute of Race Relations, and George Palmer, editor of the highly influential organ of capitalist opinion, the *Financial Mail*, and they discussed the idea of a social-welfare organisation that would fund education and skills development programmes aimed at staving off wider unrest and, potentially, revolution. Both men thought it was a "great idea". "There are little pockets of that sort of concern all around the country," Irene recalled Van Wyk saying. "Why don't you try and put them all together? Anglo-American's got this big housing conference geared up for November 1976. Why don't you see if you can move it through that?"[404]

Anglo's chairman, Harry Oppenheimer, was in England at that time and the four met Nick Dermont, his personal assistant. Dermont liked the idea and agreed to use the housing conference as a vehicle. They agreed that the new initiative would be co-hosted by a business powerhouse in South Africa focused on a "broader urban problem framework".[405] In September,

---

403 See Pallister & Lepper (n 371 above), p. 103.
404 Ibid., p. 103.
405 Ibid.

Dermont flew to England and sold the idea to Oppenheimer and Zach de Beer, an Anglo executive and ex-Progressive Federal Party member of Parliament (MP). Oppenheimer then contacted Anton Rupert, Chairman of the Rembrandt Group, who was also overseas, and won his support. Then Clive Menell and David de Villiers, former president of the South African Press Association, took a letter of endorsement that had been signed by Oppenheimer overseas and persuaded other co-hosts to back the exercise.[406]

The Urban Foundation, launched at a glitzy ceremony in November 1976 at the swanky Anglo-owned Carlton Hotel in central Johannesburg, was the result. Oppenheimer was elected its first Chairman and Jan Steyn, a judge on special leave from the Cape Supreme Court, became Executive Director. Its leadership was primarily corporate, with Anton Rupert its Deputy Chairman and Zac de Beer and Clive Menell among its 23 founding directors.[407]

But amid the tinkling of champagne glasses, it was Oppenheimer who presented the gentle face of capitalism. The Foundation's general aims, he told the elite gathering, were to establish highly visible welfare projects in black urban areas which would help steer thinking away from radicalism towards acceptance of capitalism. Modelled on the United States–South Africa Leader Exchange Program (USSALEP) and similar US initiatives in developing countries which had sprung up since the mid-1950s, the Foundation's philosophical premise was that reform rather than repression would do more to halt revolutionary impulses that had been welling up in black townships and schools since the Soweto student uprising. "As the arm and voice of private enterprise," Judge Steyn wrote shortly after the launch, "the Urban Foundation is now applying its resources to help achieve peace and stability that all South Africans seek."[408] Years later, Steyn took a more pointed view. "At stake was nothing less than the very survival of the capitalist social order," he said, "for if free enterprise was to be saved, it was imperative that businessmen were seen to dissociate themselves from racially discriminatory practices in areas where they still have some choice, such as education."[409] The *Financial Mail* took a similar tack. The Foundation, it editorialised in 1979, "was set up to search for constructive ways and means of preserving an economy endangered by African revolt against conditions

---

406 Ibid.
407 Ibid., p. 105.
408 Ibid., p. 104.
409 Ibid.

in the townships and schools".[410] A few years later, the same publication cast the Foundation's strategy in explicitly ideological terms: The creation of a "black middle class", its editors wrote, "must have a stake in stability and provide a counter to the process of socialist radicalism".[411]

This logic immediately appealed to the corporate community. Right from the start, the Urban Foundation drew support across the board: from English- and Afrikaans-speaking South African companies to foreign multinationals. Central to its strategic line was an understanding that the economic crisis of the 1970s was both a structural mismatch between the supply and demand of skills and a belief that the scope and sophistication of state repression alone would not contain township youth revolts. Coercion would increasingly have to be drawn into what the *Financial Mail* described as "an alliance with capitalism".[412]

From his position as Chairman, Harry Oppenheimer said shortly after the launch that, in the opinion of Anglo American and business in general, nationalist policy was dangerous because it led to both a skills shortage and prevented business from drawing blacks into its accumulation path.[413] Part of the Foundation's strategy, he said, was to finance education and training projects aimed at deradicalising the black youth and encouraging a culture of aspiration towards middle-class ideals. The majority of these projects were to be locally based and would include building schools and community centres.

To carry out his mission, the intellectual Sullivan now turned to the men of action, the Urban Foundation.

*

As one of its first actions, the Foundation had already co-opted National African Federated Chamber of Commerce (NAFCOC) leader Sam Motsuenyane onto its Board, and, after some hesitation, provided NAFCOC with a loan towards the establishment of Black Chain supermarkets.

Between 1977 and 1983, the Foundation launched and participated in 620 projects to the value of R47 million, a sizeable sum during that time. It

---

410 Ibid.
411 Quoted in Saul, JS & Gelb, S, *The Crisis in South Africa* (New York: Monthly Review Press, 1981), p. 45.
412 Ibid., p. 2.
413 See Sarakinsky, M, *The Changing Urban African Class Structure: 1970-1985.* MA dissertation, University of the Witwatersrand, October 1989, p. 156.

financed, or was involved in, over 250 educational undertakings, constituting an investment of over R17 million of business funds.

In 1982, the Anglo American Chairman's Fund – described as South Africa's other government because of the amounts of money it was channelling into African education and training – noted that it had spent over R25 million, of which 74 per cent had been devoted to secondary and tertiary educational projects.

These initiatives by capital in the provision of education and training had not, as Linda Chisolm argued at the time, been simply designed to meet the economic need for technically qualified manpower. The purpose, she declared, had been as much to wed workers more firmly to capitalist values in an attempt to win the "hearts and minds" of Africans.[414] Through the intentions of business and the state, limited upward mobility, facilitated by the removal of job reservation, might come to be regarded as a possibility, if not a reality.

*

Despite hostility by the government towards the Foundation's 'liberal' stance on education and urban development, the urgent need to address the question of power-sharing since the Soweto uprising led the government and the Foundation to cooperate around the formation of African 'community councils' as substitutes for a national political voice for urban blacks. Judge Steyn played a leading role in drafting the Black Local Authorities Act, the legal basis for the councils which would become a source of rebellion by black youths once more in the early 1980s.

Notwithstanding radical opinion, it was an extraordinary compact between business and government. By 1977, the erstwhile foes seemed to have swung round to the same objectives. As Leon Louw, who had dabbled in big business but set greater store in small business through his Free Market Foundation, put it: "The foundation was created by big business and it was created to secure its interests; it wanted to appease blacks; it wanted genuinely to bring about black advancement."[415]

Far from seeing African middle and capitalist classes as a destabilising class of black Englishmen and radicals, elements within the white ruling

---

414 Pallister & Lepper (n 371 above), pp. 69-70.
415 Interview with the author, Johannesburg, August 2011.

party and economic power bloc were beginning to see that the longer-term survival of capitalism depended on the development of this class. And they conveyed this to the government, which was not unresponsive to their suggestions, many of which pre-figured PW Botha's 'total strategy' in the late 1970s. Urged by Samuel Huntington in 1977 and published in the White Paper on Defence that year, the total strategy was a combination of repression and reform in the state's attempt to regain control of the political arena – to combat what was termed the 'total onslaught' of communism facing the country both internally and externally after the collapse of Portuguese colonialism in neighbouring Mozambique and Angola.[416] In fact, the total strategy was the focal point around which a new ruling political alliance between the white capitalist class, the military and the National Party emerged. It embodied measures included in the Wiehahn and Riekert commissions to recognise the permanence of urban Africans and disarticulate them from radical Africans by granting them privileges and co-opting a stratum of the black population into what would eventually become the tricameral Parliament.[417]

In their eagerness to emerge from the laager[418] and transcend the labour supply problem that had sprung from the seeds of Afrikaner mining and manufacturing capital during the 1950s, the new Afrikaner elite and English business found themselves in an awkward embrace: they wanted a third way between extreme apartheid and economic liberalism encapsulated in an earlier 1942 proposal by the liberal opposition party in Parliament called the Fagan Report. The view was that, in order to hold business against the territorial designs of Verwoerdian apartheid, it was essential for business to hold the West.

In reality, the backroom proxy fights between the Afrikaner-nationalist establishment and business were between two kinds of ugliness. The Anglo-liberal business establishment made unconvincing founding fathers of segregation; and, when Verwoerd rose to power in 1958, businessmen sympathetic to the Afrikaner-nationalist cause played a double game – midwifing the economic liberalisation process while ensuring victory for Verwoerd. In practice, economic liberalism added a gloss to an otherwise racist conviction. The Oppenheimer–liberal axis's policy on race was no different from Verwoerd's moral disposition: to support political racial segregation, even

---

416 Sarakinsky (n 413 above), pp. 158-159.
417 Ibid., p. 160.
418 Loosely translated: a circle of wagons used by the Voortrekkers during battle.

when their rhetoric seemed to suggest economic liberalisation. This was the basis for what was perhaps their single most important contribution to the business effort in the war against apartheid: their role in planning a momentous initiative that united Afrikaner nationalists and business against the student-led sanctions campaign.

And so the government in South Africa became a genial collaboration between wealthy capitalists and a political elite. At the centre was the Oppenheimer empire which rivalled the great fortunes of Paris, London and New York. As a man who understood what he wanted, Harry Oppenheimer and the National Party now had a courtship of favours. It was an extraordinary relationship which had for years exploited unskilled black miners, paying wages below the poverty line. Now he was suggesting that blacks had reasonable prospects of advancing through education and training.

This is the point where business had become a movement, on the surface stridently invoking the ideals of liberalism, but beneath the veil the emerging elite agenda pretty much fitted the old apartheid mould. The great new political and economic experiment following the Soweto uprising of 1976 had been dissolving in red ink – wealth for a few and penury for the majority.

CHAPTER 18

Saving capitalism

NEO-APARTHEID

IF THERE WAS A QUANDARY OF THE LATE APARTHEID YEARS, A GIANT SNAG in the system that embodied all the social and economic distortions of 'separate development', it was the race–skills paradox. From Hendrik Verwoerd's aggressive drive to restrict just about every facet of economic life of blacks to Bantustans and racially segregated peri-urban townships to John Vorster's urban decentralisation scheme, much of apartheid history was a carefully orchestrated crusade against black encroachments, no matter how small, on the countryside and cities of white South Africa. Although the economic system groaned under the heavy burden of growing internal contradictions as black labour began pouring into lumbering industries and onto farms to meet the rising demand for labour by employers, the giant machine of inferior education, job reservation, segregated areas, pass laws and influx controls disrupted the natural tendency toward some sort of equilibrium, confining the skills and mobility of blacks to hovels of poverty and destitution while only partially and temporarily accommodating their presence in white areas as migrant labourers.

By the early days of state reform, in the late 1970s, the system had become an economic disaster. The rising manufacturing and services sector bore the full brunt of the underlying distortions of apartheid state planning: "Persistent and deepening mismatches between the demands of the economy and the massive systemic restrictions placed on the supply of black skills and mobility," recalled Christo Nel.[419]

From the time he was a young University of Pretoria graduate student, Nel knew that the numbers didn't add up. In 1984, he was offered a research post in a groundbreaking exploratory project set up by the University of

---

419 Hereinafter, all direct references to Nel are from an interview with the author, Johannesburg, October 2011.

South Africa (UNISA) business school called Project Free Enterprise. Nel did not see himself as yet another apartheid policy wonk or bureaucrat, and took the job eagerly.

At that stage, the Business School was conducting research into perceptions of black people about economic systems generally. The specific mandate of Project Free Enterprise was to investigate the scope for black enterprise development within the developing apartheid economy. From his position as a researcher, Nel now had a bird's-eye view of the system, one that gave whites abundant opportunities and resources to become fabulously wealthy. Not only were they given the best schools, universities, art, theatres, infrastructure, and recreational facilities, but also jobs and business opportunities.

Not surprisingly, Nel's initial research showed that black workers viewed free enterprise as discriminatory. They saw big business as 'hugely exploitative' and small-business opportunities – private property, markets, small shops and merchants – as unevenly developed and skewed in favour of white enterprises. They demanded the abolition of laws which restricted the size and scope of black income and business opportunities. And they developed strong antipathies to the system of capitalism, which they saw as the root of exploitative and discriminatory patterns of social relations.

And so Nel's research contract was extended and his mandate broadened to include an investigation into alternative economic models and processes for identifying and teaching black people that free enterprise was a system worthy of support. To accomplish this task would have required their participation in the system. But there was just one problem: Nel sensed that the ground was trembling. "The problem of perceptions was a product of the system itself," he recalled. "What we were seeing and hearing on the ground was the cumulative crisis of apartheid."

*

For some reason he never explained, wrote Allister Sparks, who was editor of the *Daily Telegraph* in the late 1970s, Verwoerd named 1978 as the year when the tidal influx would turn and the ebb of black people back to the homelands would begin. "It was a date that acquired the status of an Oracle's prediction," Sparks observed.[420]

---

420 See Sparks (n 347 above), p. 200.

A year after the Amherst gathering and the student protests that followed, the government of John Vorster collapsed under a dark cloud known as the Muldergate scandal. The swift rise to power of his Bonapartist successor, PW Botha, was the opening salvo in an era that would come to be defined by a 'Total Strategy' – a lethal combination of both 'economic liberalisation' and state repression. Over the course of the next decade, the reform of corporate environments would be one of the Botha government's main defences against both the impact of Bantu education and the ideological appeal of radical ideas among black students and workers.

By the time Botha came to power in 1978, South Africa had already entered the twilight years of the apartheid experiment. The independence of the homelands automatically meant the denationalisation of black South Africans associated with them, summed up by the words of Dr Connie Mulder, Minister of Plural Relations, when he observed in 1978 that "one day there would be no black South Africans".[421] He was wrong, of course. The enthusiasm with which the state bureaucracy sought to label every black South African as belonging to some or other independent or self-governing homeland was matched by the determination of many city-based blacks not to be so labelled.[422]

As part of the deal that propelled him upward, Botha's first public act was to guarantee Afrikaners a place in the sun. In Botha's world view, it was apartheid's mission to prevent black encroachments on whites. But the grand apartheid dream of Verwoerd was over. As we shall see, it was the economy of skills shortages and economic demand, and the chaos of apartheid planning that would be the next test case.

In his first speech to Parliament, Botha outlined plans for the reversal of urbanisation. The essence of the new scheme was that, instead of transferring land to the homelands, the emphasis would be on creating jobs. The government had encouraged industry to move to the homelands before Botha's accession, but the incentives were inadequate. While the apartheid state theoretically provided for a constellation of semi-autonomous states, in reality the Bantustans were little more than impoverished dust bowls and reservoirs of mostly unskilled labour.

But throughout 1978, the basic human instinct for entrepreneurship survived in this hostile climate. The desire to survive and even thrive, to make

421 Pottinger, B, *The Imperial Presidency: PW Botha, the First Ten Years* (Johannesburg: Southern Book Publishers, 1988), p. 113
422 Ibid.

the best of the circumstances, literally drove a shadow economy of informal, small black businesses. Black retailers were beginning to set up shop in
urban areas, black taxi owners were transporting people to and from work,
black workers were entering cities and staying. There were also black spots –
essentially black settlements in white areas. 'Black spots' was once a faintly
notorious term having connections to those at the choke point of the skills
shortages. Although officially the apartheid authorities did not approve, the
truth was that the black economy grew up because the apartheid system had
created so many wants that people had found another way to satisfy them.

Yet, until the early 1970s, business knew and experienced every day the
hollowness of the promises. Apartheid provided less and less, and slow
cycles of skill shortages began, picking up pace as the 1970s plodded on.

Black professional skills were now necessary for capital accumulation.
Although the homeland policy had generally suited the needs of business,
helped by the urban-decentralisation policy of the Vorster government in
terms of which business could locate close to Bantustans, and though the
former was in considerable measure determined by the latter, it became less
functional under conditions of increased capital intensification, precipitat-
ing moves by business to ease restrictions on the education of highly trained
black labour.

These 'reforms' marked a turning point in state policy towards African
entrepreneurs. Procedures for the renewal of African trading licences were
to be brought more in line with those for whites, and Africans would be
allowed to trade in a wider range of commodities and to run more than one
business on the same premises. Partnerships were legalised; ownership of
businesses in the Bantustans no longer meant that enterprises in urban areas
had to be forfeited, and 30-year leaseholds were reintroduced. The changes
in official policy towards African businesspeople were underscored when the
National African Federated Chamber of Commerce (NAFCOC) launched
the African Bank with official permission. Its opening gave new impetus
to NAFCOC, whose President, Sam Motsuenyane, defined its major tasks
in the years to come as the "promotion of sound working relationships
between NAFCOC and both the central and homeland governments".[423]

NAFCOC's cause soon began to be taken up by groups within the white
capitalist class, in particular the Federated Chamber of Industries (FCI),
the Afrikaanse Handelsinstituut (AHI) and the Associated Chambers

423 See Sarakinsky (n 413 above), p. 170.

of Commerce (Assocom). They called for the removal of restrictions on African businesses and specifically suggested that small African industrial and manufacturing plants be established and promoted.[424] In 1977, Andreas Wassenaar, a pillar of the Afrikaner establishment and Chairman of Sanlam, the second-largest conglomerate in South Africa, published a stinging attack on government economic policy.[425] The title of the book, *Assault on Private Enterprise: The Freeway to Communism*, expressed his understanding of the nature of political intervention in the economy. Wassenaar reflected: "Why are democratic governments in some countries bent on nationalisation? Why do they disown private enterprise? Why is the RSA so prominent in this respect? ... The answer must lie in an almost inexplicable antipathy to the profit motive."[426] Wassenaar's sentiments, however, were not without irony, since his criticisms were levelled against precisely those policies which, in the 1950s, had facilitated the rapid growth of Sanlam.[427]

And therein lay the first problem: if apartheid emerged in a period of rapid economic growth, the economic crisis in 1978 presented a stark contrast with the circumstances of its creation nearly two decades earlier. Inside the apartheid planning machine, trade imbalances had been growing. By 1978, the South African economy was experiencing major impediments to the development of its productive forces. Import substitution and industrialisation inevitably came up against the problem of low skills and saturated markets. Partial economic sanctions had exacted a heavy toll. And clandestine violations of the sanctions regime – the round-tripping of currency and the illegal import of oil from Iran via front companies – were becoming unsustainable.

In the drive to shape a new class of black people liberated somewhat from the fetters of apartheid, some in the Botha government had begun to think differently.

*

In 1978, Roelof 'Pik' Botha was 46 years old. He was a law graduate and had been a career diplomat since 1953, serving at The Hague, and representing

424 Ibid., p. 171.
425 Mann, M, 'The giant stirs: South African business in the age of reform', in Frankel, P et al. (eds),
      State Resistance and Change in South Africa (Johannesburg: Southern Book Publishers, 1988), p. 52.
426 Ibid.
427 Ibid.

South Africa at the International Court on Namibia. In 1975, he had been appointed Ambassador Extraordinary in the United States responsible for both the United Nations (UN) and Washington. In early 1977, soon after the Soweto uprising, he had been brought home as Foreign Minister. He attracted at least as much public attention as PW Botha himself: in author Brian Pottinger's description, ebullient, maudlin, theatrical, as well as being a consummate political survivor.

But there was another side to Pik Botha, less visible, but no less significant than his flamboyant public persona. He had opened a discrete flank of engagement with black business leaders. "The issue was always the permanency of blacks in urban areas," Botha said to me, "and because apartheid was based on sin, and we in the National Party lived for that sin, it was like trying to sweep the ocean back with a broom."[428]

There was never any doubt in his mind, Botha recalled in speaking to me, that the economic impact of apartheid would have large consequences. The impact of sanctions on the economy, which had begun to affect the white middle class and were estimated to have doubled the country's unemployment rate, became a propaganda victory for the anti-apartheid cause in the minds of international investors.

Botha saw all too clearly, he said, "the impossibility of reversing the trend towards black urbanisation". And so, as the tough, unsentimental guardian of Vorster's Praetorian state, Pik Botha had swung round to a more moderate disposition under PW Botha. In 1978, he had quietly been meeting NAFCOC on the need for a black entrepreneurial class and professionals as functional components of capitalism.

Although the mainstream of the National Party was not dedicated to this line of thought, Botha was dedicated, as he admitted to me, "to the advancement of black business". But between his obsession with the permanence of blacks in urban areas and his actual ambitions lay an ideological gulf. Botha belonged to the neo-apartheid school of thought. In the jargon of foreign policy, he was a 'realist' dedicated to preserving the balance of power. To officials of this persuasion, the tragic lesson of Soweto did not teach hawks in the Botha government that the apartheid regime had tragically overreached and needed to learn the limits of its power. And so he concluded that accommodating the black business class was a sign of realism, not defeatism.

---

428 Hereinafter, all direct references to Botha are from an interview with the author, Pretoria, November 2011.

In our conversation, Botha brushed aside the term 'neo-apartheid'. The realist tradition in Botha's genealogy upheld a policy that reflected co-option and incremental reforms. The real target of his activism was a stratum of black business leaders who could resolve precisely what Christo Nel and his team at Project Free Enterprise had discovered as the key barrier to the continuation of capitalism: the lack of ideological purchase by blacks.

Seeking to revive the spirit of entrepreneurship, Botha reached out to influential figures in NAFCOC. He began privately meeting Sam Motsuenyane and Soweto businessman Richard Maponya at the Union Buildings from time to time through 1978 to 1980. "Luckily as minister there was no obligation on me to report to the Cabinet or anyone else whom I saw," he said. "And I can confirm that I had some of the most pleasant lunches with Motsuenyane and dinners in Maponya's house, better than any hotel could serve because the conversations could be conducted between two South Africans who almost knew what was inevitable."

Motsuenyane remembered numerous informal exchanges with Botha, but exactly what transpired during those meetings – the nuances, the inflections, the precise words – may never be known for certain. It was in the informal nature of the meetings, he told me, that no records were kept. For his part, Motsuenyane, Botha said, was not against the concept of economic development in rural areas. "His major concern was your smaller black businessman in white areas and black townships who had no skills, no financial assistance, and no organisation, and were restricted to doing business within the compounds of those black locations. That was his struggle."

Despite this qualified backing of black business, Botha still did not find it easy to disentangle the economic logic of liberalisation from the racial politics of influx controls. The question to him was not an indulgence in the senseless 'what if?' It was 'what now?' And what better way to weather the storm than to haul the scattershot economy into the narrowed field of diplomacy? This seems a sharply intuitive reading of Pik Botha's mind at the time. At this game, he was a virtuoso; for to move against urbanisation might set off a disastrous chain of events.

Still, Botha seemed to genuinely believe that black professionals and business – the emerging generation of private owners – who had a stake in the system would be the best ones to legitimise the system. At least theoretically, he thought, they were the ones who would become forces for peaceful change. By 1978, he began to think that NAFCOC offered the best chance of preserving the balance of power.

Paradoxically, however, the new reform programme contained a built-in recipe for conflict. As the 1980s dawned, the state called for large-scale township development, including increases in the budget allocation to black education, to overcome 30 years of neglect. But it was unable to pay for any of this. Despite PW Botha's reforms, the contradiction sharpened in the early 1980s as economic recession set in. By 1984, black urban communities were reacting. Then another kind of crisis hit.

In September 1984, black townships in the East Rand lit up like a beacon in an inferno of revolt and state repression. Images of burning barricades flashed across the globe in newspapers and televised broadcasts. Black communities themselves were protesting as well they should have. Once again school students led the charge, supported by workers. It was a fearsome time. In the months that followed, Botha's government sailed into the storm.

By mid-1985, it had become apparent that the process of reform had been in tatters. This fed business anxiety about international perceptions of South Africa as an unstable, high-risk banana republic. In the United States, students at universities staged protests and demanded boycotts against South African businesses and disinvestment by US companies doing business in South Africa.

A new era was dawning.

In January 1986, the FCI, which represented the majority of the manufacturing sector, issued its so-called Business Charter of Social, Economic and Political Rights.

This was where Project Free Enterprise came in.

BY THE TIME I MET CHRISTO NEL ON A WINTRY DAY IN 2011 AT HIS Melrose, Johannesburg, apartment during one of his weekly business commutes from Cape Town, he was greying behind a receding hairline, bespectacled, tall and rangy.

He was 30 years old at the height of PW Botha's Total Strategy in 1984 when he began working on a research report for the project led by a UNISA professor named Martin Nasser. Nel knew that his assignment to Project Free Enterprise was yet another desperate attempt by policy experts at UNISA sympathetic to the government of the day to save the apartheid capitalist system from extinction. But he leaped at it wholeheartedly and began a journey that would lead him to take his first, tentative steps out of apartheid.

As lead researcher of the project, Nasser had done the initial work and Nel was retained to explore policy options. Nel had his own vision of capitalist South Africa. A social democrat, he had already come to the conclusion by the time he accepted his research brief that 'free' enterprise was as illusory as the promise of equality under a capitalist system. "But in mid-1980s South Africa, the eradication of institutionalised racism in education, labour and business was the first stage in the stabilisation of the system," he told me of his ideas. Like other left-leaning democrats, he figured that eventually some semblance of equilibrium would be reached in the economy. "Some become rich, others lose," he said. "But the system would be deracialised until state control became necessary again. The whole point of the project I had embarked on was to deracialise the economy, unlock talent and opportunities."

Apart from the disastrous consequences for liberal reforms, government officials were concerned that deracialisation also in a sense meant dismantling apartheid. The idea never had a chance in the politically volatile and repressive atmosphere of 1984/1985 when the Botha military state was at its ugliest.

As Nel's research report took shape, Chris Ball, who by that time was Chief Executive Officer (CEO) of Barclays (before its disinvestment from South Africa), became a major champion of Nel's work. Soon the pair got together a group of mentors, a few powerful CEOs who were willing to back the process.

Then something extraordinary happened. Although it wasn't apparent then, it was in hindsight a major turning point, Nel recalled. Within three months of the preliminary results, he reported to the Project Reference Committee and Trustees that it was not possible to explore ways of teaching blacks the benefits of free enterprise if their context was one of "oppressive authoritarianism". "What they did was very rapid," Nel recalled. "Through their interventions, and those of the business school, organised industry and commerce opened their doors to us and we very quickly held a range of dialogue sessions throughout the country, posing the question: So why?"

A prime mover behind the dialogues was a man named Bokkie Botha, then the Human Resources Head at AECI, and the Industrial Relations Labour Subcommittee of FCI, which was later merged with Assocom to become the South African Chamber of Business (SACOB). Under Bokkie Botha's influence, the project started investigating the legal environment. "The answers to the question 'why' that came out were just overwhelming,"

Nel said. "They were captured in the final report entitled 'Economic participation in South Africa: A strategy for survival and growth'." The report eventually sold a record 15 000 copies.

In rough outline, it found that the laws of the day, principally influx controls and Bantu education, often went hand in glove with the defence of white privilege and consequent economic distortions. "Roughly speaking, the system prohibited entry by blacks into senior positions," recalled Nel. "You had in those days situations like Boom Street in the Pretoria Central Business District which essentially was a black environment. But companies like OK Bazaars were not allowed to appoint black managers in their branches because of the Group Areas Act. And whereas some employers tried to buck the system, black skills were wanting."

The report had come to the conclusion that the permanence of blacks in urban areas was an immutable fact. During the 1960s, there was a consolidation and expansion of the manufacturing sector accompanied by significant changes in the pattern of employment of both white and black workers. Between 1963 and 1969, manufacturing increased its contribution to the country's gross national product from 20.8 per cent to 23.4 per cent, while the shares of agriculture and mining (the main sources of foreign exchange earnings) declined from 28.3 per cent to 21.2 per cent. The number of black workers in manufacturing increased from 308 332 in 1960 to 2 513 000 in 1970. The total number of manufacturing firms during the period increased by over 1 000 to 13 121 in 1970, but the average number of employees per firm increased from 70 to 83. Manufacturing was characterised by a large number of relatively small and uncompetitive enterprises using outmoded technologies and employing low levels of skills enabled by tariff barriers and ample supplies of cheap black labour.

By the 1980s, deskilling of manufacturing operations and the ability of employers to absorb black labour at lower levels of organisations were no longer sustainable. Nel suggested radical reforms to the system, "without which black buy-in to the free enterprise model would be impossible. I told them that we actually have to investigate what has to be changed in order for blacks to experience free enterprise," he said to me, adding: "'Don't go teach them about free enterprise; it's a worthless cause,' I said."

Nel's proposal went to the top decision-making bodies in business, a group of 100 companies and 3 000 CEOs and managers who sat on the Board of Trustees of Project Free Enterprise. Standing at a podium, Nel outlined his plans to an audience of about 150 top industry players. What he was proposing was dramatic – "a 180-degree turn," he said. His idea was immediately accepted.

*

What had been a modest step to rescue the system had turned into something of a revolutionary act. Nel was 30 years old, but nothing at the time marked him as a prominent personality. He had taken a courageous leap in an atmosphere that did not permit initiatives that challenged apartheid dogma. Because 'A strategy for survival and growth' came out as a dual process starting at a macro-level (political and economic level) and at a micro-organisational level, Project Free Enterprise was given some leeway. Amazed at the reaction he was getting, Nel suggested a modest experiment in individual initiative – allowing black people to start their own private businesses and cooperatives.

Then he went further. "In order to get more blacks participating in the system," he once told a business gathering, "and linking very shocking statistics and facts, a quantum shift in the private sector in terms of managerial styles, attitudes, and values was needed." Finally, he proposed to draw business for the first time into making a very powerful commitment outside organised industry and commerce and underwriting a recommendation calling for the abolishment of separate departments of education. Instead, he suggested the establishment of a single department alongside the scrapping of pass laws and the Group Areas Act, which were major impediments to the project business had just signed up for.

The research was also a concrete demonstration of a new model of capitalism. But the model was not what government officials had in mind. The angle of inquiry and recommendations could only have intensified Nel's fears that the project was going to blow up in his face. To build support in government would have required more willpower than Nel and his team could summon, and much more than the system could stand. "We would have had to ask government to abandon apartheid," Nel recalled.

Oddly, it was UNISA representatives who felt Nel had overreached his mark. By the time the report entered its final stages, Nel presented it to the governing body and proposed to meet Archbishop Desmond Tutu, who had just won the Nobel Peace Prize. Realising the broad and potentially damaging implications of the report, UNISA promptly shot it down and buttonholed Project Free Enterprise. "I was not allowed to meet with Tutu,

269

which tells you something about the context of the time. And the business leaders in the reference group were not willing to override it," Nel recalled. "So when we look at the context of the 1984–85 period, your big business leadership was profoundly on the side of the National Party and they were not willing to rock that boat."

Regardless of the fate of Project Free Enterprise, it started the debate within business on a brand new era.

"IF BANTU EDUCATION AND THE BANTUSTAN SYSTEM ARE THE MAIN PROBlems, the search for a way out of the economic crisis must mean a bold new engagement by business, not with Bantustan leaders themselves but with legitimate black liberation movement leadership." It was the summer of 1985, and Nel had just snared the supposedly futile assignment by FCI to draft the practical guidelines of a Business Charter when he uttered this remark to Professor Martin Nasser at UNISA where Nel had been teaching part-time. Nel, recalled Nasser, who had a practised eye for strategy, told him that an economic solution was in fact possible without the kind of bold political curtain-raiser he was suggesting.

Nel felt "doomed". "This was a defining moment which, good or bad, would have an impact for the next decade or so," he said to me. "If it went bad, the consequences would be more bloodshed and economic ruin."

That same day he took out a blank sheet of paper in his office and drew up a list of pros and cons. The cons leaped off the page. The reform agenda of President PW Botha and his predecessor John Vorster had one thing in common: to co-opt a new class of black professionals and entrepreneurs. And indeed the reforms had at the height of the Botha regime in the early to mid-1980s begun to touch the lives of a few career bureaucrats and black professionals in the homelands and some black entrepreneurs in NAFCOC. But, in the next step forward, momentum towards deracialisation came up again and again against the limits of apartheid. Nel got a glimpse of the problem during his research stint at Project Free Enterprise. Every day, quite literally millions of blacks experienced first-hand the folly. Bantu education and the Group Areas Act were structural barriers to labour supply and small-business development.

As 1985 drew to a close, the country turned violent. The state found itself confronting not only a battered economy and a haemorrhage of support to the far right but an erstwhile partner upon whose loyalties it could no longer rely. "Chase Manhattan, Barclays and other foreign companies had just disinvested. In black townships, schools were on fire. Opposition to Bantu education was a rallying cry among youth and student organisations," Nel recalled.

If one thought of the FCI initiative as an open-ended political–economic undertaking more vast than anything business had undertaken, Nel had the right stuff. While conservative elements in business and government were engaging in limited interventions, he was contemplating something grander. "I thought to myself at that moment, I cannot take the FCI agenda forward without reaching out to the other side. What good were bold initiatives if they didn't bring freedom to those excluded from participation?"

That meant stepping into underground politics. The mere thought of a young white Afrikaner reaching across a vast ideological and racial divide was bizarre. But if this was a moment of acute crisis, there was also a special thrill for Nel. "I was in my thirties, idealistic, adventurous, energetic," he said to me. "The choice was easy. There was no turning back."

*

Right after accepting his FCI assignment to draft the practical guidelines of a Business Charter, Nel stormed into literally hundreds of meetings with business leaders, including Bokkie Botha who was then involved with the FCI. "I was working round the clock engaging, engaging, engaging, engaging," he recalled. "I knew that engagements with organised business formations were fruitless. They were essentially toothless and their collectives tended to be very conservative. So you wouldn't see Assocom within a hundred miles of a political or controversial statement."

In the next few months, Nel got 103 CEOs to underwrite the search for practical market solutions, what he described as "a sea of Afrikaner nationalist folly". "It was a major feat getting business to step out of the past," he said.

That summer, he met Bokkie Botha of the FCI. Botha, Johan van Zyl, Marinus Wiechers, and John Wilson of Shell and President of the FCI at that stage were actively lobbying against the forced removal of people from what was called Okasie, an old black township at Brits outside Johannesburg, which was within walking distance from the nearest industrial area. Over time, Okasie became a black spot surrounded by wealthier white suburbs.

Residents of Okasie were forced to move 40 kilometres away. When Botha led an FCI charge against the removal, Chris Heunis, who was then Minister of Constitutional Affairs, sent the group a telegram saying it was clear that the FCI was "no longer part of the solution; it was part of the problem".[429] "It didn't help that Wilson in his capacity as President of FCI called for the lifting of the state of emergency and the release of Nelson Mandela," Nel recalled, laughing.

Nel figured that the recommendations of the Charter, "the practical guide-lines", had to consider the implications for business of apartheid education and segregated areas. Roughly two-thirds of potential value was trapped in black communities. Nel had an idea. If the Group Areas Act was scrapped, education would follow – and perhaps unlock opportunities for business. It was a revolutionary thought, and he immediately went to work on it. He asked business to "go beyond their traditional boundaries and become social activists for change". But big business did not like it. In a reactionary shudder, the response that came back shook the FCI. Within months, major contributors to the FCI withdrew their funding and essentially bankrupted the organisation. The FCI was then merged with Assocom to become the SACOB, headed by Raymond Parsons, whom Nel described as "quite honestly a government lackey and arch conservative ... antagonistic in those days towards the type of stuff that firstly Project Free Enterprise was doing and then FCI".

Nel recalled Parsons accusing him and the FCI group of "violating business's core business" by steering the sector into politics. But the Parsons broadside was a disguised blessing. "A kind of paradigm shift occurred when Chris Ball, who was CEO of Barclays, approached me and said he and a few business leaders had come to the conclusion that bodies of organised industry and commerce were toothless and were not going to engage actively in breaking the deadlocks and the extraordinary big crisis that the country was in at that stage," Nel recalled.

Ball had assembled a small group of business leaders to establish contact with the legitimate, popular mass-based black leadership. Nel had survived his commission. Now he and his team were being thrust into a dangerous era. They would have to give up their single-minded approach at the time, of extracting political concessions from government, to achieve the larger goal of radically transforming the institutional and economic basis of apartheid.

---

429 This quotation is attributed to Nel.

Some time in 1986, a full-page advert appeared in a Sunday newspaper calling for the unbanning of the African National Congress (ANC), an end to the state of emergency, and the scrapping of segregated areas and Bantu education. It was a consolidation of the group's thinking into a stirring manifesto, with Chris Ball financing the advert, and, for his political transgressions, getting sacked from Barclays.

It's hard to think of a less auspicious moment for a radical manifesto than the summer of 1986. The economy was in free fall. Large banks, led by Chase Manhattan, had disinvested and called up their debts from local creditors. Ironically, Barclays, which had just fired Ball for his transgression, was among them. And President Botha's much-anticipated Rubicon speech to a gathering of party faithful and businessmen in Durban turned out to be a political brief for further aggression against the emancipatory impulses that had been stirring in schools and communities across the country. "Neil van Heerden who was head of the secret service at that stage, had already taken a position that it was an unwinnable war. But PW wouldn't hear about it, Magnus wouldn't hear about it. So it was a terrible logjam," Nel recalled. In 1986, as far as Botha and Malan were concerned, the rest of the world disappeared.

Yet here were Ball and his activist group of businessmen writing combative statements and summoning radical change. Over the next two years, the group grew in size and stature and included Ball himself, Mervin King (who, after apartheid, would go on to write the King Codes on Corporate Governance), Niel Chapman, then head of Southern Life, Mike Sander of AECI, Zach de Beer, who headed up one of the divisions at Anglo, and Judge Anton Mostert, reputed for blowing the whistle on the Info Scandal that brought Vorster down. Within two years, a few others joined this little group. Chris Saunders, who was vice chancellor at the University of Cape Town (UCT) at the time, came on board, then one of the big breakthroughs was to get Don Massen on board. Massen was the first Afrikaner leader and Broederbonder to join. Then Leon Cohen, who headed PG Bison, which was also predominantly owned via Monde by Anglo, joined and offered Nel a directorship as cover for the operation they were about to embark on.

Convinced that the status quo was unsustainable, the group now turned its attention towards the overhaul of Bantu education and the Bantustan system that buttressed it. In fact, the operation was less an economic weapon than a political gambit by Nel and his network to build mass support for radical change. "This is how we understood the situation," Nel said to me.

"It didn't matter whether government was not ready for it. It was imperative to break the deadlock between the government and the legitimate black
leadership at the time because the black leadership the government held up
were the homeland leaders."

Sceptics like Leon Louw, who by then was something of a maverick engaging
the group from a small-business-development perspective, regarded this turn
to black leadership as Afrikaner business's attempt "to appease black political
formations in order to secure their interests during the transition". "Here we
find big Afrikaner capital's first effort ever to curry favour with the ANC alliance against English capital and the extreme right in government," he told me.

When I put this to Nel he shrugged, saying the ANC had already been
engaging with Anglo and other businessmen on the broad preconditions of
a negotiated solution. "We were aware that leadership had begun to think
that a broader alliance with business was possible in the heat generated by
stalemate," he said to me.

Through 1987, Nel specialised in finding intellectual allies and connecting
them to the group. "At the time, I had set my priorities on establishing contact with black leadership. My mandate was to find them and engage them
and get a dialogue going."

IN MID-1986, NEL MET TWO JOURNALISTS, MIRANDA AND ROGER HARRIS.
The couple had been working on a series of progressive television docu-
mentaries for the Scandinavian market on the anti-apartheid struggle. The
Harrises' plot in Honeydew just outside Johannesburg was a safe and con-
vivial environment for an impressive list of anti-apartheid activists in the
United Democratic Front (UDF). Naturally, the Harrises were very cautious,
and only when they felt Nel was 'legitimate' did they start introducing him
to activists.

It was there that Nel met Murphy Morobe, UDF Treasurer Azar Cachalia,
and Mohammed Valli Moosa, who were on the run.

In the months that followed, the tenor of engagements softened from cold
calculations into warmth and even friendship. "The basis was business can
play a major role in breaking the stagnant positon," Nel recalled. "I said
there was a small group of businessmen who are willing to connect, who
through a small consultative business process wanted to establish a cohesive
voice against apartheid."

But as the parties discussed possible means of taking the initiative forward, they kept coming back to the same idea: the possible usefulness to their cause of numerous ANC exiles now living in London. As well as being exploitable for ideological purposes, such engagements could be deployed in subsequent talks with the apartheid regime.

Nel recalls driving at night with Cachalia, edgy and exhausted, to see Cas Coovadia, who headed up the ANC-aligned Transvaal Indian Congress:

> I would have chats with Azar and you'd get a call at whatever time of the
> day or night and they would say, 'Are you available right now?' This one
> particular time Azar and I had gone to see Albertina Sisulu in Soweto.
> And while we were there he got a telephone call saying Cas was willing to
> come out of hiding. We met in the old Fordsburg area between Fordsburg
> and the city.

At 11 p.m., Cachalia stopped at a fountain in the old Fordsburg district. "Go and talk to him," he told Nel, pointing to Coovadia. The two men talked for 30 minutes and Coovadia agreed to initiate a meeting with the exiles.

The week prior to Nel's departure was not without high drama. "I'll never forget the fear I felt when I was pulled over driving home one morning from one of these meetings," he recalled. "There was suddenly a car behind me and a car in front of me. About six white guys in balaclavas got out, put a 9 mm pistol to my head and said to me, 'We'll come and fetch you whenever we want to.'" A few days later, the Harrises' home was raided at night. Roger Harris was detained on charges of aiding and abetting terrorists.

Undeterred, in early 1987, Nel flew to London from Johannesburg to meet Aziz and Essop Pahad. At the meeting, the Pahads insisted that business would have to form a broad business collective, a task that was near impossible given the vastly disparate views of the various business chambers. Through a mixture of flattery and cajolery, Nel convinced the Pahads that the task of lobbying business would have to fall on a group of "change mavericks". He also laid on an exhausting programme of activities, including one-on-one meetings and a forum of sorts as a vital tool to kick off a process of talks around the details of a post-apartheid economic policy.

The venture proved highly profitable. When Nel returned to South Africa and relayed the ANC position to the UDF and business, Cachalia suggested a loose structure of business. "It doesn't have to be a collective, but business would have to form a structure because visions inspire people, structures move them," Nel recalled Cachalia telling him. "He had a pragmatism about him. He was in his early thirties, but he was incredibly astute," Nel said.

These astonishing feats were accomplished against a background of growing revolutionary fervour and suspicions of betrayal among rank-and-file supporters of the trade union movement COSATU (Congress of South African Trade Unions) and the UDF inside South Africa. "The ANC was seen as a revolutionary movement married to the communist party, COSATU was flexing its muscle and talking socialism, and the UDF had pockets of left-wing elements in it," said Nel. "But there was a startling receptiveness to engagement."[430] Jay Naidoo, who was General Secretary of COSATU at the time, confirmed talking to Nel and his business mavericks, "because they were important players and they had the potential to be positive or negative". "My work was to go into the trenches," Naidoo said to me.

> And, yes, by that point I was also convinced that nationalisation was not the magic panacea and that we were really dealing with the reality of an apartheid economy in which we had to improve the role of the state as an instrument to deal with poverty and inequality. I remember several meetings behind the scenes where we discussed a broad coalition to try and build an environment in which we could go forward.[431]

For his transgressions, Naidoo took flak from the COSATU Central Executive Committee. "I felt at that point that we had to start talking to capital about the post-apartheid economy because we couldn't wish away the employers. Hell man, you could see the signs on the wall in East Germany and the Soviet Union, and I had to justify that we had to negotiate on some of the deeper structural challenges that we faced."[432]

As it turned out, this was in fact the start of a major push towards a National Economic Forum which would become the 'economic CODESA (Convention for a Democratic South Africa)' on a future economic dispensation. At that stage, the UDF and COSATU leadership agreed to endorse the initiative on one condition: it had to bring together an adequate grouping of business leaders.

*

430 Interview with the author, Johannesburg, July 2011.
431 Ibid.
432 Ibid.

Although it lacked the left-wing aspect of socialism – indeed its social implications were distinctly conservative – the discussions that followed fit the emerging economic consensus. Fortunately, Nel had a few advantages in facilitating dialogue. "The principle was you need to comprehend the other person's history. And you must not react to what you hear. You must explore what is meant by what you hear. But what made it possible – and I think that's one of the lessons for me – was the intensity of the one-on-one dialogue."

Between February and July 1988, Nel stacked up more than 1 000 meetings, and, in July 1988, a date was set for what became known as the Broederstroom Encounter.

> One of our starting points, certainly on the business side, was that we would not start anything unless it was in a collaborative context – that part of the problem historically is you had these entities being created without the rigour of conflict, of dissent, of opposing perspectives and, while it was accepted in COSATU that the exiles could not publicly endorse the effort, it would have no life outside collaboration. So both sides had to break their traditions.

Nel then enlisted Cachalia and Chris Ball to court the patronage of the UDF and small-business leadership, respectively. "At that stage, Leon Cohen had made me an offer to become a Director of PG Bison. Part of the reasoning was to provide air cover because the government never jailed senior businesspeople who were seen as a bulwark against communism." Nel was given a basement office at PG Bison's Main Street head office in mid-town Johannesburg. "It was a perfect cover. We would be downstairs meeting Jay Naidoo, Murphy Morobe and others, and upstairs the Lubners would be having lunch with Magnus Malan," he recalled with a chuckle.

The first encounters proved, by general agreement, a tremendous success. As the group coalesced, Cachalia's Bertrams, Johannesburg, home became their operating office. The crowning achievement of 'Nel diplomacy' came in August 1988, when 80 business leaders, academics, and UDF and Cosatu leaders assembled in an atmosphere of brooding enmity at the Gencor Training Centre in Broederstroom for a two-day encounter. "At that stage the business voice had become quite different to the Anglo-Barlow big capital axis which had been either tacitly supportive of the government or passive," said Nel.

On the first day of the Broederstroom gathering, a business leader stood up and, pointing at the door, said, "I don't trust that bunch of communists who want to nationalise my business." The freezing atmosphere soon thawed and the group settled into awkward policy questions. After lunch, Jay Naidoo, who had acquired a reputation as a firebrand socialist, stunned the business delegation when he said they'd given him a way to think differently. "And there I learnt the power of narrative; how do you create words, phrases, metaphors which enable antagonists to start creating a shared vision," said Nel.

On Sunday morning Nel, Cachalia and Chris Ball – who were bridge figures between contending ideologies – placed the formation of a business structure squarely on the agenda. The issue divided the gathering and the meeting deadlocked.

By 3 p.m. Nel and Ball led the business leaders outside. After a two-hour caucus under a tree, individuals swung round to a consensus. When the group returned to the main auditorium, Willem van Wyk of Iscor stood up and said, "I do not know what this means going into the future. But I do know is it is better than we have at present. So I endorse the route of creating a structure." There were no objections. The group committed to one person, one vote and the elimination of racial laws.

Nel conveyed the business position to Cachalia, who took it to the COSATU and UDF leadership. At 4 p.m., Cachalia announced the new structure. The group called themselves the Consultative Business Movement (CBM). Without a moment's pause, there was sustained applause from the gathering.

*

In September 1989, when FW de Klerk succeeded PW Botha as the country's president, South Africa was a melange of economic turmoil. The rand had fallen to its lowest in a decade, unemployment lines were growing daily, the inflation rate stood at a whopping 16 per cent, and the country's national debt stood at USD20.5 billion.

That September, a multiparty meeting in Paris presented for the first time a draft economic policy document. The leading proponents of the UDF and COSATU were Alec Erwin, Jay Naidoo and Moses Mayekiso. On the ANC's side, Thabo Mbeki and Tito Mboweni led discussions. Representing the CBM, Murray Hofmeyr once joked snidely that COSATU appeared more capitalist than capitalists in the room. "I'm quite shocked at what you are saying," he told the COSATU delegation.

Next, it was the turn of *Sunday Times* editor, Ken Owen, who was vociferously anti-COSATU. Nel recalled Owen saying his view had not changed, "so yours must have because I can say I now agree with you". When Owen proposed to endorse COSATU's position in his newspaper, the room fell silent. In Nel's recollection, COSATU requested a caucus. "When the delegation returned, they said if Ken Owen and business start endorsing ANC economic policy then we will be accused of selling out," Nel recalled of the meeting. "So they came back and essentially the deal was that Owen would not endorse them because it would eliminate everything they've done; it would destroy their own credibility. It was a funny situation and in a way it said to business don't make us look too good in the eyes of business."

The appearance of progress, however, was deceptive. Soon after the Paris meeting, Anglo American's Gavin Relly and Michael Spicer led an attack on left-wing elements within the CBM whom they regarded as "too militant". "The view of members like myself and Chris Ball was that if you do not intervene in the economy then existing economic patterns will prevail," Nel surmised. "And that's where the ANC fell on its face. Mandela was simply too old to catch up quickly enough. I think that's why he in all probability supported Cyril Ramaphosa to become deputy. But the interest of big business prevailed because Mbeki was a more useful guy for them. They were secretly meeting with Mbeki between 1991 and 1992 to prevail on him to leave the private sector intact."

Despite the significant role he played in the early stages of engagements around structural reforms, Nel was ousted from the CBM under pressure from Anglo in 1993. In Nel's recollection, any awareness of this episode would have to take account of the fact that "opportunism had lured all kinds of opportunity seekers to the CBM". As far as the larger pattern of reforms to which the ousting of Nel points, several conclusions seem possible, apart from the perhaps obvious point that the story of Christo Nel and his free-enterprise crusade was emblematic of the tension between economic apartheid and political power that had been a dominant theme in late apartheid history. One is that, like awkward alliances conjured into existence by the early 1990s phase, the economic consensus was driven by a desire within the Anglo American bloc to protect its interests, strongly echoing the neo-liberal New Economic Policy of the Botha government.

Even worse, Nel's nightmare scenario, neo-liberalism – when apartheid inequalities are entrenched in liberal reforms – was fast becoming a policy reality. By the end of negotiations in the National Economic Forum, the CBM (or at least the enlightened Afrikaner flank) was a defunct body. "The deal had been struck," Nel ruefully observed.

*

In the spring of 1993, Nelson Mandela met Harry Oppenheimer to discuss business's engagement with the ANC on macroeconomic policy. The so-called Brenthurst Group, led by Oppenheimer and Anton Rupert, was formed. Under the auspices of the South African Foundation, the group crafted the Strategy for Growth and Development, which would mirror the Growth, Employment and Redistribution (GEAR) strategy of the ANC in all but name. The strategy highlighted five areas that had to be focused on: a reduction in crime, the liberalisation of education, a reduction in exchange controls, export incentives, and labour deregulation; hence the undeniable conservatism of a strategy that formalised an agenda business had set already. Not for the first time, blacks were being summoned not to destroy apartheid but to save it.

PART VI

From Lost Generation to Lost Opportunities

1994–2012

CHAPTER 19

Into democracy

NEW INSIDERS, OLD OUTSIDERS

It was a raw and gusty dawn, as bleak as the times. In early April 1993, thousands of people, riotous and combative, marched through the streets of Johannesburg. The atmosphere which surrounded South Africa was comparable to that which might be found in a beleaguered country in wartime. A sense of anxiety had settled over the land, intensifying fears even among those in the white business establishment who from greed or cowardice during apartheid, or love of privilege, now endowed the African National Congress (ANC) with spurious virtues.

There was by then a new variable. Assassinations were common during the 1980s, atrocities that were restrained after 1991. Now it seemed a recessive gene was reasserting itself, changing the country's character utterly. Across Johannesburg, in Soweto, the sense of crisis was underscored by angry young men fingering their guns during the funeral of Chris Hani, the popular South African Communist Party (SACP) chief who was gunned down by a crazed right-wing fanatic on 10 April outside his home in Dawn Park, Boksburg.

By mid-morning a hard rain washed the city. As SACP boss Joe Slovo rose to address the mourners, a crackle of gunfire erupted. It *did* feel like war. In the tortuous journey to 1994, stories of violence and instability thronged newspapers across the country. Coming on the heels of the surge in protests during the early 1990s, these reports added fuel to the debate over the future of the country's youth beyond apartheid.

Meanwhile, the country, too, was reacting. With horror, as well might any country; but South Africa felt a foreboding repugnance. All through that year the confidence that South Africa was transcending its past and was different from some of its tormented African neighbours – that trust was vanishing.

Then something extraordinary happened. As 1993 gave way to 1994, a new, guarded optimism settled over the land. On 10 May 1994, the day of his inauguration, Nelson Mandela descended the shaded veranda of the presidential offices in Pretoria to address a crowd of tens of thousands that had gathered on the lawn. He began in Afrikaans, the language of his white former gaolers: "Wat is verby is verby!"[433] (What is past is past!)

Mandela looked over the sea of human diversity. "We are moved by a sense of joy and exhilaration, when the grass turns green and the flowers bloom," he said. "The time for the healing of the wounds has come. The moment to bridge the chasms that divide us has come."[434]

At a stroke, the foundational myth of the 'Mandela factor' had been set. For Mandela's audience, it was a moment, to recall Dan O'Meara's memorable phrase in the conclusion of his treatise *Forty Lost Years*, "of absolution and unity", the likes of which the country had never seen. "The foundations and symbols of their new 'rainbow nation'," wrote O'Meara, "had been marvellously crafted."[435]

Later, when Mandela disappeared into the Union Buildings, most in the crowd felt reassured. A numbing comfort had settled over the land. The violence and power vacuum of the early transition subsided, but there was another sea – a generation of blacks who had entered democracy via different routes were restless.

The new age that gave rise to this generation might have begun on that drizzly May morning in 1994, but its roots were in a group of black-struggle militants and school dropouts tied together by the 1976 and 1981 to 1986 revolts that, ironically, the ANC itself helped create.[436]

*

On the day the apartheid regime fell to the ANC in 1994, a quotation describing the apartheid generation of blacks began doing the pro-forma rounds in newsrooms: "The lost generation." The words were Gertrude Stein's depiction of the shattered young men returning home from the trenches of the First World War.

433 Mandela, N, 'Statement at presidential inauguration', Union Buildings, Pretoria, 10 May 1994.
434 Ibid.
435 Quoted in O'Meara, D, *Forty Lost Years: The Apartheid State and the Politics of the National Party, 1948–1994* (Johannesburg: Ravan Press, 1996), p. 414.
436 Bennell, P with Monyokolo, M, 'A lost generation?: Key findings of a tracer survey of secondary school leavers in South Africa', in *Educational Development*, Vol. 14, No. 2 (Johannesburg, South Africa: Education Policy Unit, University of the Witwatersrand, 1994) pp. 195-206.

In 1981, the next generation, following the Soweto youth, of high-school pupils rekindled the resistance to apartheid and sparked a nationwide rebellion. During the revolt, which lasted five years, the historian Mark Swilling wrote 'The United Democratic Front and Township Revolt in South Africa',[437] an excellent account of the revival of organised mass opposition to apartheid since 1980. Its polemical edge was turned primarily against the United Democratic Front (UDF), which had emerged in January 1983 in the crucible of a widespread schools boycott in Cape Town in 1981/1982 and mass-based community and factory struggles in the Transvaal.

These spontaneous struggles from below steadily consolidated a new political culture that articulated the principles of non-collaboration with government institutions, non-racialism, democracy, and mass-based direct action aimed at challenging white minority rule, but within a climate of legal pressure tactics expressed in the UDF slogan, "Apartheid Divides, UDF Unites".

Swilling concluded his analysis thus:

> The significance of this phase was that the UDF was operating primarily on a terrain determined by the state and hence its politics can be described as reactive. The objective, therefore, was not to pose alternatives to apartheid or seriously establish organisational structures designed to sustain a long-term struggle for social transformation. Rather, the UDF was keen to counter the divisive tactics of state reforms by calling for the maximum unity of the oppressed people and urging them to reject Apartheid simply by refusing to vote.

This bold conclusion was the picture of the revolution which was to materialise in 1985. The picture sprang partly from rebellion against a moderate politics, in which the spontaneous mass anger of the 1981 to 1983 student and worker upsurge was curiously blended with a reformist line taken by the UDF.

It was in response to this drift to a politics of 'legalism' – of petitions and peaceful pressure tactics by the UDF – that more rebellious youths stepped in to brandish a militant culture and combative politics of 'ungovernability'. The deepening economic recession – which began to set in during the first quarter of 1982 – not only undermined real wage levels, but also limited

---

437 Accessed at http://abahlali.org/files/swilling.udf_.pdf.

the state's capacity to subsidise transport and bread prices, finance housing construction and the provision of urban services, and upgrade educational and health facilities. The illegitimacy of state reforms and, in particular, the failure of the new tricameral Parliament and Black Local Authorities to attract support from black communities meant that economic grievances were rapidly politicised and the struggles that resulted articulated the need to overhaul the structure of political power as a precondition for resolving the crisis of urban life.

By September, the youth revolts had new features which signalled a turning point in the recent history of black protest: they managed to mobilise all sectors of the township population, including both the youth and older residents; they involved coordinated action between trade unions and political organisations; and they were called in support of demands that challenged the coercive, urban and educational policies of the apartheid state.

This was the first time, Swilling wrote, that any black group laid, on behalf of the liberation movement, open claim to power or to the immensity of its aims. Swilling observed "community struggles becoming increasingly militarist" as large groups of youths began protesting the army's occupation of the townships in late 1984 in running street battles that claimed hundreds of lives.[438]

Fearing a repeat of 1976, when the revolutionary spontaneity of youth overtook the ANC, the President of the ANC, Oliver Tambo, in a January 1985 Radio Freedom broadcast, called on black militants to "make townships ungovernable" by destroying the Black Local Authorities. Councillors and police were asked to resign their positions in a climate that was nothing short of a battlefield of insurrectionary ferment – "of bus boycotts, rent boycotts, school boycotts, squatter revolts, housing movements, labour strikes[;] [the] extent of these actions coalesced into an urban uprising that took place largely beyond the organisational controls of the UDF's national and regional leadership".[439]

The combativeness of the youth, hot and impulsive, outstripped the organisational preoccupations of older UDF activists and heightened their concerns that, if the youth revolt pushed the battle lines beyond pressure tactics to an open seizure of power, the government might respond with violence and repression.

---

438 See http://abahlali.org/files/swilling.udf_.pdf.
439 See http://www.sahistory.org.za/article/people-armed-1984-1990#sthash.TNwWzk44.dpuf.

And sure enough, on 20 July 1985, President PW Botha declared his first state of emergency in many parts of the country. Within six months of the declaration, security forces received expanded powers of arrest and detention and full immunity for their actions.[440]

Within this poisonous atmosphere, the government used township vigilantes, or criminal gangs of youths aided and abetted by the security forces, to infiltrate and destabilise mass organisations. In numerous well-publicised incidents, the symbol of the new wave of resistance became the 'necklace' – the petrol-soaked tyre placed around the neck of an alleged collaborator who was tried on the spot by accusers and then set alight.

Sweeping through the townships, the police apprehended and held hundreds of activists and detained thousands of youths and children, some as young as nine years old. These onslaughts came in the wake of the smuggling of arms for the arming of internal MK (Umkhonto we Sizwe) units between 1986 and 1987. Limpet mines, hand grenades and firearms were increasingly used and landmine incidents occurred frequently in the Northern and Eastern Transvaal and in Northern Natal. The People's Army concept was further developed with the establishment of self-defence units and combat groups, with locally based MK members as the core.[441]

But this flowering of revolutionary fervour was soon to be nipped, not by Botha's security forces but by business. In 1986, various prominent white South Africans – from leading English-speaking businessmen and Afrikaners, to Progressive Federal Party politicians and clergymen – began travelling to the headquarters of the ANC in Lusaka, Zambia, and Dakar, Senegal, to explore a negotiated 'transition' to democracy.[442]

It isn't such a great leap from this insight to the settlement between the ANC and the National Party government that led to the election of Mandela as the first democratic president.

IN FEBRUARY 1991, AN ARTICLE IN *TIME* MAGAZINE CARRIED AN INTERVIEW with a youth activist going by the pseudonym 'Che Guevara'. In the mid-1980s, he walked out of school as part of a boycott and never returned. At age 22, he claimed to be a "hardened veteran" of the struggle against

440 Ibid.
441 Ibid.
442 Ibid.

apartheid. He had killed "enemies of the people" and was prepared to kill again.[443] When leaders of the liberation movement sought to make the townships "ungovernable", the article noted, Che became one of the enforcers. "If I caught a family paying rent to municipal authorities in defiance of the rent boycott, I would serve them with an eviction notice. If they refused to go," he told journalists, "we'd speak to them in the language of the struggle. We'd kill them and burn their house down."[444]

As the struggle gave way to the new political era, this generation of youth, trained in guns and the politics of resistance, had high hopes that democracy would open the doors of learning and unlock opportunities previously denied to them. But where once they embraced the slogan 'liberation before education', they were discovering that liberation might yield few benefits for them without the education they eschewed for the flames of revolution.

The slogan was a powerful emblem and harbinger of the profound cynicism, disdain and anger that characterised the Soweto generation's attitude to the apartheid government, Bantu education, and the official statutory structures and social-engineering propaganda that dominated their lives.

If the ANC brazened through the absurdities of the early 1990s, it now had its hands full with another, more immediate problem. Among young township militants and MK combatants, galvanised by the call to 'make South Africa ungovernable' which characterised the post-1983 era and legitimated and popularised the use of violence against one's political opponents, there was now talk of betrayal. By the time the ANC took the reins from the National Party government in 1994, there were literally thousands of men and women who had returned home after fleeing into exile during the 1970s and eighties. Millions more township militants who once spent their days marching in ANC camps were now in limbo; they were impatient and idle. Where once the promise of liberation meant more than theoretical rights, there was now little room to find themselves in schools and universities.

In black townships, municipal infrastructure and schools lay in ruins, with devastating consequences for the quality of black school leavers. Principals and teachers in the majority of secondary schools had lost control over highly politicised students who openly rejected Bantu education. Schools had been burned down or badly vandalised. By 1994, school spirit was the only thing intact at Morris Isaacson High School, a cradle of South Africa's

---

443 Hawthorne, P & Macleod, S, 'Lost generation', *Time* magazine, 18 February 1991.
444 Ibid.

long freedom struggle. "The dusty cluster of brick barracks," observed one journalist, "where black students led the 1976 Soweto uprising, had few books or chalkboards. Vandals had broken most of the windows, ripped out the light fixtures and punched gaping holes in the walls and ceilings."[445]

The same reporter recalled seeing destruction. "The toilets are smashed, filthy and reeking. There are no maps, typewriters or computers. There are no soccer fields or basketballs. There was a science laboratory, but thugs destroyed it."[446]

Unable to continue their education, countless students like Che dropped out of school altogether. For those who remained, attendance was subject to constant disruptions. Until the end of the school boycotts in 1987, students only attended school for a few hours a day. Matric pass rates among African school leavers plummeted to around 30 per cent.

Those activists and township youths who miraculously survived Bantu education were met at best by an indifferent job market, or at worst (this constituted a significant proportion) by a hostile one which sought to keep them in their place. They were seen as a long-term risk for the country's economy, which was trying to reduce an accumulated debt and grow its tax base as it funded increased social spending.

Archbishop Desmond Tutu factored a paradigm shift in his portrayal of the young lions when he delivered a Harold Wolpe Memorial Lecture. "We had a noble cause and almost everyone involved was inspired by high and noble ideas," he said.

> When you told even young people that they might be teargassed ... and even killed, there was a spirit almost of bravado as they said, 'So what?' 'Don't care what happens to me as long as it advances our cause.' They spoke of their blood watering the tree of our freedom. It was breathtaking stuff, and yes they really meant it, that the cause was the be-all and end-all and they were ready to sacrifice anything, even pay the supreme sacrifice for this noble cause.[447]

Writing in the *Weekly Mail*, Murphy Morobe, the then UDF acting Publicity

445 *Los Angeles Times*, 'Police fire teargas at 150 black children', 21 August 1991. Accessed at http://articles.latimes.com/keyword/south-africa-education.
446 Ibid.
447 Tutu, D, 'Real leadership', Harold Wolpe Memorial Trust Tenth Anniversary. Memorial lecture, 23 August 2006.

Secretary, echoed this sentiment when he observed:

> For many of the youth, the struggle has meant simply to shoot your way
> to Pretoria ... . We acknowledge that the degree of the political education
> has not been commensurate with the degree and extent of political mobili-
> sation that we have been able to generate. And that brings to the forefront
> an important and serious contradiction. You draw into the movement
> battalions of Young Lions and there are slogans after slogans, hearts in
> the right place, determined to become part of the struggle, but often they
> don't understand the basic political positions of the movement.[448]

Whether in response to grief and anger at what they saw as a betrayal or the
failure to grasp the political position of the ANC, old ties of political connections and comradeship were snapping. At the Second Joint Enrichment
Project Conference on the Youth held in Broederstroom near Pretoria in June
1991, Mamphela Ramphele warned with prophetic foresight that "the youth
could develop into a force which, because of its anarchic, sporadic, and
unorganised ways would sabotage the process of building a new society".[449]

In many ways, then, 27 April 1994, the day South Africa celebrated its
freedom, offered a tangible metaphor for a grander narrative caught between
circumstance and power. With the old apartheid dominion virtually on its
knees and the ANC hardly in control of the country's economic destiny, the
lost generation would inhabit the space in between – a ubiquitous terrain
known as 'the transition' – to brandish their own drama in an opaque world
somewhere between illusion and reality, between conspiracy and a newly
emerging moneyed class.

Once again, the reality had passed them by.

*

The first few years of the Government of National Unity produced a new
vision of social transformation. But the ANC and National Party had negotiated a truce that presented a serious strategic plan from ever being written
by the ANC.

By 1995, it had become clear that the ANC was going to fill in the blanks

---

448 *Weekly Mail*, 26 January 1990.
449 Ramphele, M, 'Social disintegration in the black community', in Everatt, D & Sisulu, E (eds), *Black Youth in Crisis: Facing the Future* (Johannesburg: Ravan Press, 1992).

left empty by the lost generation who had imagined that freedom and democracy would arrive ready-made through the barrel of a gun. The new plans included technical goals and timetables, the writing of a new constitution, the creation of new government structures, economic reform, and educational reform: in short, a legal overhaul of apartheid, culminating in a gradual transition in which the old elite would keep their wealth. As former Minister in the Presidency Essop Pahad once told me, "It was a pragmatic response to an understanding of the facts on the ground."[450]

With such an ambitious undertaking, the ANC faced, and in some ways didn't face, a paradox that was unavoidable. The ruling party was trying to rebuild South Africa in a way that allowed blacks, for the first time in their history, to take control of their destiny. But, if power, money, and ideas remained with white capital, how would all the plans ever lead to control?

As yet, though, the complexities of governing lacked any ideological purchase beyond a small number of black youths. What recent tradition of engagement with the new order there was among the lost generation belonged mainly to militants more familiar with a gun than the art of diplomacy.

Those youths were aged 16 to 30. A case study during the mid-1990s, based on a cross-racial sample of 2 200 youths nationwide, found that a staggering 3 million of the country's 11.5 million youths between the ages of 16 and 30 were jobless. Of these, 2.9 million were black and "marginalised" or "lost" – completely outside the social safety net. Forty-three per cent (4.7 million) were "at risk", showing signs of alienation and in urgent need of help.[451]

Some joined criminal networks. Still others carried about them a palpable air of frustrated ambition. They yearned to make it to some new land. They longed for opportunities for material advancement, consumer goods and luxuries which the apartheid system refused to give them and the new order could not.

Yet the ideas of the architects of educational reforms produced consequences as tangible as state violence, home-made bombs and gutted buildings. Those consequences must be understood above all in the attempts by the democratic government to influence the minds of the black youth.

Clearly, the government had to look elsewhere for allies. And when the

---

450 Interview with the author, Johannesburg, June 2011.
451 See National Development Plan: 2030, National Planning Commission, 2012.

ANC looked around, it turned to the capitalist ferment on the street. The time had come to supplement the opportunities granted to black individuals during apartheid with a more practical approach to understanding the larger problem and defining additional mechanisms through which a larger universe of institutions and individuals could affect change.

Fortunately for the ANC, the same developments that had made the battle for hearts and minds during the Cold War – anti-capitalist revolt – had also produced moderate black leaders.

In the drive to shape a new middle class, liberated somehow from radical ideologies and functional to the needs of business, the government sanctioned a moderate experiment in capitalism. In fact, what started out as the first, faltering steps toward reform eventually proved to be a bold gambit. The experiment worked – and years later went farther than its planners had expected. It unleashed enormous, unexpected forces of change.

While the black elite and ANC had regarded each other with an equal measure of suspicion, in the post-1994 period this tradition merged with the exigencies of the government and business to produce a new paradigm. In this era, the ANC enlisted a black elite, and the government anointed them as its experimental capitalist sons.

And so, when the doors swung open to new opportunities, a handful of aspirant blacks rushed through with gritty fortitude.

IT COULD BE ARGUED THAT THE CREATION OF A BLACK ELITE BEGAN IN the 1970s, when the National African Federated Chamber of Commerce (NAFCOC) ascended the scene, but was set in motion some time in the late 1990s when the ANC government became an unholy alliance between an ambitious black elite in office and an old white elite still in control of high finance.

First it fell among an old moneyed elite – apartheid's beneficiaries – who after 1994 strutted over the Rainbow with the crown jewels safely locked away, knowing they could do as they cared. Then it came into the clutch of an interesting assemblage of men: a new generation of beneficiaries that had taken shape under Nelson Mandela's presidency. They were the poster boys for the disaffected black youth. In the spring of 1991 when men like Cyril Ramaphosa, Marcel Golding and Patrice Motsepe were ascending the national stage, a 5-year-old future ANC Youth League leader named Julius

Malema was learning multiplication tables in school.

A handful of families controlled 80 per cent of the wealth. At their centre were billionaire families who rivalled the great fortunes of London and New York – the Oppenheimers, the Ruperts – and so wealth remained in the tight grip of a few families. Gold and diamond mining generated many of these fortunes in a perverse way.

In concept, the black elite was rigidly medieval, but, under the cover of black empowerment, members of the elite club became masters of an older oligarchy's insecurity. Black empowerment was a well-oiled pretence. By 1997, newly minted, black-empowered dynasties were slowly starting to emerge – such as the Ramaphosas, the Motsepes, the Sexwales – which formed alliances to further their ends.

Yet, as these and other members of the liberation generation ascended the scene, it was difficult to imagine a time when a black oligarchy stalked South African capitalism. In reality, men like Sexwale, Ramaphosa and Motsepe were no more than outsiders peering in. Their rise had at its core a quick-profit ethos that was forged in a peculiar co-option paradigm with the explosion of a handful of politically connected black businessmen in cosy corporate deals with large white-owned businesses, reaching full strength in the frenzy of leveraged shares doled out by finance institutions and mining houses, and ripening into a caste of black capitalists by the new millennium. Its architects called it 'black economic empowerment', but its critics knew it simply by the pejorative moniker 'oligarchy' – a politically connected elite of black businessmen. Black economic empowerment, to be sure, was engineered by the ANC and business not to spread wealth from white business to the poor but to enrich a clutch of black tycoons and legitimise the new face of South African capitalism.

Such was the suddenness and the magnitude of the stony and tortuous path ahead.

THE YEAR 1998 ENDED HALTINGLY, WITH SOUTH AFRICA RIDING HIGH. The cold winter melted into an early spring of hope – and then despair. In this new era, an underclass on the margins found themselves negotiating not the end of an old era but the dispatch of its legacy into a new frontier.

Barely a few months before, newspapers were still fawning over the Mandela icon. During his five-year tenure as head of state, Nelson Mandela indulged white South Africans across the ideological spectrum; he even established links to the Afrikaner right wing and, despite their own narrow agendas, paid slender allegiance to governments that had steadfastly opposed the ANC and, at least nominally, backed apartheid.

In the four-year interregnum, South Africa had become a turbulent place, the scale of which would yet surpass all expectations. But it must have seemed that way to a handful of men with rare insight into the internal machinations of the ruling party at precisely the moment the grand fiction of the rainbow nation was dissolving into a menacing climate of suspicion and fear that would mark the tipping point in the storyline of this book and heave the country nether and tether towards a revival of conflict and revolt.

For if the 1990s had produced men like Tokyo Sexwale and Patrice Motsepe, it also produced another sea besides. For every black beneficiary, there were thousands of black youths who were left out. For one thing, there remained in South Africa an undercurrent of deep mistrust; feelings that grew as the poor came to blame the democratic government for the country's lost generation.

For those left out, it was a generation of lost opportunities. They were young and their dreams even younger. To the lost generation, democracy was no more real than the promise of a better life.

CHAPTER 20

Freelance buccaneers, luxury cars and sushi parties

THE YOUTH LEAGUE CABAL

THE REVELATION SLIPPED OUT UNEXPECTEDLY ONE SUMMER AFTERNOON in December 2010. Sitting in the courtyard of a restaurant in the Cape Town suburb of Wynberg, the former African National Congress (ANC) military combatant known as Jan Peterson divulged his role in a secret network of information peddlers controlled by a mystery man: a short, chubby, Soviet-trained ANC intelligence operative with a thick crop of shoulder-length black hair named Bheki Jacobs.

An Umkhonto we Sizwe guerrilla during the 1980s, Peterson looked every bit the picture of an old struggle establishment more familiar with an AK-47 than a pen. He was a bear of a man, swarthy and gangly, at least 6 foot 2 inches, broad-shouldered with a large, square, roughly handsome head and thick black moustache that rolled over his lip and turned his face into a British colonial official's circa 1925. His features and physique prepared me for a blustery ex-military combatant. Instead, sipping tea across a table from me, Petersen spoke in soft, reflective sentences that were frequently interrupted by long pauses. Now in his mid-fifties, he had come to understand early in the transition from apartheid that moral codes and political loyalties were no substitute for the chessboard of get-rich schemes that had become a defining characteristic of a generation of youths who fled South Africa into exile. By the time the ANC took the reins from the National Party government in 1994, old comradely bonds had already begun to melt into moneymaking networks, where the only currency of note was treachery and betrayal. In the mid-1990s, the networks had produced men like Bheki Jacobs and Peterson; they also produced a muckraking 'front' company run by Jacobs known as Congress Consultants.

In the coming decade, Congress Consultants would cultivate the image of an interlocked private intelligence apparatus of Thabo Mbeki with a few hundred spooks spread across the country unofficially on its payroll. In reality, it was a tightly controlled one-man show with Jacobs at the helm, recalled Peterson. "Most of the 'intelligence' was gleaned from dirt gathered by former Umkhonto we Sizwe operatives disillusioned with the way things were going," Peterson said. "A lot of it was made up."[452] Some of it was from a network of right-wing Recce types from the old apartheid Military Intelligence apparatus – frightening and precise in some instances, plain black propaganda in others.

That summer afternoon in 2010, Peterson's revelation broke silence on an enduring legend. At some point Bheki Jacobs had 'turned' on the ANC, Peterson told me in a hushed tone. It might have been shortly before Jacobs vanished into exile in 1984, still in his twenties, along a circuitous route from the port city of Durban to Swaziland; thence on to Mauritius and his final destination, the Zambian capital of Lusaka. Maybe it was after his return to South Africa a full decade later from Moscow where he claimed he was taught the black art of surveillance and counter-intelligence. His handler during the early 1980s was a talent spotter for the ANC's Natal underground named Mo Shaik. Shaik was chief of the South African Secret Service in early 2011 when he told me what he had suspected all along. "The signs had been there when I recruited him in the early 1980s," he recalled. "He was brilliant, with an IQ of 152, by the way. He was a loner, restless, not an organisational person, prone to conspiracies, and in my opinion a divisive and therefore destructive influence on the ANC. He could split anything, you know, maybe even an atom."[453]

Most knowledge of Bheki Jacobs was always anecdotal. He was one of those mavericks who, it seemed, could do everything. He was an excellent high-school student, and was regarded by his professor at Moscow State University during the 1980s, Irina Filatova, as a complex and lateral mind. "He wanted to help the poor, not become one of them," she said.[454] So he decided to trade careers.

Nobody had joined up the dots. Nobody *could* in the heady atmosphere of the time. Brazenly, Jacobs's crew of 'guerrilla intelligence operatives' – a hardy band of former Umkhonto we Sizwe (MK)

---

452 Hereinafter, all direct references to Jan Peterson are from an interview with the author, Cape Town, December 2010.
453 Interview with the author, Pretoria, August 2011.
454 Interview with the author, Cape Town, December 2011.

operatives-turned-freelance-buccaneers – sustained the bizarre legend of an enigmatic character trained by the KGB.

On that cloudy December afternoon, I wanted to know what was behind the legend. There was only one way to finally find out. I told Peterson that high-minded talk about the myth Jacobs had left behind was tainted by negative public perceptions of his acquaintances. It was time, I offered, to set the record straight.

For several minutes Peterson shuffled awkwardly in his chair, avoiding eye contact and babbling softly about a "just cause" some in Jacobs's network were fighting. And then a strange thing happened. He leaned back and a gleam of interest came into his eyes, as if he'd been weighing the implications of his response. He first encountered Jacobs as a youthful ANC firebrand in Angola in 1988 and was lured to his 'network' in 1997, three years after the democratic election that ended apartheid, by the promise of money. How and when exactly the idea came about we don't know, although Jacobs had witnessed first-hand the free fall of the Soviet Empire into Boris Yeltsin's bandit capitalism and was perfectly primed to see South Africa's capitalist Leviathan coming out of the fog.

"The model for his network was Yeltsin's Russia after the collapse of communism," Peterson said. As a young 28-year-old exile in Moscow in 1991, he had already come face to face with an underworld of crooked Russian politicians and businessmen. The KGB had successfully circumvented the West's trade embargo against the Soviet Union during the Cold War by enlisting the Russian mafia to illicitly move, through a network of dummy companies, vast quantities of diamonds, gold and oil to the West in return for hard currency. Later, in post-communist Russia, the mafia would enlist the KGB to control the nation's economy. Thus it was, when Yeltsin took the reins in 1991, that the KGB–mafia merger produced not only lucrative fiefdoms – a clutch of powerful Russian businessmen who became known as 'oligarchs' – but also shady power alliances that eventually paved the way for the rise to power of a taciturn KGB officer named Vladimir Putin.

The swashbuckling Jacobs brought the same entrepreneurial gusto to his covert operations in South Africa, Peterson recounted. "He foresaw the youth, the young lions and MK liberation fighters doing the same thing here after the collapse of apartheid."

*

Bheki Jacobs had been stalking Thabo Mbeki since 1995, posing as his deniable asset. He had chosen his prey well. Mbeki was one of the younger 'pragmatists' in the ANC top brass wary of his more radical detractors in the party and its left-wing allies, the Congress of South African Trade Unions (COSATU) and South African Communist Party (SACP). To party hardliners, Mbeki represented the worst of the new government – an intellectual scion of Britain's University of Sussex who had rejected the radical ideological moorings of the radical left and the get-rich-quick schemes of nationalists in the ANC to tilt at windmills instead. If Mbeki's opponents provided Jacobs with the protein nutrients for his muckraking cause, it all may also have provoked a sharp backlash 13 years later.

The basic facts as they emerged were incontrovertible. As the scramble for power began in 1994, the lure of money became ever greater.

Those harbouring ambition in the transition who needed this unregulated swath to snatch whatever they could were all too familiar with the raw power of the state security apparatus.

"Bheki decided that he could make money from peddling dirt on them to certain officials in the upper ranks of the ANC," Peterson continued. "At first, he badly wanted to establish a reputation as Thabo Mbeki's trusted man, as his secret agent. It seemed a crazy idea at the time, but that was Bheki, always plotting and scheming. I mean you're talking about a time when digging up dirt on Mbeki's political opponents who had gone into business in the mid- to late 1990s would have convinced anyone that Bheki was the real deal."

For Mbeki, the euphoria was temporary. The story told by those close to Jacobs is that Thabo Mbeki knew the reality and the paradox. In Peterson's version, Jacobs knew how entwined political power was becoming with criminal forces, even before he returned to South Africa in 1994.

The moment belonged to a different generation of politics and business, a different century even, conditioned by a lust for power and vast fortunes.

IN 1998, GOING ON FOUR YEARS SINCE THE END OF APARTHEID, SOUTH Africa emblematised, perhaps more acutely than other geographic locations, Mbeki's 'Two Nations' thesis: one wealthy and white; the majority, black and poor. More than a doctrinaire right to a place in the post-apartheid order – a state, to be sure, in which artificially frozen racial identities were dissolving into social inequality – the quest for national unity meant something more.

Certainly for the lost generation, their decampment on a new frontier since 1994 may have been legitimised by democracy but was also circum-scribed by a borderless economic chasm inscribed in the social typography of the landscape and overlaid by a form of sociopolitical amnesia.

And here we need to remind ourselves of the fact, the author Ivor Chipkin wrote, that the white elite by and large "were allowed to retain ownership of the factors of production and their wealth in exchange for universal fran-chise and some form of redress".[455] The fractured communities frozen in 10 ethno-national identities during colonialism and apartheid would yet have to remake themselves out of a vast culture, and indeed a vast econ-omy, of misrecognition that had been entrenched all the more firmly during apartheid as much by liberal advocates of 'deracialisation' among the white propertied classes as by conservative Afrikaner opinion.

Thus it was that the optimism of the Mandela era was tempered by the dystopia that South Africa was an unequal, deeply divided society, where opportunity continued to be defined by race, gender, geographic location, class and linguistic background.

At a more profound level, as Tom Lodge argued, "the distinction ANC leaders made between governing and exercising power expressed a convic-tion that majoritarian democracy required something more than control of the executive and domination of representative institutions."[456] These con-siderations, according to Lodge, were based on the belief that "power – *real power* – was invested somewhere other than in government".[457]

By the time the Mandela presidency had reached its denouement, in late 1998, all the grim simplicity of an unresolved historical legacy had begun to strike with numbing abruptness within the new political establishment. South Africa had the superficial trappings of democracy, but in every rel-evant respect its legacy of racial hierarchies, now transposed on economic relations of exploitation, remained.

Inequality had begun to breed serious resentment, a movement of vio-lent protests over undelivered services, strikes, fatalism. This movement from "the underside" of humanity represented, according to Nigel Gibson, "Franz Fanon's visionary critique of a post-colonial 'living politics' based

---

455 See Chipkin, I, *Do South Africans Exist?* (Johannesburg: Wits University Press, 2007), pp. 173-187.
456 Lodge, T, *Politics in South Africa: From Mandela to Mbeki* (Cape Town: David Philip, 2002), p. 19.
457 Ibid., emphasis added.

on a democratic form", which could be understood as "building counter-hegemony from below that opens up spaces that fundamentally change the political status quo and contest the moral and intellectual leadership of the ruling elites".[458] Thus, Gibson argued, the attempt at corralling the "real movement" of the poor against deep-seated economic and social inequalities in a social compact with the state and capital "took on a class character" during the Mbeki era and beyond.[459]

By 1998, there was the emergence of a new politics of protest against unrealised constitutional rights, individualised within an overarching ethos of national unity: on the one hand, constitutional notions of individual rights and national identity as an elite pact between old and new social formations; on the other hand, their literal meanings as abstract rights in communities on the margins. Against a rising neo-apartheid accumulation paradigm this "meant that old divisions encouraged by apartheid would remain or reappear".[460]

If by the time the government of Thabo Mbeki was nominally invested with power, in early 1998, inequality was a central cause of black discontent, South Africa was in danger of becoming a social concert of black and white elites, on one level, and a glut of poor outsiders on another.

For black communities generally – the vast swathe of poverty in urban squatter settlements and rural areas at any rate – the transformation of the country's political–economic system exemplified, in 1998, a 'passive revolution', occurring through the individualisation, monetisation and commercialisation of social and economic relations. A politically connected black business class slowly evolved, and, along with it, a complicated array of 'deracialised' post-liberation identities which saw the "bridges" to which justice minister Maduna alluded in his 1996 address to Parliament being built, but between hegemonic economic interests of different skin colours.

Once a shining example to the outside world of peace and reconciliation, South Africa had, by 1998, become a place of darkness. What distinguished those early months of 1998 was that only a handful of men in the ANC could imagine a collaboration of elites in a future capitalist system. The economy had slid into a protracted economic recession. Hundreds of thousands of people were unemployed. On reflection, that would be seen as a

---

458 See Gibson, N, 'Upright and free: Fanon in South Africa, from Biko to the shackdwellers' movement' (*Abahlali baseMjondolo*), in *Social Identities*, Vol. 14, No. 6, November 2008, pp. 683-715.
459 Ibid.
460 Ibid.

high and low point. In the metropolitan cities of Johannesburg, Cape Town and Durban there were marches, some of them violent, and scenes of police pushing back desperate men and women hungry for jobs. People were expectant. People were angry. They blamed the government. They blamed the black elite. And who could blame them?

*

What all this represented was not just an elite coup against the poor but a grander historical shift. The Mandela consensus was all but over. By mid-1998, months before Mbeki formally took office, power had merged with wealth to become the order of the day. And an obsession with betrayal and conspiracy – of plots, traps, subterfuge and high treason – became a numbing pathology of the political mindset.

Until late 1998, Bheki Jacobs had been rumoured to be Mbeki's protector in this jungle of business and fierce internal sniping within the ANC, an invisible bridge over which all important intelligence went to the Union Buildings.

It has been a subject of much media speculation as to whether or not Jacobs was working a Machiavellian agenda. He knew the story. The silent coup, he once told his associates, was all about money, billions of rand looted during the apartheid era and the immediate post-liberation period. In fact, at least part of the loot was duly passed up the line to senior apartheid officials in the De Klerk government and, later, some members of the ANC.[461] And Jacobs, along with his associates in the right wing, was looking for anything on the financial set-up and dealings of the elite.

Whether in response to the political watershed in December 2007, when Thabo Mbeki was beaten by his rival Jacob Zuma in the battle to lead the ruling party, or the intervention of a sinister hand, Bheki Jacobs was close to death in September 2008, his body frail and limp.

There is no record either way. But, from his sister Suraya Jacobs's account, it is possible to trace his dying moments.

*

---

461 For more insight on this, see CIEX, 'Operations on behalf of the South African government', August 1997.

It was in early August 2008, a month before Mbeki's removal from office, that Bheki Jacobs had an epiphany, Suraya recalled in the dim light of her Harrington Street, Cape Town, office at the South African National Institute for Crime Prevention where she was Chief Executive Officer (CEO).[462] Jacobs watched from his palatial family home in Constantia – an upmarket Cape Town suburb of terraced estates nestled on a gentle slope at the foot of Table Mountain – the embattled antagonist he had helped destroy, to the point of his dramatic dismissal by Mbeki as the country's deputy president in 2006, re-emerge from a messy corruption scandal. He was gesticulating wildly at the character on television – "*Him*! *Him*!" he exclaimed, his finger jabbing the air at footage of Jacob Zuma, almost like some catastrophic premonition – before slinking back into a discreet silence.

Even in his frail state he was able to see a darkness that began growing around Jacob Zuma, Suraya told me. But if he knew what was round the corner, his lips were sealed. "That was typical of him, secretive to the very end," she recalled.

Nobody in his immediate circle I spoke to could – or *would* – answer the question, why? No one imagined he was bemoaning Mbeki's imminent demise.

Whatever the exact details, all who knew him agreed, the political storm that had broken in 2008 was also the theatrical denouement of his life. Bheki Jacobs knew that prostrating himself to Mbeki – even claiming a direct line to the highest office in the land that involved gathering scurrilous scraps of intelligence on Mbeki's political opponents – was a way to sustain the illusion. As long as the grand metaphor – 'the transition' – was floating above the confusion of power struggles in the ruling party, the bigger picture would at best be elusive, and no one in the inner sanctums of power bothered to challenge that.

Then came the unexpected. At 7:30 p.m. on Sunday, 21 September 2008, a pale-looking Thabo Mbeki gave a terse 15-minute resignation speech to the nation on national television, a full 15 months before the end of his term. The broadcast was carried live on all channels at a time when the country seemed adrift, bereft of leadership and torn apart by social and political divisions. Mbeki was capable of an unusual tenacity to stage fightbacks, but now he was outmanoeuvred and, apparently, fading out of view as he sat motionless and spoke in a low-pitched monotone, his eyes lowered, his

---

462 Hereinafter, all references are to an interview with the author, Cape Town, December 2011.

expression downcast. Amid all the disbelief and denial, here, finally, was proof that a seismic tremor had shaken the political foundations of the country; the main protagonist was vanquished and a secure future, which Jacobs had hitched to the Mbeki presidency, had all but vanished.

In the two years before he died, Bheki Jacobs had already been drifting in and out of obscurity, along with Mbeki. As Mbeki's star waned and a new era opened up, Jacobs had little to offer. Where he once could talk up a storm of Le Carré-esque conspiracies, his information was dismissed as worthless and unreliable. On the day he died, in September 2008, his lumbering bulk had been transformed into a lifeless soul. Like the faltering legend of his close association with Mbeki, he bade farewell to his family – his life ending as suddenly and prematurely, at age 47, as Mbeki's 10-year reign – and sank into posthumous ignominy.

Some say he may have paid the supreme price for his guile and lack of judgement, veering off a 'righteous cause' into muckraking threats to extort money from powerful people. Very likely. He may have died at the hands of dangerous men. South Africa, after all, had become a place where the settlement of disputes sometimes inspired violent reaction. In the end, he may have angered far too many people – his primary targets in business, his fake cut-outs in political office, his covert sponsors in foreign intelligence, his alleged handlers in the old apartheid security establishment, his own associates included. That's the double-edged sword of spooks and conspirators. And yet, in truth, the dissolution of the whole Mbeki enigma into a more tangible constellation of forces may have tipped his tawdry career into a vain obsolescence.

As I concluded my conversation with Jan Peterson on that December afternoon in 2010, the clouds burst in a heavy downpour. Another foreboding, I thought, as I strained to follow the thread of a story that began long before Bheki Jacobs appeared on the scene, and was still unfolding into a grim and uncertain future long after he disappeared.

WHEN BHEKI JACOBS HAD HIS PREMONITION IN AUGUST 2008, HIS FEVERED mind might have raced ahead – from the halting indecision that followed Thabo Mbeki's defeat at Polokwane in 2007, to his removal from high office in September 2008 and the sheer chaos of his successor Jacob Zuma's presidency.

By May 2009 the newly elected government of Zuma was in control; a guarded optimism was expanding, at first haltingly, and then by leaps and bounds after Mbeki's early removal from office, and a new unabashed clutch of black tycoons were swopping thrifty sports jackets for designer suits, expensive eateries, showy sushi parties and exquisite champagne.

They had good reason for optimism. Though Zuma never openly expressed it, his kingmakers at the ruling party's Polokwane conference in the ANC Youth League expected nothing less than the disavowal of an earlier period of black elitism – of oligarchic capitalism – that had taken shape initially under Nelson Mandela and then Mbeki. The previous system, forged in the mid- to late 1990s, had enriched a handful of politically connected black tycoons in cosy corporate deals with large white businesses, reaching full strength in a frenzy of leveraged shares doled out by banks and mining houses, and ripening into a wealthy caste of black capitalists by the new millennium.

Its critics knew it simply by the pejorative moniker 'oligarchy'. But the term oligarchy was strictly speaking a misnomer. Perhaps it was not obvious then, but the march of the real black oligarchy – those who would amass wealth to seize political power – had only just begun by the close of the first decade of the millennium. A fundamental rule of South African capitalism in the 2000s – control over the state – was directed less at a handful of black winners than their moneyed beneficiaries in the ANC Youth League in a new push for a more dramatic makeover of economic power relations. In hindsight, the frustrations of the previous decade – the resentments of every group that had felt ignored, marginalised, helpless, slighted – were being taken out on an older generation of ANC stalwarts, black businessmen and their corporate benefactors. Party discipline – the most tangible measure of the Mbeki era – was wilting and waning. But what that really spoke to was rising anger among a vast constituency of urban black youths about deeply entrenched wealth. And South Africa, remember, is a country were the white business community has been largely well established. What's unquestionably real are the numbers. Despite frenetic activity in deal flow by 2010, we had seen something in the order of R200 billion committed to black-empowerment transactions over the previous four years. Yet the private sector had amassed around R5 trillion in total.

Since Mbeki's downfall, the overriding theme of party unity had been dissolving into rival power blocs. Unity in fact was by then heavily contested by competing interpretations of post-apartheid history: both colluded in revisionism but none were willing to express the simple truth that leadership was driven less by stability and a unifying ethos than the search for a clear-cut political patron of vested interests beyond the ANC's 2012 Mangaung conference. It was a bewildering array of overlapping alliances and frequent conflicts subdivided and recombined into several groups previously united by the singular object of removing Mbeki in 2007.

Apparently, black economic empowerment had entered a new murky phase since the ousting of Mbeki from office. What worried more moderate ANC leaders ahead of the 2012 elective conference was the possibility that the party's history, values and principles were being discarded. Young Youth League members, Rand Merchant Bank's Peter Vundla told me, had moved in. "They think of the present and future, not the past. They're less interested in a nation's transformation than the cars they drive and mansions they live in."[463]

Given a chance, many in the Youth League would tell you what was wrong with the new South Africa. "When a black person drives an SUV it's called elitism, but when a white person flaunts money it's called success," the League's then president Julius Malema once told a gathering of supporters at a league rally.[464]

That simple sentiment was a defining moment in a 17-year battle to transform the economy – and of early 21st century South African capitalism. After 1994, when South Africa abandoned apartheid, the drive for economic stability and growth after years of stagnation and fiscal excesses provided an overarching purpose that, for many years, shaped the country's economic destiny during the Mandela and – more acutely – Mbeki years. Stability was South Africa's greatest achievement of the previous decade – greater even than its Rainbow invention during the first five years of Mandela's tenure.

But was this a country being reborn? There was a striking undertow of populist grandstanding in the run-up to the ANC's 2012 conference: there was no grand vision, no mission, no ambitious vision of remaking South Africa – or the African continent for that matter.

As the party prepared for its 2012 conclave and the national election in 2013, the miracle had become not just a metaphor for what the country could do but also what it had left undone – of vast inequalities, obstinate racial fissures and lost opportunities.

---

463 Interview with the author, Johannesburg, April 2012.
464 Malema, J, Address at ANC Youth League rally, Polokwane, October 2010.

The ANC Youth League, formed when the ANC was a moderate organisation, later radicalised as the Afrikaner National Party took power in the late 1940s. In 2012, it was home to a thriving elite that, in some respects was an almost inevitable consequence of the failure during the Mbeki administration to deal entirely with the limits of the Mandela era. It had become fodder in the new Zuma era of disaffected ANC activists who had got short shrift from the country's corporate sector. There the problem sat as old anxieties and new enmities rose. To understand what was really going on, we have to swoop back to the political blizzard that swept Zuma to power in 2005 to 2007.

*

Until 2009, there had been hints of what Zuma's kingmakers were up to, but never a full picture. Perhaps a full picture was impossible, since the always-secretive black tycoons born in the empowerment frenzy of the 1990s were never a cohesive group.

Lumbering out of the confusion and chaos in the first two years of the post-Mbeki government, a new capitalist Leviathan was visible, but its true nature was hard to discern. Apparently, the election of Zuma hardly changed their thinking. But, in mid-2009, South Africa was in trouble again.

The older priorities of the ANC were being replaced – not totally, but swiftly – by new issues. For a while, some thought tough restrictions on the market – including nationalisation – were the key. But like an unstable compound, this issue has had a tendency to explode and burn those who handled it roughly. Though all ANC leaders shared a belief in redistribution, a simplistic, exclusive emphasis on those themes served only to confirm the worst ANC stereotypes. For their political patrons, the economic record required a mobilising platform. Here, finally, was the grand vision they'd been looking for. "There will be no compromise on nationalisation," Malema emphatically told animated delegates at the League's national conference in 2011 to thunderous applause. "We don't care who says what. Nationalisation will become the policy of the ANC," he said during a memorial lecture at the University of the Witwatersrand (Wits) commemorating former president Nelson Mandela's release from prison. "And we will not stop until what belongs to us is restored to us."[465] (More applause.) Nationalisation was a clear political tool, the ambitious work of an aspirant, youthful black elite.

An economy may have been dying, felled by corruption. For some in the conspiratorial cliques of the ANC it was a death that had been inevitable from the moment Mbeki tilted at corruption. For others like the older black-empowerment stalwarts, it raised another question: what other motives were there?

It was a sign of just how dysfunctional the state had become. By every observable measure, South Africa was sinking swiftly into a sinister phase of the transition; a terrain where the scramble for wealth and power was cutting an anarchic, even murderous, swathe across the country. The first signs that something was amiss were hints of a new form of enrichment within the state procurement system that had been steadily expanding from a few localised episodes during Mbeki's government into an acidic pattern of larceny on a grand scale after his removal, adding a sombre depth to the story.

As confidence in the survival of Jacob Zuma's presidency beyond the December ANC elective conference began to falter, in mid-2012 corruption stories thronged the front pages of newspapers. Coming on the heels of a spate of mysterious high-profile murders ahead of the party conference that year, the reports fuelled media speculation of a silent coup, where control of the state and security apparatus had by then become the battleground of rival factions in the ruling party. Standing above all others in the scramble for power was a new clutch of black tycoons who wanted nothing less than the disavowal of an earlier period of elitism; they wanted control of the state and its resources. Their chief foe close at hand was Zuma, and he knew them better: they were in plain view. They had hoped to bend him to their will after Mbeki's removal, but, if they could not bend him, they decided, they must break him.

They had publicly charged that Zuma betrayed his promise at the fateful party conference that toppled Mbeki in 2007. The 'Tenderpreneurs', the South African press catchily named them: a cabal of 20 or so ANC Youth League leaders and powerful and increasingly wealthy ANC activists, politicians and businessmen.

Most notable of this group was Julius Malema. He was 31 years old in

---

465 Marrian, N, 'Malema: Nationalisation will become ANC policy', *Mail & Guardian Online*, 15 February 2010. Accessed at http://mg.co.za/article/2010-02-19-malema-nationalisation-will-become-anc-policy.

2012, a man who seemed, for a while at least, to hold most of the strings in the largely rural province of Limpopo and wanted to hold them all in the country. Malema was a neurotic bundle of energy, his boyish appearance ageing behind a bloated face. A man of daring ideas, he was a phenomenon in an age of phenomena: businessman, virulent nationalist, presidential kingmaker, and now anti-Zuma conspirator. Most of his time since Mbeki's ouster in September 2008 was spent raking up muck on Zuma at every opportunity. His eyes were fixed not on the presidency but on state resources, on what lay beneath the ground as well as the assets above. Having been unable to survive an earlier move by Zuma to expel him from the ANC, there was mounting suspicion that he had joined up with a Zuma rival, and one of the richest black businessmen in the country, for the presidency. As they loomed up in popular consciousness, these men gave the impression of a united, tightly-knit group.

On the other side there remained, especially in South Africa where abuse of state security and intelligence during apartheid continued with ever-penetrating and pernicious force beyond 1994, an undercurrent of deep mistrust of law enforcement; feelings that grew as high-ranking officials in the security establishment had become the target in the media of obloquy and citizens came to blame the police and crime intelligence for some of the country's brutal crime. Behind the appearance of a crime wave was a mafia gang in control of the security establishment led by a man named Richard Mdluli with alleged connections to the notorious apartheid-era death squad, the Civil Cooperation Bureau, in the 1980s. With access to state surveillance equipment and largesse, men like Mdluli were all too familiar with the raw power of the state security apparatus. They were a formidable presence in the country's police, crime intelligence and national intelligence structures in 2012, backed by Zuma who viewed control of the security apparatus as the first step towards control of the country's politics.

*

The first years of the Zuma government coincided with some important changes in the ANC's generational mix. It was as if a huge historic conflict had suddenly become a calumnious feud between individuals over wealth. "The ANC," the country's then deputy president Kgalema Motlanthe observed in August 2012, "was being taken over by alien tendencies."[466]

Rapidly it became clear, by 2012, that the rise of the Youth Leaguers was part of a much bigger question, one whose answer was already shaping an entire generation of youths. What may have marked the end of an era for one generation in South Africa's post-1994 transition was for another merely the continuation of an old agenda by other means.

That South Africa had achieved so much in a relatively short period after apartheid – stability, democracy, wealth – paradoxically highlighted its failings in respect of the vast swathe of society that had been excluded from the success story. The country had memorials everywhere, indicative of the earnest expression of the government's desire to acknowledge its difficult history. Yet, for every memorial, there also was a theme-park rendition of the past: Mandela Square in the middle of upmarket Sandton where you can have your picture taken next to a towering bronze statue of Nelson Mandela mounted in the midst of a faux Rainbow nation of wealthy whites and blacks. "It's disgusting," Winnie Mandela, ex-wife of the icon, bluntly told a British interviewer in 2011.[467]

Roger Southall, a sociologist at Wits in Johannesburg, argued that the success of the Mandela era revealed a dangerous form of amnesia. "It is the success of the new era." But he added the warning: "It means we can't learn from history."[468]

That historical lesson, it seems, was the combustible issue that Thabo Mbeki confronted but did not quite succeed in redressing and that incensed Youth League hardliners in the ANC and a glut of poor youths in urban areas of Johannesburg and black townships such as Soweto where – according to one survey – 50 per cent of inhabitants are unemployed.[469] For it was here – where popular expectations have been amongst the highest – that a showdown with South Africa's post-1994 legal and economic dispensation had revealed just how far some radical party activists were prepared to dig in.

That's arguably the all-important point. At a time when poverty was

---

466 Motlanthe, K, 'Organisational report on the occasion of the ANC National Elective Conference', Mangaung, December 2012.

467 See 'ANC looking for Winnie', News24 Archive, 3 September 2010. Accessed at http://www.news24.com/SouthAfrica/Politics/ANC-looking-for-Winnie-20100309.

468 Southall, R, 'South Africa's fractured power elite', (nd). Accessed at http://wiser.wits.ac.za/system/files/seminar/Southall2012_0.pdf.

469 Seekings, J, 'Race, class and inequality in the South Africa city', Centre for Social Science Research Working Paper No. 283, November 2010. Accessed at https://open.uct.ac.za/bitstream/item/22646/Seekings_Race_classinequality_2010.pdf?sequence=1.

fuelling economic crime and corrupt money was flowing into politics as never before, the ANC's National Executive Committee at the party's Luthuli House headquarters in Johannesburg was concerned not only with the country's economic stability, but also with the potential for popular antagonism.

It seems the failure to provide opportunities for all was another way in which the Mbeki government's pragmatism and failure to act big hurt it. For the congenitally pessimistic Mbeki, transforming the economy couldn't have been more than a castle in the sky, a long shot, best-case scenario. But he surely recognised that the grandiosity of the vision of a new economic order would resonate with a section of the black population. For Mbeki, the boldness of vision has a constant allure. Remaking SA Inc. via broad-based black empowerment was just the kind of game-changing idea he went for. But visions, like mirages, melt away.

Yet nowhere had history been so thoroughly defanged than by the association of Youth League militants in the ANC of Mbeki with first-generation black-empowerment recipients of white corporate largesse as moral justification for nationalisation. Jurgen Kogl, a quick-witted former stockbroker and one of Mbeki's early advisers during his deputy presidency and close associate during his presidency, told me, "What we saw by 2009 was a power grab by a younger generation in the Youth League who first mobilised a campaign against Mbeki and are now doing the same."[470]

---

470 Interview with the author, Johannesburg, April 2012.

CHAPTER 21

Lost opportunities

THE POST-LIBERATION GENERATION

"HELLO, SIR. HOW ARE YOU? YOU HERE TO TEACH US, SIR? YOU'RE welcome."

These words, uttered to me by a Grade 6 pupil at a school in Hammanskraal north of Pretoria, captured the reality and lie about black township education in South Africa since 1994. It helped explain the psychology of hope and despair that young black learners felt a decade after 1994. When I arrived at the school in February 2000, summer was going full blast. The temperature usually passed 32 degrees Celsius by mid-afternoon, and on some days it reached 36 degrees. The shade in the prefabricated classrooms offered some relief from the blinding yellow light, but the heat of the day hung oppressively. If you tried to keep going through the day, a moment came around midday when a surge of dizzying inebriation accosted you and you felt that you might faint.

In the very first hours of my visit to the school, one of the first things that struck me was the look of the faces beneath the decrepit surface of things. I was aware of the abrupt intensity of the youth's stare. It came from the constant fear of failure, of hardship, and of resigned disappointment and defeat, and even more from the sense of a transformation project going horribly wrong every minute of every day: a generation of black youths thrust together into something uncertain and new. Physically, the school appeared to be stricken, or decaying from a grave affliction. For a while, it was mordantly effective at a basic education level, but it now had the quality of a malevolent and inescapable free fall, turning everyone into hapless casualties.

I remember driving southbound across the sun-blasted township to a private school in Johannesburg and being stupefied that all the high-altitude arguments about transformation and equity had actually led to this – this privatised oasis. At an annual fee of R20 000 (by 2015, R70 000), the cost of enrolment was a haven of wealthy white exclusivity. There was a handful of blacks, like 17-year-old matriculant Kaletso Mutloatse whom I met during my visit to the school. But, by 2000, there was a discernible flight of qualified white teachers and pupils from newly integrated former Model C public schools to private schooling. It was hard not to be impressed by the splendid vista of this private college, stretched between rows of trees and blazes of flowers in Observatory, Johannesburg. In reality, the two schools still nestled in the bosom of apartheid.

Twenty years ago, we gazed as many of the country's black youths, politicised during the 1980s insurrection, stepped into a brand new era. By 2000, education was a non-stop crisis, and a new generation of youths existed in a sort of temporal bubble; any attention to a past or future was vanquished. There was only the present.

*

On my next visit to Hammanskraal, in late 2006, I found the school still shrouded in the shadow of the past that lay so heavily on the township's youth, as if it had been frozen in time. The place combined all the cruelty and injustice of the old regime with some of the austerity of the new, a product no doubt of apartheid state planning perverted by the prohibitive class dynamics that had settled into the social fabric of the country since 1994. The youths were told they were born-frees; they expected to experience freedom; they had been waiting for years to be free – but they still didn't feel free.

One month before the end of his term in 1998, President Nelson Mandela had declared in a visionary speech that integrated education would become a democratic model for the country's youth. The youth heard him, and as an unemployed matriculant in Hammanskraal told me, "We expected returns. That's why we didn't fight. And we are shocked, as if we've gone back to apartheid. We feel betrayed."[471]

'Betrayal' was in fact many acts: the economic crisis, limited resources, elitism, corruption – but also the ingrained sense of racial inequality. With it came disappointment at what the government could achieve, and the disappointment in youths' minds was only heightened by the performance of the education system. Each year, quite literally thousands of school leavers

---

471 Interview with the author, Hammanskraal, October 2006.

– a generation of potentially key players in any successful economy – were either failing the grade or dropping out of the education system, fuelling an already crippling skills deficit.

At the cost of dysfunctional school leavers, thwarted hopes and aspirations, and a deep sense of betrayal, the massive growth in tertiary entrants and black graduates predicted in the early 1990s had quite patently not materialised. The public education system that once appeared full of promise was failing the grade.

Some writers have termed the born-frees "our new lost generation".[472] The phrase captures the truth about black youth in the years following 1994. It helps to explain one of the great myths after the end of apartheid: why the moment of good feeling was short – a worrying trait, given the vision the government had signed up for.

To a generation of born-frees, the world began on 10 may 1994 when Nelson Mandela became president and a new optimism settled over the land. A handful of the youth was encouraged to succeed, a triumph no doubt of a culture of aspiration in the new South Africa. But outside the porous perimeters of Rainbow nationalism, the world looked like a different place. There were 27 million youths who bemoaned the new order.

From his vantage point at the Treasury, Iraj Abedian, one of Mbeki's hand-picked technocrats, began to see that something was wrong. It was late 1995 and Abedian, freshly minted by the University of Toronto, had experimented, using econometrics formulas, with data on a flip chart late into the night and kept coming back to the same conclusion. The economy had been haemorrhaging skills, subsidising white labour and racking up debt by the day. "The situation," he told me, "was unsustainable. The policy measures advocated by the Reconstruction and Development Plan [RDP] were like trying to heal a patient standing up when the patient was horizontal and needed oxygen.

"Essentially, we drew the conclusion that economic growth was not going to deal with the unemployment problem and poverty was not going to be alleviated through redistribution because of massive structural imbalances

---

472 See, for example, Leibbrandt, M & Green, P, 'Our new lost generation?', *Daily Maverick*, 23 June 2015. Accessed at http://www.dailymaverick.co.za/article/2015-06-23-op-ed-our-new-lost-generation/#.V7GGSc6cHIU.

inherited from apartheid."[473]

The Growth, Employment and Redistribution (GEAR) macroeconomic plan was the result – a sequence of austerity measures initially stitched together under the clumsy title, Framework for Macroeconomic and Financial Policy for SA, and – literally a night before the document went to press – changed to GEAR by a committee headed by Gill Marcus.

As opposed to the RDP, which was mainly concerned with the poor, implicit in GEAR was the understanding that redistribution would take place when growth had taken off. This was a trickle-down understanding of development.

For this kind of growth to occur, the argument went, people had to save by spending less so that money could be ploughed back into the economy. But, for as long as there was no economic growth, development would be given the last preference.

One of the casualties of GEAR was education.

*

For someone who always evoked a mystical air, Mbeki's legacy was as complex as the man himself. Before 1994, South African education was a ramshackle polyglot of inferior schools and universities for blacks. By and large, it was Mbeki who brought the level of efficiency, professionalism, and centralised control that became notoriously associated with his presidency.

The thinking that reformists in government and corporate South Africa could do business, and that a growth as opposed to a redistribution doctrine could lead the way to reorienting the country towards development and redress certainly ran high up the policy chain.

But Mbeki's accomplishments will forever be sullied by rationalisation exercises that did more to close the space for youths to progress through the education value chain. Jay Naidoo, then minister in charge of the RDP, recalled a process of "dissembling policies and structures" set up to promote redistribution. "When I look back, one of the things we took for granted is the notion that if you put more money into health you get more public health; if you put more money into public education more people get educated, etc. In effect, we underestimated the policy impact of GEAR, which

---

473 Interview with the author, Johannesburg, September 2011.

was to reduce the state's capacity to intervene,"[474] he said.

In fact, education expenditure was increased from R300 million by the time GEAR was at its peak in 1999 to R1.2 billion in the year 2001.[475] It had become apparent by then that GEAR would not help reduce educational inequalities in South Africa precisely because it was not a strategy to distribute income and wealth equitably. The restructuring of the public sector had led to many civil servants, many of them teachers, taking voluntary severance packages. Among those remaining in the profession, morale was very low. This was not surprising, since, with reduced expenditure, teachers' workloads increased – larger classes, more periods, a lack of teaching materials – and salaries declined in real terms.

By the end of the Mbeki government in 2007, the education system was a moveable feast of massive local-level corruption, resulting in thousands of students in public schools without desks, chairs or books, declining standards, teacher absenteeism, delinquency and graft, watchdog Transparency International highlighted in a 2008 report.[476] The net effect was a grossly underperforming system. Basic reading scores in 2008 showed that only 20 per cent of Grade 6 learners could do maths at the appropriate grade levels and only 40 per cent on language of instruction.

Earlier in 2006, a report released by the education department revealed that more than half of Grade 6 pupils fell below the standard of reading and writing required by the national curriculum – and maths was worse. Despite high enrolments since 1994 – well above the global average – poor results persisted. In a study centred on teaching skills, conducted in 1998 by Nick Taylor, Chief Executive of an education service organisation called JET Education Services, curriculum coverage of maths and literacy by the end of the year was on track among just 45 per cent of teachers in a sample of 24 schools. "The average score in maths tests for 25 teachers was seven out of 24 points," Taylor found.[477] In other words, pupils could hardly be expected to matriculate with anything qualitatively better than that.

All the while the private schooling and higher-education sector tended to reject any information that supported the thesis expounded in the White Paper on Higher Education that the transformation of the education system

474 Interview with the author, Johannesburg, June 2013.
475 Manuel, T, 'Budget speech to the National Assembly', Cape Town, 17 February 1999. Accessed at http://www.gov.za/budget-speech-trevor-manuel-minister-finance.
476 Ray, M, 'Educashen crysis: Wanted 68 000 engineers/artisans', Finweek, 7 February 2008.
477 Ray, M, 'Blade runner: Nzimande's free-for-all higher education spells a freefall in standards and will run into R18bn for taxpayers', Finweek, 11 June 2009.

towards greater equity between traditionally black and white schools and learners was the top priority. Overall, most of the rest of the education system was simply dysfunctional.

In short, a technocratic view of how the education system would change displaced national priorities. Whatever did corroborate it, the education department embraced with little regard for the source of the problem – a misguided and short-sighted logic.

IF THE APARTHEID ERA PRODUCED A LOST GENERATION OF UNEMPLOYABLE youths, by 2008 the ground shifting beneath South Africa's sclerotic economy was producing a generation of lost opportunities for the so-called born-frees – school leavers born after 1994 and ill-adapted to the academic rigours of higher education and the demands of a fiercely competitive modern economy.

Each year, quite literally thousands of school leavers – a generation of potentially key players in any successful economy – were either failing the grade or dropping out of the education system, fuelling a crippling skills deficit and adding to the unemployment rate.

In 2008, Mary Metcalf, an educationist at the University of the Witwatersrand (Wits), had been working on the relationship between education outcomes and employment. At the time, she had come to the conclusion that an unemployment youth bulge was developing. "Between the end of 2005 and 2007, the education system ejected 535,000 young people from school with no passing certificate and into a very uncertain future," she said. "The majority of these will join the ranks of the unemployed – young people between the ages of 20 and 24 comprise 14 percent of the labour force but are overrepresented at roughly 27 percent of the unemployed."[478]

The flip side of fiscal prudence was rising unemployment and a lost generation of unemployable graduates. About eight in 10 unemployed youths had not completed secondary education or had just made it through high school. And only 6 per cent of South Africa's jobless had a university degree, a study from the South African Institute of Race Relations revealed.[479]

The sheer scale of the problem far exceeded expert predictions in the

478 Ray (n 476 above).
479 Ibid.

mid-1990s of a groundswell of mainly black entrants into universities. In 2007, 21 500 matriculants had failed in Gauteng alone. Of 564 775 who wrote the year-end exam, more than 20 000 failed, prompting then education minister Naledi Pandor to publicly bemoan the drop in the national pass rate. In fact, the pass rate had dropped each year since 2004: In 2007, the pass rate was 65.2 per cent compared with a 2006 rate of 66.5 per cent and a 73.3 per cent success rate in 2003.

In early 2007, Pandor told a parliamentary sitting that just under half of the 675 132 learners who began high school in 1999 made it to matric in 2003. "The higher education level endorsement rate has declined from 18.2 percent in 2004 to 15.1 percent in 2007," she said.[480]

These statistics were a snapshot of the hard reality of a delinquent education system and its economic corollary: acute shortages of skilled black professionals were adversely impacting on services and industries identified by the government's Accelerated and Shared Growth Initiative for SA (AsgiSA) programme as key to unlocking growth and increasing the labour-absorption rate of the economy.

At stake was nothing less than the failure of the education system to face up to the changes of global competition in the 21st century, Servaas van den Berg, a Stellenbosch economist who had sat on the labour subcommittee of GEAR during the mid-1990s, told me. "We're probably talking about an effort – assuming for argument's sake we get the education system functioning optimally now – lasting an entire generation before we see the results of a well-educated society working its way through the labour market and economy."[481]

The picture then emerging was a distressing one of national expectations of rapid delivery utterly out of whack with the pace, quality and volume of talent churned out by the schooling system: a teaching corps ill-equipped to produce quality outcomes, a rising incidence of HIV/AIDS among teachers and consequent high rates of teacher absenteeism, shockingly low numeracy and literacy levels throughout the schooling system, and the cumulative impact of a quality deficit stealthily working its way through the economy.

Of course, the big fear was that the system's failure to meet the demands of industry would check economic growth or, worse, become self-reinforcing. Remove the best-educated members of a new generation, perhaps

---

480 Ibid.
481 Interview with the author, Stellenbosch, December 2011.

forever, and any economy would falter. To be sure, a surfeit of surveys at the time suggested that a knowledge economy – into which South Africa had been evolving – couldn't survive without skilled graduates who figured disproportionately. It was nothing short of a "vicious cycle", Van den Berg told me. "A lack of skills reduces demand and vice versa."[482]

Indeed the problem was so dramatic that it was, by 2010, prompting many economists to call into question the long-term growth and employment implications of the evolution of the entire education edifice over the previous decade. A Standard Bank economist told me that the education system had been fuelling a structural crisis on the supply side that was not going to ease overnight.[483] That's not to mention the effect on the unemployment rate – by then haemorrhaging at roughly 40 per cent despite the perverse shortage of skills. The fact of the matter was the kind of foreign investors needed to sustain economic growth want skilled personnel – tough to supply when the education system is failing.

In the disciplines underpinning an increasingly footloose global knowledge economy – maths, science and engineering – South Africa was steadily losing its global edge.

*

Therein lay the rub. "What matters is not the national obsession with the total school enrolment rate of 95 per cent or pass rate of 70 per cent each year which does not include a massive dropout rate, but the number of school and university graduates with maths and science who meet the demands of the economy," Haroon Bhorat, Director at the University of Cape Town's (UCT) Development Policy Research Unit, told me.[484]

Growth and labour market economists like Bhorat were fretting that the overall pass rate was a slippery slope in the employment-growth debate. "Just look at the skills needed in the economy – there's no question that the growth targets set by government will continue to be challenged if output is affected," he said.[485]

Those needs were dire. Mandi Olivier, Director at the South African Institute of Chartered Accountants, spoke with good authority when she

---

482 Ibid.
483 Ray (n 477 above).
484 Ray (n 476 above).
485 Ibid.

318

told me there was ample anecdotal evidence that government and the private sector were facing a massive supply bottleneck of chartered accountants. "When the economy was growing in previous years the reality was that we simply did not have enough matriculants with higher grade maths to enter BCom programmes at university and then get them through the system to CA level," she said.[486]

Between 1999 and 2004, an average 4.4 per cent of matriculants achieved mathematics passes adequate for entry into natural sciences at university level. Broken down by race, 0.5 per cent of blacks and 3.9 per cent of coloureds got matric passes that enabled them to apply for university study in natural sciences, commerce or engineering – the cornerstone of participation in a modern economy. The majority below the pass mark were black. In 2006, only 4.8 per cent of Senior Certificate candidates passed higher-grade maths, and just 5.7 per cent passed higher-grade science.

From her vantage point at Wits, Metcalf saw warning signs. "When the class of 2008 was in Grade 3 in 2001, the national survey of performance showed that 30 per cent did not achieve the required standard of numeracy, and 54 per cent did not achieve the required standard of literacy," she said. "For the class of 2009, for example, the 2005 Grade 6 evaluation showed that only 28 per cent performed at the required standard of numeracy. For literacy, only 38 per cent."[487]

Thus numerous economists alluded to international test results indicating that South Africa's public-school performance had been among the worst in the world – especially in subjects where technical employment has really mattered.

You'd think that, in the face of a predictable paralysis, any forward-looking government would adjust policy fast enough to get positive results in the education system – or at least turn to interventions to fill the skills gap.

Things weren't so simple, however.

*

If by 2008 the energy crunch that had just begun to impact on the mining sector had trumped the triumph of a new economic dynamism, another calamity was threatening to finish off the ever elusive 6 per cent growth rate.

486 Ibid.
487 Ray (n 477 above).

The golden years of the commodities boom, straddling the early to late 2000s, was nearly over and the growth rate on the back of skills shortages had begun to turn negative. A stupendous shortfall of 68 000 engineers and artisans – across the engineering and trade disciplines – had emerged on the back of the spectacular growth cycle since 2005, according to estimates by the Joint Initiative on Priority Skills Acquisition, or JIPSA, a government effort to identify priority skills in the economy. Exact figures were always scarce but that was a conservative supply target, the JIPSA survey concluded, with actual shortages perhaps twice, even thrice the number.[488]

This was despite the fact that, by 2007, increases in education expenditure began to display significantly higher levels of schooling. In 2008, a seminal study mapped correlations between parents' earnings, occupations and education and their children's. In terms of education, the correlation between parents and their children was low. Children attained significantly higher levels of schooling than their parents did. In an analysis of the first wave of data (collected in 2008), the figures showed that South African children had on average more than 10 years of education, compared with five to six years for their parents and just three years for their grandparents.[489]

Moreover, the astonishingly high apartheid racial gaps in education were shrinking. This was mainly because white attainment levels could not get much better than they were and African, and to a lesser extent coloured, educational attainment had improved considerably. Granted, roughly two-thirds of university students were black youths, but here's the worrying bit: even though most had done better in terms of education than their parents, they had done no better in terms of occupational status. "The correlation between a parent and a child in terms of occupation is high," the study concluded. "This tells a bad story. It says that if your mother was a domestic worker, the chances are you will be one too. Or if your father was a blue-collar worker on the mines, you will probably be too or, even worse, you could be unemployed."[490]

Although the black middle class had grown, so had unemployment. The proportion of the working-age population that was actually employed had dropped from 46 per cent in 2001 to 43 per cent in 2014. Unemployment among male born-frees of working age (including discouraged workers) was

488 Ray (n 476 above).
489 The annual *South Africa Survey* published by the South African Institute of Race Relations. References to *Fast Facts* are to the monthly bulletin published by the Institute, April 2015.
490 Leibbrandt & Green (n 472 above).

running at 67 per cent, and among their female equivalents at 75 per cent.[491]

Among 35 emerging markets, South African males had the second-lowest labour force participation rate. Unemployment had risen from 3.67 million in 1994 to 8.33 million in 2015, or from 32 per cent to 36 per cent, according to Statistics South Africa data. These figures included 'discouraged' workers, who were unemployed people available to work but not taking active steps to look for jobs. The number of discouraged workers of all races increased by 40 per cent in the past 14 years. The increase would include not only some of the parents and grandparents of born-frees, but also born-frees themselves eligible to enter the workforce as they turned 15.

The result has been a mix of economic and political alienation which some commentators have regarded as a detonator for rebellion. For the youth, like the black majority presently, the failure of the economy to create jobs, as the National Planning Commission (NPC) cautioned in its 2011 report, "directly threatens the delicate balance between the constitutional imperative for redistribution and the need to escape the shadow of the past and build inclusivity for all – both black and white". According to the NPC, "The Constitution is South Africa's foundation, that which binds the nation. [Yet] ... unequal experience of the law and unrealised rights undermine this foundation."[492]

Here was the final irony: notwithstanding the rapid rise in access to schooling over the past decade, widespread poverty has sat bizarrely alongside the concentrated wealth of apartheid's beneficiaries whose ownership and control of the economy has had its roots in a battery of repressive legislation since the Land Act of 1913.

The problem had two obvious triggers. First, the assumption that a reprioritisation of the national budget towards education was enough to resolve the problem of poverty and inequality in the schooling system – including the lack of physical and human resources at previously disadvantaged schools and lack of access to schools. Second, increasing the education budget and revamping the schooling system by pouring more cash into it would right the wrongs of the past and miraculously solve the education and skills crisis.

---

491 *South Africa Survey,* April 2015.
492 See Republic of South Africa, The Presidency, 'National Planning Commission: Diagnostic overview', 2011. Accessed at http://www.education.gov.za/Portals/o/Documents/Publications/ National%20Planning%20Commission%20Diagnostics%20Overview%20of%20the%20country. pdf?ver=2015-03-19-134928-000.

IN REALITY, GOVERNMENT WAS PURSUING HOSTILE POLICIES THAT IT FOUND increasingly hard to defend in the ensuing melee of economic crisis. Twenty years ago we gazed as many of the brightest beneficiaries of apartheid entered the world of work; by the end of the first decade of the new millennium, key science and technology resources faced a retirement crisis.

When I asked Derick Boshard, a partner at the international executive-recruitment firm Heidrick & Struggles in Johannesburg, what he thought of the supply side of the skills equation, he brooded. "We face a retirement crisis within the next ten years," he said. And as other countries created the learning centres and jobs to hang on to their best and brightest, Boshard lamented South Africa's loss of a dependable pipeline of talent. "Already a commitment to education is paying dividends to other countries," he said.[493]

Jonathan Crush, an independent labour market analyst, similarly argued that sourcing skills from outside the boundaries of developed countries was an increasingly important method of making up for domestic training and experience shortfalls in what's been euphemistically called 'replacement recruiting'. In particular, structural shifts within the South African economy towards a knowledge society capable of competing globally had brought the added variable of a shortage of technical and entrepreneurial information and communications technology (ICT) skills, with a stupendous 200 to 300 ICT-skilled opportunity seekers per month heading for the airport and perhaps a new life abroad, a 2005 UNISA study found.[494]

As usual, the costs were considerable. As a matter of fact, the loss of each skilled professional in South Africa had cost up to 10 unskilled jobs, the UNISA study found. "Just as alarming," Boshard said to me, "is the fact that we're doing astonishingly little to educate and train a next generation of scientists and engineers."[495] Since maths and science are entry-level requirements for natural science, commerce and engineering degrees, Boshard said, "the number of black accountants, doctors, engineers, managers and other technical professions the current schooling system can produce will have a proportional impact on economic demand in the next decade."[496]

A weaker pipeline was especially worrying precisely because the science and engineering workforce was greying. For instance, records of the Engineering Council of South Africa showed that, of 50 570 students

---

493 Interview with the author, Johannesburg, May 2006.
494 Ray (n 476 above).
495 Interview with the author, Johannesburg, May 2006.
496 Ibid.

enrolled at universities for engineering courses between 1998 and 2005, 8 900 graduated at a rate of 17.5 per cent across all engineering disciplines. The graduation rate for engineers was even lower at universities of technology: between 1998 and 2005, there were 139 820 graduates – a rate of 10 per cent across all disciplines.[497]

Artisanal training in the construction industry, which had been fuelled by the global infrastructure boom between 2000 and 2007, displayed the same trend. "This meant that the industry consisted predominantly of professionals who were aging out of the system," Boshard said. "Add to that the fact that the average age of artisans is 53 and we get a measure of the magnitude of the problem."[498]

*

The economy was like a patch of gravel that caused the education system to skid out from under it. More than two decades since the dawn of democracy, a yawning chasm still separated the world inside the education system from the world outside. As Metcalf, who in 2008 was also education MEC for Gauteng, put it, "We fail the most vulnerable through the inequality of quality and a vicious cycle of unemployment."[499]

The Centre for Development and Enterprise (CDE) in a 2008 survey on maths and science in schools explained this phenomenon in a colder light. It diagnosed a severe case of "inefficiency", concluding that the Department of Education had failed to make tough, politically difficult choices aimed at getting higher levels of competence in literacy, maths and science, especially at the senior-secondary level.

Only in 2009 was there a realisation that the scale of woes went far deeper than apocalyptic newspaper headlines about student fees, or institutions on the verge of financial collapse, or wrangles about transformation, though these were significant indicators of a system under stress. There was a growing belief that the spectacular failure of schools and tertiary institutions to get results portended more than just a transient glitch in the system. If there was any doubt, according to the education department database at the dawn of democracy in 1994, a total of 495 408 learners wrote matric, rising to 552 384 in 1998. Some 88 497 attained exemption (18 per cent) in

---

497 Ray (n 476 above).
498 Interview with the author, Johannesburg, May 2006.
499 Ray (n 476 above).

1994, dropping to a low of 63 725 (or 12 per cent) in 1999. In 2003, out of 440 096 who wrote the exam, 26.7 per cent failed, 54.6 per cent passed without endorsement, and 82 010 (or 18.6 per cent) passed with endorsement.

What this illustrated was precisely the politically difficult conclusion drawn by the CDE report – that the education crisis was not a result of a lack of access to schools. "The public education system is simply characterised by high enrolments and low quality," the report concluded.[500]

Meanwhile, the government introduced the National Skills Development Strategy and JIPSA programmes to catch up, with the focus on developing and recruiting priority artisanal and technical skills and, in the short term, developing a graduate-employment strategy and recruiting retired specialists and expert mentors. Previously, the labour-intensive nature of the mining industry encouraged the mines to 'sink their teeth into' unskilled black workers. Now that mines were no longer the key to national riches, new industries were emerging on the ashes of the old and new ways of working had long since declared unskilled workers expendable. An implicit policy thrust of government by that time was to place the onus on the private sector to retrain and employ unskilled workers. The youth were encouraged to start small businesses. A learning culture rather than CV-making culture was in vogue as a substitute for qualified professionals and unemployment.

To deal with a generation of black youths who had been left out of the education system, AsgiSA proposed to fill the gap through Sector Education and Training Authority (SETA) training programmes, apprenticeship programmes and on-the-job work progression initiatives funded by a skills levy on businesses.

But that was hardly enough to address the developing crisis.

National Business Initiative researcher Glenn Fisher, who was looking at priority demand for top-end skills over the previous three years based on extensive consultation with industry, put the JIPSA target for the period across engineering disciplines at an additional 3 000 – or an average of 1 000 a year. That was a conservative estimate, Fisher said of the 65 per cent of engineers across the board that would have had to be made up. "The country should have aimed to graduate at least 3 000 to 4 000 a year in the medium terms," he said.[501]

The target for artisans was a whopping 30 000 across engineering and

---

500 Ibid.
501 Ibid.

construction disciplines – or an average shortfall of 10 000 a year over the previous three years. Quantifying the supply constraints for trade was just as dire, with a deficit of 45 000 based on the rate at which we could expect projects to roll out into the 2012 financial year. Fisher admitted at the time that the supply target by JIPSA was a "plausible consensus" between government, industry and tertiary education institutions. "It's an underestimate so as not to stretch the target beyond the capacity of higher education institutions to produce graduates."[502]

But the SETAs were no sooner in operation than they descended into disarray, racked by mismanagement and strategic confusion. By 2012, the SETAs and apprenticeship programmes at Further Education and Training colleges were a black hole of corruption and incompetence. Even the tacit acknowledgement by government that too much was expected of the Department of Trade and Industry's (dti) Skills Development Framework – "which has expanded to include too many functions across too many fields"[503] – was an admission that the education department's efforts had become a much wider Band-Aid intervention to address the failure throughout the secondary- and higher-education system.

*

The question haunting many South Africans today is whether we are breeding our own lost generation – a desperate, directionless, unemployable mass of young people who see no future for themselves.

The point, in the end, was this: The skills shortages identified in the JIPSA report spelled crunch time for an economy where the notion that a 5 per cent or even 4 per cent growth rate was possible was increasingly derided by some economists as the 'false optimism' fallacy. More tellingly, it was bad news because it skirted a talent gap that was clearly structural and generational – what Boshard contended was a classic case of a country where "the hunger for economic growth had perhaps been exceeded by inappropriate policies".[504]

Typically, GEAR displayed a distrust of popular initiatives and a comparable veneration of the state. But while the post-GEAR push for new policies and direct state action in transformation moved to the fore initiatives capable

---

502 Ibid.
503 Ibid.
504 Interview with the author, October 2009.

of rendering services and enabling them to influence policies, it also introduced new difficulties. One was the marginalisation of the constituencies those processes were supposed to serve as Mbeki quashed dissent and (as political analyst Hein Marais astutely observed in an earlier estimation of the trend) adopted a singularised world view and political identity, purged of paradoxical or contradictory interests in its rank and file.[505]

Other layers of difference – notably class – were played down in less ambiguous ways in a developmental agenda built on the central theme of civic nationalism. In fact, it was into that blind spot that the government appeared to have slid. The irony, as most liberation movements in other societies have discovered, was that a propensity for strictly technical solutions both depoliticised and repoliticised the problem at hand. Once decoded into purely rational terms, the resultant decisions, by overlooking those dynamics, reinforced and legitimised them. Differences – which Mbeki warned would 'explode' if left unresolved – did indeed erupt to the surface in 2004 as community protests about service delivery gained ground, but with a difference: there was now a new constituency of youth born after apartheid for whom democracy was no more than a chimera. By the end of the Mbeki presidency, in 2010, the ruling party faced a groundswell of protests. Coursing through the African National Congress's (ANC) ranks by the time the government of Jacob Zuma took power were burgeoning anti-market sentiments that, increasingly, were allied to an aversion towards dissent and heterodoxy, an antipathy rationalised under the rhetoric of 'stability' and 'unity'.

In other words, as the government made forward-looking adjustments to address the limits of the transformation of the education system, such as the dti's Skills Development Strategy and JIPSA, it had merely postponed the reckoning for the failures of the real gravedigger of black aspirations and growth – the state of the school system.

505 For an analysis of this line of thought, see Marais, H, *South Africa: Limits to Change: The Political Economy of Transition* (Johannesburg: Zed Books, 2001).

PART VII

Reform and Rebellion

2003–2016

CHAPTER 22

Campus concoctions

INSTITUTIONAL MERGERS

ONE TUESDAY MORNING IN EARLY 1999, A CROWD OF BLACK STUDENTS barricaded the entrance to the University of the North West in Mahikeng, blocking staff from entering the campus. Earlier that morning, I received a two-page press alert at the *Sunday Independent*, where I had been a journalist, from the North West branch of the South African Students Congress announcing a campaign to disrupt operations at the university. The statement announced a campaign to disrupt operations at the university, denouncing the lack of institutional transformation, the high fee structure, and the university's drift to 'neo-apartheid'. On the day I visited the campus, the landscape looked abandoned and ominous, with windblown clouds blocking out the sun. A handful of students carrying placards milled around the main entrance in a funk, dancing and chanting slogans.

My designated guide was Madondo, a lanky second-year political science student and leading figure behind the protest action. Previous efforts by the students to appeal to the university council, he said to me, had elicited a weak response. Their attempts to strike a chord in the media similarly failed. In those days, student protests at historically black campuses were cheap theatre for the media. Certainly, among the predominantly white middle-class readers of the *Sunday Independent*, few seemed to recognise, much less care, about student and academic concerns at apartheid's 'bush colleges'.

It was close to midday when Madondo gave me a tour of the campus, which had the severe aspect of a barracks designed to demolish rather than liberate young minds. By this time, the place had the heightened, vivid sense and confused quality of a bad dream, washed in the relentless yellow sunlight and the dust skidding off the land. There is something symbolic about the position of the campus. Built during the 1970s as one of the bush colleges in the homeland of Bophuthatswana, the geography of the landscape, to adapt George Packer's devastating portrayal of Iraq, is tailor-made for 'psychological demolition'. Shielded by a ridge of rocky outcrops, the campus was a colourless place set on a scabrous landscape that typically defines the topography of the place. Nearby, the sprawl of teeming townships, where the haze of sulphuric smoke from paraffin-fired stoves hovered like a grubby shroud at dusk and dawn, is a symbol of extreme exploitation. Here, dispirited, weather-beaten faces show grim self-reliance and a sense of self-defeat. The shadows are abstractions in a land that has guaranteed tangible rights, but where survival has always been an act of desperation. It is from these settlements that many students had poured into the university hoping to escape the sorry and shabby reality. In this ill-defined, quiescently illiberal milieu, one sentiment was felt very keenly: a wistful yearning for all the opportunities freedom promised.

But freedom was an abstraction. For almost a decade, neither the government nor the university did anything about it, and few journalists bothered to reveal it.

I conducted my interview with Madondo crouched on a narrow verge of grass where students sometimes gathered. Some students swarmed and drew close, intrigued by this curious sight of a journalist. This was something new to them. "We have been raising issues for years," Madondo said in a slow, hesitant tone.[506] But five years of democracy had not changed the institutional and power structure of the campus. "Issues of academic representivity, and the democratisation of the council and the curriculum are much of the same."

He went on to compare their situation to that of the former homeland. "Under the apartheid regime, bush campuses were built in Bantustans, controlled by white Afrikaner academics with the purpose of training black bureaucrats and professionals to run the Bantustan administrations," he said. "The council is still dominated by white Afrikaners from the old era, to be very objective."[507]

*

We concluded our conversation, and he escorted me to see a professor of mathematics named Matthew Kambule who had been expecting me. Sitting

---

506 Interview with the author, North-West University, March 1999.
507 Ibid.

cross-legged in his office, Kambule cut a large, wary-looking middle-aged figure with a gravel voice and polite smile behind intense eyes. He had been teaching mathematics at the university for a few years since his return from the United States, where he had been in a sort of self-imposed exile during apartheid. Fearing the danger of reprisals from officialdom, Kambule spoke off the record. "The problem," he told me, "is that the curriculum is still Calvinist and the institutional culture is still rooted in the apartheid past. I returned from the US thinking I could change that and contribute to the transformation of the country. But the problem is that we have a council of white Afrikaners who are not willing to transform the power structure and academic staff profile of the institution."[508]

"Was the problem raised in council?" I asked.

"Yes, but the council is dominated by conservative Afrikaners," he said. "And here bear in mind we're dealing with a university built for the purposes of apartheid."

Like a self-fulfilling prophecy, the university stepped into the post-apartheid order fit for purpose. And like a crude expedient, the Afrikaner elite, imperious and apparently utterly impervious, entrenched the status quo.

And so, when students began their protests, Kambule and a handful of black academics quietly supported them. "These kids deserve better, far better," he said. "But transforming the place means confronting the entire system, academically and geographically."

Kambule keenly felt his professional isolation from the university senate and council and had made his goal the transformation of the power structure. His pedagogical intensity and disenchantment with what he saw as an entrenched racial legacy helped turn a generation of black students into a sort of cultural pessimism. He felt that, in order to understand the situation of blacks on campus, I needed to meet students. I thanked him and bade farewell.

Madondo escorted me across the campus to the Student Representative Council (SRC) office occupied by five youths. For two hours, they spoke of fees that were prohibitive for students born in the impoverished townships that surrounded the area, of the lack of institutional transformation and of the prevalence of white professors and departmental heads.

All that week, tension had been building up. There were already minor

---

508 Hereinafter, all direct references to Kambule are from an interview with the author, North-West University, March 1999.

skirmishes between campus security and striking students. Within this climate of tension, the old guard, having already built up a formidable presence, held the balance of power.

In the turbulent days that followed my visit, the *Sunday Independent* ran the story. There were no garish banner headlines – only 300 words hived off in a far corner of page 4, accompanied by a picture of students at the barricades. Hardly anyone noticed. There the story ran cold, along with the protest. But the problem remained.

I didn't realise it then, but the demonstration at North West was the opening salvo in a conflict between students and university authorities for institutional transformation and free education. Over time, the university disappeared behind a security zone and beyond its perimeters there was a proliferation of student protests and strikes on other bush campuses, and everything began to deteriorate. Financially mismanaged, academically weak, and dominated by white Afrikaner professors at the level of senate and council, pressure for change was festering.

The media played the story as a case of rambunctious youths with scant interest in earning a degree, and once again the story ran cold. Over the course of the next five years, the transformation of higher education would become one of the government's main defences against the more radical ideological appeals of a complete overhaul of the system and a dominant institutional force in academic life.

IN 1999, THEN EDUCATION MINISTER KADER ASMAL, IN HIS USUALLY JOCULAR manner, publicly toyed with an ambitious political agenda to deal with two niggling challenges in higher education: advancing redress and equity for black students by facilitating their access to institutions of higher learning, and fast-tracking and retaining a new generation of black scholars.

In 2001, Asmal assembled a team of experts, known rather prosaically as the National Working Group, to explore the reconfiguration of the 36 racially and spatially segregated universities and technikons built during the 1960s and 1970s as part of the apartheid government's segregation policy. For a while it looked as if a generation of black tertiary institutions would finally turn the corner after years of racial inequity and political maladministration had forced them to the brink of collapse.

On 28 May 2002, Cabinet approved Asmal's proposals for a restructured system of higher education. 'Creating Comprehensive Universities in South Africa: A Concept Document', released by Asmal in January 2004, recommended the consolidation of 36 institutions and two national institutes in the Northern Cape and Mpumalanga into 23 institutions through a process of mergers and incorporations legally enacted over a period of two years. A significant part of the restructuring plan was the creation of six 'comprehensive' higher education institutions offering a combination of technikon and university programmes with the express propose of extending the availability of technikon programmes, especially in rural areas where these hadn't previously been on offer.

Treasury made R3 billion available for restructuring the higher-education sector. Half of that amount was used for the recapitalisation of some institutions and the remainder divided between meeting direct merger costs and ensuring the long-term viability of institutions on the basis of an assessment of their institutional and operating plans.

Then came the real test of that gambit: could a far-reaching institutional and organisational reconfiguration of the higher-education system do the trick? To the Department of Higher Education, the single digit '6' was arbitrary, yet tidy – certainly more expedient as a decimal rounded off to a single digit than the surfeit of so-called bush colleges that once peppered South Africa's higher-education landscape. The same goes for the statutory council on higher education, the body responsible for driving the reorganisation of higher-education institutions.

Of course, for all the setbacks there were what Asmal described as the "birth pangs of integration". Once almost exclusively white, universities reflected more than ever before the racial demographics of the country, with more people from groups disenfranchised by apartheid climbing the ladder with a degree or diploma. But, at the same time, the number of people living in poverty had changed little since apartheid ended, with no remedy in sight given the structural problems in education.

But, if the restructuring exercise *was* a response to unequal institutions, between its architects and students lay a financial and philosophical gulf too vast for the mergers to close. Asmal had belonged to the Mbeki school of economics. In the jargon of policy, he was a 'social democrat mugged by reality', which meant he believed in preserving the balance of power.

*

In the five years following the mergers, between 2004 and 2009, a debate ensued mainly in white academic circles that clearly attempted to redefine the academic and financial logic of the new institutional set-up – from one centred on historical redress to one that placed the quality of academic output at the fulcrum of future planning. At the same time, there seemed to be broad acceptance in government and the corporate sector that something had to be done to halt the decline in tertiary output.

Some erstwhile proponents of the restructuring strategy in the education department and Council on Higher Education – a statutory body that advises the minister on higher-education issues – even quietly acknowledged (as one official put it to me) that the department "wrongly assumed the potential for structural transformation as an immutable substitute for black academic advancement", lending succour to the emerging view that restructuring was the only instrument for transformation.

By that time, the emerging consensus between white academics in historically white universities would seem to have been that, instead of forced marriages between institutions, the focus should have been on academic outputs. Even Asmal's successor, Naledi Pandor, under pressure to cap student fees, had asked Higher Education South Africa, the vice chancellors' association, to probe the wisdom of the restructuring strategy to achieve economies of scale and so bring down the fee structure.

There had also been talk among the African National Congress (ANC) and its allies, the Congress of South African Trade Unions (COSATU) and South African Communist Party (SACP), about whether the mergers and incorporations of polytechnics with universities (i.e. like institutions with each other) and campus incorporations had been successful.

The problem was that all this was happening in a familiar pattern: standards and admissions were faltering, resources were overstretched and black academics were powerless in the face of the sclerotic system. As one sceptic who was quoted in a 2008 statutory audit report on university restructuring laconically put it, "It's like flying an airplane while still building it. We're simply throwing cash at a burgeoning problem."[509]

Proof of that assertion came in an announcement by Pandor that same year that R3.6 billion would be allocated to a number of universities that had the potential to increase their enrolments and graduates – especially black graduates from poor backgrounds – during the planning process for

---

509 Interview with the author, November 2009.

the three years to 2010.

Around that time, Cheryl de la Rey, Chief Executive Officer of the Council on Higher Education, told a journalist that government would be reviewing the "size and shape" of the restructuring strategy – which had already cost higher education more than R3 billion in just four years – to determine whether the system had the capacity to produce the number and quality of graduates the country needed. "The council's higher education quarterly committee [has] been in the process of gathering information through audits of institutions that will assist in assessing the success of individual mergers," she said.[510]

Yet, what each predicament and proposed solution by the government really spoke to was the exponential growth in the cost of propping up a fundamentally flawed strategy. "The trouble is the economic impact of institutional failure in higher learning was never part of Kader Asmal's opening gambit when he announced sweeping changes to the system," Jonathan Jansen told me.[511] Certainly, while the education department had been ploughing billions of rands since 2004 into consolidating and fortifying newly merged universities against everything from low and qualitatively deficient research outputs to overstretched resources and financial barriers to entry by black students, the scale of investments was being systematically rolled back by a diminishing return as the cost of maintaining the system's failure continued to mount. On that basis, a 2007 Human Sciences Research Council (HSRC) report reached a startling conclusion: despite laudable efforts by the education department to make the mergers work, the dropout rate was costing the Treasury a stupendous R4.5 billion in grants and subsidies to higher-education institutions without an adequate return on investment.

That should intuitively have fuelled fears of an impending calamity, if weak black student access and pass rates were a proxy. It certainly worried the corporate sector that South Africa had been lagging behind global estimates of knowledge production, accounting for an average one-third of increases in the gross domestic product of a country. In business's view, the same forces responsible for the surge in costs over the previous decade now threatened the smooth functioning of the economy. It's a perception shared by most human resources managers and company executives I interviewed.

---

510 Ray (n 477 above).
511 Interview with the author, Johannesburg, June 2009.

"We're finding increasingly that students coming out of disadvantaged and merged universities aren't prepared for the world of work," Felleng Magolgoa, a human resources director at Simba Snacks and Beverages, told me. Tiger Brands training and development and personnel manager Peter Lyles agreed. "We've noticed a definite decline in quality in recent years within the former technical colleges," he said.[512]

*

Indeed, by 2009, the result of the mergers and incorporations appeared to be a fragile and limited success – perhaps even outright failure if the measure of success was the access rate and quality of academic throughputs and outputs of amalgamated institutions.

That same year, the Pretoria-based research institute Ask Afrika conducted a survey of the performance of the newly merged institutions. Judging from the responses of seven vice chancellors interviewed in the survey, critical voices had dissipated in the face of what Jansen, one of a few outspoken critics of the system, had described as "perhaps the greatest challenge to universities and technikons: the fundamental restructuring of the higher education landscape through new funding formulas, new governance regimes, new institutional cultures and new policies on institutional applications".[513]

As universities struggled to adapt to the new institutional landscape, the pundits agreed: universities were then, and continued to be, in a shambles. Only now, they were torn apart by badly conceptualised mergers and incorporations that had left amalgamated institutions academically disabled and therefore worse off.

"As things stand, the ANC is wreaking untold damage on our children and, consequently, on the country's future, just as apartheid education did in the past," wrote Barney Mthombothi, editor of the weekly *Financial Mail*, of the restructuring exercise.[514] The statement was typical of the *Mail*'s repartee. The proof, as always, was in the results. Only 38 per cent of students admitted to university were likely to obtain their three- or four-year degrees within five years.

---

512 All citations in this paragraph referenced to Ray, M, 'Stable crisis – a survey of the SA tertiary terrain', *Finweek*, 26 February 2009.
513 Ray (n 512 above).
514 Ibid.

Some 51 per cent were unlikely to graduate at all, the Ask Afrika survey found.[515]

By no coincidence, most of these students were from historically disadvantaged universities and technikons. By contrast to the country's top three institutions – all historically white campuses left untouched by the mergers – merged and incorporated institutions piled into the bottom 10 worst performers. None of the merged traditional and amalgamated universities of technology – previously technical colleges for black apprenticeships – made it to the top three spots in teaching and learning and research-performance indicators. And those that did feature in the top five of the financial sustainability and resources indicators did so because they received disproportionately large subsidies from the government as part of the Department of Higher Education's transformation agenda.

Education bureaucrats preferred to grant the system limited success, saying the country's universities were in the throes of what had become euphemistically known in the jargon of education work as a 'crisis of normalisation' – a rather oblique reference to a system that was in fact faltering under the combined strain of growing numbers of financially and academically ill-prepared students and an untransformed crop of academics.

When I asked then vice chancellor of Rhodes University Salim Badat in February 2009 what he thought of the mergers, he said, "You need to look at the results before and after the mergers."

Those results were in obvious reference to the number of black students that had entered the system since 2004. A new cohort of black students was in fact pouring into the system, with several universities reporting annual overruns of up to 20 per cent in first-year enrolments.

Of course, barely six years later, in 2015, those effects were in full view as students rose up in a blaze of protest action. But that was in the future.

*

The question then being asked was: restructuring for what? Black academics and students saw the issue in social terms. Since much of the country's knowledge was created within institutions of higher learning, government's strategy meant more than a rationalisation issue: if the restructuring of higher-education institutions was being driven by the transformation

---

515 Ibid.

imperative, it now threatened transformation. Inevitably, enflaming over-stretched institutions was not the only trap awaiting universities forced to operate within the inherited geopolitical blandishments and segregated structures of the apartheid system. The restructuring exercise seemed to be no more than disguised retribalisation.

Perhaps the most pertinent statement of the education department's intentions was to be found in the National Plan for Higher Education which saw the aim as "the development of a single national coordinated higher education system which is diverse in terms of the mix of institutional missions and programmes".[516]

Drawing on the Higher Education White Paper, the National Working Group, the body charged with drawing up the restructuring plan, had also emphasised "fitness for purpose" and the associated principles of equity, sustainability and productivity.[517] In 2002, the government explicitly expressed its goals in a discussion paper on restructuring higher education as the achievement of equity between black and white institutions, economies of scale in newly merged institutions, and black academic advancement.[518]

That scale was important to South Africa's education environment was irrefutable; everyone agreed some form of institutional reform was needed after decades of misaligned resources and racial imbalances in the old apartheid economy. However, at a very early stage in the process, anxieties were expressed about whether the goals of the exercise made any sense. At a Centre for Development and Enterprise (CDE) panel discussion,[519] those goals provided a reasonable proxy for an answer to the same question: Restructuring for what?

Among the panellists was Thandwa Thembu, one of the few black deputy vice chancellors at the University of the Witwatersrand (Wits). She argued that "the apartheid government in a number of cases had allowed institutional management and governance to deteriorate beyond redemption – and the ANC government was now looking to mergers to solve those problems". Thembu and other panellists roundly criticised the National Working Group for focusing too narrowly on "rescuing a number of irrelevant and spatially segregated institutions of the old era" and, therefore, using the

---

516 Ibid.
517 Ibid.
518 Ibid.
519 Ibid.

single instrument of merger without any prior experimentation".

When I asked Jansen what he thought of the mergers, he defended Thembu's sentiment, with a difference, however: "When the restructuring strategy was first publicly mooted by Minister Asmal in the nineties there was never any doubt that this was about anything other than political expediency," he said. "Aside from obscure references to restructuring being necessary to sort out the country's geopolitical problem – whatever that means – I couldn't find a single statement in any of Asmal's public statements during that time on academic productivity." It's a system, Jansen said, "designed to succeed on racial lines and fail academically" – lurching from the management of one costly crisis to another, adding: "Because it was primarily a political exercise there was never an academic and economic logic."[520]

Of course, there were more than a handful of black students opposed to the restructuring exercise for the very reasons Thembu articulated. They accused Jansen of defending white privilege and institutional culture.

At first, government's stance may have appeared to focus on a constructive engagement with the problem. It was apparently an attempt by the Council on Higher Education to come to terms with wide-ranging flaws in the "size and shape" of the new institutional landscape. While that sounded impressive enough, it warranted closer examination. First of all, the Council's position was a reaction to the slow pace of black academic advancement characterised by weak access and graduate output rather than the creation of globally competitive universities. And so, while the Council slammed as "problematic" the slow and uneven pace of delivery within newly configured universities, it had yet to come to terms with the root cause of the delivery problem. As Thembu put it, "You can't find solutions within a logic that wasn't intended to produce radical outcomes."[521]

True, but outcomes were a relative measure in the cut and thrust of transformation: between academic excellence and black graduates; between black access and financial barriers; between segregated and integrated institutions. Perhaps the most striking conclusion of the Ask Afrika survey wasn't what it set out to immediately identify, but the hidden contours of an incipient pattern of poor performance among most merged and (coincidentally) historically black universities and technikons incorporated into well-heeled

520 Interview with the author, Johannesburg, June 2009.
521 Ray (n 512 above).

ones. Most vice chancellors I interviewed dared not say that openly lest they evoke the ire of students. Their views were tempered – outwardly sanguine – but guardedly critical nonetheless.

"In most need of attention is a national perspective to determine what works and does not, especially with regard to differentiation between universities and technikons and research and teaching universities," Antony Melck, a social adviser to the University of Pretoria's vice chancellor, said to me.

If anything, what the mergers proved was that the size and fit of merged institutions may well have been wrong from an academic-output standpoint, but the disparities in the range and quality of both resources and capacity on different campuses of merged institutions also posed major challenges. The decision to keep open all campuses and sites of delivery meant that all institutions involved in mergers or incorporations now had multiple campuses. That posed significant management and administrative transformation challenges in some cases where capacity was limited.

Recapitalisation funds did not necessarily redress imbalances. However, there were other differentials even more intractable: differences in the quality of teaching and learning, research outputs, and financial sustainability – arguably the most important benchmarks of any university's performance – were by 2013/2014 beginning to manifest themselves.

The biggest challenge lay in strengthening restructured historically black universities. The National Working Group appointed by Asmal had explicitly recommended that weak institutions should receive additional resources. In fact, all policy documents in the early 2000s, when the strategy was being formulated, related to promoting staff and student equity; building administrative management; governance and academic capacity; enhancing sustainability by ensuring the effective use of resources; consolidating academic programmes; and creating news institutional cultures.

But the big problem seemed to lie in the curricula and institutional culture of comprehensive universities. At issue was whether they brought together different kinds of knowledge and the different knowledge cultures that support them. The proposals left the strongest of the advantaged universities untouched. They were able to consolidate their already considerable strengths, particularly in research productivity and third-stream income generation. In a sector heavily market-dependent, that left those institutions merged at a disadvantage; it also provided a breeding ground for black student anger at the slow pace of transformation.

IN 2008, THE COUNCIL ON HIGHER EDUCATION REPORTED ITS AUDIT FINDINGS on the merger process.[522] The entire exercise, the report said, was onerous: some universities were trying to manage distant campuses, rising demand for access and financial aid by black students, and an untransformed teaching corps. Nelson Mandela Metropolitan University, which resulted from a merger of technikons and the University of Port Elizabeth, was stumbling over logistical and administrative issues and course programmes. The Council on Higher Education concluded that the combinations were clearly not working.[523] But the most crucial functions were those that constituted their core business: teaching, learning and research.

In other cases, such as the University of Johannesburg (UJ), academic programmes of technikons and universities were being consolidated to provide common curricula with common criteria and modes of assessment while still trying to cater for the needs of students who embarked on their studies prior to the merger.

I asked Adam Habib, deputy vice chancellor in charge of academic affairs at UJ in 2009, what he thought of the process. "It's about massifying universities," was his response.[524] However, what Habib, who would go on to become vice chancellor of Wits and oppose the very thing he advocated in 2009, didn't concede was that academic as opposed to administrative mergers were already proving to be a headache as institutions battled to move towards establishing a suite of programmes in line with their new missions and creating the appropriate administrative units to house them: colleges, faculties, schools and departments.

The sheer scale of the problem was hard to quantify at the time, but there were hints of what was around the corner. One early clue was an institutional review in 2005 by an independent panel comprising three foreign research experts and three local panellists of the National Research Foundation. Over a 12-day period, the panel interviewed more than 400 stakeholders in three cities. The panel was highly critical of the research-rating system and subsidy formula and identified the main problems as student access; a lack of coherence with assessment instruments; relationships between ratings and funding; operational problems; concerns about systemic sources of bias; and difficulties with the 'one-size-fits-all' model.[525]

---

522 Ray, M, 'Campus concoctions', *Finweek*, 26 February 2009.
523 Ibid.
524 Interview with the author, Johannesburg, February 2009.
525 Ray (n 522 above).

Such revelations became increasingly controversial over the years: government routinely groused at those who defended past privileges. Even the Council on Higher Education in its audit reports roundly chastened institutions for failing to restructure and transform fast enough. "More than 10 years into the new democracy the University of Pretoria is still wrestling with the important challenge of locating its strong academic identity with a range of new social identities developing in contemporary South Africa," the audit report concluded.[526]

This was not another failure of imagination. "What's true," Ask Afrika business manager Amelia Richards told me in 2009, "is that there seemed to have been an overall improvement in the pace of transformation."[527] But as the problem of juggling different institutions and traditions grew, universities were all the while floundering in a strategic impasse.

Perhaps the deeper truth was that performance was being subverted by financial crises, low rates of student access and untransformed academic norms and teaching corps. It would be a matter of time before the meshing of these issues would produce a powder keg.

---

526 Ibid.
527 Interview with the author, Pretoria, January 2009.

CHAPTER 23

High-altitude abstractions

THE PROMISE OF FREE EDUCATION

IN THE AUTUMN OF 2009, THE NEWLY APPOINTED MINISTER OF HIGHER Education carried a distinguishable title in an office on the fourth floor of Cosatu House in Braamfontein, Johannesburg. The sign on the office door said 'Chairman'. The offices were the headquarters of the South African Communist Party (SACP).

Blade Nzimande cut a sturdy figure with a round face and shrill voice that soared to operatic crescendos in reflective speeches frequently interrupted by quips and qualifications whenever he spoke. His thinking during the 1970s and eighties, when he was an anti-apartheid activist in Pietermaritzburg, Natal, had been shaped by the philosophy of Karl Marx and Frederick Engels. His learning process in higher education was fitful and halting. His PhD, oddly in human-resource management, was exploratory, but it showed a keen interest in the models that influenced thinking about economic power relations in society. It was not the kind of dissertation written to land a job in the private sector, and, after a few years teaching at the University of Natal, he promptly abandoned an academic career. His interests were out of favour in the field. A life spent teaching and analysing would be difficult.

That autumn in 2009, he had just been given the responsibility to run the Department of Higher Education. Top ministry and department officials may not have shared his socialist ideals, but they were mostly African National Congress (ANC) cadres who supported the transformation of the higher-education system. By the close of 2009, talk of radical change was in the air. The government of Jacob Zuma had just been inaugurated on an electoral platform of radical economic transformation; the problems facing the higher-education system were by then a slow burn; the students were hopeful, and Nzimande was trying to see the academic year to its close. He had just announced his intention to open the doors of higher education and free up tuition.

The students heard the message.

*

For a while, it helped that Nzimande was new to his job. He had a clean slate and little incentive to defend the old way of doing things. The Zuma presidency gave policymakers plenty of work. Unlike Thabo Mbeki's presidency, when university amalgamations were bywords for rationalisation exercises, the new order would be driven by a strategy of radical transformation. Education would be a priority, and beyond education lay a course whose agonies and failures had been on full display.

In early 2010, Nzimande addressed a gathering of students and academics at the University of the Witwatersrand (Wits). Like all skilled actors in government, he was keenly aware of his audience. The view of those opposed to free tuition, he said, leaning forward with an apologetic smile, had been a selfishly privileged one. The instinctive mistrust among some academics present was reciprocated, with interest. But there it was. One by one the others agreed.

Having laid much of the intellectual groundwork for the government's new assertive policy, Nzimande now described a new era in which South Africa's higher-education system – still staggering from the department's botched 2004 institutional restructuring efforts – would be overhauled root and branch. But if Nzimande's opening gambit to introduce free undergraduate tuition came naturally, he being a Marxist, it also came like the second punch of a one-two punch knockout.

Since late 2007, protests about fees were on vivid display at the universities of the Witwatersrand and Johannesburg and, in February 2008, there were demonstrations at the Durban University of Technology, the University of Limpopo, in the northern reaches of the country, and at the Tshwane University of Technology in Pretoria. In 2009, students at UNISA's Pretoria campus threatened to make the university 'ungovernable'. David Maimela, then President of the South African Students Congress (SASCO), said, while education was a right according to the Constitution, in fact higher education was neither accountable nor free. As a result, before and after democracy in 1994 "the single most important demand from students remained access to education".[528]

In theory, the broad thrust of free tuition – what Nzimande believed was the right prescription – could only be lauded by a glut of poor citizens left out of the hallowed halls of higher learning. And that was precisely the problem. What Nzimande did not know then was that his flirtation with left-wing policy ideals would produce consequences his department wasn't prepared to handle. After all, university tuition is a costly affair: these days, students can expect to pay between R20 000 and R40 000 a year for undergraduate degrees and even more for specialised professional degrees, such as law and medicine, University of Stellenbosch economist Servaas van den Berg told me. "Take the 2008 total matriculation cohort of 533 000, multiply the 333 000 pupils who passed matric by the mean average annual undergraduate fee of, say, R20 000 and the total cost to government is around R6 billion per annum."[529]

Even here, though, the picture wasn't quite complete. National Student Financial Aid Scheme (NSFAS) support covers funding for general undergraduate studies as well as special funds for scarce skills, said Van den Berg. "But it excludes the cost of accommodation and books, which usually adds up to about R50 000 per student per year – or twice the cost of tuition fees. Add on top of that the cost of subsidising an extra year for many poor youngsters who don't score an exemption or qualify for a mainstream degree and are identified through selection processes as having the potential to succeed academically."

The result is that the cost of free tuition alone, excluding books and accommodation, was closer to R17 billion in 2009, in addition to the 2009 budget allocation for higher education for salaries and overheads.

At a national undergraduate dropout rate of 35 per cent by then, the net effect was a prospective loss to the fiscus of R6.3 billion. If department officials were worried about these costs, there was little outward evidence of it. In fact, Nzimande seemed rather apoplectic. In May 2010, he sounded the alarm when he pledged his department's allegiance to poor students "who can't write their exams because of prohibitive tuition fees" and warned that, unless additional resources were sought to bolster the student financial scheme, a more far-reaching review of the funding arrangement would have

---

528 Quoted in MacGregor, K, 'South Africa: Student protests turn violent', *University World News*, 10 February 2008, Issue No. 15. Accessed at http://www.universityworldnews.com/article. php?story=20080208090147857.
529 Interview with the author, Stellenbosch, December 2010.

to be undertaken. "We'll have to broaden that review to look at how we implement the ANC manifesto commitment on beginning to introduce free higher education at least for the first degree of poor students but who are deserving," he said.

If Nzimande had taken as an article of faith that any student who welcomed change would agree, the university authorities quivered. That Nzimande's commitment was constitutionally sound didn't matter. The question for the university top brass, those at historically white institutions at any rate, was: why – when the department had already sunk billions of rands into undergraduate failures – should Nzimande bang on so relentlessly about free tuition? And when the department had until then shown itself lax at managing even plausible risk among low-income students from the perspective of the NSFAS?

*

In truth, Nzimande was walking a fine line, alternately telling disadvantaged black students that the demands of SASCO would be met while assuring university bureaucrats that costs would be met. Yet, it may also have been that he genuinely believed a pioneering proposal such as free undergraduate education would help eliminate persistent financial hurdles to access and thereby pummel through the education system more skilled black graduates needed to re-engage the country's stalled economy and get the skills locomotive chugging along.

If that was the case, Nzimande may have spoken too soon, Van den Berg told me. "He should at the very least have spent some time absorbing the numbers before making a bold public announcement."[530]

Van den Berg may have had a point. Even if undergraduate education was fully funded, the potential costs and benefits would be onerous. A 2008 Human Sciences Research Council (HSRC) study of universities found that nearly 50 per cent of all undergraduate dropouts aged 18 and 20 were black first-year students.[531] The real humdinger, the survey found, was whether funding could really be faulted for the calculation, however cold, that 50 per cent of undergraduate students were not prepared for higher education.[532] To be sure, education has increasingly topped public-expenditure priorities,

---

530 Ibid.
531 Ray (n 477 above).
532 Ibid.

particularly in the light of the historical mismatch between high investment and poor outcomes. Since 2005/2006, Treasury has increased the total allocation to higher education by an average 16.7 per cent per year. Many of the poorest had been supported by the NSFAS, which, in 2008, doled out grants to 125 000 students, and, in 2009, disbursed loans and bursaries worth R1.8 billion – double the amount granted in 2008.

But these numbers quickly led to the much thornier issues of race and class that tended to ritually shape the contours of the dropout crisis. National statistics on the topic were blunt: by 2009, around one in three of the country's nearly 800 000 university students were graduates from substandard schools and low-income black families. Data from various national surveys, including the education department, showed black students were more than six times more likely to drop out of first-year university than students from the highest quarter. And, in some sample surveys conducted in 2008 in the Western Cape, every undergraduate dropout voiced a similar hassle: courses were too tough.[533] Or in a more nuanced version of the same refrain: "The schooling system doesn't do enough to prepare us for university."

*

Alongside the slow boil of protests by black students and Nzimande's policy gambit came a deluge of evidence showing up the waste, inefficiency and poor quality of primary- and secondary-school level education. A 2007 report published by the National Business Initiative (NBI) documented a distressingly high level of undereducated pupils between Grades 6 and 8.[534] "What the study found is Grades 3 and 6 learners aren't operating at the appropriate levels," said NBI Director Judith O'Connell. "In fact, about 60 percent of Grade 6 pupils were operating at Grade 3 level."[535]

In 2008, a committee set up by education minister Naledi Pandor to recommend methods by which schools could be evaluated and developed heard "harrowing stories about official instructions to raise test scores across the board to compensate for curriculum failure".[536] Chaired by Jonathan Jansen, the committee expressed deep concern at the examination system

---

533 Ibid.
534 Ibid.
535 Ibid.
536 Ibid.

used in South African schools and labelled its integrity "questionable".[537]

When school principals and union officials of various provinces were interviewed by the committee, they spoke of "artificial inflation" of results as requested by senior officials in the department. "That was said repeatedly and with such passion that the committee was adamant it occurred," Jansen recalled when speaking to me. "These people spoke of how officials would come up with ways to inflate marks."

In early 2009, Aslam Mukadam, a founding member of a small but hardy band of researchers and educators called the Concerned Mathematicians Group, published a scathing report on the 2008 matric results that peeled back the layers of statistical legerdemain, exposing how officials stood by while schools handed in patently misleading results. Pouring over the raw data, they asked themselves a basic question: what percentage of matriculants who failed biology and science passed maths? The answers led Mukadam and other education researchers countrywide to place the national pass rate for maths substantially below the 50 per cent mark.[538]

The knock-on effect at universities was a 50 per cent dropout rate of undergraduate students that Nzimande had not factored into blanket tuition grants.

THERE'S AN IDEOLOGICAL TROPE GOING ON HERE – NOT THE EFFECT OF seeing the limits of transformation as a reflection of historically white academic norms, but the mistake of seeing student access in populist terms. The ruling class is stable, wrote Karl Marx, the bête noire of communists, only to the extent that it is able to draw the best minds into its service.

Something like this was what had shaped the ANC's thinking of the black middle class since the late 1970s, when business and the apartheid government had set out to co-opt an elite stratum of blacks in the bantustans. As a multiclass organisation, the ANC set out to counter the strategy of business and government by turning to the mobilisation of this stratum. That ideal gained ground in 1994 when the ANC made black economic empowerment and employment equity a strategic priority of the democratic government. It is what President Jacob Zuma promised to deliver as he swept into control

537 Ibid.
538 Ibid.

of the party and government, propelled by the support of the unions and Nzimande's SACP. The new order would be 'pro-poor'. The government would 'deliver'. Better state interventions were needed if more poor students were to have access to higher education, Zuma told a conclave of students and academics at a University of Zululand graduation ceremony in May 2009.

Zuma was responding viscerally at an extremely high altitude of abstractions, where details become specks. Meeting that commitment required bold and speedier transformation, to be sure: but in a context of inequalities and financial constraints to access this meant universities were perilously close to becoming shock absorbers for structural inequalities.

And that's the core issue. For several years, education officials had warned government that South Africa's schooling system was the thin edge of the wedge in the battle to increase academic output and meet the country's higher-education and skills challenge. For several years, government dithered about how to proceed. Rather than addressing problems of qualified and under-resourced teachers and poor management, new curricula were introduced, much to the chagrin of educators.

Underlying that conviction was perhaps the most surprising statistic: just how many dropouts reported being overwhelmed academically. As predicted, the crisis eventually hit universities – hard. Studies on the performance of the newly merged institutions show that fewer than 30 per cent who matriculated were ready for university-level maths and science.[539] That was especially true of black matriculants. So, while financial aid had clearly been a factor in both actual student dropout rates and potential access to higher education, there was a more fundamental problem – the failure of the schooling system to produce university entrants. The blunt conclusion: the problem of access required a lot more than money.

*

In the early days of the Zuma presidency it may have been commonplace among university authorities to blame the higher-education crisis on schooling – but that was only half true at best. The impetus for free education, on top of a skills deficit and the paltry rate of academic output, may have been

---

539 Ray (n 522 above)

a lethal combination. As Adam Habib once pointed out to me,[540] the principle of free higher education would probably turn on the kinds of trade-offs between access and funding that the department was prepared to make. But there didn't seem to be plenty of scope to push for a better bargain for the amount of money already spent on disadvantaged black students. That was apparent not only from Nzimande's insistence that the relatively low graduation rate of black students was not a problem of quality and standards, but also from his own public reservations since becoming minister about racism within tertiary institutions. "There's talk of academic freedom, and, yes, we want academic freedom. But some universities are silent about the need to transform these institutions," he told a congress of the National Union of Metalworkers of South Africa (NUMSA) in May 2009.[541]

Many formerly white universities were still racist and unequal, he said, adding that talk about "academic freedom" amounted to "human rights fundamentalism". "That's where you only emphasise your rights but you don't take responsibility."[542] To validate his argument, Nzimande sought relief instead in statistics by Higher Education South Africa (HESA). In June 2008, HESA told a parliamentary briefing that the explosion in access was being undermined by a deepening financial burden borne by students that fuelled a high dropout rate and that equity in outcomes "still very much eludes the sector".[543] Well under a third of the intake in contact universities completed their courses in regulation time and one in three graduates did so within four years. Only seven out of 23 institutions met the success rate norm of 80 per cent in terms of students who passed their course and there were huge disparities between black and white students' performance, with black students accounting for fewer than 25 per cent of all graduations in regulation time. In fairness, South Africa's prolonged state of economic turmoil since 2009, interest rate hikes, and skyrocketing inflation had all contributed to the glum fact that many potentially successful students would not, by virtue of socio-economic factors, be able to see their educational dreams to fruition.

Drawing on a 2007 study by the HSRC, HESA concluded that "many students enrolled at tertiary institutions were from extremely poor homes – with a paltry household income of between R400 and R1 600 per month

---

540 Interview with the author, Johannesburg, February 2009.
541 Ray (n 522 above).
542 Ibid.
543 Ibid.

– and so landed up taking on part-time jobs to try and meet both the educational and daily survival obligations[,] with their studies being invariably affected and them ultimately dropping out".[544]

"The real trouble is that the problem of racism and financial affordability is tough to referee when its magnitude is wilfully ignored by research data and universities," Nzimande told the NUMSA gathering.[545] If the premise of ill-prepared black students was a foregone conclusion, Nzimande said, facts were found to confirm it. A new method of evaluating the problem was urgently needed, starting with the higher insights of transformation rather than evidence from pass rates.

Unfortunately, it was those higher insights of political philosophy that may have made Nzimande a victim of his own ambitions. It's the (false) promise of free education; of students tugged gently along the path of learning towards a hopeful future.

544 Ibid.
545 Ibid.

CHAPTER 24

Occupied Wits

THE FEES MUST FALL MOVEMENT

IT WAS THE END OF THE 2013 SCHOOL YEAR AND, LIKE MANY YOUNG BLACK youths of his generation, Mpho Ndaba was having difficulty reconciling his desire to break out of the cycle of despair and poverty of Rammolutisi, a poverty-stricken black township in the conservative Afrikaner town of Kroonstad in the Free State. The 18-year-old had passed matric with enough credits to earn him a university entrance. But in the nightmarish jungle of tertiary education, he knew that a university entrance was not a free pass to graduation. Tertiary education could be academically onerous and costly, even for black students who qualified for financial aid. Young and ambitious, he nevertheless half-heartedly applied to the University of the Witwatersrand (Wits).

Then came news from the university admissions department. Was he interested in pursuing an undergraduate degree? The opportunity immediately appealed to the young man, not just because it meant filling a hopeless void that township life was intent on fashioning – with relentless facility we might add – in young black minds, but because it also offered an outlet for the idealism awakened in him. "I'm the first generation in my family to go to university, and the opportunity pushed me to question what it meant to succeed as a black youth in South Africa today," he recalled.[546]

Indeed, a generation of black youths born after apartheid was encouraged to succeed, a triumph no doubt of a culture of aspiration in the new South Africa overlaid by a form of historical amnesia. Yet it had become normal, two decades into democracy, to remember a time when blacks were denied basic human rights, education and economic opportunities. After all, they experienced first-hand the bitter harvest of apartheid in townships,

---

546 Interview with the author, Johannesburg, February 2016.

informal settlements, schools and workplaces.

Not so for a generation of white youths. After decades spent in the washing machine of mythology, history had been bled of all reality, to the extent that few white youths born after apartheid knew, much less acknowledged, that apartheid was a diabolical system of discrimination against blacks, legalised and institutionalised over centuries by a hierarchical, geopolitical and segregated framework of laws brutally enforced by the government.

For black youths like Ndaba, their differential inclusion in a post-apartheid state mocked, even abandoned, any pretence of social bonhomie. And so it was in urban public spaces, such as work, schools, universities and shopping centres, that black encroachments on white cultural and social spaces had taken on the physical dimension of racial prejudice.

Racism without the legal trappings of apartheid, we might conclude about post-liberation South Africa. For to view South Africa's tentative steps to reinvent itself through remedial measures has meant encroachments by upwardly mobile blacks on the historical insularity of whites. By 2014, those measures had become breeding grounds for mental and cultural prejudices at universities among mainly white youths as larger numbers of black students entered traditionally white institutions.

It was in this tense atmosphere that Ndaba arrived at Wits in early 2014 to begin his first year in the humanities.

*

Outwardly, Wits is a sprawling edifice of grey-stone colonial buildings, replete with tall gabled columns at their entrances, high-ceilinged rooms adorned with paintings and photos of colonial luminaries, and baroque early 20th-century furnishings. Completed in the 1930s, the university cuts through the heart of present-day South Africa like a pathologist's blade. It exposes the country's underlying conditions, and reminds those who care to see of unfinished business. Like a clumsily retouched image, the place fades out of the real South African picture. But its grim shadow remains, and with it the fractures in South African society: generational fissures, cracks between an older generation of white academics and their black peers, between privileged white and poor black students who feel slighted.

The origins of the place lie in the South African School of Mines, established in Kimberley in 1896 and transferred to Johannesburg as the Transvaal Technical Institute in 1904, becoming the Transvaal University College in

1906 and renamed the South African School of Mines and Technology four years later. Other departments were added as Johannesburg grew, and, in 1920, the name was changed to the University College. Full university status was granted in 1922, incorporating the college as the University of the Witwatersrand in March that year. Seven months later, the inauguration of the university was duly celebrated. Prince Arthur of Connaught, Governor General of the Union of South Africa, became the university's first chancellor, and Professor Jan H Hofmeyr its first principal.[547]

From the outset, Wits was founded as an open university with a policy of non-discrimination on racial or any other grounds. This commitment faced its ultimate test when the apartheid government passed the Extension of University Education Act in 1959 enforcing university apartheid. The Wits academic and student community protested strongly and continued to maintain a firm, consistent and vigorous stand against apartheid, not only in education, but in all its manifestations. These protests were sustained through the 1960s and seventies as more and more civil liberties were withdrawn and peaceful opposition to apartheid was suppressed. The consequences for the university were severe – bannings, deportations and detentions of staff and students, as well as raids on the campus by riot police to disrupt peaceful protest meetings.

Since 1994, the strongest impulse has been to avoid big changes, to hold the campus steady as she goes. From their lofty perch, university authorities sat back and watched the country's transformation without playing by fundamentally changed rules of the game. But it's also safe to assume that such caution speaks to another side of the story: a yearning by a generation of outsiders for whom life in a new era has not proved kind, but which has created more radical impulses for change.

By 2014, Wits had quite a different academic and student population. Two years earlier, in 2012, its shareholders appointed the first black vice chancellor. An ideological scion of the Left during the anti-apartheid struggle, Adam Habib had as a student at the University of Natal during the early 1980s embraced Marxism and the anti-Stalinist politics of the slain Soviet outcast Leon Trotsky. Habib was a transformation change agent, he was fond of saying, and somewhere in his politics he was still – in one terminology – a 'Trotskyite' who disliked talk of state interference in academic freedom, and showed a keen interest in the philosophies and values that

---

547 See more at: https://www.wits.ac.za/about-wits/history-andheritage/#sthash.S1Ewkj4R.dpuf.

influenced free thinking about knowledge production and power relations in society.

There was also something obsequious about his character; he was the sort of academic who longed for a scene of action broader than the elite confabs of academia. It may have been the Trotskyite in him. As he once told me during his tenure as deputy vice chancellor at the University of Johannesburg (UJ), "massification" would be the key to breaking down the elite monasteries that characterised universities in years gone by.[548] It was a mild critique of the limits of the institutional mergers and incorporations by the government in an attempt to integrate and create greater parity between traditionally white universities and bush colleges. Whatever drove Habib, in 2015 Wits was a test case: The merger process had created unintended consequences. Those consequences were black students like Mpho Ndaba pouring into the hallowed halls and lecture theatres, changing its complexion completely since 2004. Beneath the serene surface, its institutional culture and class structure were a seething cauldron of racial enmity between black and white students, academic and non-academic staff, rich and poor.

It was almost inevitable that Habib should make one of his first orders of business, as he told an audience during his 2015 Imam Haron memorial lecture, "transcending the past and reimagining the future". He concluded by rejecting the "essentialisation of race" or "racial federalism" in which "students and staff come to interact with each other as individuals and not as representatives of racial or cultural interests".[549]

The gambit seemed to have worked. The white student and academic community settled into an uncomfortable consensus. But not a few black students and academics knew better. If episodes like the Reitz incident at the University of the Free State, when white students coaxed five black workers into eating food laced with urine, was a provocation, Habib's attempt at a social compact was also a gross miscalculation. No revolutionary assignment had been awaiting him.

Paradoxically, the vision Habib had for Wits produced results the Trotskyist in him wanted to avoid. From his seat as vice chancellor, he now changed tack. Where once he championed socialism, embracing a Marxist critique of government's transformation policies, he now preferred

---

548 Interview with the author, Johannesburg, February 2009.
549 Habib, A, 'Transcending the past and reimagining the future of the South African university'. Speech on the occasion of the 8th Annual Imam Haron Memorial lecture, University of the Witwatersrand, 30 September 2015.

to indulge the restructured higher-education system with baseless merits, often inferring that the country's universities were in the throes of transition – a rather oblique reference to a system that was in fact faltering under the combined strain of growing numbers of financially and academically ill-prepared students and an untransformed crop of academics. No matter, Habib now spoke the language of 'academic excellence'.

*

Living a fairly marginal life as an 'exiled black' in Johannesburg, Mpho Ndaba was plagued by academic and financial hardship. It was, perhaps, predictable that there would be a period of adjustment from township schooling to the rigours of academic and city life. What was less expected was that the alienation he felt as a youth growing up in Rammolutisi in the heart of white Afrikanerdom would become ever more pronounced at this bastion of academic freedom.

His earliest memories of detachment from the pockets of integration middle-class suburban life in the cities offered, he said to me, was the occasional trip as a boy to the bank in Kroonstad with his family. "My memories of going to the bank, where they spoke in Afrikaans and we spoke in seSotho and they regarded you as subordinate, those memories came back," he recalled. "When I arrived at Wits, I was made aware of racial divisions."

No matter how tightly Habib tried to manage the transition from an essentially white to a predominantly black institution, he did not seem to have a handle on the clash of classes and cultures integrated campuses like Wits were becoming. Ndaba recalled, shortly after his arrival at Wits, his first brush with racism on a bus from the university residence to the Wits campus. "There were a lot of incidents that left me baffled about race relations," he said.

But nowhere was the impact of racism on him more evident than in the lecture halls. At first, the university's programmes seemed straightforward, even crudely non-racial. "You learn the teachings of foreigners, and even embrace it, until something happens that forces you to question all of it," said Ndaba.

To a certain extent, the liberal ethos of Wits appeared to have given rise to a false consensus – of common values and interests based on a shared identity – which transcended the tensions of the past. And yet it was the sense of an idealistic dynamic, even noble cause, that Ndaba tried to articulate to me. "There was never a consensus," he said. "There was no need for that because blacks were a negligible presence on white campuses until quite recently.

"The things that pushed us to fight, like unemployment and a lack of access to the mainstream economy were a challenge to the whole notion of born-frees," he said, adding: "Nothing indicated I am born free. The assumptions – that we are ahistorical, that we have nothing to fight about, and the attempts to create a utopia of monuments and symbols – were false."

*

An older generation of white South Africans knew the lie. Even though South Africa had experienced a dramatic process in 1994 in which the old despotism was shaken, its legacy of psychological horror and social hardship remained an embarrassment to those who directly participated in and benefited from apartheid. So much so that, as former head of intelligence, Mo Shaik, once told me, "It is hard to find a white racist in South Africa today," adding: "For the history of South Africa is, to recall that pregnant first sentence of a 1992 United Nations report, littered with some horrendous occurrences – the Sharpeville and Langa killings, the Soweto uprising, Boipatong and Sebokeng."[550]

Racism had either been privatised at dinner tables or reinvented through liberal discourses that had done more to disguise unequal power relations. In fact, with the exception of overt racism, it was largely among white youths that the hereditary element of racism had been pervasive, exemplified by the Reitz incident, the humiliation by a white student at the University of Cape Town (UCT) of a black worker, and the unsympathetic and sometimes violent response by white students to ongoing black student protests, to name but a few.

Thus it was that the translation of government policy interventions since 1994 into durable propositions of national unity became a matter of simple economics: the greater the degree of structural inequality between black and white communities generally, the greater the extent of racial disharmony. Corrective measures by the African National Congress (ANC) government such as black economic-empowerment and employment-equity policies popularised this hypothesis and created new discourses of social inclusion

---

550 Interview with the author, Pretoria, June 2011.

to characterise it.

The problem thus posed was inherent in policy endeavours to transfer the legacy of inequality and terms of subordination from their apartheid origins to a 'deracialised' market.

And so it was in urban public spaces, such as work, schools, universities, and shopping centres that racism was a live germ. In other words, while material inequalities were tangible, it was within deracialised spaces of inter-action between whites and blacks that racial prejudice was prevalent. By this I mean the interstices of black encroachments on white cultural and social spaces (distinguishable from the ghettoised poverty of the black majority) in which racial prejudice had taken on a physical dimension.

Racism without the legal trappings of apartheid, we might conclude about post-liberation South Africa. For to view South Africa's tentative steps to reinvent itself through socio-economic transformation and the con-struction of emblematic attributes and iconographies is to miss the point; it is to misconstrue form for substance, appearance for reality. It has the superficial trappings of democracy, but in every relevant respect the deeper legacy of racial prejudice, now transposed on individual and social relations among the youth, remained.

By and large, black students like Ndaba at former white campuses like Wits were an underclass, liberated, visible but slighted and marginalised. They belonged to a different generation from their parents – a different era even. But for all the surface contrasts – black students, black managers, black academics, and a black vice chancellor – Wits in 2015 was not so different from the elite cultural monastery it epitomised during the apartheid era.

SPRING REACHES SOUTH AFRICA IN SEPTEMBER. FROM THE DUSTY KAROO to the Highveld of Johannesburg, storm clouds usually break amid claps of thunder. Streaks of lightning blaze across the evening sky and, for a fleeting moment, a hard rain washes over the land.

In mid-September 2015, heavy storm clouds sagged low over the city, nudged along by gusts of wind, but there was no rain. Throughout the spring and summer that year the city's landscape was hot and dry. A crip-pling drought had settled over the land, water shortages now adding to a devastating energy crunch that had already battered the economy and driven thousands of workers into a life of unemployment and destitution. All that year, there were strikes and community protests, some of them violent scenes of police pushing back desperate men, women and youths.

As September gave way to October, there were other clouds besides those over Johannesburg. Six months earlier, the Rhodes statue at UCT had become a lightning rod for student resistance and opposition against symbols of the colonial and apartheid legacy when a fourth-year political science student named Chumani Maxwele staged a one-man publicity stunt by desecrating the statue with human faeces. On Friday, 20 March, a procession under the banner of the slogan 'Rhodes Must Fall' was led from the main campus to the university administration building, Bremner, where the vice chancellor's office is located. Midway through an address, the student-driven contingent occupied the administration building and took up residence in a historic room curiously named the Archie Mafeje room after the black academic who resigned under a cloud. By April, the university capitulated. The statue was eventually removed in a staged event that bore all the hallmarks of a minor coup.

Similar protests spread to traditionally white campuses across the country, rapidly gathering force as students began raising more deep-seated demands for transformation. In early October, a black student lit a bundle of dry, yellowy roots on the promenade of the Great Hall at Wits. The ritual was in deference to his ancestors. A clutch of black students stood by, watching. Their white peers ignored the spectacle. The ritual was also a minor act of theatrics no doubt, an ingenious provocation designed to get people's attention, for it epitomised the cultural and socio-economic chasm between black and white students on campus.

What distinguished those early days of October 2015 was that so many black students had no money or hope of ever surviving the financial and academic rigours of university life. The prolonged economic downturn since the 2008 global economic crisis had sunk into a ruinous recession. Thousands of black parents lost their jobs, or were hit hard by debilitating wage freezes in the face of a weakening rand and soaring inflation. On reflection, that summer would be seen as a low point. Across the city, thousands of black children were homeless, begging bowls in hand at street intersections, their faces scorched from the scalding sun and emaciated from malnourishment.

To black students, they were a generation who were 'born free' but still did not count. If they did not count, they surmised, another human sea did. In Habib's drive to cut and prune expenditure, black workers at Wits had been shut out of permanent employment, their employment outsourced and their wages and conditions 'flexibilised', an embraceable term among employers who saw outsourcing as a better means of slashing labour costs and disrupting trade union organisation. Habib had quickly gained notoriety among workers and students, who saw his plans less as a reflection of his personal brashness, a character trait described to me by several students I spoke to, than a mandate from the university's financial stakeholders to turn an academic institution into a commercial concern run on business principles.

The students wanted social justice. They wanted the university to pay decent wages to non-academic staff. And they wanted free education for the children of workers. "We found our cause," Ndaba said to me.

I now understood the context. But I wanted to know how student grievances had developed into a mass movement.

*

It was a grey Wednesday afternoon in late January 2016, and I had been waiting to meet Shaeera Kalla at the Wits cafeteria. At 3 p.m., the clouds burst in a heavy downpour. At just that moment, I received a text message from Kalla. She was held up in traffic, not because of the rain. All that week Kalla had been flitting between meetings into the late hours of the night. The student protest movement had become the major preoccupation of the country: there were marches and sit-ins at universities across the country protesting fees and racism, and Kalla had by then become a familiar face in households, revered and reviled by parents of students for her pioneering role in the protest movement.

Unlike typically poor black students involved in the protest movement, Kalla was something of an anomaly. Her family were cut from well-heeled Indian entrepreneurial stock, she told me. "My father is the third of three generations of family business and could afford to pay for my fees. There was no point in my life where I had to worry about where my next meal was going to come from."

Elegant and articulate, the 22-year-old BCom honours student was also a poster of a characteristically existential-looking figure. Beneath her privileged upbringing and polite manner lay a fierce intensity and political philosophy that belonged to an older generation. "Even in that privileged environment I felt as if I did not belong in Laudium," she said.

Going to a privileged school like Crawford gave her a keen sense of race and class. "An ordinary person will say, okay it's a rainbow nation. I saw the lie," she said matter-of-factly.

I was a little embarrassed to sit with her and hear her ideas. It was awkward to be confronted with this fierce passion, intellectual rigour and activism all at once, to sympathise with her hopes and yet keep a guarded distance. Kalla reminded me of the selfless commitment shown by many brave activists during the anti-apartheid struggle. There was defiance too. Her first act of defiance was to pursue graduate studies in the humanities rather than in commerce, as her father wanted. She eventually compromised and enrolled for a BCom, majoring in politics. The decision set the course of her public-spiritedness, first as President of the Student Representative Council (SRC) and then her second act of defiance.

When she arrived at Wits, Kalla's mission was tailor-made. She flinched from the university's vulgar colonial history and snobbish distinctions. It belonged to a different era, she told me. "So many students go to study but only 18 per cent go further because they struggle financially," she said. "It's not like free education is something we suddenly woke up to. It's something we really need for people and the future of our society."

Kalla began the 2015 academic year as President of the SRC after sitting President Mcebo Dlamini found himself in trouble with the university. She had shot to prominence as a driving force behind the "One Million in One Month" campaign in early 2015 that raised R4.4 million to pay the registration fees of poor students. "It was still a drop in ocean," she said. "Wits alone now needed about R109 million, leaving aside government funding. So I realised that charity was not the answer to what were clearly structural problems of inequality."

Serving on the SRC was a "scarring experience", she said. "You are confronted by students who have to sleep in libraries, who are not empowered to succeed. It's not that people are not smart enough. Language and the poor quality of schooling were also major factors."

When the Rhodes Must Fall protest at UCT became a national movement in March, tens of thousands of students turned their attention from symbolic issues of transformation to more tangible measures on campuses. "The removal of the statue, while largely symbolic, was a rallying cry to tangibly address the practical implications of so-called 'transformation' and re-imagine what the role and function of an African university should be," Kalla said.

With the student movement stirring, signs that a new phase of engagement around bread-and-butter issues had begun multiplying. Kalla recalls numerous discussions with the university about fees. "We were in discussion for months and everything just flew over their heads." What was needed, she decided, was greater organisation and student activists responsible for research, media, and mobilisation around the fees issue.

Eventually, Kalla and others presented a report compiled by actuaries and accounting students to a council meeting in October, exposing the costs to workers and benefits to the university of outsourcing, the lack of transparency, and the considerable cash reserves the university had accumulated. The report also highlighted the inadequacies of the National Student Financial Aid Scheme and the roughly 20 per cent "missing middle" that could neither afford tuition nor qualify for financial aid.[551] It was Kalla's final council meeting as SRC President and the beginning of a brand new phase of activism. Predictably enough, the university responded by rejecting the report and proposing a 10.5 per cent fee increase for the 2016 academic year.

Dismayed by these developments, Kalla tried lobbying members of council in a last-ditch effort to challenge the increase. "There was no support because the council is a complacent structure, hardly decolonised and entirely undemocratic," she said.

*

Eventually, a day after the October 2015 council meeting, the university officially responded in a memorandum announcing a 10 per cent fee increment. On 2 October, Kalla and other student representatives in the university council lost a vote over student fee increases. "I was infuriated," she later recalled in speaking to a journalist. "I didn't sleep that night, plotting to see what we could do, because we just weren't satisfied with the reasons they gave us for why fees needed to increase. If you look at the composition of council, it's quite scary the kind of people who make decisions for black students yet understand so little about the struggles that these students go through."[552]

Kalla immediately called incoming SRC President Fasiha Hassan and proposed a meeting with Progressive Youth Alliance (PYA) structures to discuss a course of action.

On the evening of 5 October, Kalla, Hassan, members of the PYA and some academics met at the university to decide on a course of action. In the early hours of 6 October, a group of black students, academics and workers

551 Wits SRC report on student fee increases presented to Council, September 2015.
552 Morrissey, K, 'Young woman on a mission to see university fees fall', *The Star*, October 2015.

blockaded the main gate in Empire Road to "symbolise how inaccessible universities are", she said. They knew they needed only 20 students to shut down the gates and they used cars as barriers until more supporters arrived. Part of the plan was to "kill the label 'born frees'" that her generation carried, she told journalists that morning. "When things affect white monopoly capital, it seems to get a very different reaction."

By 6 a.m., the protesting crowd had swelled, and included academics sympathetic to their cause. At that moment, a white student got out of his car and yelled, "Who's in charge here?" Kalla stepped forward. Moments later, the student launched into a furious tirade, attacking the protestors in a fight that was quickly ended by campus security. Kalla again stepped forward, urging non-violence, until a white driver ploughed into the gathering and students retaliated.

Later that morning, the protestors marched across the university, gathering support along the way. The university was coming to life, cars and buses skidding up Yale Road, students milling about and bespectacled academics walking around campus with an air of dishevelled preoccupation. All across the campus, heads turned as the strange phalanx strode across the open spaces. At its peak, about 5 000 students, academics and workers joined the march.

Later that day, students met at Senate House to assess the day's activities and discuss a programme of action. The following day, the PYA led a large contingent of students to the bus rank to raise awareness. They rallied under the slogan 'Wits Fees Must Fall'.

"In the end, we didn't get what we demanded in the petition," Kalla told me, "but we mobilised the beginnings of something big."

Whether in response to the students' ancestors or student leadership, a new movement was stirring.

"WE WANTED ADAM," A THIRD-YEAR ACTUARIAL SCIENCE STUDENT NAMED Ali exclaimed.[553] Harsh and defiant towards authority – or, as students themselves mocked, towards a black vice chancellor claiming a revolutionary pedigree but whose entire character was ensnared in bourgeois habits and prejudices – the student movement focused on Adam Habib, who became its most visible target.

---

553 Interview with the author, Johannesburg, January 2016.

The story related to me by Ali is that students initially told Habib to drop the 10 per cent increment to 7 per cent. The students, sick with unfulfilled dreams, were incensed. On 5 October, students and workers drafted a petition against outsourcing and the abysmal condition of non-academic staff at the university and delivered it to Senate House.

"Adam Habib didn't want to listen, and that angered students," Ali recalled. "We then said we want zero upfront payments. The more he didn't listen, the more students got angry."

On the evening of 5 October, as Kalla and others met late into the night, a mild tremor rippled through the hallowed corridors of Senate House. The key themes were an end to outsourcing and free tuition for disadvantaged students. The following day, 6 October, a large crowd of students gathered at Senate House, now renamed Solomon Mahlangu House. The gathering was so well attended that speeches had to be broadcast via bullhorns to an overflow crowd. They denounced the corporatisation of the university and demanded Habib's resignation.

When he was appointed to the top position, Habib had promised far-reaching changes, which now seemed shockingly porous. The students had given Habib a certain amount of time to prepare for these changes, but there was never any real effort to transform things. If Habib remained indifferent to the point of negligence, it had become clear to students paying attention that the university wasn't remotely prepared for dealing with transformation. The chief beneficiaries of higher education, they charged, were white academics and students who had no interest in allowing a new institutional culture to emerge. In fact, by 2015, the university authorities were decades away from meeting the goals they had committed to.

*

On the evening of 14 October, television news channels aired dramatic footage of Adam Habib on his haunches in the entrance hall of Senate House looking crestfallen and being confronted by a crowd of angry students.

Social media was abuzz with the symbolism of the image. The story of what looked like a hostage scenario is a little obscure. One eyewitness account denies the prosaic character of the connection between Habib on his knees and Habib the hostage. It describes students marvelling "at how power had been unseated, brought to its knees, and, symbolically, students had brought Habib to their level in order for fair negotiations to happen".[554] "The air," wrote student activist Anele Nzimande in an op-ed piece in *The Star*, "was a miasma – hope, fatigue, despair were all thick."[555]

This account seems, on internal evidence, truthful. Habib realised the university was not going to function. By the time he eventually arrived at 3 p.m., students were in a funk. They sang songs and chanted slogans calling for fees to fall. They demanded Habib's resignation and commanded him to sit on the floor.

Habib replied that he couldn't decide on fees without consulting the chair of council, who was in Durban. Students demanded the chair fly to Johannesburg. By the time the chair eventually arrived later that evening, deliberately awkward questions by students became a rallying cry.

The October Movement, as it came to be known, brought one of those sudden commotions which marked the upheaval of mass struggle. Video footage shows students gassed that day with pepper spray thrown into Senate House. "It was a miracle that students remained peaceful," Kalla recalled. "We were sitting peacefully and all of a sudden students were running around. I remember running around with milk and pouring it on people. It wasn't as if this was a national movement. It felt as if one wrong move on my side and students could get hurt."

Then the video footage pans to a student leadership corps. Having upended their audience's settled categories, the students went on to describe their vision of transformation in a nine-point manifesto drafted by the PYA. The speaker was coming to the end, his voice growing stronger and there was a sudden ungrounded energy in the hall. He had everyone's attention.

Here, one might say, was in a nutshell the hallmark of the student revolt, by which they themselves would eventually be cut off. The Wits occupation seemed to give political sanction to students' disillusioned anger. The spark of rebellion had been kindled in the young leaders. They called themselves the Wits Fees Must Fall movement, a name, in Ali's recollection, that was the idea of Shaeera Kalla – but the Wits occupation did not much resemble a national movement yet. The students were no more than a few thousand on one campus and Kalla was sometimes their public face.

*

---

554 Nzimande, A, 'Students are leading the need for transformation', *The Star*, 6 November 2015.
555 Ibid.

On the morning of 12 November, Habib met students and agreed to the principle of 'insourcing' and committed to the appointment of a task team for the implementation of resolutions. "There was a small sense of justice shared by everyone present in the room," recalled Anele Nzimande.[556]

But Habib was a shrewd negotiator. In the days that followed, he met a group of student and union representatives. He proposed a Workers Charter and drew up a document that set up a platform for engagement with students and workers and portrayed Wits as a university well on its way to stability and transformation. It was the Marxist in him. But now he was in a positon of power. And power has a way of arbitrating radical impulses through the agency of moderation. To students, he had become the institutional embodiment of the money elite. They were not buying it. What had been conceived as a swift resolution would become a prolonged battle.

Shortly after student and worker delegates met Habib, Kalla and other elected representatives met to discuss a course of action against Habib and his deputies, but the question that divided them was politics. Their chief foe was Habib. And their policy on transformation was local and still isolated, even when university authorities on other campuses were committing similar discriminatory acts against workers and students.

Still the idea and language of politics took hold in the minds of students like Shaeera Kalla: fees and wages were only half a world view; the other half was ideological, a faith in the transformational power of ideas. And in this regard, power, such as it was, was in the figure of Blade Nzimande, who had already been Minister of Higher Education for six years. Nzimande had watched the protests unfold with shock and apprehension. The revolt, he knew, might have been a wakeup call to universities but it also brought with it an ideology that could disrupt government.

Yet, it was true that, at this time, the student movement could not advance a single step without national integration. The idea of realigning the Wits movement was proposed and adopted by the Fees Must Fall group. And when they looked around for a way to think about the uncharted era that began on 6 October 2015, there was already one available.

Wits began to spill over into other parts of the country. The student fees crisis, the horrors that outsourced workers experienced – a reduced quality of life because of low salaries, no medical benefits and low savings – all this was something that resonated on other campuses. "Through a collective

556 Ibid.

conviction," recalled Anele Nzimande, "and a deep knowing that many voices together would amplify the plight of both students and workers, we echoed the calls made from different parts of the country to decolonise the education system."[557] All those who experienced it were to understand that.

The political clouds were heavier than ever; universities were aquiver.

[557] Ibid.

CHAPTER 25

The storm breaks

REVOLT AND REACTION

ON WEDNESDAY, 21 OCTOBER 2015, THE FEES MUST FALL MOVEMENT STAGED its most dramatic provocation since the start of the protest. In the preceding days, there were rumours that a student–worker alliance at the University of Cape Town (UCT) was planning to protest fee increases and outsourcing at national key points. Some of the more radical elements in the alliance were speculating about a national shutdown and a march on Parliament.

In the early hours of that Wednesday morning, Parliament was awakened by the clatter of armoured police vehicles and a small gathering of singing students. In Plein Street, where a security cordon between the entrance and the parliamentary precinct ran, armed guards lined the side of the street. On that day, the Fees Must Fall campaign was garnering massive support amongst students and workers on campuses. On De Waal Drive, one of the busiest crossing points to the city, buses carrying students headed toward Parliament.

The light of dawn revealed police slowly erecting a cordon on De Waal Drive. A few metres back, ringing the parliamentary precinct, they openly took up positions – and waited.

*

An air of taut suspense hung over the chamber of the National Assembly as news of the possibility of a sit-in spread. The students had chosen their target well. Cabinet ministers and members of executive councils (MECs) were assembling to listen to finance minister Nhlanhla Nene's first medium-term budget speech since his appointment to the post. Nene held the purse strings to the country's beleaguered economy. He had been in office barely a few months, but he already had enemies, lots of them.

As Nene sidled up to the podium in the chamber, a column of police vehicles moved up De Waal Drive. Student activists from UCT were singing as they made their way to Parliament to join Cape Peninsula University of Technology and University of Western Cape comrades. In his recollection of the event, Busisiwe Nxumalo, one of the protestors, recalled the bus transporting UCT students on De Waal Drive being met by police blocking access to Roeland and Plein streets in the city. Other vehicles were allowed to proceed. Armed with stun grenades and tear gas, police ordered the bus to turn around.

"When the protestors tried to disembark, police blocked them from exiting," Nxumalo recalled. "Tempers flared with police shouting and becoming physical." Undeterred, the students managed to disembark and joined fellow protestors on the streets. Before the group could continue their march, police announced: "You are not allowed to gather in groups of more than five." Protestors drew together, fearing arrest. One of the students was pulled from the crowd and bundled into the back of an awaiting police van.

"Release our comrade. He has done nothing wrong," the crowd shouted. Police responded by saying, "This is an illegal gathering. You are not allowed to gather in groups of more than five." To which a black woman retorted: "This is not apartheid."

Perversely, it *was* reminiscent of apartheid.

The crowd eventually reached Parliament, protesting and chanting, "Fees must fall" and, "End outsourcing". A day before, student groups rejected a proposal by the Minister of Higher Education, Blade Nzimande, to cap increases at 6 per cent. They wanted Nzimande to address their demands.

Meanwhile, a group of supporters of the Economic Freedom Fighters (EFF) disrupted the chamber, preventing Nene from delivering his speech for more than 40 minutes. They demanded the postponement of the budget in order to address the countrywide shutdown of universities over proposed double-digit fee hikes for 2016.

Hours later, unarmed students holding their hands above their heads entered Parliament's grounds. The police pushed the crowd back. However, a small group slipped past the security cordon and sat in front of the stairs leading up to the National Assembly, chanting, "We want Blade."

Moments later, police, accompanied by the riot unit and six snipers, opened fire on the crowd. Stun grenades and tear gas were thrown. Several protestors were physically assaulted, screaming as they retreated in the mist

369

of pink smoke.

After Nene's mini budget speech, Nzimande, flanked by some of his Cabinet colleagues, stepped out of Parliament and tried to address the angry protesters amid shouts of "Blade must go!"

When the dust settled, the crowd regrouped with their hands in the air and sang the national anthem to show that they were protesting peacefully. The police again opened fire, wounding some activists.

In the end, about 23 protesters were arrested on possible treason charges, and for staging an illegal gathering, public violence and trespassing.

In the week that followed, protests continued at other campuses around the country. The students wanted zero fee increments for the 2016 academic year and free education.

*

As President Jacob Zuma came under increasing pressure, some in his government had begun to consider launching a pre-emptive strike. On Thursday that week, the Presidency released a statement saying that Zuma would meet with the management and leadership of universities as well as student leaders to discuss practical steps towards addressing concerns behind the ongoing protest action.

On Friday morning, Zuma launched a vigorous lobbying campaign to position government as something more. Hours later, in a closed session, he announced a moratorium on fee increases for 2016.

But, for students, the reprieve was temporary. All that year, government's future hung in the balance and the fracas outside Parliament marked a turning point in the student struggle. On that day, student–government relations had taken a turn for the worse.

Yet no one seemed to anticipate the consequences. When the Rhodes statue was removed, government was still waiting for an operational plan from the Department of Arts and Culture to deal with the removal of the statue and neutralise tensions between black students and university authorities that had begun to spread across the country. The debate on colonial statues and symbols seemed to preoccupy the minds of government and society at large.

The last vestiges of the Rainbow era had turned to fear on campuses as fees and institutional culture became the latest in the fight and heat that began with the Rhodes protest. For if the fall of Rhodes had drawn a symbolic line under a turbulent era, the Fees Must Fall movement was its intellectual and ideological expression. At that same moment, the protest suddenly exploded into a full-scale movement.

*

In the weeks that followed the chaos outside Parliament, I never found the questions about it easy to answer, and the manner in which the country argued with itself wholly inadequate to the nearly interminable build-up to the day. Why were the police ordered to take such drastic action? Who, or what, was behind the student movement? And why did UCT and the University of the Witwatersrand (Wits) become the leading cause of the student movement? Student protests had received no special attention during the late 1990s and early 2000s; they were barely mentioned in newspapers or in the writings of authors and academics. Now, two decades since the end of apartheid, the plight of black students replaced crime and corruption as the overriding concern of the country.

During the months of September and October 2015, the fall of Rhodes at UCT and the movement for free education pushed the government close to its old isolationism of the years before Jacob Zuma. But, throughout the first decade of the 2000s, another current ran alongside the mainstream.

The student protests over fees caught the government and university top brass by surprise. It shouldn't have. The Fees Must Fall movement did not emerge suddenly. It evolved slowly at first, later gathering force. It started as a battle of ideas, and, to understand how and why Rhodes became such a powerful detonator for student protests, one has to trace their origins.

There are no straight lines in the history of events, but let's start with 2004.

WHAT MARKED THE PROTEST MOVEMENT WAS ITS OUTBREAK AT HISTORICALLY white universities. There was a perception that universities such as Wits and UCT were exclusive or "special", Shaeera Kalla told me.[558]

The chief beneficiaries, she went on, of the failed strategy to merge and integrate historically white and black universities were white students who had no interest in allowing a new society, under black leadership, to emerge from the ruins of apartheid's legacy.

---

558 Interview with the author, Johannesburg, February 2016.

There was no contingency for historically black universities. And as long as former white universities remained untouched by the tertiary restructuring project Kader Asmal began in 2004, their beneficiaries were content to sit back. None of the traditionally white elite universities, except perhaps for the University of Johannesburg (UJ), noticed, let alone faced the difficult facts unfolding on the ground of the higher-education terrain even as they begrudgingly embraced Asmal's strategy. What had been left out of the planning, however, were black students themselves.

Flush with the triumphalism of his restructuring plan, Asmal regarded black student protests over institutional culture and fees with guarded wariness. In the view of others in the Mbeki administration, but above all Mbeki himself, freedom was the absence of intellectual dissent and revolt.

For Kader Asmal, this view might have been problematic, but it was also a matter of cynical pragmatism more than anything else, since nothing during his term of office suggested he had given the more complex subject of overhauling the entire apartheid edifice of higher education any meaningful thought. For others, including those working under him in the National Working Group responsible for producing and implementing the restructuring plan, it was something of an article of faith, and when their critics used the word 'neo-liberal' – as they often did – to describe the approach to spreading democracy in higher education, they weren't completely wrong. This faith defied both history and clear evidence of racialised elites at historically white universities. It led directly to the assault on higher education by disaffected black students who had gradually poured into historically white universities since 2004 when the mergers and incorporations began.

By 2009, two developments made a response to the problem all the more urgent. One was an escalation in racism at elite universities. Images of white students plying urine to unsuspecting black workers played particularly badly on racially integrated campuses.

By this time, black students had begun to take up issues of human rights, and the problem of racism became an important agenda item in the following years. Universities themselves were hesitant, and if there was a consensus among others, they were taking a cautious line: openly condemning racism while quietly doing nothing to remove it.

The other development was a world apart from former black universities: the continuing entry of black students into former white universities and the ensuing battle over fees. In the broader context of the higher-education landscape, then, the restructuring exercise left the institutional set-up and structural inequality between white and black universities intact and at the same time unleashed unintended, less certain forces.

In 2009, there were already warning signs that portended a far greater crisis. It looked like a throwback to the anti-apartheid struggle. But this was the future.

In the early light of a February morning in 2013, students started queuing at the entrance of UJ. By 8 a.m. that morning, the queue snaked along Kingsway Road for about five kilometres. They were restless and convulsive, as if the promise of free education had introduced a virus into the organism and a fever was burning through the institution. At 9 a.m., a group stormed the gates of the university. Among the students, some broke open the locked gates. Others scaled fences. One youth died in the chaos. On that morning, I visited the campus. Wandering out of the petrifying chaos, I felt as if the stampede had induced a kind of post-traumatic stress disorder – not just at UJ but across the country. It was a new kind of syndrome for students.

*

When the Fees Must Fall movement began in earnest in October 2015, it was grudgingly embraced by leading officials in the Zuma administration, for whom the appetite to radically transform higher education was scarcely stronger than the desire to meet the constitutional imperative to open the doors of learning. While the administration of Mbeki was willing to turn a blind eye to the South African higher-education quandary, at least the Zuma administration seemed to care.

To lend succour to government's support for students, Zuma appointed a task team to look into the feasibility of free education. Meanwhile, the problem of structural inequality that Asmal's strategy seemed to have reinforced would become a key priority – in theory. In reality, in the weeks and months after the sit-in at Parliament, the student movement had lived under a virtual state of emergency, with police patrols and reports of unlawful arrests and harassment on campuses.

By now I had the argument down cold, but it was striking to spend a few hours in students' inner circle and feel the breezy certainty, the sense of a generation riding a giant wave of history into a future that belonged to them.

By April 2016, the student revolt was rarely on the front pages of newspapers. But another story was playing out. While the stated aim of the 'militarisation' of campuses was to mark indelibly the perimeters of the state and universities, the clampdown signalled the start of a new incendiary phase of protest politics.

More than a battle for free education, this was a larger political and ideological battle against the institutional restructuring exercise and its corollary – the entrenchment of disparities between historically white and black universities.

CHAPTER 26

Helter-skelter

THINGS FALL APART

"Asife isitja esifayo," a student scowled outside Senate House, which had been renamed Solomon Mahlangu House. The SeSotho phrase, loosely translated, means "Let the breakable dish break." It was a warning shot at members of the University of the Witwatersrand's (Wits) top brass. "They want the university leadership to fall," a student remarked to me.

It was Wednesday, 20 January 2016. I'd completed my interview with students and walked out of the building at 12 midday to a glorious summer afternoon with cotton clouds floating in a turquoise sky. A small crowd of mainly student activists from the Economic Freedom Fighters (EFF) quietly gathered on the main concourse outside the building. Hoisting four mattresses in front of the entrance, they began a symbolic sit-in. They had closed down the administration offices and planned on disrupting face-to-face registrations at Solomon Mahlangu House, the centre of the Fees Must Fall campaign at the university in October and November 2015.

Outside the building, Ali and Mpho Ndaba began the following conversation:

Mpho: "What do you think about the direction the movement is taking?"

Ali: "I left the movement because it became politicised."

Mpho: "But we can't abandon it."

Ali: "The question is what united us as students. Why did we start this movement in the first place? I'll consider joining the movement again if personal and political interests are removed."

Mpho: "But the EFF is raising valid issues. Politics is part of the struggle."

Besides showing how disaffected with the university students had grown, this dialogue revealed two important developments in the opening weeks of 2016. One was a sense that the Fees Must Fall movement had induced a kind of nervous disorder – a sense that the original intent had been taken over by political interests. The other was a more fragmented movement based on political and personal interests of some groups for whom Solomon Mahlangu House began to take on a different meaning.

A few metres away from the crowd of students on the main concourse, a dozen private security guards in black riot gear were arrayed at the entrance to Solomon Mahlangu House. Their orders were to enforce an urgent interdict granted by the Gauteng High Court to Wits management barring students from entering the building and disrupting registrations.

Along Yale Road leading to the university security gate, police lined the pavements. They were not allowed on campus, but their orders were to intervene if things got out of hand. The campus had a heightened sense of siege, which in a sense was the case.

Just after midday, the silence was broken by a scuffle with security guards. It was over in minutes.

*

In previous chapters, we traced the main thread of policy continuity since the 2003 restructuring exercise which led to unintended consequences. A similar subtle thread connects the tense stand-off between students and authorities in January 2016.

Facing the EFF role in the growth of the protest movement beyond the initial core group at Wits first required facing the demands themselves. But, in Pretoria, there had been no plan for free education. It was a measure of the system's inability to achieve its goals that a student like Mpho Ndaba, who had everything to gain from government's transformation policies and the opportunities it opened up, now felt himself pulled toward a militant opposition.

*

By mid-January, Blade Nzimande showed signs of wanting to deal with the student rebellion, but not its root causes. Students charged that the education crisis had been on the government's books but never in Nzimande's heart. The students seemed to understand better than government that the battle was for the loyalty of people over the causes of racism and exclusion at universities. The Zuma administration, seeing an exit strategy in partial concessions, failed to look at institutional leadership and governance at previously white universities. Instead, government kept issuing utterly misleading figures on fee allocations.

All that January, Nzimande had been preparing for a meeting with the student leadership. Though students were wary of Nzimande, their reasons for going to the meeting were in a sense strategic. "Our analysis was that we really were at a turning point in the movement. We felt that this was a defining event which, good or bad, would have an impact," Shaeera Kalla said to me. In her view, Nzimande had to be convinced that he had no choice but to concede their demands.[559]

But Nzimande, like his South African Communist Party (SACP) comrades, no longer thought entirely in categories of sudden changes. He also believed in the leadership of the African National Congress (ANC) – the idea that a multiclass movement presided over a project of national unity and social cohesion and that, since the founding of democracy, the ANC's role in transformation was something higher than radical left-wing politics or sectional interests. He differed from the students less in what he thought than in what he did. His idealism was tempered by a minister's attraction to moderation and pragmatism. And so he began to seek those with similar views and concerns; but, in so doing, he at once stepped out of the sheltered environment of high office.

As STUDENT REGISTRATIONS DREW TO A CLOSE IN LATE JANUARY, GOVERNMENT and universities seemed convinced that the student movement had come close to playing out its role. They were not altogether mistaken. But there was a new variable.

From the outside, the students gave the impression of being a united, even tightly knit group. The Fees Must Fall movement's backbone – its organisers, leaders and public spokespersons – was students united by a demand for free education. But the character of the student movement was more complicated than its origins whose moment had by January 2016 all but passed. The student movement remains poorly understood in part because it defies easy categorisation. Students' motives were varying and overlapping: resentment over racism, poverty and inequality, decolonisation of universities, regime change.

---

559 Interview with the author, Johannesburg, February 2016.

So their opponents thought – and they had many opponents. As they loomed up in public consciousness, by the start of the new year the Fees Must Fall movement was an instantly recognisable slogan to parents, academics, government and ordinary citizens alike. Their foe was Nzimande – and he knew them better. The students were not a united group.

When I went to see students at Wits in mid-January, the great question of the day was whether or not to support the ANC government and its policies, and this question divided them. On the one hand, there were those who hoped for government support against the university authorities: Shaeera Kalla was one, Ali another, as were students who supported the Progressive Youth Alliance (PYA). On the other side was a burgeoning group of radicals – mostly supporters of the EFF and, marginally, the Pan Africanist Congress (PAC) – who increasingly chafed under the moderation of government. The identity of the EFF was no accident. Those most vexed by the ANC were those with the deepest commitment to regime change.

The initial weeks of November had answered that. Only a few weeks had passed since the beginning of the student movement, and the whole edifice of the economy was battered. The sudden dismissal of Nhlanhla Nene as Minister of Finance by Jacob Zuma had struck the country with devastating force. The saga revealed the instability and the acute crisis of democracy. Confidence in the Zuma administration had plunged to an all-time low. The state of the poor was, of course, even worse. The blows that fell on them utterly disorganised and weakened their capacity to stage a political challenge. Yet students appeared to have achieved a degree of inner cohesion which they had hardly ever attained in the recent past. In its mass, it seemed, and to some extent was, united in the hostility with which it confronted white privilege. Its antagonism towards university authority overshadowed inner divisions between militant and moderate currents.[560]

But as it became clear that the government was in no mood to retreat, warming up instead to university authorities, the unity of the student movement crumbled; the long-subdued but now stoked hostility of the EFF towards authority came back into its own. Deprived of an ally in government, the movement was all the more strongly torn apart by centrifugal forces and splits between conflicting ideologies, calculations and sentiments; between ANC supporters and the EFF.

---

560 Special editorial: 'The Wits protest is not just about university fees', in *Editorial*, 16 October 2015.

White campuses became students' leading cause because the country's education policy of restructuring and quotas seemed to be failing; but for a larger reason, too. They saw white universities as a test case for their vision and ideas about transformation and decolonisation. They began to charge that universities like the University of Cape Town (UCT) and Wits represented the worst failures of neo-liberalism and the first opportunity of the Zuma government. They collected information and discussed it. But they did not go beyond that. They were not in a position to gauge the import of the new movement, and they seemed to have only a hazy notion of their own critique of neo-liberalism.

The student movement had by this time taken on characteristics that government had feared. The January Statement by the Fees Must Fall movement was one of those rhetorically overwrought left-wing agitations, something new in the movement. "Due to the neo-liberal nature of contemporary racial capitalism, the outsourced workers had no prima facie relationality with the capitalist class as per crude logics of Marxist analysis of class struggles. The nexus of the relationship gave them no political currency under the discourses of trade union economism."[561]

And therein lay the rub. Students who had initially gambled on winning a struggle for free education decided to take political action against government.

*

By the time Nzimande met students in Midrand in late January, the consequences of his wilful blindness were as real and dire as the false promise of free tuition: "Unless our demand for free education is met, our action continues," the students shot back.[562] There was nothing more to be said. Those who remained, Kalla said, were beneficiaries of the National Student Financial Aid Scheme (NSFAS).

In February, Nzimande acknowledged in an opinion piece that government was faced with a classical political campaign. The students on the ground were now far ahead of the political leadership in government in recognising the vulnerability of government. Even the sharpest of planners in government had no ready-made model for understanding the student rebellion.

---

561 'Wits fees must fall manifesto', January 2016. Accessed at http://www.feesmustfall.joburg/ manifestos/.
562 Interview with the author, Johannesburg, February 2016.

"This isn't a movement about fees only; we're seeing a different face," a government official told me around that time.[563]

Many of those who professed radicalism were indeed adopting a simplified and sometimes parodied Marxist creed in their will and determination to fight. Despite the absence of a clear ideological mooring, what the student movement lacked in coherence it made up for in demands that seemed to strike a nerve among poor black students and workers. Having thrown himself into the controversy, Mpho Ndaba told me that he had by this time turned his allegiance from the ANC-aligned PYA to the EFF. "I didn't see much merit in becoming a cheerleader for an organisation [the PYA] that became part of the problem," he said, his eyes filled with that afterglow of a victorious prizefighter.

If politics had prevailed on the Fees Must Fall movement, none of this was good news for government. In the seemingly eternal void that followed the failed meeting between student leaders and Nzimande it was as if universities were putting the finishing touches to the interior of the building while arsonists gathered outside.

At Wits, where it all began, Adam Habib's infamy among students was by February at its low point. He watched intensely the waves of discontent rising and beating against the walls of the university. The disconnect, it should be remembered, not only beat against the walls of Senate House; it breached them.

One evening in February, Habib appeared on national television and admitted that all universities were "caught napping in October 2015". Then he issued a caveat to students: "Do not play around with public institutions. These are important assets that we built. We should not be playing short-term political gains with these institutions."[564]

Presumably at the senate's prompting, Habib had earlier that day issued a statement reminding students that "political parties were entitled to have differences but must not compromise universities". Moving towards free education, Habib went on, "does not mean we should destroy the higher education system to advance political agendas".[565]

These allegations sounded plausible enough; but it was puzzling that Habib should have come out with them. When Habib said universities were "caught napping", he might have meant something else. There was a studied

---

563 Interview with the author, Johannesburg, February 2016.
564 SABC panel discussion on the student protests, February 2016.
565 Ibid.

malice in his caveat. Although government bore a major responsibility for disproportionate disbursements to universities, former white institutions were prepared to enjoy the weather – until the trouble started. If, as Habib contended, the cost of education was rising, the statement was intended to accomplish what the university had failed to do.

He was in fact addressing the hubris of the entire academic enterprise. Committed as he was to work for the transformation of the university, not for its destruction, he had to appeal to students, because only the poorest students, composed almost entirely of black students, could start a reform process in a less virulent manner. And here we need to realise that Habib was in effect prompting the student leadership to turn its hostility to government rather than the university. "Government's additional R6.5 billion – that's a first step," he went on to say. "But that's not enough."[566]

Several universities had already mounted effective public-relations campaigns, arguing that the funding gap from government placed the problem outside their hallowed halls. According to media reports, Universities South Africa, which represents higher-education institutions, complained that the 2015 financial year's equitable share to universities from government – approximately R22 billion – was still about R12 billion short of the R36 billion they needed to meet all their financial needs.

In effect, universities had passed the buck, but their response was overwhelmed by the speed of student reaction. It was not the hard-won gains of the ANC that the student movement – now teeming with heresies and factional struggles – was at loggerheads with. Students came to suspect that, in directing the problem at government, the university authorities had slyly aimed at claiming legitimacy. Of course, it didn't help students' cause that party politics had infected the student organism. But beyond student political affiliations, campus politics was a game played out of public view. The university power structure was a creation of apartheid, and negotiating with it, one student said, was "like asking an arsonist to put out a fire".[567]

Such, then, were the complex circumstances in which universities parleyed government to carry out their will.

---

566 Ibid.
567 Author's interview with Wits student, Johannesburg, January 2015.

"You will find little support for the government here, and much less for the ANC," Mpho Ndaba said without a hint of equivocation.[568] He told me how workers and ANC sympathisers like him had finally done the unthinkable and turned their backs on the party.

For some time, student leaders had not concealed the desirability of regime change. Those backing the PYA hoped to bend the ANC to their will. Zuma had the power to change things, but, if government would not do their bidding, he must go.

A meeting of students at Wits, Ali once told me, turned into a political rally when EFF students disrupted a speech by a former Student Representative Council (SRC) president, who had been dating Zuma's daughter at the university. "The EFF student spoke of the deliberate policies of the ANC, and sarcastically told students that the ANC had christened the born-frees but had failed to adopt them."[569]

If the Zuma administration started out backing student demands, no one in charge was asking the most basic question: How would free education be sustained without fundamentally transforming the structural and institutional legacy of apartheid?

In government's grim world view, there wasn't much room for talk of radical change outside the ruling party's universe – especially when opponents of the ruling party put talk of human rights and transformation at the centre of opposition to cronyism and corruption in government. This talk seemed to the ANC leadership truly dangerous; for it undermined business and investors whose behaviour we might not like but whose survival was essential for growth and stability.

To students' ideas about transformation, the ANC added a theory of its own: conspiracy. This wasn't a mere sleight of hand.

Shortly after the day students stormed Parliament, rumours spread within the ANC that a third force was fomenting the protests to destabilise the ANC.

The South African Students Congress (SASCO) produced a voice clip calling for a revolution. On it, an unidentified man who was allegedly a member of the UCT Rhodes Must Fall movement indicated he had been mandated to propose a national strategy to "capitalise" on campus unrest. He suggested the occupation of "key points" such as Parliament and the

---

568 Interview with the author, Johannesburg, January 2016.
569 Interview with the author, Johannesburg, January 2016.

Union Buildings.[570]

Screen grabs of messages on the Rhodes Must Fall WhatsApp group three weeks later revealed a call for general destabilisation, indicating that violence was on the agenda.

Around this time, ANC Secretary General Gwede Mantashe described a work of dangers and power struggles in which the ANC had to remain the stabilising force for transformation, for its own hegemony and for stability in the country. The key phrase was 'vital national interest'. The rise of the student movement was cause for concern because it upset the balance of power. The mainstream of the ruling party was dedicated to this line of thought, but, once the student protest was in progress, party leaders seemed uncertain about what course to pursue – especially with local elections around the corner.

*

When I met Mpho Ndaba in February for the second time since the protests began, he was an EFF convert. He had joined the protest as an ANC sympathiser only when the university's behaviour made it impossible to cooperate. The ANC was the country's liberator, but the radical nationalist ideology of the EFF which had now taken hold in the student movement had a seductive lure for students like Ndaba. It had been spreading in a particularly virulent form – the default world view of a deposed group.

Ndaba spoke for the dispossessed and blamed the education crisis on an elite the ANC had fastidiously cultivated. "We have a right to expect something better from the second, liberated half of our lives," he said.[571] As well as protesting the legacy of history, the young South Africans were trying on a historical identity, inhabiting the anger their parents had expressed decades earlier.

The student rebellion proved some of the Zuma administration's assertions false and it made others self-fulfilling.

The first signs of political agitation surfaced during the occupation of Solomon Mahlangu House at Wits in early January. Two representatives of the SRC were shouted down by students in the room, who complained

570 Farber, T et al., 'Rhodes must fall fires back on unrest', *Times Live*, 18 November 2015. Accessed at http://www.timeslive.co.za/thetimes/2015/11/18/Rhodes-Must-Fall-fires-back-on-unrest.
571 All direct references hereinafter to Ndaba are from an interview with the author, Johannesburg, February 2016.

that the SRC had been too lenient on the university authorities, that whites received more privileges than blacks, and that the student movement had been infiltrated by "leaches". Posters and graffiti carried anti-government propaganda. "Fuck the ANC," read one poster. Among that group were a number of EFF members. The SRC's Fasiha Hassan, whose PYA is aligned to the ANC, suggested political opportunism was at play. "I think we must just be cognisant of the fact that a local government election is upcoming in the next few months and there are very opportunistic situations and parties and groups seeking to hijack things," she said outside the building.[572]

Finally, an EFF student leader named Vuyani stood up and usurped the SRC chair. "There are snakes and leaches amongst us," he said, grabbing the microphone. The university power structure was controlled by "white monopoly capital" – this was his real objection.[573] The government sacrificed legitimacy for control, and it ended up with neither.

There wasn't much room for manoeuvre outside a context of economic decline – especially when the ANC put talk of investment at the centre of its economic policy. And so the government's position on the protest was no different from that of university authorities: to support the academic industry in the national interest, even when the industry was committing social and economic genocide against students and workers. Thus it was that, in the weeks leading to the start of the 2016 academic year, students and workers regarded with dismay the government's turn away from the poor.

The problem more acutely lay in the Fees Must Fall movement retreating from a root-and-branch transformation of universities, Ndaba said. "What was required was to get two basic things right: free education for the poor and an end to outsourcing." But when the movement gained momentum, there wasn't the follow-through to pare down the activists and focus on the two key things. Instead, this machine kept grinding on, creating long-term agendas that looked more like an ideological crusade.

At base, I heard the same thing from virtually every student I talked to. The sentiment extended beyond the university power structures to the student command. And media seemed to devote copious amounts of airtime and newspaper copy to the stand-off between moderate students in the PYA and their more radical opponents in the EFF.

Within this climate, the Fees Must Fall campaign was an opportunity for

---

572 Nicolson, G, 'Fees must fall: Reloaded', *Daily Maverick*, 12 January 2016.
573 Student video footage of the gathering, January 2016.

black students to expand their politics over the university. "It was an opportunity, you understand, because it upset the balance of power that the ANC
had held," Ndaba said to me.

*

When I returned to Wits on Wednesday, 20 January, and met a group of
PYA students, a mood of battle fatigue had set in. Days had passed without
consensus on what had to be done to resolve the impasse. The protest had
by then drawn the attention of government and university authorities but
the objectives were subsumed under a calumny of party politics. As PYA
students retreated, the more militant wing of the Fees Must Fall movement
pushed ahead, albeit with less pugnacity than at the height of the protests
during October 2015. With it came an expectation that new impulses for
rebellion would come from universities and workers if the underlying problems were not addressed.

They already were. There were by this time new battalions that had
spared them disappointment: As PYA students retreated from the politically
charged atmosphere of the campaign, the now long-subdued but stoked-up
anger of casualised workers in the civil service towards state-run institutions
came back into its own. On 17 January, municipal workers joined the protest
against outsourcing.

Students, those outside the PYA at any rate, now had the backing of
some workers, and it was easy to recognise an ideological canon of black
nationalism incongruously combined with ultra-left tactics in the démarche.
On 16 January, students and unions, such as the National Union of
Metalworkers of South Africa (NUMSA) that had been expelled from the
ANC-aligned Congress of South African Trade Unions (COSATU), and a
group of civil-society activists met in Johannesburg. They called themselves
the Johannesburg Region of the United Front. They issued a statement criti-
cising the capitulation of the PYA and demanded an end to outsourcing
in all public institutions and the decolonisation of education to serve the
working class.

This was something new. An ultra-left undercurrent combining the race
and class politics of students and workers – the classical desiderata of revolutionary politics during the anti-apartheid struggle – could be discerned
in the United Front. For if, as Ali had articulated to me, there was in 1994
an act of betrayal, was the United Front of workers, unions, students and

communities not a movement against the terms of the 1994 settlement itself?

As I concluded my interview with Ali, I asked him whether the source of divisions within the student movement was between the beneficiaries of financial aid and those who felt excluded.

"It's not as simple as that," he said. Throughout the protests, there was a sharpening of contradictions in society. This was not just a protest. At that point it was difficult to go back to things as usual. "Its politics, it's the politicisation of the movement," said Ali.[574]

There was politics all right, but in whose interests? I pressed.

"As I understand it, the United Front was an attempt to unite students and workers around common demands for free quality education for all disadvantaged blacks and decent working conditions for workers," Ali explained. "But there are those who believe that the demands of students – for free education – cannot be met within the limits of capitalism."

And if your demands are not met within those limits? I asked.

Ali balked, as if the question had unsettled him. Then, after a long silence, he sighed. "This place will explode again, eventually. It will be a matter of time."

AMONG THE ARSONISTS AND LOOTERS WHO FOLLOWED ON THE HEELS of the Fees Must Fall movement, some vandalised and pillaged university property. Besides the looting, arson became a new virus spreading across campuses by April. A lecture theatre at Wits and an auditorium at the University of Johannesburg (UJ) were gutted. At Wits, the landscape looked ominous. Anti-establishment graffiti was now part of the university landscape; so, too, was the presence of armed private security guards.

This was a grand exclamation: it demonstrated the way in which, from the very first moment the demand for free tuition presented itself, the frustrations of the last two decades were being taken out on the ruling party and university elite. In this milieu, a kind of rhetorical hysteria thrived on all sides. I knew instinctively that there were layers of deception that prevented the real story from being told. For, after all, who or *what* was behind the violence?

Although the immediate response of the ANC leadership to the arson

---

574 All direct references hereinafter are from an interview with the author, Johannesburg, February 2016.

attacks implied a third force, on the canvass of extreme poverty, conspiracy was a tiny speck, but it stayed with me as other, more significant, events have not.

All through the first half of 2016 there had been a sinister build-up of violent conflict. The media was less invested in political preconceptions of what was really going on, and, though they were often woefully ignorant of the country, the nature of hard news forced them to stick to 'the facts'.

Later, I asked Ali what he thought of allegations about a 'hidden agenda' behind political parties such as the EFF. The way he tells it, the period that followed the removal of the Mbeki government scrambled everything, and turned many old truths on their heads. The ideas were that vital strategic interests would be secured through the agency of soft power, or strategic deception.

Did this mean that an anti-government cabal had insinuated its way into the student movement and taken hold of the initiative to serve their interests? Was the slogan 'Fees Must Fall' another term for disruption and destabilisation of the ANC government? Was revolution a byword for strategic deception? Or was this crackpot stuff?

*

As a liberation movement, the ANC had fought apartheid and colonialism. Now in government, the party had a new foe. The goals of students, many of them ANC backers, might have been legitimate. But it also brought with it old foes – socialists and militant nationalists.

In September 2015, President Zuma told a gathering on Heritage Day that the ANC had used protest action to combat and defeat apartheid. It was not acceptable, he said, that a democratically elected government should defend itself against those it liberated.

The notion that bad planning, a half-hearted commitment and incompetence on the part of the government accounted for the anarchy simply wasn't believable, he said. How could black students think that the same government that once fought Bantu education and offered a free and transformed education system as a model for the country's tertiary-education landscape contributed to the crisis? Deliberate sabotage made more sense. The conspiracy theories were an attempt to make sense of the moment.

Yet, in the heady flush of controversy courting the ruling party, what was once subversion – or treason beyond 1994 – increasingly became the 'historical birthright' of a generation of black youths. As the ANC turned its back on their revolution, they stepped forward as the makers of a new order.

Epilogue

'A TRAGIC OPTIMISM'

THE RISE OF THE FEES MUST FALL STUDENT MOVEMENT AND THE SUBSEQUENT clampdown by the South African government clearly mark the end of one era in student–university–government relations and usher in a new and more volatile period. Among the most ominous symptoms of these tense relations were the violent reactions of state security forces, the arrest of more than a dozen student protestors outside Parliament in late 2015, and the dramatic surge in acts of arson under highly suspicious circumstances on some university campuses in early and then late 2016.

The student revolts and demands for decolonisation should not, however, have provoked the shock and awe that apparently marked the reaction of the government and society generally. For more than three decades after the rise to power of the National Party, black students had waged militant protests against the political edifice and social consequences of apartheid education and racial segregation. The consistent reaction of the apartheid government had been harsh, often brutal repression. Soon after the banning of the African National Congress (ANC) and other liberation organisations in the repressive conditions of the 1960s, a militant generation of black students consisting mainly of members of the South African Students' Organisation (SASO) stampeded onto liberal campuses to brandish an intellectual nous and ideological facility for a new combative politics never seen before. After the creation of SASO, these nascent groups coalesced under a new black political movement from 1971 to 1976 – first among black university students themselves and then school-going youths in Soweto – taking as its leitmotif the philosophy of black consciousness. Without suggesting that the analogy is complete, the Fees Must Fall movement has operated in much the same fashion more than two decades since the end of apartheid. Of course, there are several important differences between SASO and the Fees

Must Fall movement – SASO represented a disenfranchised black minority at segregated universities whose demands could not be accommodated within the political and institutional constraints of the apartheid system, while the majority of student activists in the Fees Must Fall movement were, for lack of a better term, 'born free'. However, the liberalisation and 'integration' of traditionally black and white universities and their corollary – corporatisation and financialisation – evoked the resulting black and white public furore. Poor black students unable to cope with the academic and financial burden of universities now joined in protests and confrontational demonstrations against untransformed colonial institutions and the entire post-1994 legacy of neo-liberalism. The values of black pride and self-reliance were once again stressed in slogans and graffiti and on social-media platforms, adding a new political dimension to the previous indifference of black students.

A combination of factors, including the structural form of racial inequality in our society, the dissolution of the legal appurtenances of apartheid and their replacement with a new form of cultural insularity and identitarian politics, overt racism, and the growing number of financially disadvantaged black students on campuses preclude indifference to recent events. What our response should be depends upon an analysis of trends within the education system and their effect on black students. An approach to the problem of fees that has had particular appeal to the government in recent months is a policy formula to fund the 'missing middle' who neither qualify for financial aid nor can afford a university education. A notable argument for this position has been enunciated in numerous radio and television interviews and newspaper columns by the head of the National Student Financial Aid Scheme (NSFAS) Sizwe Nxasana. It is my contention, however, that even a revised version of the current financial aid scheme will not advance the policy objective of free education.

This epilogue responds to the need to find long-term solutions to current student protests over tuition fees at higher-education institutions across the country, and to the more recent commitment by government to investigate lasting measures to fund higher education in our country beyond the government fiscus.

A number of implications for government policy flow from this conclusion.

*

Because government's funding formula has attracted some attention both within university management structures and in the student movement to have become a counter in the debate about transformation, certain key arguments will be used here in discussing this approach.

The focus on funding has been targeted by the government for several years now as a way to ensure adequate financial support for students. The Department of Higher Education and Training's (DHET) White Paper for Post-School Education and Training sets out a vision of a transformed post-school system which is equitable, much expanded and more diverse than it is at present, and which will include a key role for employers in the provision of education and training opportunities.

In general, the DHET has embraced the concept of an integrated and accessible education system. The DHET believes that improving student access, success and throughput rates "is a very serious challenge for the university sector and must become a priority focus for national policy and for the institutions themselves, in particular in improving access and success for those groups whose race, gender or disability status had previously disadvantaged them".[575]

Its main policy objectives are:

- A post-school system that can assist in building a fair, equitable, non-racial, non-sexist and democratic South Africa;
- A single, coordinated post-school education and training system;
- Expanded access, improved quality and increased diversity of provision;
- A stronger and more cooperative relationship between education and training institutions and the workplace; and
- A post-school education and training system that is responsive to the needs of individual citizens, employers in both public and private sectors, as well as broader societal and developmental objectives.[576]

Guided by the National Development Plan, the White Paper reaffirms that graduates of universities and colleges should have the skills to meet the present and future needs of the economy. Pursuant to this goal, a three-pronged policy approach has been adopted. Firstly, as the university and post-school sector grows, it will be essential to facilitate student access to institutions. The Central Applications Service (CAS) is a crucial move

---

575 The Presidency, 'Draft press statement', April 2015.
576 See the revised White Paper for Post-School Education and Training, 2013.

towards supporting informed access to universities and other post-school opportunities for students, and to making the choices and placements of students across the system more effective. Its primary aim for the university sector is "to offer advice and support to students applying to university, to allow them to pay a single application fee, and to facilitate their application to more than one institution if necessary".[577]

The CAS is designed to be student-centred and to promote greater equity of access for all students, particularly the poor, for whom multiple application fees can be prohibitive. It will also offer a clearing-house service that will allow students not accepted into one university to be redirected to other universities or post-school institutions. Over time, the CAS will replace all other application systems, preventing student walk-ins and building a national culture of applying early for university study.

The second approach is the provision of student financial aid for the poorest students to access university studies and to increase equity through the NSFAS. In the short term, government has shown a commitment to finding a compromise by convincing students to accept a capped fee increase in the current academic year. In the long term, government believes access to education might be best served by strengthening the allocation of funding to the NSFAS and opening new universities in Mpumalanga and the Northern Cape and the Sefako Makgatho Health Sciences University in Gauteng.[578]

Thirdly, partnerships will be essential to the success of student-funding initiatives. These will include intragovernmental partnerships, such as cost-recovery support from the South African Revenue Service (SARS), scholarship support from other government departments in scarce-skills areas, and government partnerships with the private sector and international partners. In this way, government hopes that student funding, though not a sufficient condition for academic success in itself, may progressively support greater levels of academic success.

That's good news if the measure of success is the demographic profile of the student population. South African universities are changing – demographically and institutionally. Not only is there a new institutional landscape, but the fault lines between historically black and white post-secondary institutions have also eased as the annual average student intake for

---

577 Ibid.
578 Ibid.

the first time reflects a larger black student cohort. But there the optimism dissolves in an institutional quagmire of gloom. For one thing, since the start of the student revolts in 2015, this approach has been directed toward demonstrating that the DHET policy equation of 'student access' with 'free education' is likely to fuel protests and resistance to any sort of practical settlement and that the government and universities ought, on the contrary, to direct their influence toward the achievement of some sort of goal that the missing middle does not find unacceptable. On this score, both DHET Minister, Blade Nzimande, and Nxasana have warned that student pressures are an unachievable end.

Yet participation rates in universities are expected to increase from the current 17.3 per cent to 25 per cent – that is, from just over 937 000 students in 2011 to about 1.6 million enrolments in 2030. Additionally, South African universities are characterised by relatively low success rates – 74 per cent in 2011 compared with a desired national norm of 80 per cent. Despite overall demographic changes in the student bodies of universities, cohort studies have shown that black students, particularly those from poor backgrounds, are still disproportionately affected by poor graduation and throughput rates.

One theme has run like a strong thread in this book: institutions incorporated and merged in 2004 and 2005 as part of government's grand restructuring plan appear to have lagged woefully behind their more cloistered peers in elite universities in the struggle to adapt to the new set-up. Despite the interracial marriages between black and white institutions, the worst overall performers are institutions that either merged or were incorporated in 2004/2005. This has resulted in an average year-on-year graduation rate of 15 per cent – well below the international norm of 25 per cent for students in three-year degree programmes in contact education. This not only raises serious concerns about the productivity of the system and the high costs to government and institutions from poor student success rates, but also raises substantial equity issues.

To compound matters, the poor living conditions of many students, a grave shortage of student accommodation in universities, as well as poor living conditions in many of the existing residences are negatively affecting student outputs. Very low numbers of first-year black contact students are accommodated in university residences, which is likely a contributing factor to poor performance in the first year of study.

*

Manifestly, the pattern is a system torn between historical redress and its consequences: massive barriers to access and a dropout and failure rate pulling
in the opposite direction. In fact, the restructuring plan introduced by former
education minister, Kader Asmal, in 2003 has succeeded in one respect only:
the rigid racial profile of students on traditionally white campuses is wither-
ing away. But the veneer of integration masks a more variegated picture: the
net effect of the absorption by historically advantaged universities of poor
and academically unprepared black students is not, as education department
bureaucrats have maintained, a qualitative improvement in overall access;
neither is shared infrastructure and academic expertise necessarily an improvement in the level of academic output by previously disadvantaged universities.
It is certainly not a panacea for centuries of oppression and indoctrination by
successive colonial and apartheid governments.

Despite relatively favourable circumstances of rapid demographic change,
the government has used the post-2003 reform period progressively to lib-
eralise and enforce a new kind of separation through the Higher Education
Act, which established a very broad definition of access and integration.
Paradoxically a major bulwark of late-apartheid liberalisation, the commercialisation of university access was elaborated during these years. Thus
the argument that mergers will drive integration and access is demonstrably
flawed. During a period of growth and relative stability, universities were
moving deeper into their defensive structure, and fortifying it energetically –
until economic conditions declined and students began protesting.

Unlike many of their parents, the born-frees were thus born into a recov-
ering economy that has turned pear-shaped. Although the black middle
class has grown, so has unemployment. Among 35 emerging markets, South
African males have the second-lowest labour force participation rate.[579]
The proportion of the working-age population that is actually employed
dropped from 46 per cent in 2001 to 43 per cent in 2014 using the expanded
definition. These figures include 'discouraged' workers, who are unemployed people available to work but not taking active steps to look for jobs.
The number of discouraged workers of all races has increased by 40 per cent
in the past 14 years. The increase would include not only some of the parents and grandparents of born-frees, but also born-frees themselves eligible
to enter the workforce as they turn 15.[580]

---

579 *South African Survey*, 2014/15, pp 216-218.
580 Ibid., pp. 87-90.

Although very large numbers of born-frees have grown up with theoretical rights to education and economic opportunities, high and rising unemployment is the dominant reality. Two-thirds of all the unemployed have been jobless for more than a year. The result is a mix of economic and political alienation which some commentators regard as a potential threat to stability.

In sum, available evidence, from history and recent events, would indicate that skirting the problem is tantamount to postponing the eventual reckoning. In fact, the history of transformation since the late 1990s has been characterised by movement in one direction – revolt by black students on the one hand, and a defensive structure founded on the progressive consolidation of white privilege through the financialisation of higher education, on the other.

What, then, is the solution? Since President Jacob Zuma's announcement of a Presidential Task Team in late 2015 to investigate solutions to the crisis, students have repeatedly declared that government has no timetable or formula in mind for achieving radical change. Blade Nzimande himself admitted the same point in a late-2015 television interview, saying his department had never put forward a plan for free education because it did not have one.[581]

If access and throughput rates are to improve, as they must, it is clear that large-scale targeted interventions must be expanded in all tertiary institutions, with the support of the state. Improvement of access and undergraduate throughput rates – and therefore access – is a key strategy for increasing graduate outputs, for providing the skills needed by the economy, and for ensuring that larger numbers of students are available for postgraduate study.

Much as we have been concerned with problems that have beset higher education, this is also, to borrow the Polish radical Isaac Deutscher's adaptation of Sophocles to describe the Soviet Union at its low point of internal opposition and Stalinist show trials in the 1930s, an 'optimistic tragedy', one in which the student movement now occupies the minds of all concerned about the future of South Africa.

Our primary concern is with the lack of an effective mechanism to equalise access and open the doors of learning to all. We have the right ideals. However, on account of a combination of structural constraints and

---

581 *eNCA* special broadcast on student-fee protests, 14 October 2015.

historical factors such as racial inequality and poverty, our strategic agenda in the education sector towards radical outcomes may be losing ground. In our drive to overcome these problems, a new approach is urgently needed.

IN ITS IMPLICATIONS FOR TRANSFORMATION, THE CRUX OF THE PROBLEM IS that the government and university establishment have restricted themselves to what would not be unacceptable to the missing middle. The creation of a funding policy of separate but equal – perhaps starting with the upgrading of traditionally black campuses, the building of new ones, the easing of restrictions on black students who do not qualify for financial aid, and a gradual dismantling of university autonomy over issues of access – is seen by government as doable.

A major semantic difficulty with this argument is that government's definition of access in particular and transformation generally seems to differ widely from that of black students. Whereas government uses the term 'access' for signifying a deracialised hierarchy of power, as well as perhaps a broader base of access, the understanding of the student community, led by the Fees Must Fall movement, is that the funding model should not prejudice all financially vulnerable students. It means bringing to an end the harsh decree that denies access to blacks who cannot settle debt. To be fair, Nzimande does talk frequently of ending elitism, but most of government's definition would constitute for students the central core of neo-liberalism and is therefore non-negotiable. Thus a new model would have to mean free education and not a mere renovation of its petty face.

The underlying problem with government's stance, however, lies precisely in the fact that centuries of history have demonstrated that inequality is unacceptable to the black youth. Even now, the integration of universities, the liberal embodiment of neo-apartheid in South African terms, demonstrates the reality of what 'integration' means to the ruling South African establishment.

*

Central to the higher-education crisis in South Africa is the ideological paradigm within which the transformation agenda has been cast. The formula for fees, in order to represent the expression of student concerns about their future, must represent more than the missing middle. Time is running out. For, while protests have reached a lull at the time of writing this epilogue, black student politicisation has been greatly spurred by the demonstrably raw power of mass mobilisation and the prospect of regime change should the government not heed the warning signs.

In general, the reverence of black students toward the ruling party is largely diminished. They have become increasingly impatient for radical change. The events of 2015/2016 on campuses painfully demonstrate that rhetoric and abjuration have been most ineffective in inducing movement toward the goal of an inclusive and transformed education system. If anything, the impotence of the government in the face of student revolts has demonstrated the efficacy of a new use of black consciousness. The related gutting of black public schools in Vuwani and violent protests in the build-up to the 2016 local-government elections may constitute an equally significant turning point toward the radicalisation of black communities. A violent and protracted collision with the ruling party and established order seems inevitable unless a combination of policy measures, resources and practical interventions can be used to enlarge the ambit of what is acceptable and possible.

But it is asserted that government, students, universities and the business community in South Africa contain as yet untapped reservoirs of transformative potential and that the exercise of this community's economic power can bring about results satisfactory to students, universities and government. Left to their own devices, however, stakeholders in South African society appear to possess neither the will nor the foresight to effect fundamental alterations to the structure of the higher-education landscape. Indeed, until the onset of the current economic downturn, the primary characteristics of South African business was its enormous profitability and relative exclusion of the majority of blacks from its largesse. Yet, in an age of the knowledge economy, the wellspring of that profitability is not hard to discern: skilled labour. It is simply no longer sustainable to continue on a path of exploiting the vast black labour pool relative to that of skilled whites. Thus, whereas profit-making enterprises have shown little propensity to commit economic suicide by misconceiving the structures that best serve their interests, the present and future economy requires radical structural changes.

The real issue is whether substantial change can be induced without regime change. The unthinkable must be thought – what should be the position of all parties in response to the crisis?

IN DISCUSSING POLICY OPTIONS, WE SHOULD FIRST LOOK AT REAL OR PERCEIVED issues shaping or constraining policy.

The factual premise of student access to higher learning and related protests over fee hikes is directly related to the apartheid legacy of skewed resource distribution and funding shortfalls. An essential element of higher-education transformation policy and the challenge of redress has been complicated and subverted by a market-based system, which, in turn, has perpetuated a distorted (racial) development paradigm. This has meant that funding shortfalls are a symptom rather than a cause of a distorted development paradigm.

More substantial constraints on the scope of transformation are current bleak growth expectations of 0.5 per cent for 2016, compounded by ballooning government debt and corresponding tax revenue shortfalls, thus exposing a deeper structural malaise in the higher-education funding and governance model.

The ongoing discord over fee increments is therefore over racially skewed patterns of wealth distribution in the economy and control in universities that are bound to entrench a vicious cycle of low graduate outputs, unemployment and jobless growth unless structural problems besetting higher education are resolved.

A related constraining force on government policy is the cost of university education. All 23 institutions rely on state financial support for varying proportions of their operating costs, and most receive some form of third-stream income, though this varies enormously. However, all universities also charge student fees, which are essential to institutional survival in the current funding environment. Fees have risen substantially over the past two decades, as overall government funding to institutions has not kept up with the financial requirements of the system. Rising student fees continue to pose a major barrier to access for many students.

The structure of our higher-education system is best understood as Western-centric where fees and access perpetuate elitism. In this context, the Fees Must Fall campaign will continue to gain momentum. The points of disagreement are whether there are grounds for the continuing consequences of fee increases.

Despite the commitment by the DHET to transforming institutions of higher learning and 'massifying' access to universities, successive fee hikes have made it increasingly difficult for black students to enter universities or complete degrees for which they enrol. Though the problem of fees has

always been present, it has become more pressing in the context of elitist Western notions of higher learning, as these notions limit the range of
opportunities to facilitate access while simultaneously limiting transformation to liberal interventions which do more to entrench the status quo.

In this regard, university claims of rising costs should be treated with
caution. It seems to be discredited by recent data, which show a largely
untransformed staffing and resource-allocation pattern in a context of concentrated ownership and control. A recent report by BusinessTech shows that
universities in South Africa are not as broke as they claim to be. According
to the report, government's allocation for higher education is around R30
billion, which represents 0.72 per cent of the country's gross domestic product (GDP). The NSFAS received more than R9.5 billion of that R30 billion
in 2015 alone. The remaining R21 billion went to universities.[582]

In 2015, the University of the Witwatersrand (Wits) received R1.148 billion, the University of Cape Town (UCT) got R1.074 billion and Stellenbosch
University received R1.177 billion. That was just government's portion: the
Wits 2014 annual report shows the university generated a whopping R1.5
billion from tuition fees. There are other sources of revenue that are reflected
in its annual report resulting in a surplus that went to reserves.

Another constraining force on transformation is the challenge of governance which, while highlighted as a challenge to be overcome in the White
Paper, is more deeply embedded in the structure of the economy and the
institutional design and funding model of the university system. University
councils are responsible for fee hikes, as they oversee institutions' financial
and corporate governance. Despite strong grounds for assuming that the
higher-education system relies heavily on fees to survive and meet its academic output targets, the problem with the current policy approach is that
it posits an administrative solution (namely the CAS) and limited financial
aid in a context of massive inequality and scarce resources as a solution to
a structural problem.

On a macro-level, the knock-on effect of limited access and high dropout rates (of up to 50 per cent at undergraduate level) as large numbers of
deserving black students struggle to meet the burden of tuition fees is a massive cost to the economy as business struggles to match demand with skills
in a fiercely competitive global economy.

---

582 'Fees must fall leaked: See what SA universities earn annually', *City Sun*, 21 October 2015. Accessed
at http://citysun.co.za/feesmustfall-leaked-see-what-sa_20/.

In fact, the benefits of higher education are only marginally captured by the economy as a result of a skills deficit, massive unemployment and a narrow domestic tax base. Moreover, the higher-education sector itself has been bleeding local, mainly white, talent to global markets given the supply–demand mismatch, leading to a massive outflow of resources in which South Africa invests.

Given the ongoing legacy of discriminatory practices in higher education – principally ownership patterns and power relations – it is by now evident that the market does not counterbalance structural imbalances. Although basic education access has increased to 99 per cent since 1994, only 15 per cent of black students are able to enter higher-education institutions due to financial barriers.

Despite the noble intentions of the White Paper to effect the broad transformation envisaged in the Freedom Charter, a closer examination of power relations highlights the pervasive constraints presented in the form of non-equitable distribution of benefits inherent in their implementation.

Thus, the underlying model has resulted in a distribution of resources intended for transformation purposes being tied up in skewed, limited and costly student loans. The crucial point here is that the tension over an elite higher-education system does not only refer to the reality of material obstacles which sustain the status quo but, above all, to the reality of socio-economic inequalities and antagonisms, unequal power relations, and cultural hegemonies which brand the space for transformation with a twist. Crucial here is the blurring of the distinction between policy and practice in which the social position of black students is obliterated.

*

Given structural problems, economic constraints, and the deeply divided nature of South African society, what is possible as a realistic policy? My basic point of departure is that short-term solutions to the university funding crisis such as caps on fee increases, development grants to enable institutions to become financially stable, and revised funding formulas to accommodate the missing middle are tantamount to kicking the can down the road. A bold engagement with underlying problems of funding and access, and clearer guidelines on how to effect radical change, is therefore needed.

Notwithstanding the strain on higher education due to rising costs and the elevation of education among government's apex of priorities, the issue before us comes down to the structural problem driving up higher-education costs and foreclosing opportunities to broaden access. From a socio-economic and growth perspective, a 'business-as-usual' position risks further instability in the higher-education sector, where compromises by stakeholders with vested interests won't resolve the problem of access and its corollary, unemployment and the talent deficit facing the economy, in a context where growth is expected to remain depressed for quite some time.

Recognising the problem of the market paradigm, government seems to believe that it will become obvious that these contradictions cannot be resolved without radically transforming economic and social power relations. But there are a number of policy inconsistencies in higher education that have developed within the current policy position. For instance, in the light of the emphasis on accelerated transformation, there has been no clarity on what distinguishes a radical approach from a reformist approach to transforming universities and colleges. The current policy position of subsidising universities and supporting disadvantaged black students through financial aid is not a sustainable approach; it will not resolve the underlying challenge of democratising and transforming education.

In fact, consideration of ways of controlling fee increases is a short-term palliative. There is therefore a danger of misconstruing, or even redefining, what is necessary in the light of what is possible within the current funding paradigm and, worse still, of doing this without effective strategic assessment and analysis. This strategic confusion sometimes produces contradictory outcomes within our policy architecture, sometimes accentuated by the illusory pursuit of policies that bear no workable radical outcomes.

Because higher education is an important form of investment in human-capital development, it can be regarded as a high level or a specialised form of human capital: it helps in the rapid industrialisation of the economy by providing individuals with professional, technical, and managerial skills.

Our objective should be to maximise the developmental impact of higher education through labour-absorbing growth and development to, inter alia, capture the value derived from employment and business development, invest in long-term knowledge and physical infrastructure, and create more jobs through circulating value captured.

The investment and participation of all stakeholders in higher education must be harnessed in order to build our economic potential domestically and realise our competitive strengths globally to overcome our massive unemployment time bomb. To do so, it is essential that graduate outputs are aligned to the national imperative of transforming the actual structure of the economy. No country has successfully built a mature economy without significant and sustained investment in knowledge, research and development. Thus a prerequisite for success is a dramatic enhancement of the quality of our education system and the increased production of graduates by overcoming barriers to university access.

In order to achieve this, we need to locate the problem of access and affordability at the heart of a development strategy. In the view expressed here, the question of advocating radical transformation cannot be substantially resolved within the current market paradigm.

Finally, our aim must be to generate value and capture this for social and economic development. Generating value requires significant investment and risks in a partnership between the public and private sectors along with students. The public sector needs to deploy resources and various development instruments to facilitate the equitable growth of the higher-education sector and capture an equitable share of the value generated. In order to do this, we must overhaul the current higher-education funding system with respect to the terms and conditions of the private sector's participation (particularly the regime of power relations that this entails).

Rather than a reformist, market-based approach, a radical approach is recommended in which universities become national assets open to all students, and in which there is skin in the game for all stakeholders, including students.

It is clear that radical transformation as a concept can only be meaningful relative to a given objective function. Radical transformation in the context of the proposed framework refers to the socio-economic basis of our national policy imperatives. So, if we understand radical transformation very generally to be what a policy does in relation to our objectives, and if we define the task at hand to be the creation of radical outcomes, then a good policy in the context of this framework simply refers to socio-economic outcomes (in business, the public sector or other sectors within the economy) that are conducive to the overall transformation of the country.

What matters, ultimately, is that policy positions and interventions need to be understood in the context of our strategic objectives. This means that policies must be filtered through a framework for radical transformation. We now have an opportunity to overhaul the foundation of the current education paradigm based on unequal power relations and wealth and replace it with a system premised on the thinking of 'community' in which government, the private sector, unions and students cohere for the achievement of common goals.

RECOMMENDATIONS

The Higher Education White Paper introduced the concept of free education for the poor in South Africa. Accordingly, "Everything possible must be done to progressively introduce free education for the poor in South African universities as resources become available."[583]

This principle is valid, as it takes forward the agenda of opening learning to all. A recent study commissioned by the Minister of the DHET found that "free university education for the poor in South Africa is feasible, but will require significant additional funding of both NSFAS and the university system".[584] While developing the necessary mechanisms and levels of investment, the DHET believes the system must progressively support access for students of varying financial means.

While this approach responds to the competing imperatives outlined in the White Paper, with regard to increasing enrolments and improving throughput and curriculum relevance within a system and infrastructure that will continue to be under strain despite plans to expand it substantially, it does not provide a long-term solution.

Shifting the paradigm

The core challenge facing us is that of ensuring full participation in education based on the principle of free and unfettered access. This requires bold interventions to transform the structure of the system and the thinking that entraps universities in elitist and racially cordoned enclaves.

Having diagnosed the problem as that of elitism in a context of unequal power relations and racialised inequality which perpetuates both Westernised curricula and languages as mediums of instruction, the solution lies in a new paradigm which democratises education by removing funding obstacles to equitable access. For, if the problem of access comes down to racial inequality, a radical approach means increased state and private-sector participation in this sector. Participation can be broadly defined to comprise a range of options from 100 per cent equity participation, through partial

---

583 Revised White Paper for Post-School Education and Training, 2013.
584 See Hall, M, 'Creativity in contradiction' (nd). Accessed at https://martinhallfacilitation.org/author/martinjohnhall21/.

equity arrangements, to equity participation without financial obligation. Higher education has long been viewed as a national asset. It is a sector in which the state often believes it must have a high degree of control. In a number of countries, this control has been exercised through direct state participation.

Towards a Nation Building Fund

Nationalisation of a special type

The principal outcomes desired are full access to higher education (through the introduction of a Sovereign Wealth Fund) and the development of a funding pool in which all stakeholders (business, government, unions and students) have skin in the game.

There are broadly three types of SWFs: government holding companies, development investors, and savings funds. In the proposed model, increased sophistication in equity participation as a means of raising revenue can be accomplished by establishing a national pool into which stakeholders invest money.

A sovereign, publicly listed fund would then have to be established in order to pool state assets, as well as contributions by business, unions and other stakeholders, which could be realised by ring-fencing all revenues. In this regard, we could draw on the efficiency of this model in other countries such as the Swedish Division of State Enterprises under the Ministry of Enterprises which operates as a holding company of state-owned enterprises (SOEs). Finland has a similar type of holding company, Solidium Oy, for holding state assets.

In effect, then, the Nation Building Fund would nationalise access and remove the responsibility of fees from universities, leaving the latter to focus solely on education outputs.

Skin in the game – building a virtuous cycle

In essence, the crucial point here is that the problem of tuition increments must be overhauled by decreasing fees to a zero base. However, this is not to suggest the collapse of university funding sources. An incremental approach over the coming five years to reducing fees to zero must be proportional to the rise of the Nation Building Fund.

In contrast to the current system of vested interests and unequal power relations within university councils, the proposed funding model creates a virtuous cycle of equitable education and quality outputs, growth and value circulation. As a solution-driven fund, the Nation Building Fund is not welfarist or grant-driven; it is based on the idea that each stakeholder (government, business, unions, students) will have skin in the game. Money can be recycled through the fund.

The following three components constitute a virtuous cycle of development which we believe is sustainable in the long term:

Value creation
- In effect, companies would be investing in future cohorts of human talent and the latter's contribution to growth.
- Students who benefit from fund fees would be required to invest two years of their working lives in the private sector and an additional two years in the public sector.
- They would also derive benefits from gainful employment and business ventures through seed funding beyond university, thereby circumventing the global problem of graduate unemployment. The White Paper already directs the DHET to explore community engagement to "answer the call of young people for constructive social engagement; enhance the culture of learning, teaching and service in higher education; and relieve some of the financial burden of study at this level".[585]

By extending this model to include the above, the concept would be less abstract and more concrete.

Value capture
Currently, value is not created and captured by the community and state. In fact, government's contribution to universities is in the form of tax and subsidies to universities. What value capture exists is off a low tax base. By investing in larger student numbers, and aligning education to the demands of the economy, we would be capturing a larger share of value in business development, job creation and innovation.

Value circulation
In contrast to the current paradigm in which value circulates within a narrow, racially skewed economy, value captured from a growing economy and larger tax base can be invested in equitable growth and development.

---

585 Revised White Paper for Post-School Education and Training, 2013.

Key issues for consideration

- *The Nation Building Fund should be sovereign:* Decision-making powers over the use of cash flow should be the prerogative of the board and not the Treasury. It is particularly important that sufficient reinvestments are made to secure the long-term performance of the fund.
- *Full transparency:* The fund should be fully transparent and follow the most stringent reporting rules, even if it is not required to do so from a formal point of view.
- *Clear and transparent non-profit goals:* Long-term government strategic goals such as inclusive growth, employment and development have to be coordinated and set in line with the fund's abilities and its other priorities. These goals should be clearly stated and be transparent.

In making monies available for the fund and removing the burden from the remit of universities, universities would be left to focus on the core business of academic development.

By transforming the model of higher education, we can ensure that transformation assumes the depth necessary to change the following:

- the governance of the universities benefiting from the Nation Building Fund;
- the management profile of universities;
- the academic staff profile of universities; and
- research outputs of higher-education institutions through greater diversity.

In addition, authentic Afrocentric content and innovation can be guaranteed.

Bibliography

This is mainly a book of reporting. In addition to interviews, I depended for information on newspaper reports and online media. For historical background material, I also benefited principally from the following publications:

Books

Ballinger, Margaret. *From Union to Apartheid: A Trek to Isolation* (New York: Praeger, 1969).

Chipkin, Ivor. *Do South Africans Exist?* (Johannesburg: Wits University Press, 2007).

Cummings, Richard. *The Pied Piper: Allard K Lowenstein and the Liberal Dream* (New York: Inprint.com, 1985).

D'Oliveira, John. *Vorster – the Man* (Johannesburg: Ernest Stanton Publishers, 1977).

Davis, John Lewis. *George Kennan: An American Life* (New York: Penguin Books, 2011).

Driver, CJ. *Patrick Duncan: South African and Pan-African* (Cape Town: David Philip, 1980).

Du Plessis, J. *A History of Christian Missions in South Africa* (London, 1911).

Epstein, EJ. 'Chapter 18: The American conspiracy', in *The Diamond Invention: The American Conspiracy* (Hutchinson: 1982). Accessed at http://edwardjayepstein.com/diamond/chap18_print.htm; also see Pallister et al.

Everatt, David et al. (eds). *Black Youth in Crisis: Facing the Future* (Johannesburg: Ravan Press, 1992).

Fanon, Franz. *Black Skin, White Masks* (New York: Grove Press, 1967).

Fanon, Franz. *The Wretched of the Earth* (New York: Grove Press, 1968).

Frankel, Philip et al. (eds). *State Resistance and Change in South Africa* (Johannesburg: Southern Book Publishers, 1988).

Gerhart, Gail. *Black Power in South Africa: The Evolution of an Ideology*

(University of California Press, 1979).

Gevisser, Mark. *Thabo Mbeki: The Dream Deferred* (Johannesburg: Jonathan Ball Publishers, 2007).

Giliomee, Herman. *The Afrikaners: Biography of a People* (Johannesburg: Tafelberg, 2003).

Kallaway, Peter (ed). *Apartheid and Education: The Education of Black South Africans* (Johannesburg: Ravan Press, 1984).

Keegan, Timothy. *Colonial South Africa and the Origins of Racial Order* (Cape Town: David Philip, 1996).

La Guma, Alex. *Apartheid: A Collection of Writings on South African Racism by South Africans* (New York: International Publishers, 1971).

Lipton, Merle. *Capitalism and Apartheid: 1910–84* (Taylor & Francis, 1985).

Lodge, Tom. *Politics in South Africa: From Mandela to Mbeki* (Cape Town: David Philip, 2002).

Majeke, Nosipho. *The Role of the Missionaries in Conquest* (APSUSA, 1986).

Marais, Hein. *South Africa: Limits to Change: The Political Economy of Transition* (Johannesburg: Zed Books, 2001).

Marchetti, V & Marks, JD. *The CIA and the Cult of Intelligence* (New York: Dell, 1974).

Massie, Robert Kinloch. *Loosing the Bonds: The United States and South Africa in the Apartheid Years* (New York: Bantam Doubleday Dell, 1997).

McNish, JT. *The Road to El Dorado* (Cape Town: Struik, 1968).

Mokoena, Kenneth (ed). *South Africa and the United States: The Declassified History* (New York: The New Press, 1993).

Moss, Glenn. *The New Radicals: A Generational Memoir of the 1970s* (Johannesburg: Jacana Media, 2014).

Murray, Martin J. *City of Extremes: The Spatial Politics of Johannesburg* (Johannesburg: Wits University Press, 2011).

O'Meara, Dan. *Volkskapitalisme: Class, Capital and Ideology in the Development of Afrikaner Capitalism* (Johannesburg: Ravan Press, 1993).

O'Meara, Dan. *Forty Lost Years: The Apartheid State and the Politics of the National Party, 1948–1994* (Johannesburg: Ravan Press, 1997).

Pallister, David et al. (eds). *South Africa Inc: The Oppenheimer Empire* (Simon & Schuster, 1987).

Pottinger, Brian. *The Imperial Presidency: PW Botha, the First Ten Years* (Johannesburg: Southern Book Publishers, 1988).

Rotberg, Robert. *The Founder, Cecil Rhodes and the Pursuit of Power* (New York, Oxford University Press, 1988).

Sarakinsky, M. *The Changing Urban African Class Structure: 1970–1985*. MA dissertation, University of the Witwatersrand, October 1989.

Saul, JS & Gelb, S. *The Crisis in South Africa* (New York: Monthly Review Press, 1981).

Sletz-Kessler, Robert. *Sylvia, Rachel, Meredith, Anna: A Novel* (Durham: Thatcher Forest Publishing, 2007).

Smuts, Jan Christiaan. *The Basis of Trusteeship in African Native Policy* (South African Institute of Race Relations, 1942).

Sparks, Allister. *The Mind of South Africa: The Rise and Fall of Apartheid* (Ballantine Books, 1991).

Stubbs, Aelred (ed). *Steve Biko: I Write What I Like – a Selection of His Writings* (Johannesburg: Picador Africa, 2004).

Suzman, Helen. *In No Uncertain Terms: A South African Memoir* (Knopf, 1993).

Swanepoel, Piet. *Really Inside BOSS: A Tale about South Africa's Late Intelligence Service (and Something about the CIA)* (Self-published, 2007).

Talbot, David. *Brothers: The Hidden History of the Kennedy Years* (London: Pocket Books, 2008).

Wilford, Hugh. *The Mighty Wurlitzer: How the CIA Played America* (Harvard University Press, 2008).

Wilkens, Ivor & Strydom, Hans. *The Super-Afrikaners: Inside the Afrikaner Broederbond* (Johannesburg: Jonathan Ball Publishers, 1980).

Documents and journals

Bennell, P with Monyokolo, M. 'A lost generation?: Key findings of a tracer survey of secondary school leavers in South Africa', *Educational Development,* Vol. 14, No. 2, pp. 195–206, 1994. Education Policy Unit, University of the Witwatersrand, Johannesburg, South Africa.

Cohen, Herman J. 'A perspective on fifty years of US-Africa policy: The Nixon legacy', in *American Foreign Policy Interests.*

Department of Arts and Culture. 'Creating a caring and proud society: A national strategy for developing an inclusive and a cohesive South African society', 7 June 2012.

Department of Higher Education and Training. White Paper for Post-School Education and Training, 2013.

Educational Development, Vol. 14, No. 2, 1994. Education Policy Unit, University of the Witwatersrand, Johannesburg, South Africa.

Gibson, Nigel. 'Upright and free: Fanon in South Africa, from Biko to the shackdwellers' movement' *(Abahlali baseMjondolo)*, in *Social Identities,* Vol. 14, No. 6, November 2008.

Gool, Jane. 'The crimes of bantu education in South Africa' (Unity Movement Publication, 1966). Accessed online at http://www.apdusa.org.za/wp-content/books/crimes.of.bantu.education.pdf.

Hawthorne, P & Macleod, S. 'Lost generation', *Time* magazine, 18 February 1991.

Johnson, R. 'Really useful knowledge: Radical education and working class culture, 1790–1848', in R Dale et al. (ed), *Politics, Patriarchy and Practice: Education and the State*, Vol. 2 (Basingstoke: Farmer Ford/OU Press). Accessed online at http://www.arasite.ord/johnson.html.

Kamen, Scott. *Competing Visions: The CIA, the Congress for Cultural Freedom and the Non-Communist European Left, 1950–1967*. Honours thesis submitted to the Western Michigan University, May 2008.

Leibbrandt, M & Green, P. 'Our new lost generation', *Daily Maverick*, 23 June 2015.

Magubane, Bernard. 'From Union to a democratic South Africa: Change and continuity?' *Focus,* Issue 57, May 2010.

Mandela, Nelson. 'Statement at presidential inauguration', Union Buildings, Pretoria, 10 May 1994.

Mbeki, Thabo. 'The state and social transformation'. Discussion document submitted to the ANC's 1997 National Congress.

New Left Review, No. 227 (London: January–February 1998).

O'Neill, E. 'Paulo Freire: Revolutionary thinker', *Socialist Voice*, January 2016. Accessed online at http://www.communistpartyofireland.ie/sv2016-01/09-freire.html.

South Africa Survey published by the South African Institute of Race Relations. References to *Fast Facts* are to the monthly bulletin published by the Institute. April 2015.

Tutu, Desmond. 'Real leadership', Harold Wolpe Memorial Trust Tenth Anniversary. Memorial lecture, 23 August 2006.

Venter, JJ. 'HF Verwoerd: The foundational aspects of his thought', *Koers* Vol. 64, No.4, 1999

Index

UWC *see* University of the Western Cape

Van den Berg, Servaas 317–318, 345–346
Van der Kemp, Johannes 24–25
Van der Merwe, NG 72
Van Eck, Hendrik 156–159, 165, 172
Van Heerden, Neil 273
Van Rooyen, JC 59–60
Van Wyk, Freddie 253
Van Wyk, Frederick 172
Van Wyk, Willem 278
Van Zyl, Johan 271
Verwoerd, Hendrik
    apartheid 81–82, 97–106, 124, 163–164,
        181–182, 243, 257–258
    assassination of 204
    background of 65, 67–68, 75–80
    Extension of University Education Act 108–
        112, 114–119
    homelands 94–96, 260
    USSALEP 160, 173
Verwoerd, Willem 75
Viva FRELIMO rallies 210–214
Voice of Free Hungary 138
Volkelt, Hans 76–77
Volkskapitalisme 58
Volkskongres 78–80
Voorbrand Tobacco Corporation 117
Voortrekker monument 67–68
Vorster, John 184, 204, 209, 227, 239, 249
Vundla, Peter 305

Wallace, Jimmy 137
'Wall Street Rule' 241
Warsaw Pact 138
Wassenaar, Andreas 263
Waterboer, Andries 17, 19–20, 32–33, 35–36
Waterboer, Nicholas 36–37
Webster, Eddie 195, 204

Weekly Mail 289–290
Wellesley College 252
Welsh Committee *see* Interdepartmental
    Committee on Native Education
Wentworth 189–190
Wentzel, Ernest 153
Wesleyan missionaries 31–32
Western Cape Youth Organisation 218
White Paper for Post-School Education and
    Training 391, 399, 400, 403, 405
White, Walter 136
Whyte, Quintin 172
Wiechers, Marinus 271
Wilberforce, William 24, 27, 29, 30
Wilford, Hugh 134–136, 141, 169
Wilkins, Ivor 57, 101, 117, 120
Wilson, John 271–272
Wilson, Woodrow 139
Wisner, Frank 135, 138
Wits *see* University of the Witwatersrand
Wood, Michael 170
World Court *see* International Court of Justice
World Federation of Democratic Youth 137
World, The 217, 222
World University Service 153
World War I 56–57
World War II 64, 67–68, 79
Wretched of the Earth, The 199

Xhosa people 24–25, 30–35
X, Malcolm 198

Yale University 252–253
Yeltsin, Boris 297
Young, Andrew 251

Zimele Trust Fund 215
Zuma, Jacob 1, 5–7, 301–304, 306–310,
    348–349, 370, 373, 378, 382, 387